ISLAMISTS AND THE GLOBAL ORDER

Edinburgh Studies of the Globalised Muslim World

Series Editor: **Frédéric Volpi**, Director, Prince Alwaleed Bin Talal Centre for the Study of Contemporary Islam, University of Edinburgh

This innovative series investigates the dynamics of Muslim societies in a globalised world. It considers the boundaries of the contemporary Muslim world, their construction, their artificiality or durability. It sheds new light on what it means to be part of the Muslim world today, for both those individuals and communities who live in Muslim-majority countries and those who reside outside and are part of a globalised ummah. Its analysis encompasses the micro and the macro level, exploring the discourses and practices of individuals, communities, states and transnational actors who create these dynamics. It offers a multidisciplinary perspective on the salient contemporary issues and interactions that shape the internal and external relations of the Muslim world.

Available titles

Salafi Social and Political Movements: National and Transnational Contexts
Masooda Bano

A Political Theory of Muslim Democracy
Ravza Altuntaş-Çakır

Literary Neo-Orientalism and the Arab Uprisings: Tensions in English, French and German Language Fiction
Julia Wurr

Why Islamists Go Green
Emmanuel Karagiannis

Islamic Modernities in World Society: The Rise, Spread and Fragmentation of a Hegemonic Idea
Dietrich Jung

Islamist Movements during the Tunisian Transition and Syrian Crisis: The Power of Practices
Teije H. Donker

Islamists and the Global Order: Between Resistance and Recognition
Hanna Pfeifer

edinburghuniversitypress.com/series/esgmw

ISLAMISTS AND THE GLOBAL ORDER

Between Resistance and Recognition

Hanna Pfeifer

EDINBURGH
University Press

To JuM

Edinburgh University Press is one of the leading university presses in the UK. We publish academic books and journals in our selected subject areas across the humanities and social sciences, combining cutting-edge scholarship with high editorial and production values to produce academic works of lasting importance. For more information visit our website: edinburghuniversitypress.com

Edinburgh University Press Ltd
13 Infirmary Street
Edinburgh EH1 1LT

First published in hardback by Edinburgh University Press 2024

Typeset in 11/15pt EB Garamond by
Cheshire Typesetting Ltd, Cuddington, Cheshire

A CIP record for this book is available from the British Library

ISBN 978 1 3995 1585 6 (hardback)
ISBN 978 1 3995 1586 3 (paperback)
ISBN 978 1 3995 1587 0 (webready PDF)
ISBN 978 1 3995 1588 7 (epub)

This publication has been supported by the Leibniz Open Access Monograph Publishing Fund and the Research Initiative 'ConTrust: Trust in Conflict – Political Life under Conditions of Uncertainty', funded by the Hessian Ministry of Higher Education, Research, Science and the Arts.

CONTENTS

ACKNOWLEDGEMENTS

This book project started with a misgiving about the articulation of a supposedly irreconcilable difference between Islamists and the West in 2013. Since then, the project has been an exercise in proving and studying the existence of grey where there is supposedly only black and white. My observation is that thinking in binaries and antagonisms comes rather naturally to me and, I suppose, to many others who have grown up in the West. It is indeed hard to think in relative rather than absolute terms, to escape 'either/or' logic and replace it with 'both/and' assessments, nuance and ambivalence. In this sense, the book is also the undoubtedly imperfect result of my struggle to reorganise my habits of thinking, to learn to bear the inescapable complexity of the social world and to find ways of doing justice to it, by making modest but well-founded and carefully researched claims. If, with this book, I can hope to have made a good attempt at achieving these goals, this is thanks to two factors: time and social encounters with long-term companions and erstwhile strangers who became valuable interlocutors, colleagues and friends. Such encounters are sometimes confrontational and troublesome and have regularly demonstrated to me how limited and erroneous my thinking is. Luckily for me, virtually all of these encounters have simultaneously been underpinned by mutual respect, academic and social curiosity, and sometimes friendship and love. In this sense, I can only hope that more such discomforting encounters await me and thank all those from whom I have had the honour to learn. Not all of them can be mentioned here individually but they can nonetheless rest assured of my gratitude.

Even as a child I dreamt of writing a book some day. But back then I did not think it was going to be an academic one. It feels quite wonderful, if somewhat unbelievable, to have written a book and I have many people to thank for having supported me in this endeavour, not least because it took me more than ten years from start to finish. The first person to whom I would like to express my gratitude is my PhD supervisor (*Doktormutter* as we say in German), former boss, mentor and colleague Anna Geis, who, I am proud to say, has also become a trusted friend over the years. Then a supervisor for my MA thesis, Anna recruited me from Munich in 2012 to become a member of her team at Otto von Guericke University Magdeburg and, later, Helmut Schmidt University/University of the Federal Armed Forces Hamburg, where I received my PhD in 2017. Anna has many admirable qualities including meticulousness, humour and modesty. She also possesses an impressively broad and substantial knowledge of very diverse social science debates. From her, I have learnt to connect bodies of literature, to gain overviews of fields and to combine them in new ways, as well as to consolidate what we know across different areas. But most important to me is her unbreakable sincerity and ethics, even in the more difficult situations that academic life can bring. I am grateful to her for being such an excellent role model to me and others.

Before starting a PhD in political science, I was encouraged to work in academia by Elif Özmen, for whom I worked as a student assistant and tutor in practical philosophy and ethics at the University of Munich. Elif also wisely urged me to develop a thicker skin if I intended to embark on the journey of an academic career, which is something I tried and am still trying to do. I am grateful for this honest piece of advice and for the female power with which Elif's appearances and encounters are always imbued and which has always been an inspiration to me.

While I held my first university job at the Munich School of Philosophy and over the coming years, I had the opportunity to discuss the relationship between politics and religion with Michael Rederm and I learnt a lot from him. During this time, Stephan Stetter from the University of the Bundeswehr Munich accompanied me as my second PhD supervisor and Wolfgang Merkel from the WZB Berlin Social Science Center acted as my mentor. Gabi Schlag, now working at the University of Tübingen, was my closest colleague and taught me everything I needed to know about the 'IR business' and community. I presented some of the very early stages of my work to the different participants of the colloquia Anna organised in Magdeburg and Hamburg. I also had a wonderful reading group, consisting of old friends from school and university, Steffen Murau, Lukas Rudolph and Kilian Spandler, who can all boast impressive career paths and great achievements in their respective academic fields. I am grateful to all of them for having enriched my intellectual perspective and academic work, but also my personal life.

During my PhD research, I had the pleasure of spending some time – albeit less than I would have liked – in Lebanon and Tunisia. I felt more than welcome in both countries and was met with hospitality and generosity, as well as much humour. As a PhD fellow at the Orient Institute Beirut (OIB) in 2014 and 2015, I not only conducted field research but also worked alongside brilliant young colleagues who, like me, were writing their dissertations, among them Sheryn Rindermann from the University of Leipzig and Samer Ghamroun from the Saint Joseph University in Beirut. Sheryn and I spent many hours in the OIB garden, smoking and whiling away the hours discussing our projects. Meeting Samer meant that I got to know many sides of Lebanon and Lebanese society that would otherwise have remained hidden to me. But more than that, he is one of the sharpest intellectuals and activists I have ever met. I am honoured to count him among my close friends.

Thanks to an invitation from Mathias Rohe, I was able to spend a month as a guest researcher at the Erlangen Centre for Islam and Law in Europe, where I got to know Jörn Thielmann. Together with Moncef Ben Abdeljelil from the Université de Sousse, Jörn implemented a project entitled 'The Struggles over Identity, Morality, and Public Space in Middle Eastern Cities' for which the late Christoph Schumann had acquired funding from the Volkswagen Foundation. They generously let me participate in an insightful workshop at the Université de Sousse in 2016. This not only helped me with field access later on, it also introduced me to yet another circle of wonderful colleagues, including Firas Ben Nasr, Oussama Bouffrikha (both Université de Sousse), Durgham Shtaya (An-Najah National University), Abdulsalam Al-Rubaidi and Nina Nowar (both Friedrich-Alexander-Universität Erlangen-Nürnberg).

Besides these companions, colleagues and friends, I would also like to express my deep gratitude to the interlocutors who were willing to share their assessments of Ennahda's and Hezbollah's views on global order, as well as of Tunisian and Lebanese politics respectively, all of whom remain anonymous in this book. Owing to their generosity, the time they spent answering my questions and sharing their knowledge, I gained many insights about two lifeworlds which I had previously only known from the literature and primary sources. Their perspectives also helped me correct my analytical hunches and sometimes biases. I would also like to thank Stefan Leder, Said AlDailami and Takouoi K. for their invaluable help in finding interlocutors and arranging interviews.

For the final stages of this publishing project, I was accompanied by my esteemed colleagues in Frankfurt, both at Goethe University and at the Peace Research Institute Frankfurt (PRIF). I discussed my introductory chapter with the members of PRIF's research group on terrorism at the time: Damaris Braun, Mustafa Karahamad, Amr Sakr, Regine Schwab and David Weiß. David also helped me to prepare and format the final manuscript. Felix Anderl gave me indispensable feedback on the book proposal that I submitted to Edinburgh University Press (EUP). Antonia Witt provided wisdom and moral support whenever needed. Irene Weipert-Fenner acted as my cheerleader urging me to submit the final draft of this book to the publisher before Christmas 2022, as a gift to myself. It is thanks to her and all my other wonderful colleagues that the email with the manuscript that would later be accepted for publication reached Louise Hutton and Frédéric Volpi on 24 December at 2.26 p.m. – right before my family and I left for our traditional Christmas Eve walk. Besides Louise, I am grateful to Emma House, Isobel Birks and Eddie Clark from EUP for their outstanding support and the absolute professionalism with which they have accompanied the publishing process. Besides Frédéric and the EUP Press Committee, I would like to extend my gratitude to two anonymous reviewers whose keen observations and prudent suggestions helped me improve the manuscript. Finally, I am grateful to Carla Hammes-Welch, whose editorial work has made the book a more pleasant read and who helped me find the words to best express my ideas, and to copy-editor Jonathan Wadman for the final polishing of the manuscript and his exceptional eye for decisive details.

I wrote this book in various places, the most important of which were libraries. I have a lot of affection for these places, their smell and atmosphere. Sincere thanks are owed to the Bavarian State Library in Munich, the library of the Munich University of Applied Sciences, the central library of Goethe University Frankfurt, the libraries of the Orient Institute Beirut, Friedrich-Alexander-Universität Erlangen-Nürnberg and Clare Hall, Cambridge, and the small library of the Arnold-Niederer-Haus in Ferden for hosting me and my laptop for many days and months. For funding at different stages of this project, I would also like to thank the German Academic Scholarship Foundation (Studienstiftung des Deutschen Volkes) and the Max Weber Foundation/OIB for supporting my research through PhD scholarships, PRIF and the research initiative ConTrust: Trust in Conflict – Political Life under Conditions of Uncertainty at Goethe University Frankfurt for financing the language editing of this book, as well as the Leibniz Association and ConTrust for allowing me to make this book available as an open access publication.

Much like many other professions, academic work is sometimes exhausting, given the job uncertainty, long working hours, mobility requirements and, well, the constant need to acknowledge and overcome one's own limitations. It can be as stressful as it is rewarding. I am lucky enough to be part of an incredible group of friends with whom I can share these feelings and whose love, care and laughter I can always count on. Just before starting to revise my research to write this book manuscript, life also gave me a brilliant partner in crime. Thomas tickles my academic mind and makes my heart chuckle. I thank him for the joy and ease he brings to me every day. Finally, I am deeply grateful to my beloved parents, Maria and Joachim, who never let me doubt that I could pursue an academic career – and who, when I did anyway, assured me of their unconditional support and belief in my abilities. From them, I learnt to be curious and thorough. It is to them I want to dedicate this book.

Hanna Pfeifer
Frankfurt, September 2023

ILLUSTRATIONS

ABBREVIATIONS

AKP	Adalet ve Kalkınma Partisi (Justice and Development Party)
AMU	Arab Maghreb Union
ANSA	armed non-state actor
CNN	Cable News Network
CPR	Congrès pour la République
EU	European Union
FSA	Free Syrian Army
GCAD	Global Coalition against Daesh
GCC	Gulf Cooperation Council
GDP	gross domestic product
GWOT	'global war on terror'
HIROR	Haute Instance pour la Réalisation des Objectifs de la Révolution, des Réformes Politiques et de la Transition Démocratique (Higher Authority for the Realisation of the Objectives of the Revolution, Political Reform and Democratic Transition)
IDF	Israeli Defence Forces
IR	international relations (academic discipline)
IRGC	Islamic Revolutionary Guard Corps
ISF	Internal Security Forces

ISIE   Instance Supérieure Indépendante pour les Élections
              (Independent High Authority for Elections)
ISIS   'Islamic State of Iraq and Syria' organisation
JCPOA   Joint Comprehensive Plan of Action
JN   Jabhat al-Nusra (the Support Front, also known as the
              Nusra Front)
MENA   'Middle East' and North Africa
MTI   Mouvement de la Tendance Islamique (Movement of
              Islamic Tendency)
NCA   National Constituent Assembly
NGO   non-governmental organisation
PCVE   preventing and countering violent extremism
PLO   Palestine Liberation Organization
QCA   qualitative content analysis
R2P   responsibility to protect
RCD   Rassemblement Constitutionnel Démocratique
              (Democratic Constitutional Assembly)
STL   Special Tribunal for Lebanon
UAE   United Arab Emirates
UGTT   Union Générale des Travailleurs Tunisiens (Tunisian General
              Labour Union)
UN   United Nations
UNESCO   United Nations Educational, Scientific and Cultural
              Organization
UNIFIL   United Nations Interim Force in Lebanon
US(A)   United States (of America)
USSR   Union of Soviet Socialist Republics

SERIES EDITOR'S FOREWORD

Edinburgh Studies of the Globalised Muslim World is a series that focuses on the contemporary transformations of Muslim societies. 'Globalisation' is meant here to say that although the Muslim world was always interacting with other societal, religious, imperial or national forces over the centuries, the evolution of these interconnections constantly reshapes Muslim societies. The second half of the twentieth century has been characterised by the increasing number and diversity of exchanges on a global scale bringing people and societies 'closer', for better and for worse. The beginning of the twenty-first century confirmed the increasingly glocalised nature of these interactions and the challenges and opportunities that they bring to existing institutional, social and cultural orders.

The series is not a statement that everything is different in today's brave new world. Indeed, many 'old' ideas and practices still have much currency in the present, and undoubtedly will continue to in the future. Rather the series emphasises how our current globalised condition shapes and mediates how past worldviews and modes of being are transmitted between people and institutions. The contemporary Muslim world is not merely a reflection of past histories, but it is also a living process of creating a new order on the basis of what people want, desire, fear and hope. This creative endeavour can transform existing relations for the better, for example by reconsidering the relations between society and the environment. They can equally fan violence and hatred as illustrated in the reignition of cycles of conflicts over sovereignties, ideologies or resources across the globe.

The Globalised Muslim World series arrives at a challenging time for any inquiry into Muslim societies. The new millennium began inauspiciously with a noticeable spike in transnational and international violence framed in 'civilisational' terms. A decade of 'war of terror' contributed to the entrenching of negative mutual perceptions across the globe while also reinforcing essentialist views. The ensuing decade hardly improved the situation, with political and territorial conflicts multiplying in different parts of the Muslim world, and some of the most violent groups laying claim to the idea of a global caliphate to justify themselves. Yet a focus on trajectories of violence gives a distorted picture of the evolution of Muslim societies and their relations with the rest of the world. This series is very much about the 'what else' that is happening as we move further into the twenty-first century.

Hanna Pfeifer's *Islamists and the Global Order* constitutes a timely contribution to the debates about the place and role that actors identified as 'Islamists' in the policy and scholarly literature can have in the international arena and the global political imaginary. Focusing on the post-9/11 foreign affairs context in the Middle East, the book illustrates the tensions, opportunities, strategic choices and trajectories of two movements embodying different forms of political Islam which are simultaneously presenting themselves to, and being represented by, a Western-dominated discourse about world order. The subtitle of Pfeifer's work, 'Between Resistance and Recognition', highlights two crucial dynamics that have characterised multiple Islamist actors over the last few decades. In her perceptive analysis, Pfeifer details and elucidates the agency of these movements in creating a discourse and practice that is meaningful to them and that can also be accurately recognised by the main international powers of a secularised global international system.

Considering the rather different approaches of Hezbollah in Lebanon and Ennahda in Tunisia, the book analyses how those movements that have made the choice to embrace formal politics interact with national and international actors in situations of both normalcy and crisis. Delving into the discourses and positions of those Islamist actors, Pfeifer documents the strategic choices, options and dilemmas that have shaped their initiatives and responses to political events and actors over time. While Hezbollah and Ennahda have embarked on different political and social strategies – i.e. resistance versus recognition – the analysis of their specific predicaments illustrates more generally the factors that weigh heavily on Islamist actors across the board and that structure their patterns of engagement on the international scene. Hence, Pfeifer's contribution constitutes a most welcome addition to the literature on both Islamism and international affairs that undoubtedly paves the way for more research of those dynamics across more movements throughout the globalised Muslim world.

Professor Frédéric Volpi
Chair in the Politics of the Muslim World
University of Edinburgh

INTRODUCTION: ISLAMISTS AND THE WESTERN-DOMINATED WORLD ORDER – DECONSTRUCTING A TALE OF TWO ENEMIES

At the Munich Security Conference in February 2016, the late John McCain gave a pessimistic speech on recent developments in and prospects for Syria. The conference took place at a time when the 'Islamic State of Iraq and Syria' organisation (ISIS), also known as Dā'ish, had already lost significant amounts of territory in Iraq and Syria. At the same time, however, there had been several attacks against targets outside these two countries in 2015, notably in France and Tunisia. The perpetrators had claimed to belong to ISIS. In January 2016, the air strikes carried out on Iraqi territory within the framework of Operation Inherent Resolve by the Global Coalition against Daesh (GCAD), led by the United States of America (USA), had reached their peak and the coalition would from then on mainly target Syria. In this context, McCain warned:

> I watched . . . giants of our transatlantic alliance come together year after year to address the greatest challenges of their time. They believed in the value of a rules-based international order, because they knew the horrors of global anarchy. They believed in sustaining a favorable balance of power, because they had survived the collapse of it. They believed in the *West*, and its power. And they succeeded. It is *that vision of world order – our vision – that* is under assault today . . . and nowhere more graphically than the Middle East.[1]

He feared that the 'world order that we built, our dearest inheritance . . . [was] coming apart'.[2]

When McCain delivered his speech, there was the growing realisation among Western policymakers and observers that a global transformation process was underway. The United States had already declared its strategic reorientation towards the Pacific, the 'pivot to Asia' (Campbell and Andrews 2013), which was intended as a response to the global power shifts brought about by China's rise (Mearsheimer 2014a). Just a few months after this speech, the British voted for Brexit, and Donald Trump was elected the forty-fifth president of the United States. Both the rise of non-Western powers and populism in the West would be debated as external and internal challenges or even outright threats to the liberal international order in the second half of the 2010s (Ikenberry, Parmar and Stokes 2018). But McCain's address to the global – in fact mostly Western – security community was made against the backdrop of dramatic images of violence from the 'Middle East' and North Africa (MENA).[3] Back in 2016, the MENA region was still at the top of Western security agendas – contrary to the declared political will of many politicians, especially in the US.

The 'global war on terror' (GWOT), launched a decade and a half earlier by George W. Bush after the 9/11 attacks, had made MENA the prime target of Western attention and engagement in the 2000s and 2010s. The tone the Bush administration set for the deadly global campaign in the name of counterter-rorism was unambiguous: 'Bin Laden and his terrorist allies have made their intentions as clear as Lenin and Hitler.'[4] According to Bush, any effort put into a more nuanced view of Islamism would be too much. For the 'Shia and Sunni extremists represent different faces of the same threat. They draw inspiration from different sources, but both seek to impose a dark vision of violent Islamic radicalism across the Middle East.'[5] The Bush era gave rise to an antagonistic worldview according to which the West and its leader, the US, appear as 'a beacon of "democracy", "progress" and "modernity", in contradistinction to an Islamist "other"' (Mullin 2011, 264), imagined as irrational, anti-modern and religiously fervent. Bush's successor, President Barack Obama, sought to 'eschew some of the more polarised language' (Mullin 2011, 274), referring to specific rather than generalised threats emanating from some versions of Islam. Yet, ultimately, he was unable to fully shake off the legacies of the structure his predecessor had created: the ideologisation of terror, the employment of double standards regarding legitimate political violence and the conflation of Islamist movements, which went hand in hand with a tendency to frame the latter as a security problem to be dealt with through counterterrorism (Mullin 2011, 266). Until the end of his presidency, Obama maintained that 'violent fanatics who claim to speak for Islam' were up against

> a post-World War II order [which we built] with other democracies, an order based not just on military power or national affiliations but built on principles – the rule of law, human rights, freedom of religion, and speech, and assembly, and an independent press.[6]

In the age of the 'GWOT', which began in 2001 and lasted at least until the US troop withdrawal from Afghanistan in 2021,[7] 'Islamism' had come to replace communism as the spectre haunting the global order of the West's making (Camilleri 2012).

What This Book Is About

In this book, I seek to show that a dichotomous imaginary of 'Islamists' versus the 'Western world order' is mistaken.[8] The reason for this is that neither part of this conflict constellation is a unitary and homogeneous subject or structure. By deconstructing these two terms and reconstructing the different versions and meanings in all their plurality and ambiguity, what appears to be a static and intractable polarity can be subjected to an open empirical analysis: what kinds of relationship do actually existing actors dubbed 'Islamist' have with a global order under Western hegemony? The book is dedicated to continuing the important work of scholars who have invested in deconstructing essentialised and securitised images of 'Islamism' and Islam in Western discourse and in providing a more nuanced picture of them in a post-9/11 world. These scholars come from various disciplines, including anthropology, religious studies, critical terrorism and security studies, area studies and international relations (IR). This book brings together three strands of research, in particular: the interdisciplinary debate on secularism (Chapter 1), conceptualisations of (global) order and ordering from IR and political theory and philosophy (Chapter 2), and analyses of political Islam and Islamism from area studies (Chapter 3). This allows me to interrogate how Islamist actors perceive the world order, the position they adopt towards it, and why. The empirical part of this book scrutinises the world order discourse of two Islamist actors in the post-Arab-uprisings era: Ennahda, the largest Islamist actor in Tunisia, which re-emerged as a successful party after the toppling of the Ben Ali regime in 2011, and Hezbollah, a powerful Shi'i party–militia hybrid in Lebanon. Drawing on transcripts of political speeches, newspaper opinion pieces and interviews with various party elites, and official party programmes and statements between 2011 and 2016, the book reveals how Ennahda and Hezbollah position themselves towards other actors and speakers in the global discourse on world order, as well as how they have developed their own conceptions of that same order. The book presents the results of an agent-centred, critical constructivist discourse analysis (Holzscheiter 2014) of documents published by party elites for a (potential) global audience. The study sheds light on Ennahda's and Hezbollah's conceptions of sovereignty (Chapter 4) and legitimacy (Chapter 5), as well as the goals and values an order should pursue, which I call *teloi*. These *teloi* are connected to wider narratives about history (Chapter 6). In contrast to conventional wisdom, the book demonstrates that Islamists do not reject the 'Western world order'. Rather, they are mostly recognisant of hegemonic discourse on world order, but sometimes resistant to certain interpretations of and practices employed in the name of a global (normative) order.

I start by observing several problematic traits and distinctions (or rather a lack thereof) that characterise political and public discourse on 'Islamism'. Marc Lynch (2017) calls the use of the term 'Islamism' that I problematise in this book 'lumping'.[9] This concept refers to the practice of conflating a whole variety of distinct actors and phenomena under one umbrella term. Besides 'Islamists', other popular labels are 'fundamentalists' or 'fanatics' and 'radical' or 'political Islam'. Lumping not only blurs important distinctions but also tends to frame all Islamists as a security problem, as being linked to violence and terrorism (Mullin 2011). This securitising logic has even encroached on Muslim communities and Islam as a whole (Mavelli 2013). Indeed, such a narrow security perspective on Islamism is not limited to public and political discourse. Some strands of IR and especially policy-oriented approaches in the field of security and terrorism studies, too, are prone to essentialising political Islam, reverting to Orientalist clichés, obscuring differences between Islamist groups and denying that their claims have any legitimacy or even a political quality (Volpi 2010, 149–73).[10]

Reducing all Islamists to somewhat apolitical, irrational and violent fanatics does not do justice to the complexity of the phenomenon of political Islam and the plurality of its manifestations. In particular, constructing Islamists as radical opponents or even enemies of a liberal world order is overly simplistic:[11] it constructs and reifies 'the Islamist' as a more or less unitary subject. But it also conveys the idea of a single, uncontested world order that aims at implementing liberal values – a project which 'the Islamist' tries to frustrate by force. Fortunately, the literature comprises more than the 'lumping' strand, and this book can build on a very nuanced and well-established academic debate on Islamists. As the following chapters will show, Islamist movements and parties, as well as armed groups, have been the subject of numerous studies from various disciplines, including comparative politics and area studies, security studies, and peace and conflict studies, as well as sociology and anthropology. However, Islamists have so far only rarely been studied as actors in international politics – that is, as subjects that, on the one hand, have agency in politics beyond regional and domestic contexts, but are subjected to the structures of the world order, on the other. How do Islamists perceive the world order, what position do they adopt towards it – and with what purpose? Our knowledge on this issue is limited because the context for the debate on Islamists has usually been the domestic and sometimes the regional, rather than the global order.

Where authors have shown an interest in how Islamist or jihadist actors position themselves beyond their narrow domestic or regional context, the concept of 'global order' or 'world order' is not sufficiently theorised or is reduced to the 'Westphalian order' or 'state-based international system' – and the studies have focused on Salafi jihadism (Gerges 2016, Maher 2016). Salafi jihadists are sometimes subsumed under the term 'Islamists' as well. There are various reasons for and against this, as I will discuss at later points in this book. Suffice it to say here that Salafi jihadism has preoccupied the public and academia since the 9/11 attacks. In the academic study of Salafists, the suggestion has been made to distinguish between the attitudes they hold towards the state and the international order and the methods by which they try to achieve change (Maher 2016, 3–27). Only a small number of Salafi actors have a rejectionist agenda, which they pursue by resorting to violent means. Despite the fact that Salafi jihadism, defined in this way, is an ideology adhered to by a minority of Salafists and one that is marginal when considering the whole spectrum of Islamist groups, it has come to shape the image evoked whenever the danger of political Islam is publicly debated. Salafi jihadists have also been a key concern for scholars in the fields of security and IR (Volpi 2010, 149–73) and they have come to epitomise what it means for the 'Western world order' to be challenged (Mohamedou 2018). The focus on Salafi-jihadist groups, then, has come at the expense of a broader investigation and has sometimes led to a side-lining of other important political and social actors from the MENA region, including Islamists. More specifically, Islamist world order politics beyond Salafi jihadism have yet to be studied.

This book addresses that research gap, located at the intersection of area studies and IR, by assuming that Islamists, too, are political subjects and participants in a global discourse on world order. It argues that the image of a politics of rejection is an unwarranted reduction of a whole spectrum of theoretically possible and empirically observable positions Islamists hold vis-à-vis the global order. More precisely, the politics of rejection is only one of three possible forms an actor's encounter with the Western-dominated world order can take. The other two are the politics of recognition and the politics of resistance. I understand these forms as ideal types of how political actors – be they state or non-state – can position themselves towards the world order under Western hegemony. The tendency to see Salafi-jihadist actors as the archetype of 'Islamism' and, thus, to think of Islamist politics towards the Western world order in purely rejectionist terms needs to be corrected. With its focus on the Tunisian Ennahda and Lebanese Hezbollah, this book analyses two actors that are also labelled 'Islamist', but are not part of the Salafi-jihadist trend. It thereby offers new ways of thinking critically about potential (obstacles to) cooperation and about (driving forces of) contemporary conflict between 'the West' and 'the Islamists'. By investigating how Islamist actors discursively construct world order, it will show that there is both continuity and rupture with Western discourses, that Islamists' reaction to the world order under Western hegemony is not (violent) rejection and that the substantialised image of the Islamist as the 'chief ideological "other"' (Mandaville 2013, 184) of the West after the end of the 'Cold War'[12] should be revised. This necessitates the deconstruction of two terms: the 'Western world order' and the 'Islamists'.

Deconstructing the Secular, Liberal West and Pluralising Islamism in the World Order

Over the last two decades and building on insights from philosophy and anthropology, IR and related fields have problematised the stylised image of a modern, secular, liberal West on several levels. First, various authors have discussed the secularist bias in both Western politics and the academic theories on international politics. Since the mid-2000s, these authors have tried to challenge the 'oppositional binaries [that] exist within dominant understandings of religion in International Relations . . . and are used to separate religion and the secular and establish religion's subordination to the secular' (Wilson 2012, 58). As Elizabeth Shakman Hurd (2007, 1) argues, while an 'unquestioned acceptance of the secularist division between religion and politics' prevails in political and academic practice, secularism actually 'needs to be analyzed as a form of political authority in its own right'. By defining the '"proper place of religion" in a secular society' (Asad 2006, 526), secularism functions as a 'power-knowledge regime' (Mavelli 2014, 174). The Peace of Westphalia is at the core of the secular narrative: according to 'liberal mythology' (Thomas 2000, 819), it was the privatisation of religion, the secularisation of politics and the rise of the modern state that put an end to the era of religious wars – at least in the West. Based on this myth, a civilisational divide was introduced into the world, between those societies which meet standards of modernisation and those which do not (Eisenstadt 2000a). It is in this way that the 'messy' Orient was able to serve as a means of Western self-reassurance, as Edward Said argued several decades ago (Said [1978] 2003; Euben 1999). There is a discursive co-constitution of the rational, liberal nation-state in the West and an Islamism on the outside that 'has come to represent the "nonsecular" in European and American political thought and practice' (E. S. Hurd 2007, 49). The Islamist, then, appears either as 'an infringement of irrational forms of religion upon would-be secular public life in Muslim-majority societies' (E. S. Hurd 2007, 118) or as a civilisational feature of Muslim societies reluctant to modernise and secularise (Volpi 2010, 29–33).

As William T. Cavanaugh has argued, though, the 'myth of religious violence' not only serves to legitimise the liberal nation-state (Cavanaugh 2009, 3–4). It simultaneously constructs the role of the rogue, which is attributed to non-secular orders and in particular to Muslim societies. Such a categorisation, then, becomes an important component in the legitimation of the use of force against these societies on the grounds that religiously motivated violence is something that needs to be countered (Cavanaugh 2009, 59). Without suggesting that fighting 'Islamists' is the only or even the most important motive for the use of military force, it is striking that Muslim-majority societies are particularly likely to be subject to foreign intervention. Since 2001, Western states have led or been involved in military interventions in Afghanistan (2001), Iraq (2003), Libya (2011), Mali (2013), Syria/Iraq (2014) and Yemen (2015), to name but a few of the larger-scale operations. Besides this, 'smaller-scale' violent actions, such as drone strikes and targeted killings in Pakistan, Yemen, Libya and Somalia, occur on a regular basis, albeit largely unnoticed by the Western public (Bachman 2015). Through the 'war on terror' narrative, secularism operates at the very core of security policies (Gutkowski 2014, 2016). Consequently, a second strand of research has directed its attention to the securitisation of Islam in Western discourse. Increasingly, this securitisation has been extended from terrorists to Islamists in the MENA region to Muslim communities in the West and even to Islam as a whole (Mavelli 2013, Matthews 2015).

These first two strands of research have produced important results regarding the question of how secular Western power operates by creating an Other it can 'legitimately' and 'reasonably' fight. Attempts at deconstruction have been directed at the West as the hegemonic side in a postsecular power configuration. The perspective of those who challenge Western secular discourse, however, has only rarely been taken into account in academic work to date. How do Islamists perceive the West, their relationship with it and the distribution of power in, as well as the normative structure of, the global order?

To be sure, research on how Islamists view the world and the West, and their conception of a social and political order, does exist. But this kind of research is often rather disconnected from the discipline of IR.[13] Studies on Islamists frequently embrace a social-movements perspective (Wiktorowicz 2006), for example asking how mobilisation takes place (Donker 2013, Kandil 2015, Ketchley and Biggs 2017) or in what kind of social environment Islamist movements emerge (Deeb and Harb 2013). Studies from comparative politics try to classify different Islamist movements and parties (Volpi and Stein 2015) and analyse the conditions under which they become more moderate and can be integrated into political systems (Schwedler 2011, Cavatorta and Merone 2013). A question which has been passionately debated for a long time – and declared as misleading by some – is whether Islamists can become democrats or not (Hamid 2014, Dalacoura 2015, Kubicek 2015, Esposito, Sonn and Voll 2016). More recently, contributions to the debate have taken a more inductive approach, investigating contemporary Islamists' conceptions of democracy and how they combine these with, or view them as a modern extension of, Islamic principles (Khanani 2021). Taking a more historical perspective, some authors have traced the development of modern Islamic thought in an exchange with and in opposition to Western thought (Donohue and Esposito 2007, Jung 2012), or they have concentrated on how changing political conditions influence Islamist thought and practice and the forms Islamists assume (Roy 1994). This sort of research often takes into account global society and the big changes in global politics, such as decolonisation, the end of the 'Cold War', economic globalisation and the (arguably) postnational constellation (Roy 2004, Mandaville 2007, Bayat 2013).

For instance, Olivier Roy's comprehensive work covers Islamism from its emergence as an anti-colonial movement, to its split over the question of violence, to the integration of some Islamists into their respective political system as parties, often followed by phases of repression and re-cooptation, to what came to be known as the 'failure of political Islam' (Roy 2004, 2012a, Boubekeur and Roy 2012a). Islamism as a political ideology had lost its persuasive power and thus the Islamists needed to find a new platform and form of organisation. Roy predicted two trajectories which mirrored not only the programmatic crisis but also the accelerating processes of deterritorialisation of Islam. In Roy's view, post-Islamists would abandon their programmatic demand for an Islamic state and attempt to insert religious values into political discourse 'from below', thereby transforming the relationship between religion and politics without claiming the total Islamisation of the state and politics. In contrast, neofundamentalists would place the emphasis on individual piety and spirituality, appearing as quietist, political or jihadist movements (Wiktorowicz 2006). This distinction has regained relevance since the Arab uprisings, with the Islamist and Salafist spectrum broadening and diversifying to an unprecedented degree.

In this context, the transnational character of Islamism and Salafism has attracted attention again. But even more importantly, there is a growing awareness that they need to be analysed as phenomena embedded in domestic, regional and global political environments. For example, literature on ISIS now emphasises the extent to which recent political history in Iraq and Syria, as well as Western interventions in the region, created a favourable environment to disseminate the message of religious 'purification' and 'liberation' globally through the establishment of the *Khilāfa* (Isakhan 2015, Gerges 2016, Pfeifer and Günther 2021, Günther 2022). In the discipline of international relations, too, much academic effort is currently being put into understanding the radicalism and violence but also the appeal of Salafi jihadism (Friis 2015, 2018, Euben 2017, Heath-Kelly 2018). But focusing on the most destructive, most extreme, most totalitarian appearance of political Islam in this way reinforces the impression that it is all about violence, rather than working towards a more nuanced image that does justice to the complexity of actually existing Salafi-jihadist and Islamist groups. Rarely does IR seriously engage with research results from the area studies. Only recently have there been contributions that speak to the debate on or explicitly embrace the perspective of norm contestation in IR (Lecocq 2020). Centred on Hamas and Hezbollah, these studies have focused on resistance as a key norm and its consequences for political order (Koss 2018) and on how (religious) language is used in processes of norm contestation (Farida 2020). This book builds on the important contributions made by these scholars but moves beyond the focus on resistance, showing that Islamists simultaneously engage in practices of both recognition and resistance in the Western-dominated world order. It thereby responds to the desideratum of examining the relationship between Islamist and Western world order discourses (Lecocq 2020, 1079).

Islamists between the Struggle for Recognition and a Politics of Resistance in the World Order: Beyond Moderation and Rejectionism

The study of Islamists is much more nuanced in area studies than it is in IR, and has overcome the essentialism and instrumentalism traps that are still very much present in the discipline of international relations (Valbjørn and Gunning 2021). Conversely, area studies often do not make use of the rich theoretical repertoire IR has to offer in order to analyse empirical phenomena in their global environment.[14] Studies often remain at the domestic or regional level in their explanatory frameworks and contextualisation.

A very popular framework for analysing changes in the ideology or strategy of Islamist movements is the inclusion-moderation paradigm. Its basic assumption is that actors who are included in political systems become more 'moderate' (Schwedler 2011). Even though the debate within this paradigm is multifaceted, some of the thesis's more problematic traits, as well as the binary between 'moderate' and 'radical' itself, have been justifiably criticised. First, 'moderate' is necessarily a relative term: something can only be moderate in relation to a certain normative standard. Have Islamists really been more radical than the authoritarian regimes in the MENA region that suppressed them? These very regimes also used the term 'moderate' in reference to acceptable forms of public Islam, thereby simultaneously stigmatising oppositional Islamism as illegitimate (Pahwa 2017, Pfeifer 2018). This indicates that 'moderation' is also a political term with a secular bias: anything that is not religious automatically seems more moderate.

Second, and related to this point, 'moderation' is closely associated with Western democracy promotion in the region, which reinforces the concept's normative bias. It is often used as a synonym for 'more democratic' or 'more secular' (Netterstrøm 2015, 113–15). Third, an important distinction in the inclusion-moderation paradigm is between tactical (behavioural) and ideological (substantial) moderation (Schwedler 2011, Karakaya and Yildirim 2013). Whereas the former denotes a change in behaviour for opportunistic reasons, the latter refers to a 'genuine' change in political ideology. This distinction is also mirrored in the 'wolf in sheep's clothing' metaphor, according to which Islamists show 'their real face' once they are in power. Such claims are part of self-proclaimed secular autocrats' rhetorical repertoire and are typically used to fend off demands to include the Islamist opposition in the political system. The results of the Ennahda case study in this book support the critics of this distinction (Netterstrøm 2015), as they demonstrate how difficult it is to dispel the suspicion that apparent moderation is illusive and to convincingly exhibit ideological change. Once they were in power, the Islamists had to demonstrate time and again that they were willing to compromise. When they pushed for their own platform, their previous concessions were considered merely tactical, thus 'proving' how unchangeable they are.

Fourth, the inclusion-moderation thesis has been challenged by empirical cases that seem to suggest the exact opposite, namely that it is exclusion, or even violent repression, which triggers learning processes within Islamist groups. According to this logic, Islamists adapt their platform (and behaviour) because the old version did not resonate well enough in society – or even sparked opposition – and led the regime to resort to repressive measures (Cavatorta and Merone 2013). Finally, current developments related to the Adalet ve Kalkınma Partisi (AKP, Justice and Development Party) in Turkey, but also the Muslim Brotherhood's brief period of rule in Egypt have raised the question of what happens to 'moderate' Islamists once they are in power. While Tunisia's Ennahda is seen as an exception to the rule, it was claimed that incumbent Islamists would embark on a journey of 'immoderation', understood as 'a top-down pursuit of morality issues and unwillingness to compromise with the opposition' (Kirdiş 2018, 309). However, when taking into account recent studies on the governance of religion by former authoritarian regimes in the MENA region, it seems rather unclear why this 'immoderation' would be a phenomenon specific to Islamists in power (Cesari 2014).

This book presents an alternative theoretical perspective on Islamist groups which are part of their respective political system, that is they act as parties and run in elections. It allows us to analyse how they relate to a global order under Western hegemony without falling into the trap of normativity that prevails in (some) approaches in the moderation debate by explicitly scrutinising and reflecting on the normative reference system: the Western-dominated world order. I suggest that these Islamists have to navigate between two poles with regard to global order: resistance and recognition. On the one hand, Islamist parties originated in social and political movements which emerged as a form of resistance against social marginalisation, political domination and cultural hegemony – in particular where this was perceived as heteronomy and interference or imposition from the outside. Inevitably, this historical origin shapes their agendas and worldviews: Islamists do have divergent programmes, because they were opposed to colonial rule and postcolonial regimes. Moreover, the West as a former colonial power and hegemon *a priori* plays the role of an adversary. But this image is not as clear cut and unchangeable as is often suggested – not least because Islamists, too, are subjected to the actually existing power relations in the world order.

This means that, to a certain degree, they have to embrace the struggle for recognition. This especially applies to those actors which have either been labelled terrorist groups by their respective regimes in the past (Ennahda) or are still deemed such by international actors today (Hezbollah). For the terrorism label is particularly powerful at marginalising and delegitimising actors. Talking to and negotiating with actors that are considered 'terrorists' is a taboo, which reduces the options to engage them in a non-violent way (Toros 2008, Clément, Geis and Pfeifer 2021, Dudouet 2021). In order to have successful interactions with others in the domestic and international realms, and in particular to take over the responsibility of government, Islamists therefore depend on gaining recognition as political actors. They need to be seen as actors whose claims can be accorded a certain degree of legitimacy and with whom others can talk, negotiate and cooperate (Fierke 2009). Hezbollah and Ennahda, for instance, were both part of different coalition governments between 2011 and 2016. This meant that they had to struggle for the support of their coalition partners for their agendas as well as making concessions to the latter, and ensuring that their interests were respected in their states' foreign relations. They also needed to develop a position on international politics and justify this position vis-à-vis their constituency, but also to transnational support groups and international partners. A mere politics of resistance cannot be successful in an interdependent world – and this holds true for Islamists, too.

Resistance and recognition can be seen as complementary concepts (Geis 2018, 612) which lend themselves to providing a nuanced analysis of Islamists who are part of a government and thus need to engage in the world order politics to which they are subjected. Meanwhile, Islamists also adopt a critical position towards a world order under Western hegemony, a position which is historically grounded and legitimised on the basis of religious and political arguments. By using this theoretical perspective, this book makes a valuable contribution to existing literatures. First, the complementary view on resistance and recognition in Islamist discursive practice is a theoretical innovation in its own right.[15] It directs our attention to the world order discourse of actors on the Islamist spectrum who are not Salafi jihadists and, thus, helps us move beyond the idea of rejectionism. Second, the book offers a more fine-grained concept of world order, which in the existing literature is sometimes not sufficiently theorised. Rather, broad terms like 'Westphalian order' or 'state-based international system' are used to describe the rejectionist position of actors under investigation (Maher 2016, Gerges 2016). But for the analysis of the Islamist groups of interest in this book, a more disaggregated understanding of world order is needed, if we are to detect positions of recognition of, and resistance to, a global order under Western hegemony. Third, the book makes an empirical contribution by analysing Islamist world order discourse after the Arab uprisings, a period for which there is still a dearth of research on Islamists' regional and international relations. Finally, by comparing Ennahda and Hezbollah, the book also contributes to the recent debate on similarities between Sunni and Shi'i Islamist groups, in particular regarding the question of where religion 'comes in' in (world) order discourses (Valbjørn and Gunning 2021).

At first glance, treating Ennahda and Hezbollah in one book may seem odd, as there are a lot of differences between these two groups of Islamists (Chapter 3). Ennahda and Hezbollah belong to different sects and Islamist schools of thought; the former renounced violence several decades ago, whereas the latter is one of the most active armed non-state actors (ANSAs) in the region. The diverging repertoires of political activity also have consequences for their distinct internal organisational structures. The domestic contexts in which the two groups are active are quite different, with regard to both societal composition and political system, as are the conditions under which the two movements emerged. Ennahda directed its activism primarily against domestic repression, whereas Hezbollah became active in the context of a civil war and, notably, foreign intervention and occupation by Israel, against which it called for resistance.

That said, the two groups have a lot in common, too. Both have been regarded as 'statist' Islamists or as movements that have at some point started participating in domestic politics (Volpi and Stein 2015). Being both a movement and a party, they also share the hybrid quality that is typical of many Islamist groups. Most importantly, both Ennahda and Hezbollah have been met with scepticism or outright rejection from the Western world for being 'Islamist' (Chapter 1). At the same time, both actors have been exposed to the Western world order, and vice versa, by virtue of having belonged to coalition governments in their respective countries for several years, covering the whole period under analysis (Chapter 3). This makes them 'politically pregnant'

(Hansen 2006, 76) cases for this study. They have to somehow position themselves vis-à-vis the global order they encounter in their capacity as government actors. Their discourse is also regionally significant as they do not operate from a marginalised position or in a very limited local context, but rather from a position of relative power within their respective systems. What is more, both are subjected to (a certain degree of) pluralism and democratic competition in the systems in which they operate. In a competitive environment, actors have to legitimise political decisions and action. In their communication, Hezbollah and Ennahda thus tend to take positions on both everyday domestic and international political matters. Finally, the selected cases *a priori* seem to represent two ends of a spectrum with an ideal type of a politics of resistance at one end and a politics of recognition at the other. While Hezbollah calls itself the Islamic resistance, Ennahda has ultimately even tried to shed the Islamist label for the sake of gaining recognition on a domestic and international level. However, as this book will show, elements of recognition and resistance can be found in both actors' discourse on world order. They strive for recognition in the world order under Western hegemony and yet resist that same world order and aim to transform parts of it.

World Order as a Global Discourse: Assessing how Islamists Relate to the West

This book starts by identifying a dual research gap: the debate on global order in IR is missing an Islamist perspective and the debate on Islamism lacks analyses of these actors' views of international relations and specifically the world order. To address these shortcomings of the existing research, I suggest understanding Islamists not only as relevant actors in the MENA region but also as active participants in a global discourse on world order. Thus, the book takes a discourse analysis perspective to elucidate how Islamists understand world order, how they relate to the Western world order discourse and what their own conceptions of world order are.

The term 'world order' may not immediately be associated with a discourse, but rather with the institutions, rules and norms of the international system (Lipscy 2016). The liberal world order is often described as the post-World War II set of international institutions built up primarily by the US and aiming at the promotion of liberal values, such as human rights, democracy

and freedom, as well as prosperity, through economic and political cooperation and peaceful relations among states (Sørensen 2006, Ikenberry 2009).
Contemporaries expected it to experience a boost with the end of the 'Cold
War', which ushered in a phase of Western hegemony under the leadership of
the US. The activities of many international organisations and state practices
of global security, such as military interventions, were framed in and legitimised by a language of liberal norms and values and an attempt at enlarging
the 'democratic zone' in the world (Doyle 1983, Russett 1994). But failed
peace-building and state-building efforts and the disastrous outcomes of 'liberal' interventions in the 1990s and 2000s soon cast doubt on the virtues of
'liberal internationalism' (Richmond, Visoka and Jahn 2021). And with the
rise of populism in several Western countries and a perceived erosion of multilateralism and international institutions in the 2010s, some have declared that
the liberal international order is in crisis (Ikenberry, Parmar and Stokes 2018,
1). But what exactly does 'liberal' world order mean? Authors within IR have
emphasised that there is more than one understanding of liberalism (Sørensen
2011, Dunne and Flockhart 2013, Zürn and Gerschewski 2021), and the
conclusion that the liberal world order is being challenged, in crisis or being
undermined may, therefore, be misleading. What is more, the term 'liberal'
has often been used interchangeably with, or as a shortcut for, 'Western'. Not
only does this veil the numerous illiberal practices that the West has pursued in
international relations but it also creates a false image of unity and coherence.
There is no single 'Western' world order, but rather many different versions of
it (Chapter 2).

Adopting a well-established constructivist perspective where social facts
exist because of intersubjectively shared meanings, that is, 'because people
collectively believe they exist and act accordingly' (Finnemore and Sikkink
2001, 393), this book proposes a discursive understanding of world order.
While not denying that the world order is made up of institutions, rules and
norms, it focuses on the discursive practices which 'bring them to life' through
interpretation and reinterpretation. 'World order', then, is a contested term
and different actors participate in this 'struggle over meaning', that is, they
intentionally and 'actively construct, re-negotiate and transform intersubjectively shared interpretations of reality' (Holzscheiter 2014, 144, 147). By
emphasising the discursive constructedness of the concept, the idea of a single

Western-dominated world order can be left behind. To challenge the claim that Islamists are the enemies of this world order, I suggest that the concept of the 'Western world order' should first be disaggregated into competing discursive strands that offer a whole repertoire of interpretations of global order. This brings to light the great diversity within the West. It also relativises claims of radical otherness, as any assessment of difference must be more specific: different from which tradition of thought, from which line of argumentation; in opposition to which practice or norm?

To say that Western discourse is fragmented and internally contested does not preclude that it is also hegemonic. In the discursive understanding proposed here, world order is produced through the utterances of a variety of actors who are embedded in asymmetrical power relations. They are both part of and subjected to the global discursive structure. At the same time, they may recognise and reproduce that structure through their actions, but they may also oppose and challenge, reject and transgress it. The order is hierarchical in that it creates actor positions with varying degrees of power. I support the thesis that the global order is dominated by Western hegemony, which began to unfold after World War II, but consolidated after the end of the 'Cold War'. In the discursive approach to world order, this means that the West has the most powerful speaker position, even though this position may now be challenged.

On an empirical level, this perspective on world order suggests that actors' contributions to a global discourse should be studied in relation to other available meanings and will probably not be univocal, but will mobilise several different repertoires of meanings, too. This book investigates the relationship between Western and Islamist interpretations of world order, whether, where and how they differ and why. To provide such a nuanced picture of world order discourses, I investigate three key fields in which struggles over meaning take place: sovereignty, legitimacy and the goals and values an order should bring about, which I call *teloi*. These *teloi* are connected to broader narratives about history. The three fields correspond with what Hedley Bull identifies as elements of social order (Bull 1995, 3–4). Sovereignty refers to the entities that constitute the order (what are the entities to be ordered?) and thereby also identifies the level of ultimate decision-making authority. For instance, it could be argued that the world order is composed of states, only some states, peoples, or sub- or supranational entities. Legitimacy describes the discernible principle or pattern according to which the order is organised (how are the entities ordered?). It comprises ideas regarding how a certain political authority can be justified. Legitimacy claims commonly refer to the individual or a specific community as the ultimate reason and purpose which any order needs to take into consideration. However, some legitimacy claims are also based on the quality of certain processes, for instance the fairness of public deliberation or the fervour of political struggle. *Teloi* are the normative aspirations connected to the order or the substantial ideas regarding what the order should bring about (to what end are the entities ordered?). They are global scenarios that contain broad narratives on how history develops, where an order came from, where it is aiming for and what values and purpose it is built to achieve. *Teloi* can be utopian visions, for example when they involve a peaceful and just order, but also dystopian, for example envisaging orders of inequality and violence. These three fields are not exhaustive and notably do not encompass the global economic order – or at least only touch on it here and there. But in terms of the global political discourse on world order, they cover the main discursive battlefields. Importantly, they provide 'hard cases' for the thesis that Islamists do not simply reject the world order under Western hegemony. For in the simplified view that prevails in political discourse – but also some academic accounts – Islamists rely on divine sovereignty, which renders democratic forms of rule and legitimacy impossible, and they project their normative aspirations onto the afterworld rather than the here and now.

The book identifies four main traditions in Western discourse for each of the three discursive fields (Chapter 2). Contrasting these different discursive traditions of world order allows for a more nuanced understanding of a world order under Western hegemony. Based on this structured reading of the Western discourse on world order and using the four discursive strands for each field as a heuristic, Ennahda's and Hezbollah's world order discourses are scrutinised against this representation of Western discourse in the empirical part of the book (Chapters 4–6). This part of the book is the result of a three-step discourse analysis of documents issued between 2011 and 2016. The first of these steps was a qualitative content analysis 'in the service' of a critical discourse analysis (Schreier 2012, 28). The deductive category frame, representing Western discourse on global order, was inductively modified in the process of coding more than 420 documents (speeches by party leaders, party programmes and statements, opinion pieces by and interviews with party representatives in newspapers, etc.) as published by party elites for a global audience. Categories were modified and sometimes dropped, new categories and subcategories were added until the respective category frame covered all the meanings of world order identified in Ennahda's and Hezbollah's discourses (Schreier 2012). Drawing on critical and poststructuralist discourse analysis (Phillips and Hardy 2002, Hansen 2006), the second and third step involved (critical) contextualisation of the results of the text analysis, as well as an examination of images of Selves and Others found in both discourses. To illuminate the broader discursive formations the analysed texts are part of, as well as their political and social contexts, competing discourses, political processes and events were analysed for both case studies. For this purpose, a broad body of secondary literature, as well as interviews conducted in Tunisia and Lebanon between 2014 and 2017, were used.

Structure of the Book

The theoretical part of the book is dedicated to the deconstruction and reconstruction of 'Islamism' (Chapter 1) and the 'Western world order' (Chapter 2). Only then is it possible to empirically study the positioning of actually existing Islamist actors towards a global order under Western hegemony. Chapter 1 traces the emergence of the Islamist enemy image in both political and academic discourse. It shows how the study of religion and its supposed disappearance led to a preliminary secular consensus: the world (order) should and would eventually be free from religion. This changed in the 1990s, when religion appeared to make a violent comeback on the world stage, taking politicians and academic observers by surprise. These debates contributed to the image that religion and especially Islam were drivers of conflict and a danger to be contained. But they also paved the way for a critical recalibration of secularism and the relationship between religion and politics in the 2000s in academic discourse. When political discourse securitised Islam(ism) in the post-9/11 era, an interdisciplinary effort was made to challenge and deconstruct distorted images of Islam and show how they contributed to the legitimation of secular violence. This did not, however, prevent a powerful enemy image from forming and persisting: Islamists came to be considered the archetype of 'large and fervent resistance to . . . a liberal (global) order' (Zürn 2018, 1). To this day, Islamists are widely considered a threat. The chapter concludes by arguing that, in contrast to Salafi jihadists, Islamists' repertoire goes beyond rejectionism when it comes to their position towards a global order under Western hegemony: their position comprises part recognition, part resistance.

But what exactly do they recognise and what do they resist? Chapter 2 scrutinises and disaggregates the notion of the 'Western world order'. It introduces a discursive understanding of world order that is rooted in constructivism and is distinct from institutionalist approaches (Ikenberry 2011, Zürn 2018) on the one hand, and from power-based approaches (Mearsheimer 2019) on the other. I build on sociological theorists' interpretation of the deep structures of global order as intersubjectively shared principles, norms and beliefs that fulfil ordering functions, notably defining legitimate actors and rightful action in the international system (see, for example, Reus-Smit 1997, Buzan 2009). But while certain interpretations of these structures may be shared or become hegemonic, this does not imply that their meaning is uncontested. Rather, competing discourses and meanings underpin the deep structures of global order. The theoretical contribution of this book is to shift attention to this world order discourse and conceptualise it as a space in which actors negotiate and sometimes fiercely fight over the meaning of order. While, as a whole, Western discourse on world order can be considered hegemonic, it would be wrong to assume there is one Western way of interpreting world order. I scrutinise three discursive fields centred on constitutive parts of the deep structure of global order to show the degree of contestedness within what is deemed the Western world order discourse. I argue that this disaggregation allows us to establish with more accuracy and in an empirical manner whether and how non-Western actors reproduce or challenge, reject or seek to transform the global order. The chapter studies three discursive fields of world order in which the position of these non-Western actors can be observed: sovereignty (what are the entities to be ordered?), legitimacy (according to what principle?) and *teloi* (to what end?). More specifically, the *teloi* discursive field examines the concrete normative ideas about what the order should bring about. The chapter then identifies four strands of Western discourse for each of these fields: absolute, popular, shared and conditional sovereignty; individual- and community-based as well as deliberative and agonistic conceptions of legitimacy; liberal convergence and the pluriverse as utopias; and the clash of civilisations and Western hegemony as dystopias. Chapter 2 concludes with a methodological reflection on how an empirical study of the relationship between Islamist discourse and Western world order discourse can be used.

Chapter 3 introduces the empirical cases under study in this book: Tunisia's Ennahda and Lebanon's Hezbollah after the Arab uprisings. A core argument of this book is that the debate on Islamism needs more differentiation and nuance. I also hold that Islamist discourse needs to be studied in context. The chapter, therefore, presents Ennahda and Hezbollah as speakers in a global discourse on world order and as 'cases' of Islamism. It traces their historical emergence and evolution while simultaneously reconstructing the debate on Islamism as it developed in the area studies. It then zooms in on the Arab uprisings and the subsequent years (2011–16) in Tunisia and Lebanon, depicting their situatedness in the turbulent wider MENA region. Finally, the chapter discusses what constitutes appropriate material for the cases of Ennahda and Hezbollah and the analysis of their world order discourse.

Chapters 4, 5 and 6 are the empirical part and core of the book. They are organised along the three discursive fields. Besides their conceptions of sovereignty, legitimacy and *teloi*, Ennahda's and Hezbollah's construction of Selves and Others, of identity and difference, are also scrutinised. The results of the discourse analysis are presented and discussed with a view to establishing the extent to which Ennahda and Hezbollah reproduce, transform, challenge or innovate upon Western conceptions of global order. Chapter 4 demonstrates that the two Islamist groups reproduce understandings of absolute and popular sovereignty as established in Western discourse, add their own takes on shared sovereignty and reject the idea of conditional sovereignty. The anti-colonial and anti-imperial identity of both actors is reflected in their sovereignty discourse. Chapter 5 demonstrates that Ennahda is developing a sophisticated model of community-based legitimacy that it aims to implement in its model of Islamic democracy. The model also comprises institutions and rights that are grounded in considerations of individual-based legitimacy. It is combined with a methodology of consensus as the modus operandi of political decision-making which bears similarities with, but goes beyond, deliberative conceptions of legitimacy. In contrast, Hezbollah's conception of legitimacy varies depending on its scope of application. For the domestic realm, Hezbollah identifies the multireligious composition of Lebanese society as a fact with normative consequences: it calls for a political system that allows a peaceful coexistence of diverse communities rather than an Islamic state. Hezbollah's version of community-based legitimacy is combined with a dialogue- and cooperation-oriented approach to domestic affairs. This crude version of deliberative legitimacy is geared towards maintaining societal peace and mitigating domestic conflict – not least to increase Hezbollah's room for manoeuvre with regard to its core project: the transnational resistance. For, according to Hezbollah, the core question of legitimacy in the international realm, marked as it is by inescapable conflict dynamics, is: When is it legitimate to resort to violence? In Ennahda's and Hezbollah's legitimacy discourses, both recognition and resistance can be found – sometimes in rather unexpected places.

Chapter 6 shows that Ennahda has a progressive view of history as a story of the liberation of the Tunisian people and the Arab-Islamic world. In synchronicity with the unfolding of history, the Islamic movement eventually becomes a party of Muslim democrats in a free, democratic Tunisian state – recognised as equal in a global order that allows for a pluralism of domestic and regional orders. The road to this *telos*, however, is bumpy: authoritarian relapse, terrorism, foreign intervention and societal polarisation are among the dangers blocking the way. Conversely, Hezbollah has a dystopian outlook on the global order. It sees it as marked by an unescapable conflict structure between the oppressors and the oppressed. This struggle has existed since the early days of Islam and the martyrdom of Imam Husayn. Throughout this period, it has reappeared in different guises and schemes that need to be uncovered – and resisted. While this means the future prospects for the global order are, thus, somewhat bleak, there are glimpses of optimism in Hezbollah's belief in the plausibility of victory and in its visions of peaceful coexistence in the midst of difference.

The conclusion summarises Ennahda's and Hezbollah's world order discourse and the findings on recognition and resistance. Based on the empirical results, I characterise Ennahda as highly recognisant of and Hezbollah as moderately resistant towards a global order under Western hegemony. For both parties, significant overlaps with Western discourse can be seen. Both Ennahda and Hezbollah largely recognise the global order. Ennahda seeks to be recognised as a 'normal' party and for Tunisia to be recognised as a democratic state.

But it constantly – and rightfully – fears misrecognition and being forced back into marginalisation, demonisation and repression. Hezbollah performs resistance, articulately and sometimes dramatically. But this does not hide the fact that, in its own discourse, it reproduces many standards and norms found in Western hegemonic world order discourse. It also cannot deceive its antagonists about the political necessities and practical constraints the party faces. Next, I recontextualise Ennahda's and Hezbollah's discourses between 2011 and 2016 by discussing their ramifications for the now known future. The most recent history of Tunisia, Lebanon and the MENA region (2017–23) is presented and analysed with regard to its implications for the two actors' world order discourses. Finally, the conclusion discusses the broader lessons to be drawn from this study for other Islamists and the debate on a global order in transformation or even crisis. In line with other recent studies (Zarakol 2022), I conclude that world orders exist in the plural, that 'world ordering' is a practice pursued not only by states and not exclusively in the West – and that Islamists are (world) political actors more than religious ideologues or unscrupulous opportunists. They are, thus, less special than often assumed.

Notes

1. https://warontherocks.com/2016/02/the-syria-ceasefire-plan-is-a-sign-of-the-decaying-world-order/ (accessed 6 November 2023).
2. https://warontherocks.com/2016/02/the-syria-ceasefire-plan-is-a-sign-of-the-decaying-world-order/ (accessed 6 November 2023).
3. As 'Middle East' is still more common in academic accounts than the geographical term West Asia, I will continue to use it in this book. Given the problematic history of the term 'Middle East' (see, for example, Yilmaz 2012), however, it will be put in inverted commas. The abbreviation MENA will be used without inverted commas.
4. https://georgewbush-whitehouse.archives.gov/news/releases/2006/09/200609 05-4.html (accessed 6 October 2023).
5. https://georgewbush-whitehouse.archives.gov/news/releases/2006/09/200609 05-4.html (accessed 6 October 2023).
6. https://obamawhitehouse.archives.gov/farewell (accessed 6 November 2023).
7. While there are good reasons to believe that the withdrawal from Afghanistan marks a turning point for (military) counterterrorism, it is too early to claim that the 'global war on terror' era has ended. The full Russian invasion of Ukraine that

started in February 2022 has elevated interstate war and territorial defence to a priority in security discourse and policy for the foreseeable future. Among policy-makers and analysts, this war of aggression was perceived as a rupture in the global (security) order. For a moment, it seemed like the world would transition into a new era of international security – one in which the importance of 'Islamists' in Western discourse would decline, and where terrorism and counterterrorism, insurgency and counterinsurgency, as well as civil war and intervention, would gradually fade from view. However, this changed when Palestinian Hamas penetrated Israeli territory in October 2023, assaulting and killing over 350 members of the security forces, and perpetrating acts of terrorism that claimed the lives of more than 750 Israeli and foreign civilians. The Israeli government responded with massive air raids and initiated a comprehensive ground offensive. In just the first weeks of the Israeli military operations, thousands of Palestinians lost their lives, predominantly women and children, along with an unknown number of male civilians.

8. To mark the book's critical take on any substantialist idea or unambiguous meaning of the 'West', and the 'Western world order', in particular, I sometimes use quotation marks when the constructedness, deconstruction and reconstruction of these terms are explicitly addressed. To say that the 'West' has no universal and only temporarily fixed meanings is not the same as claiming that the idea has no power or real-world consequences (see Chapter 2).

9. To flag this problematic, that is, 'lumping', use of the term 'Islamism', it has so far been put in inverted commas. For the sake of readability, I will mostly abstain from doing so in the remainder of this book – except when I explicitly discuss issues of naming.

10. One pertinent example of academic 'lumping' is a study by Boaz Ganor (2015) called *Global Alert. The Rationality of Modern Islamist Terrorism and the Challenge to the Liberal Democratic World*, which appeared in the Columbia Studies in Terrorism and Irregular Warfare series. The study makes bold claims about the danger of 'Islamist terrorism', 'Islamist-jihadist terrorism', 'radical Islamists' and 'Islamic fundamentalism'. These terms are used interchangeably and are applied to, among others, Hezbollah, Hamas, al-Qa'ida and its branches, ISIS, Jabhat al-Nusra, Abu Sayyaf and Jemaah Islamiyya.

11. The complicated relationship between liberal and Western discourse is discussed in more detail in Chapter 2.

12. In contrast to what the term 'Cold War' suggests, the post-World War II era that lasted until 1990 witnessed many armed conflicts, military interventions and out-

right wars that were directly linked to the system competition between the US-led West and the USSR. See, for example, M. T. Berger (2008).

13. Exceptions include Dionigi (2014), Adraoui (2018), Darwich (2021b), Pfeifer (2021) and Stein (2021).

14. This has been a well-known diagnosis since the 'area studies controversy' at the end of the 1990s. It revolved around 'the alleged incompatibility of disciplinary-focussed social sciences and area studies', the former striving for 'a universalism that risks not properly considering existing cultural variations of specific regions', the latter tending to a particularism which 'claims that the region under investigation is unique and thus not comparable to other regions in the world' (Bank and Busse 2021, 550). See also Teti (2007) and Valbjørn (2017).

15. In his study of Lebanese Hezbollah's thought and practice until its manifesto of 2009, Filippo Dionigi (2014) follows a very similar line of thought but adopts the language of IR norms research. He argues that Hezbollah, too, is subjected to processes of norm socialisation and thereby moves beyond the idea that its politics is only about 'Islamic resistance' and, thus, hostile towards liberal norms. As Dionigi himself states, however, the events triggered by the Arab uprisings and in particular Hezbollah's violent engagement in the Syrian Civil War challenge Hezbollah's politics and the issue of norms in new ways (Dionigi 2014, 14). It is here that this book provides updated empirical evidence. Moreover, while socialisation into *and* contestation of norms (see, for example, Wiener 2018, 40–50) bear some similarities with the conceptual approach in this book, recognition and resistance refer to political (discursive) practices and thus open up a broader analytical view on Islamist politics in a world order under Western hegemony.

PART I

ISLAMISTS IN A WORLD ORDER UNDER WESTERN HEGEMONY

PART I

ISLAMISTS IN A WORLD
ORDER UNDER WESTERN
HEGEMONY

1

SETTING THE SCENE: HOW ISLAMISTS CAME TO BE KNOWN AS REJECTIONISTS AND ENEMIES OF WORLD ORDER

U ntil the end of the 'Cold War', social theorists across disciplines believed that religion would slowly but surely disappear and become irrelevant to political and social life. Secularisation was considered 'the only theory which was able to attain a truly paradigmatic status within the modern social sciences' (Casanova 1994, 17). As a corresponding normative claim, liberal and deliberative political theory in the Kantian tradition asserted that religion, on the one hand, and the state, politics and sometimes even the public, on the other, must be strictly separated from each other (Reder 2013, 63–6). In what seems like a rather drastic break with the empirical assessments of the secularisation paradigm seen in the 1990s, academics warned against 'the revenge of God' (Kepel 1993), 'the challenge of fundamentalism' (Tibi 1998) and the 'clash of civilizations' (Huntington 1993). And lastly, after the attacks of 9/11, what is often called 'Islamic terrorism' (Jackson 2007) went straight to the top of Western security agendas and, as a consequence, sparked new debates in the social sciences. In IR, for instance, the events of 9/11 triggered a critical reassessment of the structural secularism some believed to be prevalent in the discipline. These events had revealed that 'all mainstream theories of world politics . . . ignore the impact of religion, despite the fact that world-shaking political movements have so often been fueled by religious fervor' (Keohane 2002, 29). In political and social theory, too, there was analytical and normative re-evaluation, including the debate on 'postsecularism' which revolved around Jürgen Habermas's (2001a, 2009) revised position on religion. A critical interdisciplinary strand of research, heavily influenced by Talal Asad (1993), pursued an important agenda of deconstruction. It questioned the binary distinction between the religious and the secular, and scrutinised the conditions and effects of the 'politics of secularism' as a power practice (E.S. Hurd 2007). Notably, this debate successfully revealed how the figure of the 'Islamist' was constructed as the Other in Western hegemonic discourse, serving the self-affirmation of an insecure, but idealised secular Self (Mavelli 2013, 163).

This chapter uses this deconstructive lens to trace how 'Islamists' (and sometimes even Islam as a whole) have come to replace communism as the spectre that haunts the liberal world in the Western mind (Gerges 1999, vii–viii, Camilleri 2012, 1029). Of course, scholarly debates now take a far more nuanced approach to analysing political Islam, its intellectual history and its different real-world manifestations. Marc Lynch (2017) identifies two basic postures on political Islam present in policy circles in Washington, DC, but also in academia. There are the 'splitters', who 'produce finely-grained, accurate assessments of the ideological, organizational, and tactical differences among groups which share broadly-defined ideological orientations'. However, among some politicians and academics with a focus on policy and security (see, for example, Ganor 2015), a very crude, almost caricatural image of the 'Islamist' threat prevails. These are the 'lumpers', who 'typically view "radical Islam" as a coherent whole . . . from the manifestly apparent armed groups and terrorists to the underlying ideological and material support networks and broadly-held public attitudes that create an amenable environment' (Lynch 2017). This more or less monolithic enemy image of 'radical Islam' started to grow after the Iranian Revolution of 1979, gained importance during the 1990s (the 'clash of civilisations' and 'religious civil wars'), consolidated into a generalised and ubiquitous enemy image in the 2000s (al-Qaʿida and 'new terrorism'), experienced a revival in the 2010s (ISIS and the 'caliphate') and has survived to this day, especially in conservative and far-right circles in the West.

From the lumpers' perspective,[1] 'Islamists' are portrayed as suspicious, not only because of their alleged proneness to violence and the 'special character' of their ostensibly 'religious terrorism' (Gunning and Jackson 2011, 371). They are also constructed as an anachronism, as a relic from pre-modern times who stubbornly reject the principles of the Western world order as a legacy of the 'Westphalian synthesis' and the corresponding 'norms of authority' (Philpott 2002, 67, 76): the sovereign state as the only polity with authority, the proscription of intervention into the domestic affairs of other states and the consequent emergence of pluralism in international society, religious freedom and the decline of religion's 'temporal prerogatives' (Philpott 2002, 75). Islamists are said to challenge the modern state-based order because they rely on divine sovereignty (Anderson 2009, 196, Mandaville 2013, 178–9). This renders democratic forms of rule and legitimacy impossible, for 'any "Islamist" politics . . . demands a theocratic state in which there can be no debate about right and wrong, or about appropriate social order, because its aim must be "to bring about the rule of God"' (Teti and Mura 2009, 102). In this reading, Islamists' normative aspirations have to be totalitarian (Lynch 2017) and 'must eventually produce a caliphate' (Mandaville 2021). They are inextricably linked to the hereafter and do not provide room for concessions to the here and now – which makes it undesirable, indeed impossible, to negotiate with them (Nilsson and Svensson 2020, 391, Miller 2011).

Following the 'splitters', this book argues that the figure of the 'Islamist' must be deconstructed to investigate what kinds of relationship actually existing actors that are labelled 'Islamist' have with a world order under Western hegemony. I argue that the legacies of the secularisation paradigm,[2] which consists of the analytical secularisation thesis and the normative secularism claim, can still be felt in the more problematic parts of political and public discourse on Islamists and underlie the construction of the latter as the enemy of a world order deemed liberal. The 'global war on terror' further contributed to consolidating the image of an Islamist threat. Not only did it mean Muslims and Muslim communities came under a general suspicion of radicalism and potential radicalisation, it also further widened the concept of Islamism to include an increased number of more or less political forms of Islam. The 'evilisation' (Sheikh 2014, 496–7) of first al-Qaʿida and then ISIS also inflated the fear of these 'monsters' (Pinfari 2019, Bapat 2019) among Western publics. Without a clear distinction from other actors, sometimes even deliberately conflating the two, this led to the notion that Islamists are violent rejectionists (Maher 2016) of the global order – even though this is only true for a very small minority of them, namely the Salafi jihadists. Despite this, with their sometimes dramatic politics of rejection (Pfeifer and Günther 2021), Salafi jihadists have managed to hegemonise the imaginary of Islamism as being diametrically opposed to and violently fighting against the Western world order. But political Islam is a plural, modern discourse. So, while some Islamists may indeed reject parts of the world order as built and dominated by Western states, they may also recognise (and seek recognition within) this order (Geis, Clément and Pfeifer 2021) or choose to resist and transform it.

A World Order without Religion? Secularisation and Secularism in Social and Normative Theory

Some of the most important reflections on and basic distinctions in the study of religion stem from the very beginnings of sociology. Among the most influential Western thinkers of the nineteenth and twentieth century are Émile Durkheim, Max Weber, Thomas Luckmann and Peter L. Berger. These scholars all contributed, in different ways, to what came to be known as the secularisation thesis. This thesis predicts – and sometimes tacitly advocates – the decline or even disappearance of religious phenomena in modern societies. What the aforementioned authors understand as 'religion', however, varies. The search for a concept of religion (or the rejection of a transhistorically and transculturally valid definition; see Asad 1993, 17) is one of the driving forces for social theorising on religion and lies at the core of debates in sociology, political philosophy, anthropology, comparative politics, area studies and IR to this day.

One important distinction is between functionalist and substantive or essentialist understandings of religion (Pickel 2011). The former is associated with a Durkheimian tradition (Durkheim [1912] 1990), whereas Max Weber is considered a key thinker when it comes to essentialist conceptions of religion. Weber ([1920] 1972) was mainly concerned with the relationship between religion and economics. He assumes that confessions have certain characteristic elements that have specific effects on human, and especially economic, behaviour. Notably, the precursors of more elaborate sociological secularisation theories can already be found in Weber's work, too. He contends that one key driver of its eventual demise is paradoxically inherent in the history of religion (more specifically Protestantism) itself. By relocating the path to salvation to actively working in and on the world ('*aktiv asketische*

"Weltbearbeitung", Weber [1920] 1972, 263) and rejecting all magical means, Weber argues that Protestantism launched a process of internal rationalisation which coincided with the rise of rationalism in the empirical sciences. In so doing, it contributed to the disenchantment (*Entzauberung*) of the world (Weber [1920] 1972, 263) – a world in which religion itself became increasingly implausible and was relegated to the sphere of the irrational until it finally became the 'anti-rational super-personal power par excellence' (Weber [1920] 1972, 564, author's translation).

These theses about religion's self-defeat were further expanded into secularisation theory in the second half of the twentieth century. Following a Weberian tradition, P. L. Berger ([1967] 1990, 25) conceptualised religion as 'the human enterprise by which a sacred cosmos is established'. What exactly is understood as sacred varies throughout history, but it is always something extraordinary compared to everyday routine practices, and it is the opposite of both the profane and chaos. Religion bestows 'an ultimately valid ontological status' on social institutions and locates them 'within a sacred and cosmic frame of reference' (P. L. Berger [1967] 1990, 33), thereby both legitimising order and concealing its constructedness. With the rise of modern political orders, however, the status of religion changed. First, the state no longer operated as an enforcement agency ensuring religious practice but rather adopted more of a laissez-faire position. Second, the state no longer acted as an arbiter in an increasingly heterogeneous field of competing religions. Third, religion became more and more of a private matter, a '"choice" or "preference" of the individual' (P. L. Berger [1967] 1990, 133). It no longer fulfilled the function of connecting cosmos and nomos. The political order now drew on other sources of legitimacy. Through processes of marketisation and bureaucratisation, religion lost even more of its mysteriousness and awe-inspiring nature. The wide variety of different religious traditions on offer also challenged the claims of the confessions to 'unchanging verity' (P. L. Berger [1967] 1990, 145). In the end, religion was reduced to moral and therapeutic functions and subjected to 'consumer controls' (P. L. Berger [1967] 1990, 148). It was thereby de-objectivated and no longer provides 'overarching symbols for the society at large' (P. L. Berger [1967] 1990, 154). This process of the privatisation, individualisation and subjectivisation of religion is what came to be known as secularisation.[3]

Until the 1990s, the secularisation thesis that was formulated in the second half of the twentieth century remained largely unquestioned, despite empirical evidence that should have cast doubt on it much earlier (Casanova 2012). One explanation for this may be that some of the core claims of secularisation – like the separation of religion from institutions and its relegation to the private sphere – were supported by normative theories of secularism. These hold that 'religion should be confined to the private sphere' (Shah 2012, 2). In particular, they stipulate that institutions must be secular and that the democratic state must be fundamentally neutral. Such claims build on a strict separation of the public and the private sphere, as found in liberal political theory (for more recent contributions, see, for example, Laborde 2017). Following John Rawls's line of argument, for instance, religions cannot be the basis for public deliberation because they demand the acceptance of one comprehensive belief system. Modern societies, however, are marked by a plurality of reasonable doctrines, which means that citizens do not all share one single conception of 'the good'. In the public sphere, members of a society should therefore provide reasons for political action that are intelligible and comprehensible to other citizens, irrespective of the comprehensive doctrine to which they adhere (Rawls 1993, 133–72, 212–54, 1997). Such an 'overlapping consensus of reasonable ... comprehensive doctrines' (Rawls 1993, 144) can be supported by various theories of 'the good'. This liberal conception not only protects the public sphere from being captured by one all-encompassing belief system, it also protects religion by making sure that public reason 'does not trespass upon religious beliefs and injunctions insofar as these are consistent with essential constitutional liberties' (Rawls 1997, 803).

The relationship between religious language and the public sphere is also central for deliberative democratic theories. Jürgen Habermas is one of the major thinkers in this field but this is not the only reason to study him. His work on religion is remarkable because he significantly revised and adapted his position on its role in democratic societies. Originally, he had been sceptical about religion, which, he argued, undermined communicative action, as rather than allowing an intersubjective understanding to emerge from discourse, it predetermined the goals of that discourse instead (Reder 2013, 82). In his later works, however, Habermas recognises the moral role of religion in democratic societies and in the foundation of the liberal state (Habermas

2001a, 22–3). Religion bears significant semantic potential for a postsecular society. By providing a source of solidarity and motivational force for participation in public discourse, it can play a corrective role for the pathologies of modernity and a secularisation that is in danger of being 'derailed' ('*entgleisende Säkularisierung*', Habermas 2001a, 12). Habermas rejects the notion that citizens are capable and willing to separate political from religious values. He dismisses what he calls the 'Rawlsian *proviso*' (Habermas 2009, 129) as an excessive demand (*Zumutung*) made by religious citizens (Habermas 2009, 135) but still insists that rule must be neutral (*weltanschaulich neutrale Herrschaft*) and that the state give secular reasons (Habermas 2009, 136). He solves this problem by introducing a divide into the public sphere. In the 'wild' political, or informal public, religious arguments are allowed – and even desired for their semantic and truth potential (*Wahrheitsgehalte*) that help political life to flourish. The formal public sphere, however, must refrain from religious language. In order that state institutions (parliaments, courts, ministries, administrations) may both benefit from religion's specific qualities and remain neutral, Habermas introduces an institutional proviso of translation (*institutioneller Übersetzungsvorbehalt*): religious and secular citizens in the informal public sphere both have to invest in a reciprocal translation process. The former accept that their arguments have to be translated in order for them to access the formal public, while the latter open up for the truth potential of religion (Habermas 2009, 136–8). These citizens thus live in a postsecular society as envisioned by Habermas.

Religion's Violent Return to Social and Normative Theory and the Recalibration of the Secularisation Paradigm

It is no coincidence that Habermas began to rework his thoughts on religion in the early 2000s. In a speech given at the award ceremony for the Peace Prize of the German Book Trade in 2001, he shared his first ideas on a postsecular society. This was not only a reaction to the attacks of 9/11. Rather, Habermas asserted that 'whoever wants to avoid a war of civilizations has to remember the unfinished [*unabgeschlossen*] dialectic of our own, Occidental secularisation' (Habermas 2001a, 11, author's translation). Indeed, the 1990s had seen an outright explosion of publications on the supposed proneness of religions to violence (Baumgart-Ochse 2010) with a surprisingly one-sided focus on intra- and (potential) interstate wars (Huntington 1993), militancy (Kepel 1993) and fundamentalism (Tibi 1998). According to these primordialist accounts, religious convictions discretely affect world politics. They regularly create violent conflicts with unbelievers or believers of other denominations by establishing fixed images of an adversary or hostile Other that needs to be fought. While the more simplistic primordialist approaches to religious violence were quickly refuted on theoretical and empirical grounds (Senghaas 1998, Henderson and Tucker 2001, Sen 2006), other research projects were more thorough in their data collection and claims. One of the most extensive comparative studies, *The Fundamentalism Project (1987–1995)*, was published in five volumes by Martin E. Marty and R. Scott Appleby (1991–5). The project identified fundamentalist movements as groups with 'family resemblances' reacting to the marginalisation of religion and responding to the challenges imposed on them by the secular modern world. Despite the sophistication of the project, one of the investigators resentfully contended in retrospect that the project 'reinforced the perception that religion ... was becoming a significant national-security problem ... [and] the notion of a "clash of civilizations"' (Appleby 2011, 228). The zeitgeist of the 1990s was all-pervasive.

However, some of the foundations for a more (self-)critical debate which emerged in the 2000s were also laid in this period. For sociology and neighbouring disciplines had to come to terms with the fact that 'a whole body of literature ... loosely labelled "secularization theory" [was] essentially mistaken', given that the world was 'as furiously religious as it ever was, and in some places more so than ever' (P. L. Berger 1999, 2). A couple of years before Berger's famous restatement, José Casanova (1994) had presented a book on the persistence of religion in the public sphere. At the time, as he disclosed later, he interpreted this 'as an antimodern, antisecular, or antidemocratic reaction' (Casanova 2012, 25) and therefore problematic. Later, Casanova would become an important critic of secularisation on a more fundamental level.

In this sense, Talal Asad (1983, 1993) and his works on the anthropology of religion can be considered ahead of their time. His critique essentially addresses the way in which sociology and anthropology hitherto constructed conceptions of and knowledge on religion. He is particularly interested in the power involved in these processes of knowledge production. In these theories, religion is conceptualised as a system of symbolic meanings and generic functions. It thereby acquires a transhistorical and abstract character and is posited as universal – even though it has a Christian history and is deeply entrenched in social practices and power-knowledge formations which are specific to the European context (Asad 1993, 17). The validity of concepts of religion is always connected with particular traditions and historical developments, which is why Asad rejects any attempt to formulate a universal definition of religion. He sees the act of defining as a product of contingent discursive processes at a certain point in time and space (Asad 1993, 29). Asad's theory calls for analyses of the power involved in authoritatively defining religion and identifying its place in society. He became one of the reference authors, if not the central one, in a critical deconstructive strand of research on secularism in the 2000s and 2010s that will be introduced in the next section of this chapter.

More generally, what was perceived as 'religious resurgence'[4] (P. L. Berger 1999, 10) in the 1990s triggered a myriad of studies in the 2000s that revisited the secularisation paradigm from various disciplinary angles. In IR, the 9/11 attacks were read as a culmination point of religion's violent comeback and therefore as a 'challenge . . . to secularism in International Relations' (Philpott 2002). And yet, at first, mainstream publications and conferences in IR only tentatively considered religion (Kubálková 2009). Due to the dominance of positivism and rationalism, IR was not the most accommodating discipline when it came to the study of religion. What was described above as the 'Westphalian synthesis' (Philpott 2002) is deeply inscribed in IR's foundations and main theoretical strands, and 'the rejection of religion has become even stronger in IR than in most other disciplines' (Laustsen and Wæver 2000, 739).

In most realist approaches, if it is not considered entirely irrelevant, religion is either reduced to rhetoric that serves the legitimation of foreign policy (Barnett 2011, 94, Fox and Sandal 2010, 149–50) or relegated to the sphere of the irrational, 'almost always caus[ing] the state to act in ways that are counter to its national interests' (Barnett 2011, 93–4). Liberalists sometimes get caught up in a narrative of modernity which sees it as a 'linear process in which liberal formations such as capitalism, secularism, and democracy all progress together', sometimes even embracing a 'thoroughly secular ideology' and a self-understanding that is 'antithetical to religion' (Snyder 2011, 12, 17). With the rational, self-interested individual as the core analytical unit, liberalism is an obvious champion of secularisation theory – even though its ability to take non-state and transnational actors into account gives it an advantage over realism (Haynes 2014, 63). Liberal approaches which absorbed some concepts from constructivism, such as identity and norms, were more prone to accommodating religion (Moravcsik 1997, 525). Jeffrey Haynes, one of the first IR scholars to carry out substantial work on religion (see, for example, Haynes 1998, 2001), applied a soft-power approach to transnational religious actors, highlighting their ability to influence international politics despite their lack of military and economic resources compared to a state (Haynes 2008). Finally, with an empirically oriented research agenda, Jonathan Fox and Shmuel Sandler proposed reworking IR theories, especially realism as 'the most influential theory in international relations scholarship' (Fox and Sandler 2004, 167), to systematically take religion into account.

But some authors in IR remained very sceptical about such endeavours. For instance, Vendulka Kubálková (2009, 28, 29) criticised approaches that maintained a commitment to a positivist research tradition while trying to integrate religion into existing key theories. She read them as attempts at 'forcing "irrational" religion into secular and positivist categories and treating it as a culture or identity', thereby embracing an instrumentalist view of religion and reducing it to religious institutions as 'elements of transnational civil society or expressions of general cultural tendencies'. Instead, she advocated a more fundamental inquiry into the 'foundational myths and assumptions on which the discipline has been built' (Kubálková 2009, 30). Important stimuli for this agenda came from critical security studies investigating the securitisation of religious referent objects (Laustsen and Wæver 2000), and approaches in the tradition of the English School (Thomas 2000, 2005). But first and foremost, IR took inspiration from the debates in other disciplines.

In peace and conflict studies, for example, authors sought to put forward alternatives to the primordialist view of religion as violence prone (Hasenclever and Rittberger 2000, Baumgart-Ochse 2016). Instrumentalists argued that religion was merely a frame applied to conflicts that were actually about modernisation or about socio-economic grievances (Senghaas 2002). Functionalists like Mark Juergensmeyer (2008) emphasised the functional equivalence of the nation-state and religion in providing an ideology of order, which creates rivalry between them. Consequently, the 'sacralisation of political demands' occurred where the secular nation-state failed to fulfil its promises (Juergensmeyer 2008, 217). Religion emerged as a form of resistance to the nation-state, offering the 'language of ultimate order' and the interpretation of conflict as the 'drama of cosmic war' (Juergensmeyer 2008, 213, 214). Constructivists saw religion not as something external which is attached to the actual conflict after the event but rather as a cognitive and normative structure through which the social world could be interpreted in order to be intersubjectively meaningful. Religion 'provide[s] social actors with value-laden conceptions of the self and others' (Hasenclever and Rittberger 2000, 647) and it is constitutive of social action, including violence. Whether or not religion plays an escalating role in a conflict, then, depends on the behaviour of political elites who may (but do not have to) mobilise religious traditions for the legitimation of violence (Hasenclever and De Juan 2007). One important insight from this strand of research is that

> the impact of religious traditions on conflict behaviour is deeply ambiguous: they can make violence more likely, insofar as a reading of holy texts prevails that justifies armed combat . . . [but they can also] make violence less likely, insofar as a reading of holy texts prevails that delegitimises the use of violence in a given situation or even generally. (Hasenclever and Rittberger 2000, 650)

The 'ambivalence of the sacred' (Appleby 2000) with regard to violence implies room for agency and underlies pleas for interreligious and intercivilisational dialogue (Dallmayr 2002, Michael and Petito 2009).

During the 2000s, normative reassessments were made in both political theory and philosophy, beginning with Habermas's sketch of a postsecular society and soon followed by the works of Charles Taylor, who became his most important critical interlocutor in the debate on religion. Besides his genealogy *A Secular Age* (2007), Taylor also developed a normative critique of the obsession of (liberal) democratic theory with religion as its Other. He opposes '"subtraction stories" of modernity in general, and secularity in particular' which suggest that human beings slowly but surely 'liberated themselves from certain earlier, confining horizons, or illusions, or limitations of knowledge' (Taylor 2007, 22). By disaggregating what appears as a coherent story of secular liberation, he identifies three secularities, among which he highlights the one which refers to the changing conditions of belief as the most striking. He argues that not only has religious belief lost its status as the default mode of accessing the world, but it has even become 'hard to believe in God in [many milieux of] the modern West' (Taylor 2007, 539).

Although, as in the Habermasian postsecular society, believers and non-believers live side by side in the secular age, Taylor is more interested in the hierarchy that is still established between them. An epistemic distinction is drawn between secular reason, as available to 'any honest, unconfused thinker', and religiously grounded arguments, which 'will always be dubious and in the end only convincing to people who have already accepted the dogmas in question' (Taylor 2011, 53). Secular reasons are *a priori* more convincing in the field of moral and political orders because they are deemed neutral. Religion, in contrast, is seen as irrational and potentially dangerous. '[R]eligiously informed thought is somehow less rational than purely "secular" reasoning. [This] attitude has a political ground (religion as threat), but also an epistemological one (religion as a faulty mode of reason)' (Taylor 2011, 51). According to Taylor, however, it is unclear why, in principle, secular reasons should be any more accessible than religious ones:

> If we take key statements of our contemporary political morality . . . I cannot see how the fact that we are desiring/enjoying/suffering beings, or the perception that we are rational agents, should be any surer basis . . . than the fact that we are made in the image of God. (Taylor 2011, 54)

According to Taylor, the debate on secularism should therefore be realigned. Overcoming its fixation on religion, it should ask for the fitting 'response of the democratic state to diversity' – which, for Taylor, refers to any viewpoint (Taylor 2011, 36). Habermas countered this claim by arguing that religion demands from its believers that they participate 'in cultic practices in which no Kantian or Utilitarian has to participate in order to make a good Kantian or Utilitarian argument' (Habermas and Taylor 2009). For Taylor, however, these non-religious epistemic universes also presuppose certain experiences and they may be as inaccessible as religious language. Therefore, secularism's claim to neutrality should not single out religious language as unsuitable for the formal public sphere. In Taylor's words, the state's self-articulation 'can't be in Benthamite language, it can't be simply in Kantian language, it can't be in

Christian language' (Habermas and Taylor 2009). The core normative question, then, was whether or not religion had to be treated differently from other belief systems, convictions or worldviews (see also Dworkin 2013).

Sociology reacted to the empirical challenge of the secularisation paradigm in two main ways. One group of scholars considered its rejection to be premature and worked to reformulate and refine the claims of secularisation theory. For instance, Steve Bruce (2002) disaggregated the secularisation thesis into several causal linkages which can individually be subjected to empirical investigation. In the end he insists that 'religion diminishes in social significance, becomes increasingly privatized, and loses personal salience' (Bruce 2002, 30) – at least in the form of Christian, church-based religious belief seen in Western states. In other contexts, however, specifically in ethnic civil wars or conditions of rapid social change, religion may not in fact disappear. Similarly, Pippa Norris and Ronald Inglehart (2011) linked the survival of religion in some but not in other places to varying levels of affluence and existential security.

The second group of scholars took their criticism further and came up with different results. Casanova (2007, 105), like Bruce, made the case that secularisation theory needs to be conceptually divided into subtheses. For

> what usually passes for a single theory of secularization [are actually] three separate propositions . . .: 1) secularization as a differentiation of the secular spheres from religious institutions and norms, 2) secularization as a decline of religious beliefs and practices, and 3) secularization as a marginalization of religion to a privatized spheresphere. (Casanova 2006, 12)

With this disaggregation, Casanova found that only the first of these theses is sufficiently supported by empirical evidence to be defended as a core aspect of secularisation theory. But he pursued his differentiation agenda even further. He scrutinised public religion in different contexts and was able to show that the empirically observable processes of secularisation differ from one another with regard to their course and outcomes. There are multiple 'secularisms' and 'secularities' (Casanova 2009, Wohlrab-Sahr and Burchardt 2012) at work as public religion interacts in different ways with the state, politics and civil society. There is no single path leading to the secular age or, for that matter, modernity (Eisenstadt 2000b).

Casanova's work contributed to deconstructing the binary opposition between 'the secular' and 'the religious' and helped to sensitise the secularisation debate to the Western origins of its assumptions, warning, as others had done, against the universalisation of a particular experience. But as Casanova himself suggests, some ideological forms of secularism are firmly rooted in cognitive apparatuses and therefore hard to tackle, operating subtly as an 'epistemic knowledge regime that may be unreflexively held and phenomenologically assumed as the taken-for-granted normal structure of modern reality, as a modern *doxa* or as an "unthought"' (Casanova 2009, 151). He thereby formulates the suspicion that a deep-seated secularist bias may be present not only in everyday practice and discourse in Western societies but also in political and academic accounts of religion. Revealing and deconstructing this bias was the agenda of the research strand presented in the next section.

Deconstructing Secularism and the Muslim Other through Critical Theory

So far, this chapter has reconstructed the origins and main claims of the secularisation paradigm. It has also shown how what was perceived as 'religious resurgence' and 'religiously motivated violence' in the 1990s challenged the secular assumptions inherent in various disciplines. The adjustments made in the different disciplines ranged from a reformulation of secularisation theory to a normative reassessment of religion's role in society to theoretical adaptations which allowed religion to be accommodated. What many contributions to this dynamic debate had in common, however, was that they posited religion to be something which is *a priori* located and meant to be outside the realm of politics. One important strand of research addresses this tacit assumption and shows that the religious–secular distinction is inherent in a specific discourse which produces the political as a secular realm with religion on its outside. To the scholars participating in this debate, the divide between religion and politics is therefore not natural but a 'powerful political settlement' (E. S. Hurd 2012, 47). Rather than a normative political theory or ideological stance, secularism, then, is a 'power-knowledge regime . . . that shapes modes, forms, and practices of religiosity compatible with and instrumental to the reproduction of state sovereignty' (Mavelli 2014, 174). It is precisely this authority of the modern secular state to continually define religion, to draw and redraw the line between religious and secular realms, to define and redefine the '"proper place of religion" in a secular society' (Asad 2006, 526) and to 'become involved in the regulation and management of religious life' (Mahmood 2015, 3) that comes under scrutiny in the debate on the 'politics of secularism' (E. S. Hurd 2007).[5]

This debate primarily took place in IR but owes its key insights to contributions from other disciplines, especially the works of anthropologist Talal Asad. It started by deconstructing binary oppositions which not only separate the religious and the secular but also establish the subordination of the former to the latter (Wilson 2012, 58). Such oppositions include '*belief* and *knowledge*, *reason* and *imagination*, *history* and *fiction*, *symbol* and *allegory*, *natural* and *supernatural*, *sacred* and *profane* . . . [and] pervade modern secular discourse, especially in its polemical mode' (Asad 2003, 23, original emphasis). One particularly important distinction juxtaposes the violence-prone nature of religion, especially Islam 'as peculiarly [violent] (undisciplined, arbitrary, singularly oppressive)' (Asad 2003, 10), with secularism's claim that it is concerned with reducing 'pain and suffering as such', which is actually about 'the pain and suffering that can be attributed to religious violence because that is pain the modern imaginary conceives of as gratuitous' (Asad 2003, 11). In this perspective, the Peace of Westphalia is part of a 'liberal mythology' (Thomas 2000, 819) according to which peace is the benefit of the privatisation of religion, the secularisation of politics and the rise of the modern state. At the same time, however, the 'myth of religious violence' not only has the capacity to help 'marginalize discourses and practices labeled religious' (Cavanaugh 2009, 225) but can also be used to legitimise resorting to the use of 'secular' force against religious actors, especially in the context of counterterrorism practices (Gunning and Jackson 2011). For, as William T. Cavanaugh (2009, 226) puts it, 'their irrational violence must be met with rational violence', which may include the use of military force and war.

It is no coincidence that the critical debate on the politics of secularism gained traction in the 2000s at a time when the US and its allies began waging the GWOT, framed as necessary counterviolence against the threat of 'Islamic terrorism'. However, the characterisation of secularism as a hegemonic discourse on and authoritative definition of the relationship between religion and politics is a more systematic intervention and should not be limited to the empirical post-9/11 context. Elizabeth Shakman Hurd argues, for instance, that secularism can operate as a 'conceptual apparatus' (2007, 114) through which events are perceived in foreign policymaking. In Hurd's view, two variants of secular discourse inform practices in international politics and IR theorising to this day. The first discursive tradition, laicism, is a legacy of the Enlightenment and claims that religion has successfully been banished to the private sphere or has disappeared entirely. Judeo-Christian secularism, in contrast, sees 'the separation of church and religion [as] a Western achievement that emerged from adherence to common European religious and cultural traditions' (E. S. Hurd 2012, 42). Both traditions have a certain connection to Orientalism, as they were developed at least partially with the Muslim Other in mind. Today, the two versions of secularism construct political Islam as a refusal to accept the public–private divide and as a deviation from '"normal" politics' (E. S. Hurd 2007, 117):

> In laicism, political Islam appears as a superficial expression of more fundamental economic and political interests and an infringement of irrational forms of religion upon would-be secular public life in Muslim-majority societies . . . In Judeo-Christian secularism, political Islam appears as an undemocratic commingling of Islam and politics that stands in sharp distinction to the modern . . . separation of church and state (E. S. Hurd 2007, 118)

As this shows, the binary of the secular and the religious is also often linked to the 'divide between the West and the rest of the world' (Cavanaugh 2009, 205). The politics-of-secularism debate is therefore closely linked to postcolonial thought. It also clearly formulates its critique against the backdrop of the aforementioned obsession of Western secular discourse with Islam and especially 'Islamists' and 'political Islam'. Characteristic of the construction of this religious subject is that it has neither internal differentiations nor clear conceptual boundaries. Secular discourse 'equates the appearance of Islamic religion in political practice with fundamentalism and intolerance' (E. S. Hurd 2007, 118), thereby neglecting the dispute over how religion and politics should relate to each other within the discourse of political Islam (E. S. Hurd 2007, 128) and portraying 'Islamism' as a general threat to modernity.

The merit of the debate is in particular that first, it revealed the deeper roots of the Western production of Islam as its 'ultimate "Other"' (Mavelli and

Petito 2012, 932, Euben 1999, Asad 2009) in secular discourse. Second, it also provided the tools to deconstruct the enemy image of 'Islamism' which has become pervasive in political and public debate and some intellectual circles since George W. Bush declared the GWOT. At the same time, this strand of research as an 'emergent orthodoxy' (Mufti 2013, 7) in the study of secularism has been criticised in two main respects. The first is its tendency to create new essentialised images in the course of deconstructing others. This refers not only to the structural understanding of secularism, which depicts it as oddly unchangeable and free of agency. By adopting the West/non-West divide, authors in the field also run the risk of re-essentialising both sides of that divide 'in a manner that mirrors the narratives of orientalist scholarship' (Lord 2019, 688). The 'Muslim world' is portrayed, then, as being primarily inhabited by religious subjects (Enayat 2017, 92–3), which also disregards actually existing developments and advocates of secularisation in this geographical area (al-Azmeh 2020). In a 'jargon of authenticity' (Mufti 2013, 11), authors who criticise the flat imaginary of Islamism as a form of totalitarianism (Cavanaugh 2009, 222) or the idea of a 'responsibility of Islam as a religion and Arabs as a people for acts of terror' (Asad 2003, 3) may actually be guilty of undue reductions themselves. They take

> varieties of contemporary political Islam as representative of the (Sunni) Islamic 'tradition' as such . . . [and suggest] that as a spiritual, intellectual, and political culture, Islamism marks a 'return' of Islam, either uncontaminated by, or having shaken itself free of, the liberal thought and practice of the modern West. (Mufti 2013, 10)

In this way, agency is only accorded to those who systematically reject Western legacies such as secularism, while all others are somehow implicated in the logic of colonial domination and contemporary imperialism (Lord 2019, 688–9). What is more, Islamists are portrayed as untouched by modernity, 'even though their revivalist claims of religious authenticity are undeniable products of the very cultural logics they disavow and disown' (Mufti 2013, 12). Islamism and modernity are inextricably linked to each other.[6] But this trait of Islamism tends to be overlooked in the debate on the politics of secularism because authors target only secularism in their critical analysis, not (political) Islam (Enayat 2017, 93).[7] This second point of criticism contends that one-sided deconstructions make it seem like, on the one hand, non-Western intellectual traditions do not have the potential to become hegemonic or seek domination over others. On the other hand, such traditions also tend to equate liberalism, of which secularism is a part, with the West. This implies that either other Western intellectual traditions, from 'forms of communitarianism and conservatism . . . to forms of radical thinking and practice', are defined out of existence – or that liberalism 'is being utilized to indicate the culture and politics of the modern West as such, [but then] it can hardly be conceived of as a unitary intellectual system' (Mufti 2013, 13).

One does not have to agree with all the readings of and criticism levelled at key contributors to the deconstruction of secularism (for a differentiated discussion, see March 2015). For the purposes of the remainder of this book, I home in on one message from the controversy between the scholars who contribute to the politics-of-secularism debate, on the one hand, and their critics, on the other. The relationship between Islamists and the West – or in this book, the world order under Western hegemony – needs to be made more complex in two ways.

First, I see the danger of drawing an all-too-simplistic picture of both Islamism and the West, as identified by the second group of authors, the critics mentioned above. Neither secularism nor the Western world order should be conceived of as an unchangeable or unequivocal structure. Both are discursively contested from within and from outside the West – which is itself home to various practices and intellectual traditions, including several secularisms and liberalisms. The power of these structures should also 'not be understood as absolute, but hegemonic and therefore constantly open to struggle and contestation' (Mavelli and Petito 2014, 6). In this sense, Islamists – like other actors in a world order under Western hegemony – certainly do have agency. This fact has so far been neglected as a direct object of inquiry in the critical debate on secularism (March 2015, 110–11). This book aims to provide such a perspective by conducting an empirical analysis of Islamists' position vis-à-vis the Western-dominated world order. To this end, it is necessary to first disaggregate and paint a more nuanced picture of the Western-dominated world order, which is what I seek to do in Chapter 2.

Second, however, I concur with the first group of scholars contributing to the politics-of-secularism debate in their assessment that the West does have an obsession with a supposedly dangerous Islam and especially what is framed as an Islamist threat. As I show in the next section, there is an abundance of evidence of both the securitisation of Islam and the 'evilisation' of Islamism in the GWOT era. What is more, the position of violent rejectionism as held by a small group of Salafi jihadists has managed to almost monopolise the notion of what an Islamist is, what they think about the Western-dominated world order, and how they behave towards it. We might refer to this as the al-Qaʻida/ISIS effect on Western perceptions of political Islam.[8] However, Islamists' agency and the repertoire available to them transcend violent rejection, as I will argue in the remainder of this chapter.

The Stubborn Persistence of the Islamist Enemy Image

As has also been seen in other disciplines, IR, peace and conflict studies, and security studies reconfigured their theoretical understanding of religion and its role in politics under the impression of the ostensibly pervasive Islamist threat. Even before 2001, scholars of international security came to the conclusion that the alleged danger of religion 'has most keenly been felt in the form of an alleged threat from . . . primarily Islamic fundamentalism' (Laustsen and Wæver 2000, 705). With the attacks of 9/11, the destiny of what was then called 'Islamic terrorism' at the top of Western security agendas was sealed. A plethora of studies appeared, seeking to understand political Islam and in particular its violent manifestations, as well as what might constitute suitable policy reactions (for a rich and critical discussion, see Volpi 2010). Even though phenomena that relate to Islam, the 'Middle East' and North Africa, and Muslim-majority societies were (and still are) overrepresented in social science accounts of religion, empirical studies have become more varied. The 'obsession' with Islam itself became the basis for innovative theory-building and critical inquiries, as the previous chapter demonstrated. The academic attention devoted to the concepts of 'political Islam' and 'Islamism', however, entailed a blurring of important distinctions, the proliferation of definitions and, simultaneously, the interchangeable use of terms that describe divergent phenomena, actors and behaviours (Volpi 2010, 149–50).

This conceptual vagueness in academic discourse fed into but was also informed by a highly securitised public and political discourse on 'Islamic terrorism'. As concepts in use, 'Islamism' and 'political Islam' were often directly associated with jihadism, violence and terrorism. This was one effect of the aforementioned GWOT frame which George W. Bush introduced into his rhetoric after the 9/11 attacks and which subsequently proliferated – albeit not without resistance or calls for alternative framings – to European and other contexts. In the course of the GWOT, several practices, laws and institutions were established to fight terrorism in and beyond the West (Josua 2021), culminating in what has been called a 'transnational counter-terrorism order' (De Londras 2019). In the US, the GWOT frame served to legitimate several counterterrorism policies which often operated through the externalisation of the terrorist threat (Hellmuth 2021). These infamous measures included torture, offshore detention and extraordinary renditions, mass surveillance, the use of military force, including smaller-scale military and special operations, and drone strikes in several countries, as well as larger counterterrorism operations like the French-led Operation Barkhane in Mali (2014–22) with the G5 Sahel countries as partners, and finally fully fledged wars in Afghanistan (2001–21) and Iraq (2003–11, 2014–21) conducted by coalitions of Western (and Arab) states.

Stacey Gutkowski (2014, 5) calls these the '9/11 wars' and suggests that they revealed 'secular *ways of war*, habits of doing and behaving in war' (original emphasis). In her study of the British secular security habitus, she shows that the security and public discourse on Islam, Islamism and jihadism evolved over time to become more knowledgeable and nuanced. However, the initial reaction to 9/11, constructed as an 'unintelligible, insurmountable and "cultural" trauma for the West' (Gutkowski 2014, 20), was marked by hysteresis. State apparatuses were not calibrated to respond to jihadism. On the one hand, Gutkowski argues, this was visible in the way knowledge on al-Qaʻida and jihadism was produced. As she demonstrates using the British case, in their attempt to learn as quickly as possible about this previously underestimated phenomenon, security circles readily found and embraced the myths of religious violence and the clash of civilisations. This led to the 'production . . . of jihadist Islamism as a reified (and surprisingly coherent) knowledge category for British foreign and security strategists, politicians and senior officers' (Gutkowski 2014, 29). In 2001–3, the 'diagnostic period' (Gutkowski 2014, 31) of the 9/11 wars, the enemy was constructed as a 'global Islamist threat' or 'global jihad'. Even among academics it was not uncommon to equate al-Qa'ida with Islam. There was an outright 'fetishization of . . . Islamic funda-mentalism' (Gutkowski 2014, 95). But according to Gutkowski, the al-Qa'ida brand of Salafi jihadism had 'yet to pose a realistic threat to the current liberal, secular global order' (2014, 18).

On the other hand, European and US armed forces also lacked the military and tactical abilities required for counterinsurgency wars and found it dif-ficult to adapt to what seemed like an ever-changing insurgency. The 'military approach to counter-terrorism' was premised on the assumption that 'fighting them "over there" is better than waiting until terrorist attacks at home' (Boyle 2019, 385). For the war zones of Iraq and Afghanistan, this entailed a blending of counterterrorism, focused on the use of kinetic force, with the 'winning the hearts and minds' approach of counterinsurgency (Boyle 2019, 386–9) as set down in *The U.S. Army/Marine Corps Counterinsurgency Field Manual* (FM 3-24/MCWP 3-33.5), which was published in 2006.

Given the failure of the counterterrorism measures taken, the US shifted to a '"strategy against violent extremism" [to address] a wider perceived prob-lem of "support in the Muslim world for radical Islam"' (Kundnani and Hayes 2018, 6) from 2005 onwards. The turn to 'violent extremism' and 'radical Islam' exacerbated the effects of the GWOT within Western societies. Here, the idea that there was a 'direct connection between "Islam" and "Terrorism"' (Mavelli 2013, 165) increasingly took root, despite a more nuanced discourse among parts of the political elites and security circles. The fear that individuals would radicalise and become 'lone wolves' (Byman 2017), part of a 'leader-less jihad' (Sageman 2008) or perpetrators of 'stochastic terrorism' (Robinson 2021) reinforced the image of a potential threat 'from within' Western socie-ties in the form of 'homegrown terrorism' (Hafez and Mullins 2015). The shift to the 'preventing and countering violent extremism' (PCVE) terminol-ogy further blurred the distinction between violent action and ideological sympathy (Kundnani and Hayes 2018, 6), supporting the general suspicion towards Muslim individuals, communities and organisations and the securiti-sation of Islam (Mavelli 2013). Not only were Muslims increasingly subjected to extraordinary measures, such as renditions and detentions; Western soci-eties also discussed several variations of the 'Muslim question' (Mandaville 2021), such as the possibility of 'appropriate integration' of Muslims, the Muslim 'threat' to Western values such as democracy, freedom and secularism, and the fear of a cultural 'Islamisation' of European societies through the 'waves' of Muslim refugees, as propagated by anti-Islamic movements and parties (see, for example, Mavelli 2012, Roy 2013a, Nabers 2016). The GWOT, then, gave rise to Islamophobia as a phenomenon of global scope (Bakali and Hafez 2022).

Public and political discourse also fell down several slippery conceptual and normative slopes attached to the terms 'Islamism' and 'political Islam'. On the one hand, the two terms were often equated with Islam. This meant that Muslims were viewed as the Other relative to Western values because they were not able to draw a line between private faith and public politics. On the other hand, 'Islamism' and 'political Islam' were part of a larger set of labels used to describe the 'global threat' Muslims allegedly posed. These labels included 'militant Islam', 'Islamic fundamentalism', 'Islamic extremism', 'jihadism', 'Salafi jihadism', 'jihadi terrorism', 'global jihad', 'Islamic terrorism', 'violent extremism', 'religiously motivated terrorism' and so on (Volpi 2010, 149–50). And while careful and nuanced analyses were present at an early stage, and important counterdiscourses emerged during the GWOT years, too, the idea of a 'global Islamist threat' persisted. This concept was renewed and, to some degree, dramatised through the rise of ISIS in the 2010s. While the group's inception dates back to 1999, it reached the peak of its power in 2014 (Bamber-Zryd 2022). Due to its sophisticated media strategy (Harmon and Bowdish 2018, 209–13), ISIS 'captured the imagination of a global public and positioned itself at the centre of . . . security debates' at the time (Friis 2018, 244). ISIS managed, through transgressive forms of violence (Friis 2018, 256) and by making mediatisation a constitutive part of this violent logic (Pfeifer and Günther 2021), to convince a global audience that its evilness went 'beyond anything we [had] ever seen' (Friis 2015, Richards 2017, Rogers 2018, Fermor 2021).

The rise of ISIS and its considerable success in gaining and holding territory in Iraq and Syria, the attacks it committed in Europe (and, as tends to be forgotten, other parts of the world) and the military efforts by the GCAD since 2014 had an important effect: 'Islamism' was associated with the violent rejection of not only Western values and norms but the global order and its core principles and institutions per se. A lack of distinction between Salafi jihadism, on the one hand, and Islamism as well as other forms of political Islam, on the other, led to the perception that ISIS's performance of violent rejectionism was somehow representative of Islamists' position towards the world order. More generally, it also contributed to the ignorance of Islamist diversity and intra-Islamist struggles (Milton-Edwards 2014). In 2020, on the occasion of the anniversary of the 2019 attacks in Nice, the French minister of the interior, Gérald Darmanin, reminded the public that 'we' are at 'war against an internal and external enemy . . . the Islamist ideology . . . a form of twenty-first century fascism' (Lepelletier 2020). This snapshot of a strongly martial framing of the problem should not be considered typical of Western political discourse and, even though we could identify similar examples from other European and North American states, the 'lumpers' are probably a minority compared to the 'splitters' (Lynch 2017). Nevertheless, a loud minority can still have quite an effect. This is, for instance, reflected in the almost constant and, relative to actual numbers and risk assessments, highly exaggerated threat perception of terrorism among US citizens. Despite articulate and well-founded warnings expressed at an early stage that 'fears of the omnipotent terrorist . . . may have been overblown' (Mueller 2006, 8), no significant changes in threat perceptions seem to have occurred since the early years of the GWOT (Krause et al. 2022).[9]

Moving beyond the Image of Islamist Rejectionism: Between Recognising and Resisting Global Order

In light of this diagnosis, my book further contributes to developing a more nuanced view of Islamism, specifically from the perspective of its relationship with the Western world order. While no such study exists to date, the rich scholarship on non-state actors in the MENA region and on Islamism offers very fertile ground for cultivating a nuanced study on Islamists and the world order. In IR, non-state actors are still underrepresented when it comes to studying their external behaviour beyond the resort to violence or potential security threat. With regard to armed non-state actors, May Darwich (2021b, 2) recently suggested that their 'actorness and foreign relations [should be established] as a new area of inquiry for foreign policy analysis'. Indeed, research on ANSAs has so far mainly focused on their violent behaviour in the context of civil wars. In the last ten years, however, the study of ANSAs' order-building has become a lively field of inquiry. One important debate, now established at the core of conflict studies, investigates the phenomenon of rebel governance (Malthaner and Malešević 2022, Loyle et al. 2023, Pfeifer and Schwab 2023a). Something that is so far underrepresented in this debate, however, is how ANSAs establish external relations during wartime and peacetime to influence (global) politics through non-violent means. The exceptions here are studies of rebel diplomacy (Coggins 2015, Huang 2016) and, more broadly, the study of ANSAs' struggle for recognition (Geis, Clément, and Pfeifer 2021). ANSAs address international, even global, audiences (Clément, Geis, and Pfeifer 2021, Pfeifer 2021, Sienknecht 2021) and are embedded in global normative structures (Hensell and Schlichte 2021). The study of rebels as contributing to the production of order, as well as the recent attention that IR has cautiously devoted to ANSAs and their actorness in international relations, are two fields to which this study seeks to make a contribution.

The third is the academic debate on Islamism. This is mainly rooted in area studies and rarely overlaps with the other two fields (exceptions are Cook and Maher 2023, Darwich 2021a, Stein 2021). As has been argued in the context of the 'area studies controversy' (Valbjørn 2017, Bank and Busse 2021), IR only produces limited theory-oriented knowledge on the MENA region and is often reluctant to revisit its theoretical assumptions.[10] It also tends to focus narrowly on militant Islamists, which reinforces the false impression that political Islam is associated with violence. Conversely, the study of Islamism is often confined to national and regional contexts rather than being positioned in the study of international or global politics (exceptions are Dionigi 2014, Adraoui 2018, Darwich 2021b, 2021a).

One core debate in the field revolves around the meaning of Islamism, its distinction from conceptual neighbours and the questioning of the dichotomies that structure inquiries. Among such binaries is the distinction between state and non-state politics where the former is associated with secular rule and the latter with religious opposition (Cesari 2014). As early as the 1990s, some authors suggested that Islam was being used as 'the language of politics in the Muslim world' (Eickelman and Piscatori 1996, 12) by both rulers and opponents. The more common view, however, conceptualises political Islam as the politicisation and instrumentalisation of Islam by Islamist actors using religion as a tool of opposition against the allegedly or self-proclaimed secular state. A similar framing was also used by rulers who felt threatened by the mass protests in the course of the Arab uprisings and sought to delegitimise the opposition (Pfeifer 2017). But studies show that Arab states, rather than refraining from intervening in the religious sphere or maintaining a 'neutral' secular posture, had established a hegemonic status for Islam as part of their nation-building projects in the twentieth century. They nationalised religious institutions and personnel, and religious doctrine was taught in public schools. They legally discriminated against other religions in the public sector and restricted certain rights and freedoms on religious grounds (Cesari 2014, 3–18). Recently, the sharp distinction between state and non-state actors has been questioned on a more general level (see, for example, Pfeifer and Schwab 2023b). Authors in the field have argued that non-state actors should be viewed as contributing to the production of regional order and as partners in state hegemonic strategies (Stein 2021). Others have demonstrated that core concepts in Islam are mobilised by and contested between state and non-state actors alike (Piscatori and Saikal 2019). Finally, some have suggested understanding Islamism not as a label to be attached to a certain kind of actor but more broadly as a discourse.[11] For instance, Islamism is then coneptualised as 'an articulatory practice whose characterisation lies in its ability to hegemonise the whole discursive horizon by turning "Islam" into the master signifier of the Muslim communities' (Mura 2015, 25).

A second core debate in the study of Islamism concerns the question of how to classify different actors and their evolution over time. As a key author in the field, Olivier Roy defines Islamism rather narrowly as 'the explicit recasting of Islam as a political ideology ... and a stress on the need to control and build an "Islamic state"' (Roy 2012a, 19–20). It is this Islamist project of transforming society through the state that Roy concluded had failed in the early 1990s: 'The Islamic revolution, the Islamic state, the Islamic economy are myths,' he stated (1994, 27). But this 'collapse of Islamism as a political ideology' (Roy 2013b, 16) did not imply that Islamist movements would disappear. Rather, Roy predicted two developments. On the one hand, some Islamist actors would opt for a trajectory of transformation into a conservative party (along the Turkish AKP model). These actors would become post-Islamist. On the other hand, he expected some Islamists to be further challenged by the rise of neofundamentalism 'that stressed a strict return to purely religious norms' (Roy 2013b, 16). Salafists, whether quietist, political or violent, belong to this trend (Wiktorowicz 2006). In the simplest terms, Salafism is a 'philo-

sophical outlook which seeks to revive the practices of the first three generations of Islam' or which 'believes in progression through regression' (Maher
2016, 7). Salafists may use different methods, including violent ones. If they
resort to violence, they are called Salafi jihadists. The most widely known representatives of Salafism are two Salafi-jihadist groups, al-Qaʻida and ISIS. Both
are what Fawaz Gerges (2016, 24) calls a marriage between ultraconservative
Wahhabism ('Saudi Salafism') and the radical jihadism developed in Egypt in
the 1950s and 1960s by Sayyid Qutb and his disciples. Whereas al-Qaʻida was
an 'underground, transnational, borderless organization', ISIS additionally
'managed to blend in with local Sunni communities' (Gerges 2016, 223) and
made establishing statehood its core strategy. Another important innovation
of this second generation of Salafi jihadism was the reorganisation of enemy
images. The ISIS organisation created a hierarchy of these images based on
a sectarian logic, with the Syrian regime and Shiʻa at the top, thus becoming
ISIS's primary enemies (Hegghammer 2014). All this proved to give ISIS a
comparative advantage over al-Qaʻida.

The violence and visibility of Salafi jihadism overshadowed other forms of
political Islam. Militant versus non-militant became the key distinction in the
academic debate (Volpi and Stein 2015, 279–80). The controversy was also
connected to the question of whether (some) Islamists could play a conducive
role in processes of democratisation and, if so, how. As a consequence, the
radical-versus-moderate binary was *en vogue* in the 2000s and the inclusion-
moderation hypothesis gained prominence among scholars (critically
Schwedler 2011). The latter suggested that Islamists who were made part of the
democratic game would deradicalise and be socialised into the political system.
There was much criticism of the concept of 'radical Islam' (Kazmi 2022), the
distinction between radical and moderate, and the latter's normative value in
autocratic contexts, as well as the empirical validity of the inclusion-moderation
thesis (Cavatorta and Merone 2013, Netterstrøm 2015). A key problem with
the label 'radical' was that it prevented a distinction being drawn between
such diametrically opposed actors as al-Qaʻida and Hezbollah (Schwedler
2011). At the same time, it obscured ideological similarities between militant
and non-militant Salafists. To solve some of the above-mentioned issues and
escape the focus on (non-)violence and (non-)moderation, Frédéric Volpi and
Ewan Stein (2015) proposed separating statist from non-statist Islamists. The

latter are Salafist groups that used to avoid formal politics and have thus often been tolerated by the authoritarian regimes. Some of them advocate violence for ideological reasons rather than in reaction to state repression. In contrast, statist Islamists practise 'institutionalized participation in the politics of the nation state' (Volpi and Stein 2015, 282) and do not seek to overturn the existing social order. They are usually representative of a middle class and (came to) adopt a reformist discourse which also appeals to the lower middle class. In their respective authoritarian context, at some point, statist Islamists decided to participate in the system, even though phases of (illiberal) participation alternated with episodes of harsh repression against them. Over time, they gave up on certain claims, notably including the goal of establishing Islamic statehood.

In this book, I concentrate on such statist Islamists. More specifically, I am interested in Islamists that are part of the incumbent regime and therefore exposed to and required to adopt a position vis-à-vis the Western world order (see Chapter 3). For purely practical reasons, such actors do not have the 'luxury' of adopting a simple position of violent rejection as Salafi jihadists like al-Qa'ida and ISIS do. The latter are indeed 'irreconcilably estranged from the state, regarding it as a heretical and artificial unit, . . . [and they reject] constitutional politics [and] the international system' (Maher 2016, 11). But the politics of rejection is an unwarranted reduction of a whole spectrum of theoretically possible and empirically observable positions Islamists hold with regard to the global order. I argue that statist Islamists recognise the norms and conceptions of this order and seek recognition for their identity within it (Clément, Geis and Pfeifer 2021). Yet Islamists also resist some practices and principles and aim at transforming the world order from within. They do not, however, reject the order as a whole – no actor can adopt such a dissident position unless they position themselves outside that very order (Deitelhoff and Daase 2021, 128–9).[12]

These three ideal types of world order politics – rejection, resistance, recognition – are in principle not specific to Islamist actors and could be applied in the analysis of any other actor. Empirical cases will not match one ideal type perfectly. We can expect incumbent, statist Islamists to be positioned somewhere between the two poles of recognition and resistance. Groups also change their stance over time, for example leaving rejectionism behind or moving from a more resistant to a more recognisant position or vice versa. World order politics of one and the same actor vary over time, due to changes in their identity and their domestic context, but also within what has so far simply been called the 'Western world order'. This term will be explained, disaggregated and de-essentialised in Chapter 2 – along similar lines to the de- and reconstruction of 'Islamism' in this chapter. Here, I have shown that we should not simply assume that all Islamists are dangerous, anti-democratic, anti-liberal – and oppose the Western world order. I have proposed a more nuanced repertoire of positions that Islamists can take. What can, in fact, be expected from Islamist world order discourse is a combination of practices of recognition and resistance, transformation, adaptation and pushing the boundaries of the Western discursive space. It would be implausible for the statist Islamists under study here to adopt a position of simple rejectionism. After all, incumbent Islamists rule in a world which is actually shaped by Western hegemony. They cannot fully escape the order and the discourse from which it emerges and on which it is built. But this does not mean that Islamists are left with the choice of either succumbing to this order or rejecting it. Structure should not be overestimated. Rather, Islamists are somewhat complicit in producing, reproducing and transforming this very order. This means that they have agency and a whole repertoire of violent and non-violent means at their disposal.

Islamists of the sort that this book is interested in do not simply promote divine sovereignty as an alternative to the Westphalian state system. They do not base their legitimacy claims on simplistic notions of totalitarian polities, caliphates or imamates, nor do they flatly reject democracy. And they also have complex, responsive and worldly normative aspirations or *teloi* rather than projecting these ambitions onto the afterlife. Islamist world order discourse is more intricate. It is a modern and pluralist discourse (E. S. Hurd 2007) in which problems and their solutions are discussed for the here and now – including conceptions of global order. Sovereignty, legitimacy and *teloi* are also anything but unequivocal and uncontested with the Western world order discourse, as the next chapter will show.

Notes

1. All of the scholars referenced in this paragraph challenge these overly simplistic images of Islam but show that these clichés exist among policymakers and/or in some academic accounts. The references should thus be prefixed with the qualifier 'critically'.

2. This interpretation of the secularisation paradigm diverges from the understanding proposed by Bruce (2002, 30) in that it includes the normative side of secularism.

3. Even though he adopted a functionalist approach to religion, Luckmann ([1966] 1991) made quite similar claims about secularisation. As is typical of functional definitions, he employs a very broad understanding of religion. For him, the anthropological capacity of an organism to become a person by transcending its naturalness or biological nature is already 'a fundamentally religious operation' (Luckmann [1966] 1991, 87, author's translation). As religious operations are part of human nature, they will not disappear but rather change their form and appearance. Consequently, Luckmann conceptualises secularisation as the 'detachment of *institutional* norms and values from the cosmos of religious meaning-making [*Sinngebung*]' (1985, 39, author's translation, original emphasis).

4. For a criticism of the 'return' and 'resurgence' rhetoric, which presupposes a previous decline or disappearance of religion, see, for example, Mufti (2013).

5. In the literature, this strand of research is sometimes labelled 'postsecularist'; see, for example, Mufti (2013), Mavelli and Petito (2012) and Wilson (2014).

6. It is important to note that Asad himself explicitly states that Islamists should be 'understood on their own terms as being at once modern and traditional, both authentic and creative at the same time': https://talalasad.blogspot.com/2010/11/modern-power-and-reconfiguration-of.html (accessed 17 October 2023).

7. It has also been argued that the binary between an essentialised 'West' and 'Islam' was co-produced by Islamic thinkers in categories that were similar to those used by Orientalists; see Jung (2011).

8. In this way, they also essentialise the idea of the West and equate it with liberalism. For uses of the 'West', see Hellmann and Herborth (2017).

9. It remains to be seen whether this will change with the war of aggression against and full-scale invasion of Ukraine that Russia launched in 2022 and a potential readjustment of global threat perceptions.

10. In fact, exploring Islamic contributions to the field of IR and challenging the Eurocentrism of the discipline is the goal of the International Relations and

Islamic Studies Research Cohort (Co-IRIS), founded in 2013. The cohort connects its intellectual project to an agenda of a broader presence for Islamic approaches to IR in publications, conferences and workshops. See, for example, Abdelkader, Adiong and Mauriello (2016), Adiong, Mauriello and Abdelkader (2018).

11. See also Talal Asad's understanding as expressed in the interview with Saba Mahmood https://talalasad.blogspot.com/2010/11/modern-power-and-reconfiguration-of.html (accessed 17 October 2023).

12. I deviate from Deitelhoff and Daase's (2021) use of the resistance terminology in so far as I understand rejectionism, or what they call dissidence, not as a form of resistance but rather as a position towards the world order in its own right.

2

A DISCURSIVE UNDERSTANDING OF WORLD ORDER: SOVEREIGNTY, LEGITIMACY AND *TELOI*

Since the mid-2010s, IR has debated significant potential or imminent transformations of the global order. To some, the core concern was whether what they call the 'liberal international order' (Ikenberry, Parmar and Stokes 2018, Ikenberry 2020, Weiss and Wallace 2021) was going to survive, along with its institutions, norms and rules. For this order faced serious challenges, both internal and external. Scholars also tried to explain where this crisis came from in the first place. The 'surge of Islamic fundamentalism, revisionism in Russia, the rise of China, and antiglobalization movements, as well as the proliferation of right-wing populism and nationalism in Europe and the US' were named as causes of the crisis – but also interpreted as a result of the post-'Cold War' transformation of the liberal international order itself (Börzel and Zürn 2021, 286). Institutionalist approaches emphasised the legitimacy problems of global governance (Zürn 2018) or rising powers' pursuit of equal status and their varying success within existing institutions (Mukherjee 2022) as sources of conflict in the world order. Against the background of the rise of China, some even predicted an 'authoritarian century' (Ogden 2022), while others diagnosed the return of a 'great-power politics', which had never really vanished in the first place. They were concerned about the re-emergence of territorial defence on Western security agendas, at the latest since the Russian annexation of Crimea in 2014 (Mearsheimer 2014a, 2014b, Meijer and Wyss 2019) and almost exclusively since the beginning of the Russian war of aggression against Ukraine in 2022. Others still forecast that 'liberal hegemony' would come to an end and give way to a 'multiplex world' (Acharya 2017) or a 'multi-order world' (Flockhart 2016, Flockhart and Korosteleva 2022). Despite their rootedness in different schools of IR, from liberalism and institutionalism to realism and constructivism, what all of these approaches share is that they diagnose a moment of crisis in the Western world order – be it because of the challenge to liberal institutions posed by non-democratic, illiberal states; material power shifts and the return of interstate war; or the resistance against norms and values previously deemed universal but now representing just one of many possible normative orders. In one way or another, they lament or welcome the prospect that the world order is going to have to deal with a certain degree of 'Westlessness' (Flockhart 2022).

But what might the term 'Western world order' mean in the first place? I build on the understanding, from a sociological IR perspective, of the deep structures of global order as intersubjectively shared principles, norms and beliefs that fulfil ordering functions, notably defining legitimate actors and rightful action in the international system (see, for example, Reus-Smit 1997, Buzan 2009). But while certain interpretations may be shared or become hegemonic, this does not imply that the meaning of these structures is uncontested. Rather, competing discourses and meanings underpin the deep structures of global order. The previous chapter has already warned against essentialising both 'Islamists' and the 'West', including the use of these concepts with specific qualifiers (dangerous, religious, irrational, peaceful, secular, liberal etc.) and their construction as antagonistic Others. The previous chapter also questioned the structural determinism sometimes present in critical analyses of secularism or, more generally, the 'West'. Islamists are subjected to the structures of the world order, which, for instance, produces and reproduces their position as the enemy. At the same time, however, as actors in international politics (Adraoui 2018), they are subjects who have agency in politics beyond regional and domestic contexts.

This chapter aims to de-essentialise the 'West' by disaggregating the 'Western world order' discourse. It thereby identifies spaces of agency even for those actors outside the West who, at first glance, have for the longest time seemed marginal from the perspective of world order (Acharya 2018a, Zarakol 2022). Such a discursive understanding of world order suggests that it is produced through utterances by a variety of actors who are embedded in asymmetrical power relations. These actors are at once both part of and subjected to the structure of global discourse. But they also can and indeed have to interpret this order and adopt a position in relation to it. Through their actions, they may thus recognise, reproduce and even co-produce the order, or they may resist, oppose and challenge it. As we saw in the previous chapter, actors like al-Qaʿida or ISIS even try to position themselves outside this structure and choose to violently reject, transgress and fight it.

Understanding world order as a discourse does not mean discarding the material side of the world (order). Rather, it suggests that social phenomena like the world order are 'the contingent, temporary, more or less sedimented (institutionalized) product of ongoing discursive struggles' (Stengel 2020, 25). This does not mean that the world order is without material foundations, resources or practices. But it 'exist[s] only because people collectively believe [it] exist[s] and act accordingly' (Finnemore and Sikkink 2001, 393). It gains its social meaning from being interpreted in a way that is socially accessible, conceivable and, at least to a certain degree, acceptable. Discourse is the 'space where [such] intersubjective meaning is created, sustained, transformed and, accordingly, becomes constitutive of social reality' (Holzscheiter 2014, 144). Importantly, a discursive understanding of world order is also not power blind. I assume that the world order has been and still is hierarchical in that it assigns subject positions with varying degrees of power, in terms of those subjects being both able to make themselves heard (which includes material factors) and endowed with discursive authority in a certain context (Stengel 2020, 31–2).

I support the view that there is Western hegemony in the global order. This hegemony began to develop after World War II, but consolidated after the end of the 'Cold War'. By 'Western hegemony', I mean both that self-proclaimed liberal actors (the 'West' under US leadership) are in the most powerful position and that Western discourse is pervasive, albeit internally contested. Most authors focus on certain features deemed key to the Western order as the liberal international order: 'free trade; post-war multilateral institutions; the growth of democracy; and liberal values' (Acharya 2017, 272). Some have argued that (parts of) the liberal international order can survive without the West or may even benefit from its absence (Flockhart 2022).

Others have simply assumed that the liberal international order was 'bound to fail' in the first place (Mearsheimer 2019). The discursive approach pursued in this book views liberal ideas of order as one part of the 'Western' discourse on world order. Not only are there intellectual traditions beyond or in opposition to the liberal strand in 'Western' discourse, liberalism is also not exclusively reserved for the 'West' but can theoretically be used by any actor. By focusing on the discursive construction of world order, I can show that there is no single 'Western' world order, but rather many versions of it.

Revealing the nuanced and fragmented character of the 'Western' discourse on world order is in itself a step towards deconstructing sharp dichotomous distinctions: the self-perception of the world order as liberal (and therefore secular) is particularly pronounced in the construction of the 'Islamist' enemy image. If we acknowledge not only the plurality of Islamism but also the equivocality and internal contentedness of the Western world order, the notion of a binary opposition of the two becomes increasingly questionable. While the liberal is only one of several traditions present in Western discourse, the world order is also too abstract and too big a conceptual 'container' to be of analytical value. In the tradition of Chantal Mouffe and Ernesto Laclau (Laclau and Mouffe 1985, Laclau 2007), the term 'world order' could be described as an 'empty signifier' or a 'signifier without a signified ... whose temporary signifieds are the result of a political competition' (Laclau 2007, 36, 35). In this reading, the 'liberal world order' could be interpreted as one such concept with a temporarily fixed meaning or an attempt at establishing hegemony which has constructed the 'Islamist' (and some linked equivalents such as 'jihadist', 'terrorist', 'radical', 'fundamentalist', 'extremist', 'irrational' etc.; see Stengel 2020, 28–31) as a 'common other that symbolizes a threat to this order and thus embodies disorder' (Wojczewski 2018, 38).

But we should not exaggerate the pervasiveness and stability of such a constitutive or radical Other. Rather, a constructed Self can have multiple Others who appear more or less threatening and are attributed different properties and qualities over time. So, while the 'Islamist' may indeed have been the West's radical Other in some periods, for instance directly after the 9/11 attacks, its 'Otherness' changed over time, as briefly touched upon in the previous chapter. It became less threatening with the emergence of alternative Others and learning processes, which led to a partial deconstruction – only to become a radical Other again when ISIS rose to its full power. It therefore makes sense to think about Selves and Others in relative terms, as 'a series of related yet slightly different juxtapositions that can be theorized as constituting processes of linking and differentiation' and as being situated in a 'web of identities' (Hansen 2006, 37, 40).

The focus of this book is on those actors who have been placed under the umbrella term 'Islamism' and identified as Other but who do not simply accept and live with this fate. Instead, they make use of their discursive agency, challenging hegemonic constructions of world order while simultaneously being subjected to them. Empty signifiers like 'world order' are 'never completely empty but [have] an indeterminable signified in that [they] can have various competing meanings and thus serve as a surface of inscription for various political articulations' (Wojczewski 2018, 37). The struggle over (temporarily) fixing the meaning of 'world order' takes place on a global level, albeit on very unequal footing, and it takes place within the West, as well as outside the West.

Chapters 4 to 6 will analyse how two actors belonging to the realm discursively covered by the term 'Islamism', the Tunisian Ennahda and the Lebanese Hezbollah, make use of their agency and employ discursive strategies to contribute to the construction of and challenge the world order (see also Milliken 1999, 229–31). In its empirical part, the book takes an actor-centred discourse analytical perspective that focuses on the 'communicative processes in which agents actively construct, re-negotiate, and transform intersubjectively shared interpretations of reality' (Holzscheiter 2014, 147). Actors – in this case two Islamist parties – struggle to recast their image, gain recognition for their claimed identity and delineate themselves from other actors, as well as interpret the world order, position themselves in relation to it and discursively establish world order alternatives. And they do so in and against the structure of a Western discourse on world order which is simultaneously hegemonic, compared to non-Western discourse on world order, and internally contested.[1]

In this chapter, I offer a structured reading of this Western discourse, which allows me to develop a matrix that spans the discourse and approximately identifies the 'limits of the sayable' (Butler 2004, 17) with regard to world order in the West. I do not claim that all interpretations are covered. But I do aim to represent both hegemonic and marginal positions within Western discourse. I use academic accounts as a proxy for Western discourse on world order, being fully aware that this implies another limitation of the proposed matrix. Academic discourse tries to grasp what is happening in the world and could be seen as an accumulation of interpretations of reality. Despite the mechanisms of self-correction and reflection at its disposal, the knowledge produced in academic discourse is biased, power-laden and powerful. Some discourses can even become so authoritative that it is virtually impossible to transcend them, as Edward Said famously wrote on Orientalism: 'I believe no one writing, thinking, or acting on the Orient could do so without taking account of the limitations on thought and action imposed by Orientalism' (Said [1978] 2003, 4). But for the purposes of this chapter, suffice it to say that academia makes political discourses, including the 'world order' discourse, its object of study. We can assume that academic discourse reproduces, feeds into, criticises, reflects upon and analyses, but also enables and supports, and therefore in many ways encompasses, political discourse (see also Wojczewski 2018, 41).

In order to draw the contours of the available meanings in Western world order discourse(s), I disaggregate the term 'world order' into, and reconstruct different discursive traditions in, discursive fields which revolve around three concepts: (1) sovereignty, (2) political legitimacy and (3) the goals and values an order should bring about, which I call *teloi*. These *teloi* are connected to greater historical narratives. Again, I do not claim that this is the only way to think about world order, or to capture and structure Western discourse on it.[2] Rather, I follow Hedley Bull's established and pragmatic definition of order:

> To say of a number of things that together they display order is . . . to say that they are related to one another according to some pattern, that their relationship is not purely hap-hazard but contains some discernible principle . . . [Order] in social life is . . . a pattern that leads to a particular result, an arrangement of social life such that it promotes certain goals or values. (Bull 1995, 3–4)

In these three discursive fields, possible answers to the core questions of order are negotiated: (1) What is it that is ordered? (2) How is it ordered? (3) To what end? They cover the main discursive battlefields in the global discourse on world order. (1) Sovereignty refers to the entities in the order, (2) legitimacy to the principle according to which these entities are ordered and (3) *teloi* to the normative aspirations connected to world order. In the remainder of this chapter, four discursive strands within Western discourse for each of these fields are identified and characterised. These four 'ideal types' of sovereignty, legitimacy and *teloi* serve as a nuanced representation of Western discourse on the respective element of the world order to which Islamist discourses can be related. How exactly this can be done methodologically will be explained in the last section of the chapter.

Sovereignty, or What Entities Make Up the World Order

The topic of sovereignty originates in the early debates of modern political theory, as for instance represented in Thomas Hobbes's *Leviathan* (1651) and Jean-Jacques Rousseau's *Du contrat social* (1762), and has been a recurring subject of treatises in philosophy ever since. It has also been one of the key issues in the discipline of IR since its foundation. With ongoing processes of globalisation and transnationalisation, the issue of sovereignty is debated anew in normative and analytical respects, including in what has sometimes been considered a new field of inquiry – international political theory (Kuntz and Volk 2014, 9). While political philosophy used to justify political order within the nation-state and IR saw states as the basic units of the international system, such state-centred approaches are now being challenged. Binaries such as inside/outside and local/global are hard to maintain (R. B. J. Walker 1993, Kuntz and Volk 2014). In IR, the constructivist turn in the 1990s had already allowed sovereignty to be historicised as state sovereignty (Philpott 2001). As 'normative conception[s] that [link] authority, territory, population (society, nation), and recognition in a unique way and in a particular place (the state)' (Biersteker and Weber 1996, 3), state-based conceptions of sovereignty are bound to a particular temporal and spatial context. This also means that sovereignty can be constructed in different ways. I identify four paradigms of sovereignty in Western discourse: absolute, popular, shared and conditional sovereignty. Sovereignty as a discursive field contains two types of claims. On the one hand, understandings of sovereignty explain why a certain subject should be considered the (last) autonomous unit with the legitimate right to self-determination. Thus, there is an intrinsic normative quality to sovereignty claims – and they also always have a component of justification which cannot be strictly separated from claims of political legitimacy. On the other hand, by defining this last unit, sovereignty claims also determine the units which make up an order.

Absolute Sovereignty

In the history of ideas, Thomas Hobbes could be considered the founding father of absolute sovereignty. As the only possible escape from his (fictive) state of nature with a *bellum omnium contra omnes* and logical answer to the security problem, he proposes

> the generation of that great Leviathan, . . . that mortal god to which we owe, under the immortal God, our peace and defence. For by this authority, . . . he hath the use of so much power and strength conferred on him that, by terror thereof, he is enabled to form the wills of them all, to peace at home, and mutual aid against their enemies abroad. (Hobbes 1965, 132)

The sovereign has all-encompassing prerogatives and rights and establishes a monopoly on the use of force, which used to be everyone's right in the state of nature. The sovereign's only obligation is to guarantee the security of the people. Otherwise, they cannot be unjust or act against any rules – for he is the law. A more contemporary version of a philosophical conception of absolute sovereignty can be found in Carl Schmitt's *Political Theology* (1922). Sovereign is he who 'decides on the exception' (C. Schmitt [1985] 2005, 5) and is thereby able to suspend the legal order. In both conceptions, sovereignty is therefore absolute.

Absolute sovereignty is the archetype of modern sovereignty. The anarchic character of the international system, a core concept of neorealist IR theory, is due to the existence of several absolute sovereign states who know no authority above them (Philpott 2001, 16–19). Paradigmatically, Kenneth Waltz connected the concept of sovereignty to his 'like units' argument:

> To call states 'like units' is to say that each state is like all other states in being an autonomous political unit. It is another way of saying that states are sovereign . . . [To] say that states are sovereign is not to say that they can do as they please, that they are free of others' influence, that they are able to get what they want . . . To say that a state is sovereign means that it decides for itself how it will cope with its internal and external problems. (Waltz 1979, 95–6)

The structural equality of states as sovereigns makes the international system a 'self-help system' in which 'units worry about their survival' (Waltz 1979, 105).

Absolute sovereignty has an internal and an external side. Internally, sovereignty is the 'supremacy over all other authorities within [a specific] territory and population' (Bull 1995, 8). This implies final or supreme authority in the domestic arena and effective control. Besides 'independence of outside authorities' (Bull 1995, 8), the external side of sovereignty is often associated with the formal equality of states, also in the legal sense, and the external recognition of authority that grants immunity from external interference (Biersteker and Weber 1996, 2, Krasner 1999, 9–26, Philpott 2001, 18, Zürn and Deitelhoff 2015, 194–5).

These dimensions could be considered the ideal of absolute sovereignty, which most authors agree has never existed in real-world politics. The Peace of Westphalia established the state as the bearer of a sovereignty that was absolute in terms of 'the scope of affairs over which a sovereign body governs within a particular territory' (Philpott 2001, 19), as well as, arguably, the norm of non-intervention. But the geographical boundaries of this sovereignty were quite narrow, merely encompassing Europe and political entities that were labelled 'Christian states' (Philpott 2001, 30–3). Other authors have pointed to the tension between the ideal of absolute sovereignty and state and non-state practice which disconnects the external side of sovereignty from the internal one. For example, states are recognised as equal parts of the state system without effectively holding the ultimate authority within their territory (Krasner 1999, 14–20). And yet, absolute sovereignty not only continues to serve as a 'normative and conceptual aspiration in the minds of individuals' (Zürn and Deitelhoff 2015, 195). It also persists in the legal domain in the form of absolute sovereign rights (Donnelly 2014, 233–5).

Popular Sovereignty

Whereas absolute sovereignty is intimately linked to the modern nation-state, popular sovereignty is rooted in the notion of individual freedom as autonomy. In the history of thought, Jean-Jacques Rousseau was one of the first philosophers to introduce the concept of popular sovereignty as the only and ultimate source of a legitimate polity. In contrast to Hobbes, Rousseau argued that individual freedom is preserved in the *volonté générale*: 'Each of us puts his person and all his power in common under the supreme direction of the general will, and, in our corporate capacity, we receive each member as an indivisible part of the whole' (Rousseau 1994, 55).

The idea of popular sovereignty was also at the core of demands for the self-determination of peoples and, thus, colonial independence. While the participation and recognition in the international system of sovereign states used to be a privilege of European states, the colonies being mere 'extensions', a new norm emerged in the second half of the twentieth century. This norm stipulated that 'colonies [be] entitled to statehood however weak their government, however scant their control over their territory, however inchoate their people' (Philpott 2001, 35). In this way, the external and internal dimensions of sovereignty were decoupled. The recognition of a state's international legal status and sovereign equality, understood as the absence of formal hierarchy in the international system, was no longer dependent on the exercise of effective authority and control within that state's territory. Counterintuitively, then, the rise of colonial independence, while motivated by the idea of self-determination, led to a further strengthening of state sovereignty and not necessarily to what might be understood as popular sovereignty in Rousseau's sense. The norm of self-determination merely changed the understanding of what entities 'qualified' as a state, not, however, the idea that states were the legitimate polities in international society, nor their prerogatives. In this sense, statehood was the 'reward' for those peoples who made their way to freedom (Philpott 2001, 28, 35–7, Donnelly 2014, 228).

This contrasts with the many obstacles which pursuing a claim to statehood – as one possible form of self-determination – faces in reality. Self-determination as a right to independent statehood is disputed outside the context of decolonisation and tends to be considered a deviant case. But given the rewards and privileges that come with being a state, the quest for statehood, especially through secession, remains the main means by which groups try to exercise their right to self-determination (Buchanan [2004] 2007, 7, 332–3, Roepstorff 2013, 31–2, 44). Another question in the context of popular sovereignty is who the 'we' is that demands certain rights or what 'self' can legitimately claim self-determination. This is what has been referred to as the 'paradox of popular sovereignty' (Ochoa Espejo 2014, 467). On the one hand, determining who the people are is so important that it should be decided by the people themselves. On the other hand, this act already presupposes that the boundaries have been drawn around a *demos*. Historically, the most successful solution to this dilemma was the invention of the nation, although there is no causal link between popular sovereignty and the nation (Yack 2001, 517–18) – just as the nation does not necessarily exist prior to the state or popular sovereignty, but may be built after the state has already been established (Jones 2016, 628). Ultimately, this 'solution' to the paradox only shifts the problem to the question of what the nation is – and the answers to this are all problematic in one way or another (see, for example, Höffe 2007, 271–4).

Moving to the external dimension of popular sovereignty, it can be observed that not all quests for statehood are recognised as legitimate, even if they are founded on the idea of a nation, the Kurds and Palestinians being two pertinent examples here. Groups that try to create a *demos* based on something other than the nation, for example transnational identities 'such as class, ethnicity, and religion' (Jones 2016, 627), are denied sovereignty. The close association between the nation and popular sovereignty relies on the idea that 'humanity is divided naturally into nations' and has become normalised to the extent that 'any state that does not express a nation or national idea is potentially illegitimate' (Hurrell 2007, 123, 125). Accordingly, decolonisation is romanticised as a success story at the end of which formerly subjugated peoples have become nation-states and thereby 'full members of an international society ... [with] full legal equality'. Some denounce this as mere fiction, however, given the persisting inequalities in power and rights among states (Agnew 2005) and the suspicion that anarchy among equal states may actually be constituted by prior hierarchical orders (Mattern and Zarakol 2016, 631).

Conditional Sovereignty

In addition to the persistence of informal hierarchies alongside formal state equality, however, there is also a line of argumentation in favour of abandoning the idea of equal sovereignty altogether (for similar conceptions, see 'conditioned sovereignty' in Prinz and Schetter 2016, or 'gradated sovereignty' in J. M. Hobson 2012, 313–44). States that behave in certain ways internally can lose their recognition as states and their sovereignty externally. This notion of conditional sovereignty was rooted in a return to the individual as the basic unit of any sovereignty considerations. With the turn to 'human security' in the 1990s and its subsequent institutionalisation in international organisations and promotion by non-governmental organisations (NGOs) (Owens 2012), the 'universal human rights-centred language of global or cosmopolitan law . . . [replaced] the state-based territorialized language of international relations' (Chandler 2012, 214).

The academic debate soon problematised the potentially violent flipside of 'human security' in the form of 'humanitarian inventions' and, later in the 2000s, the 'responsibility to protect' (R2P). While the old security agenda had focused on containing violence between sovereign states, a state could now (temporarily) forfeit its sovereignty in the most severe cases of human rights violations. The realisation that individuals needed to be shielded from violence committed by their own state gave birth to the concept of humanitarian intervention. But according to the logic of the United Nations (UN) system, this created a tension between two core principles: equal state sovereignty and human rights (Welsh, Thielking and MacFarlane 2002, 489–90). While some insisted on the necessity of the right to intervene, for example in cases of genocide and other crimes against humanity, others favoured the old notion of national sovereignty and its primacy (Evans 2006, 705–6). The contention around humanitarian interventions was the background against which the International Commission on Intervention and State Sovereignty formulated the R2P in 2001. The most important novelty of this principle was that it introduced a new normative dimension to the concept of sovereignty, which now implied 'both [being] responsible to one's own citizens and to the wider international community' (Evans 2006, 708–9).

Some voices in the political and academic arena went even further, claiming that the 'state has a duty not only to protect its own peoples, but also to meet its obligations to the wider international community', and sovereignty 'misused, in the sense of failure to fulfil this responsibility, could become sovereignty denied', where 'direct enforcement is also an option' to ensure compliance (Slaughter 2005, 628). Arguments like this belong to a strand of thought found in parts of IR and international law which claims to stand in the liberal tradition, especially following the philosophy of Immanuel Kant, and no longer prioritises the goal 'to overcome the security dilemma' but rather 'reproduces it between liberal and nonliberal states' (Jahn 2005, 179).

Democratic peace theorists divided the world into a 'zone of peace' that would spread among democracies (Doyle 1983, 226) and a 'zone of war' where an anarchic and violence-prone state of nature was doomed to prevail, suggesting that only a 'separate peace' was possible. Drawing on this general idea, theorists of liberal international law began to promote a divided notion of sovereignty, where sovereign equality is only granted to those states that are democratically organised and respect human rights. The more radical among these theorists even demanded that those states that do not have a liberal constitution be excluded from international law and deprived of the right to non-intervention (Eberl 2008). In the early 2000s, these ideas also resonated with neoconservative agendas and led to the call for a 'Concert of Democracies' in some policy circles in the US. This kind of liberal club governance was meant to establish an exclusive circle of democracies – based on their internal normative qualities – as decision-makers on a global level (Geis 2013).

In sum, this brand of liberal internationalism sees liberal democracies as empirically more peaceful than other political systems, and protective of political and civil rights, as well as morally reliable, which makes them the 'most advanced historical form of polity' (Reus-Smit 2005, 76). These outstanding qualities of liberal democracies also justify them 'hav[ing] special rights in international society' (Reus-Smit 2005, 76), thereby reintroducing legal hierarchy to the international sphere through the idea of conditional sovereignty reserved only for those states that qualify.

Shared Sovereignty

A last paradigm of sovereignty is what I call shared sovereignty, also known as disaggregated or divided sovereignty (Agnew 2005, 441). Again, from the perspective of the state, this type of sovereignty has an external and an internal side which capture sovereignty transfers from the state to levels above or below it. The latter refers to the subnational level and such concepts as federalism as the prototype of 'shared and negotiated sovereignty' (Rudolph and Rudolph 2010, 556), which, as an ambivalent part of the process of state formation, contrasts with the ideal of absolute state sovereignty. Examples include not only the USA, Germany and the UK, but also India. More recently, the model of autonomous regions that are neither sovereign states nor simple administrative units within a nation-state has gained relevance, for instance in such contexts as Catalonia, Kosovo, Kashmir or Kurdistan (Mansour 2014).

With regard to the former (sovereignty transfers from the state to levels above), today's international institutions and organisations play a key role in international politics. It has even been argued that contemporary sovereignty 'no longer consists in the freedom of states to act independently . . . but in membership [and] reasonably good standing in the regimes that make up the substance of international life' (A. Chayes and A. H. Chayes 1995, 27). The UN, its ever-evolving system and the development of international law stand out among those institutions that have imposed limits on state sovereignty at a global scale. Notably, some international institutions have introduced 'majority decisions, thus creating the possible condition that states were asked to implement decisions to which they had not necessarily consented' (Zürn and Deitelhoff 2015, 204). While these decisions could eventually require the consent of states, international institutions being a mere tool for the exercise of state authority, the European Union (EU) and concomitant forms of international authority ('delegated' and 'pooled' authority, see Zürn and Deitelhoff 2015, 215) have to be interpreted as embodying actual sovereignty transfer, as supranational institutions can take decisions in those policy fields that are communitarised within the EU without the nation-states' consent.

A whole field of research under the title of multi-level governance has begun investigating these forms of shared or layered sovereignty and overlapping spheres of authority (Piattoni 2010, Kreuder-Sonnen and Zürn 2020). Importantly, while the EU stands out as both an empirical phenomenon and an object of academic investigation, 'integrative regionalism' (Acharya 2002) is a model that exists outside Europe. In the 1970s, it seemed that Europe and its integration in the EU stood in sharp contrast to the disintegration and advancement of the nation-state in the other regions of the world (Haas 1961, 366). Yet, the 1990s came to be known as the era of 'new regionalism' (Acharya 2014, 86). In contrast to 'old regionalism', which had mainly focused on strategic and economic cooperation, 'new regionalism' was marked by its 'comprehensiveness and multidimensional nature' (Acharya 2014, 86) and its autonomous development from within and below, without a hegemon behind the scenes. 'New regionalism' was thus not a mere imitation of the EU – on the contrary, in fact (Acharya 2014, 96–7). What all types of regionalism shared, however, was their emphasis on regional identities and the emergence of intrusive regionalism. In contrast to integrative regionalism, this 'is not always based on consent . . . [and has] a coercive element (Acharya 2002, 28) which may be military or political, but is always 'sovereignty-defying' (Acharya 2002, 28). While in some countries, the reluctance to restrict state sovereignty and create supranational bodies initially prevailed, given that these nation-states had only recently gained their full sovereignty, most regions now have models of shared sovereignty. Today, regional institutions can be considered building blocks of a global order with shared sovereignties where 'the traditional distinction between regionalism and universalism [disappears]' (Acharya 2014, 93).

Legitimacy, or the Pattern According to Which Entities Are Ordered

In this section, I will turn to the patterns according to which entities are and should be ordered or how forms of authority can be legitimised. Legitimacy can be divided into a philosophical, a juridical and a sociological dimension (Glaser 2013, 14–29). When inquiring about the conditions under which rule can be considered legitimate, philosophers ask how compatible that rule is with a normative principle that justifies the relationship between rulers and the ruled. A juridical perspective is concerned with whether authority is grounded in existing legal provisions and principles. Finally, the sociological understanding of legitimacy refers to the empirical acceptance of authority or what Weber called 'legitimacy belief' (*Legitimitätsglaube*, Weber 1922, 122). In what follows, I focus on normative conceptions of legitimacy, as this is the relevant dimension when it comes to discursive struggles over what world order should look like.

The normative legitimacy of an institution is often assessed on the basis of how its inputs are organised and what outputs it generates. The former refers to participation in and consent to a form of rule, whereas the latter looks at the effectiveness and responsiveness of institutions and policies. Input legitimacy presupposes some sense of community, collective identity or *demos*. The problem-solving dimension of output-oriented legitimacy looks for mutual benefits and relies on common interests rather than a collective identity (Scharpf 1999, 16–28). The democratic ideal in the nation-state context used to insist that these two dimensions belong together. But this view has come under pressure in the postnational constellation (Kohler-Koch and Rittberger 2007, 1–29). Today the normative debate needs to take into account the legitimacy of global governance institutions and decision-making (Peter 2021), which raises new questions about the relationship between political legitimacy, on the one hand, and democracy and justice, on the other, as the two reference ideals most typically employed (Erman 2016). Empirically, IR scholars, too, have argued since the end of the 1990s that 'legitimacy matters to international institutions and to the nature of the international system as a whole' (I. Hurd 1999, 403).

The following reconstruction of four paradigms of legitimacy will therefore take into consideration both the domestic and the international level when asking what is considered legitimate authority. The guiding question is: Why should an institution, procedure or decision be accepted by those concerned? I identify four main sources of legitimacy present in Western discourse: the individual, the community, deliberation and agonism. While these are part of normative political theorising, they can also be used by political actors for legitimacy claims and as good reasons to justify their decisions, claims to power or authority and even use of violence. The following paradigms are to be understood as covering a substantial share of the repertoire of meanings available in Western discourse on legitimacy.

Individual-based Legitimacy

Individual-based approaches to legitimacy are rooted in the tradition of contractualist argumentation, which asserts that the consent of the individual to a state, government or form of rule is the only source of legitimacy. John Rawls's (1993, 1999) political liberalism can be considered paradigmatic for such approaches of methodological and normative individualism today. Setting up a thought experiment in the form of a fictive original position – the famous 'veil of ignorance' behind which individuals do not know what position in society they will end up in – Rawls argues that a just society is the result of rational decisions taken by an individual under such conditions of fairness, and therefore a concept of justice to which everyone can consent, no matter what their respective encompassing beliefs are. For the main challenge in modern societies is the 'fact of a plurality of reasonable but incompatible comprehensive doctrines' (Rawls 2005, xvii).

Rawls proposes two solutions to this challenge. The first is the idea of an overlapping consensus of reasonable comprehensive doctrines that support the idea of 'justice as fairness . . . as a freestanding view that expresses a *political* conception of justice' (Rawls 2005, 144, original emphasis). By virtue of being political, this conception does not presuppose the acceptance of any religious, metaphysical, moral, philosophical or epistemological doctrine. The consensus is stable because it is supported by the different comprehensive doctrines, without, however, depending on any one of them, as the 'constitutional essentials and basic institutions of justice' are grounded in political values (Rawls 2005, 140). Such a purely political foundation is possible because of Rawls's second solution: public reason imposes limits on the arguments that can be made with regard to the basic structure of society. These limits are that any citizen should articulate ideas that are intelligible and comprehensible to other citizens, and they should only give reasons that are within a framework of a political conception of justice (Rawls 2005, 226). Such rationales can generally be accepted as reasonable even if they do not correspond to one's own comprehensive doctrines or beliefs. From this, Rawls derives his 'liberal principle of legitimacy':

> [Our] exercise of political power is proper and hence justifiable only when it is exercised in accordance with a constitution the essentials of which all citizens may reasonably be expected to endorse in the light of principles and ideals acceptable to them as reasonable and rational. (Rawls 2005, 217)

Compared to the domestic context, Rawls's theory of international legitimacy is rather modest. The international political sphere is ideally made up of well-ordered peoples, that is, societies that are 'effectively regulated by a public conception of justice' (Rawls 1999, 4), which need not, however, be the liberal one. Rawls does not argue in favour of an order which would transcend the nation-state or envision some kind of global polity. He does not even draw a teleological picture of an eventual convergence towards liberal societies. For Rawls, an ideal theory of political liberalism applied to the international context has to restrain itself in order to follow its 'own principle of toleration for other reasonable ways of ordering society' (Rawls 2005, 37) and only strives for a thin consensus: a law of peoples with which both liberal and hierarchical well-ordered societies can agree. This theory contains classical provisions of international law, such as the duty of non-intervention and the principle of *pacta sunt servanda* ('agreements must be kept'), as well as the respect for human rights. Rawls (1999, 36) explicitly follows Kant (1977, 208–13, orig. 1795) in suspecting that 'a world government would either be a global despotism or else would rule over a fragile empire torn by frequent civil strife as various regions and peoples tried to gain their political freedom and autonomy'.

Rawls's disciples, however, followed other trajectories in their liberal conceptions of legitimacy at the global level (Kymlicka 2002, 268–70, Pogge 2002). Such cosmopolitan theories are marked by their individualism, claimed universality and generality (Zürn 2016, 90). As most authors whose legitimacy conceptions are based on the individual also argue in favour of institutional cosmopolitanism (Peter 2021), Rawls's thin law of peoples is the exception rather than the rule. One example of an individual-based institutional cosmopolitanism is Otfried Höffe's subsidiary and federal world republic. Höffe claims that a global polity is necessary because states can no longer fulfil their duties to the individual, the 'only being empirically known as having intrinsic moral value' (Höffe 2007, 215), in an age of globalisation. A 'two-dimensional residual state of nature' (Höffe 2007, 215), among individual states and between individuals and foreign states, must be overcome through a complementary federal world republic. Deriving its power and legitimacy from both 'the community of all human beings and from the community of all states' (Höffe 2007, 219), the republic should be composed of two parliamentary chambers representing both communities. Like other cosmopolitan theories (for example, Held 2006, 305), this model does not aim at abolishing the nation-state but rather at complementing it through institutions at the regional and global level.

Community-based Legitimacy

Compared to individual-based conceptions of legitimacy, community-based approaches[3] are state-based and generally more sceptical about global institutions (Peter 2021). Furthermore, community-based approaches differ from individual-based conceptions in three important respects (Forst 1993, 196–203). First, they assume that a given community is normatively integrated through a common understanding of the good, which varies across different societies (Walzer 1983, 7). Second, based on citizens identifying with this common good, these approaches advocate participatory forms of organising the political process. Third, they conceptualise citizens as part of a culturally integrated community within which they individualise. As Michael Sandel puts it, the community is constitutive (and therefore antecedent) to the individual:

> Can we view ourselves as independent selves, independent in the sense that our identity is never tied to our aims and attachments? I do not think we can ... To imagine a person incapable of constitutive attachments ... is not to conceive an ideally free and rational agent, but to imagine a person wholly without character, without moral depth. (Sandel 1984, 90)

The individual's embeddedness in social relations means that communitarianism replaces liberalism's '(abstract) identity of the isolated self' with 'the (real) identity of the communal self' (F. M. Barnard 2001, 174).

This has consequences for the way in which legitimacy is conceptualised. Michael Walzer (1980, 1998), for example, develops a twofold theory of legitimacy which makes a sharp distinction between the national and the international sphere. As 'the state is constituted by the union of people and government', domestic legitimacy requires 'a certain "fit" between the community and its government' (Walzer 1980, 212). The people must be governed according to their traditions. The government is legitimate only in so far as it 'actually represents the political life of its people' (Walzer 1980, 214), and it is up to the community to judge whether or not it does so. Legitimacy, then, resides in acts or institutions that reflect the normative culture of a given community and arises from collective processes rather than the aggregation of individual acts of consent (Etzioni 2011, 107–9). There is no requirement for arguments and reasons given in the public sphere to be neutral. In contrast to 'antiseptic liberalism', it is the passionate play of identities and communities that is considered 'normal democratic engagement'(Walzer 1998, 300, 303).

For Walzer, international legitimacy needs to be approached in a different manner. As long as the community does not rebel against its government, a state must be considered internationally legitimate. As the only standard for domestic legitimacy is whether a state rules in accordance with the 'opinions of the people, and also their habits, feelings, religious convictions, political culture' (Walzer 1980, 216), any intervention from the outside is rejected. For this would infringe on the 'respect for communal integrity and for different patterns of cultural and political development' (Walzer 1980, 215). This is also the reason why advocates of community-based approaches to legitimacy are sceptical about any kind of cosmopolitan order and hold that national communities remain the source of legitimacy on a global level (Peter 2021). They also doubt that any universal concept could integrate differences between these communities without creating massive conflict (Bellamy and Castiglione 1998, 157–9). What is more, there is no global *demos* or converging global culture that could legitimise a global polity (Archibugi 2004, 460–1). Nevertheless, some authors have tried to combine communitarian arguments with cosmopolitan approaches (Bellamy and Castiglione 1998) or foregrounded the importance of the regional level, with its regional political identities and communities, as building blocks in (legitimising) global democracy (Gould 2012).

Deliberative Legitimacy

The paradigm of deliberative legitimacy can be considered dominant in the current literature on, as well as the gold standard for, political legitimacy. In democratic theory, deliberative models are often contrasted with and thought of as solving the problems of aggregative democracy. To deliberative theorists, legitimacy resides in the 'deliberative process itself' (Peter 2009, 52), rather than the individual or the community. To be legitimate, any form of authority 'must be based on argumentative justification through public reasoning to those subject to it' (Böker 2017, 23). The basic idea is that 'public deliberation contributes to democratic legitimacy to the extent that it enables citizens to endorse the laws and policies to which they are subject as their own . . . [and thereby] achieve political autonomy or non-domination' (Lafont 2015, 42). Two strategies of building deliberative legitimacy can be identified. Deliberative proceduralism grounds legitimacy in a 'deliberative decision-making process [that] meets some demands of procedural fairness' (Peter 2009, 69) or political equality. Rational deliberative proceduralism, in contrast, insists that there be 'some form of justification of the collective decisions themselves' (Peter 2009, 70) and thereby introduces a standard for the results of deliberation.

Deliberative democracy has become a whole field of study in its own right (see, for example, Bächtiger et al. 2018) but has been fundamentally influenced, if not constituted, by the works of Jürgen Habermas. For Habermas, legitimacy can only be achieved through the discursive rationalisation of the decisions taken by a government and administration for which 'the procedures and communicative presuppositions of democratic opinion- and will-formation function as the most important sluices' (Habermas 1996, 300). By virtue of this ideal process of deliberation and decision-making and 'insofar as the flow of relevant information and its proper handling have not been obstructed' (Habermas 1996, 296), reasonable or fair results can be obtained. Habermas sees the constitutional state as the institutionalisation of complex forms of communication. It allows for an interplay between formal, institutionalised deliberations that are regulated through procedures, deal with problem-solving and lead to will-formation, on the one hand, and an informally formed public opinion that operates anarchically as an agenda-setter, on the other. It is this discursive structure of public deliberation that produces legitimacy of political decisions or, as Seyla Benhabib puts it:

> [Legitimacy] in complex democratic societies must be thought to result from the free and unconstrained public deliberation about matters of common concern. Thus a public sphere of deliberation about matters of mutual concern is essential to the legitimacy of democratic institutions. (Benhabib 1996, 68)

Given that Habermas's approach is premised on a consensus that results from public deliberation, his version of legitimacy has been called rational deliberative perfect proceduralism (Peter 2009, 71). But for the transferability of deliberative legitimacy to a postnational constellation, the consensus condition is a stumbling block. In the face of the loss of sovereignty experienced by the nation-state, and a consequent decline in policy effectiveness, Habermas is sceptical about the introduction of a global polity or 'world state'. Instead, he argues, politics 'has to find a less demanding basis of legitimacy in the organizational forms of an international negotiation system' (Habermas 2001b, 109). But as a '"thick" communicative embeddedness is missing [on the international level]' (Habermas 2001b, 109), he attaches great importance to NGOs that participate in transnational decision-making. Eventually, though, the Habermasian version of deliberative legitimacy reaches its limits in a global context (Fine and Smith 2003).

But not all versions of deliberative legitimacy require such a discursive consensus. Other deliberative theorists have tried to take the model further and show its potential for use at the global level. John Dryzek, for instance, tries to mobilise 'diffuse communication in the public sphere that generates public opinion that can in turn exercise political influence' (Dryzek 2006, 27) for a transnational space. This sort of influence can be exercised through 'communicatively competent decentralized control over the content and relative weight of globally consequential discourses' (Dryzek 2006, 154). And yet, it remains doubtful whether a truly global public sphere can develop, let alone one that meets certain normative standards which could translate into the rationalisation of decision-making – the resurgence of populist politics in many parts of the world is just one development which makes the prospects for deliberative legitimacy beyond the nation-state seem bleak.

Agonistic Legitimacy

The last model of legitimacy is rooted in what came to be known as the 'agonistic model of democratic politics' (Benhabib 1996, 7) or approaches of 'radical democracy' (Laclau and Mouffe 1985). These approaches are all concerned with 'a mysterious phenomenon: the displacement of politics in political theory' (Honig 1993, 2). By focusing on procedures and institutions and narrowing their understanding of politics down to 'juridical, administrative, or regulative tasks' (Honig 1993, 2), political theories tend to displace conflict from its position at the core of politics. As Bonnie Honig argues, out of fear of the disruptive practices and conflictual nature of the political, such theories strive for closure. They try to develop a single model of order under the assumption that 'their favored institutions fit and express the formations of subjects' (Honig 1993, 3). In this way, Honig further contends, those who do not fit are relegated to the margins and contestation is placed outside the political realm.

Starting from the criticism of this depoliticising or even anti-political trait of liberal democracy,[4] Chantal Mouffe develops her agonistic model of democracy. For Mouffe, liberal democracy results from the attempt to combine political liberalism (private autonomy) and popular sovereignty (public autonomy) in one political organisation (Mouffe 1996, 246). It tries to reconcile or demonstrate the co-originality (*Gleichursprünglichkeit*) of democratic legitimacy as represented by popular sovereignty (equality) and the exigencies of rationality understood as liberal rights (freedom) through deliberation or public reasoning (Mouffe 2000, 83–4). Deliberative theories of liberal democracy share the belief that the performance of institutions generates a rational consensus that exceeds a mere modus vivendi because it is 'the idealized content of practical rationality' (Mouffe 2000, 86). According to Mouffe, these theories ignore the impossibility of establishing such a 'rational consensus on political decisions without exclusion' (Mouffe 2000, 89). Rather than solving the problem of difference, then, such theories ultimately opt for a 'flight from pluralism' (Mouffe 2000, 90).

In a nutshell, the concern that proponents of agonistic approaches have regarding both individualist and deliberative forms of legitimacy is that these simply relocate difference to areas where it is not considered problematic, that is the private sphere, with the aim of making politics a space of encompassing inclusion in a rational consensus that can be universally justified. Mouffe (2000, 99), in contrast, insists that 'the dimension of antagonism that the pluralism of values entails' cannot be eradicated from political theorising. Rather than aiming at an intellectual, argument-based, almost aseptic consensus which abolishes antagonism, democracy should be able to mobilise passions or, as Honig put it, 'the energy and animation and frankly, the fun, that come from gathering together around issues that are affectively charged'.[5]

Of course, antagonism itself is not democracy – but it is the central feature of what Mouffe calls 'the political'. She contrasts it with 'politics' understood as

> the ensemble of practices, discourses and institutions which seek to establish a certain order and organize human coexistence in conditions that are always potentially conflictual because they are affected by the dimension of 'the political'. (Mouffe 2000, 101)

Politics is the struggle over hegemony, that is, the moment of closure by which, through acts of power, a certain social order is objectified. Such a hegemonic order is always temporary and precarious. Pretending otherwise or seeking final closure would simultaneously kill the political. For Mouffe, the central question for democratic theory is not the abolition of power or its transformation into authority, but how to make the power play democratic. This can only be achieved by transforming relations of antagonism (that construct the Other as an enemy) into 'agonistic pluralism'. The Other, then, is recognised as a legitimate adversary or as one who has embraced the principles of equality and liberty – but who interprets these in an irreconcilably and insurmountably different way. Democratic politics is no longer democratic when the struggle over social issues takes place between enemies and takes on antagonistic forms. Democratic politics is no longer political when these differences are concealed, abolished or discounted. For Mouffe, this implies that legitimacy is based on 'purely pragmatic grounds' (Mouffe 2000, 100): a hegemonic order is legitimate by virtue of having 'been able to impose itself', which presupposes some degree of acceptance. Legitimacy is thus a question of facts, not norms.

At the global level, advocates of pluralistic agonism are primarily critical of the fact that the neoliberal model of globalisation is the only one available and that there is a lack of legitimate ways to express alternative ideas of a global order beyond practising resistance. This is accompanied by a rejection of any version of political or institutional cosmopolitanism, which would merely constitute the transfer of the Western hegemonic model to the global level. Again, such a consensus, this time of global scale, would eliminate 'the possibility of legitimate dissent, thereby creating a favourable terrain for the emergence of violent forms of antagonisms' (Mouffe 2013, 20). Instead of an 'international Leviathan', Mouffe proposes the 'pluralization of hegemonies ... [in] a multipolar world' (Mouffe 2013, 20), in which more than one order is considered legitimate. Liberal democracy with its close relationship with human rights and secularism, then, is considered a contingent historical form of political organisation that emerged in the West. Agonistic legitimacy on a global level resides in the coexistence of and encounter 'between a diversity of poles which engage with each other without any one of them having the pretence of being the superior one' (Mouffe 2013, 41). Existing differences between poles are a virtue, for they 'contribute to enhancing the pluralism that characterizes a multipolar world' (Mouffe 2013, 41). Mouffe's conception of a global order demonstrates the extent to which theories of legitimacy are premised and build upon values and goals that order is supposed to bring about.

Teloi, or Why Entities Are Ordered

Orders should help realise some common good or value. They are built with a certain goal in mind – which simultaneously marks the endpoint of a historical narrative justifying this future order. Such *teloi* and the teleological stories contributing to the order in the making, sorting and structuring a past and linking it to a future with a projected desirable or dreaded state of affairs, are what I call utopias and dystopias here: 'The utopian views humanity and its future with either hope or alarm. If viewed with hope, the result is usually a utopia. If viewed with alarm, the result is usually a dystopia' (Sargent 2010, 8). These views are often nostalgic because they idealise a past order which was lost and can either be restored (utopia) or never brought back (dystopia) (Sargent 2010, 26). They therefore always imply a certain understanding or even philosophy of history, a teleological understanding of how events evolve and bring about either a better or a worse society. An understanding of causality (emplotment) is also built into these narratives, as are its protagonists and their antagonists (see Pfeifer and Spencer 2019).

In this chapter, utopia and dystopia are used to describe the fate of and prescribe the cure for the still imperfect world order. They project the world order into a glorious or threatening future, while using the past as both an indicator of and a standard for future developments. They usually contain arguments concerning sovereignty and legitimacy, but relate these to a more comprehensive story of the evolution of the global order. The four teleological stories introduced in this chapter comprise a utopian and a dystopian version, respectively, of universalism and pluralism as values to be achieved through the world order. What they all have in common is their view that the current state of international relations is marked by a pluralism of political orders and values. Where they do not agree, however, is on the evaluation of this state of affairs and their (normative) outlook on future developments.

Liberal Convergence

The first paradigm is an optimist's outlook on liberal universalism. Here, liberal political principles are considered normatively superior to any other doctrine and seen as the most rational form of political organisation, which makes them an almost natural endpoint of history. The best-known version of this first utopia is the 'end of history' thesis developed by Francis Fukuyama (1989) at the transition from the 'Cold War' era to what came to be known as the decade of liberal euphoria. This historical change, Fukuyama held, left only 'one competitor standing in the ring as an ideology of potentially universal validity: liberal democracy, the doctrine of individual freedom and popular sovereignty' (Fukuyama 1992, 38). While the liberal democratic ideal had already come to perfection in the beginning of the nineteenth century, the collapse of communism marked 'the end of history as such: that is, the end point of mankind's ideological evolution and the universalization of Western liberal democracy as the final form of human government' (Fukuyama 1989, 1). While Fukuyama proclaimed the ideological victory of liberalism, he did not expect real-world conflicts to end or ultimately be solved. Rather, 'the world [would] be divided between a post-historical part, and a part that is still stuck in history' (Fukuyama 1992, 276). The former would be guided by peace, economic prosperity and cooperation; the latter would face conflicts driven by religion or nationalism. No significant interaction would take place between the two worlds until the best of all forms of political organisation eventually materialised everywhere. As Fukuyama put it, the 'great majority of wagons will be making the slow journey into town, and most will eventually arrive there' (Fukuyama 1992, 339).

As this version of liberalism as a 'political vision' (Jahn 2013, 12) illustrates, liberal theorists tend to assume that 'all good things go together' (Sørensen 2007, 373, Bech and Snyder 2011). Liberal democracy is supposedly accompanied by, among others, capitalism and prosperity, human rights, peace and justice. One example of this assumed convergence is the 'Kantian triangle', known from the debate on the democratic peace, that combines the democratic constitution of states with economic interdependence and shared norms in international organisation into a recipe for peaceful international relations (Russett and Oneal 2001). This belief in the co-constitution of the political, economic and normative dimensions of liberalism is rarely made explicit (Jahn 2013, 22–4). And yet it can give rise to simple political formulas which suggest that achieving one liberal good will unleash the other benefits. The democratic peace thesis as an – albeit controversial – empirical finding in academia, for instance, was translated into a political formula that became a justificatory framework for US policies of regime change in the 'Middle East' (Ish-Shalom

2006, 566). The encompassing view of liberalism also establishes a firm link with, and thereby also narrows the possible understanding of, democracy, universalising a 'historically specific understanding of what democracy is and should be, underwritten by a teleological reading of its past that seeks to validate this truth claim' (C. Hobson 2009, 637).

Originally developed for the domestic context, liberal theory pursued different strategies in order to globalise and universalise its scope and values. Beate Jahn identifies three ways of '"domestify[ing]" the international context' (Jahn 2013, 29) to build liberal international theory. The first version prioritises the liberalisation of the units that make up the international system, that is, the democratisation of states. Given the declining importance of the distinction between an international and a domestic sphere, the second version focuses on the constitution of a cosmopolitan society and global polity. The third strategy operates through the analogy between the domestic and the international realms, for instance conceiving of the American hegemon in the international system as the equivalent of the domestic government (Jahn 2013, 29–31). As the introduction to this chapter briefly discussed, proponents of this last version of liberal internationalism do see the American-led liberal hegemonic order as being in crisis. But they attribute this crisis to changing circumstances rather than 'the underlying principles of liberal international order' (Ikenberry 2011, 334).

This first utopia thus builds on the conviction that liberal normative theory offers a comprehensive and coherent ideal the implementation of which is yet to be perfected. Conflicts, tensions and paradoxical effects are blamed on problems with the practice of norms and illiberal forces beyond liberalism, rather than the contradictions of the fragmentary dynamics inherent in it (Jahn 2013, 9–10). The normative achievements of liberalism are enthusiastically embraced and seen as having universal validity. Liberal internationalists are optimists in the sense that they regard history as moving towards liberal convergence, however bumpy the road may be.

Western Hegemony

The second paradigm makes similar empirical assessments as the first but differs in its normative judgements. The paradigm is the dystopian flipside of liberal convergence, criticising liberal hegemony and problematising the liberal use of force, such as democratic wars (Geis, Müller and Schörnig 2013), as well as deconstructing liberalism's claims to a monopoly on rationality and normative superiority. Many approaches in this paradigm are grounded in a Gramscian tradition and build on his understanding of hegemony as the '"spontaneous" consent given by the great masses of the population to the general direction imposed on social life by the dominant fundamental group' (Gramsci 1971, 12). Antonio Gramsci distinguishes between civil or private society and the state or political society. Whereas the latter operates through direct domination, the former is the realm of hegemony which carries and supports the political system. For Gramsci, a political revolution would have to be accompanied by proletarian hegemony. In neo-Gramscian approaches, such subaltern social groups have often been conceptualised as counterhegemonic, as a challenge 'to an order *already constituted*' (Pasha 2005, 547, original emphasis), but the creation of a 'constitutive outside' is an integral part of the formation of hegemony, as the discussion on the Muslim Other in Chapter 1 demonstrated.

With regard to world order, these conceptual distinctions are important because hegemony is not simply domination of the global order by one state, nor is it a synonym for imperialism. In order for it 'to become hegemonic, a state would have to found and protect a world order which was universal in conception, i.e. . . . an order which most other states . . . could find compatible with their interests' (Cox 1983, 171). Thus, hegemony on a global level emerges when an already established hegemony at the national level acquires international scope through the expansion of 'economic and social institutions, the culture, the technology' (Cox 1983, 171), as determined by the dominant social class. A Gramscian reading would explain

> global tensions between a West-centred liberal order and its assumed antithesis in much of the Third World (particularly the Islamic World) . . . not simply in material terms, nor as a cultural clash, but as the cumulative effect of a culturally partitioned world of privilege and unity, want and fragmentation. (Pasha 2005, 553–4)

While there are works that critically refer to actors as hegemons, more specifically the US as the only remaining superpower (see, for example, Habermas 2004), most approaches are concerned with the structural side of hegemony. Edward Said ([1978] 2003) emphasises the intimate connection between power over and knowledge of the Orient, which makes Western hegemony both stable and subtle.[6] Hegemony or 'cultural leadership' can be challenged through postcolonialism (which detects colonial practices in new guises) and postmodernism (which questions the universalisability of both moral claims and the legitimation of political orders) on the level of knowledge production (Said [1978] 2003, 7, 350–1). Mouffe sees the globalisation of the neoliberal economic model as problematic to the extent that any arguments from the critical left are drawn into and have to argue within the logic of neoliberalism (Mouffe 2000, 118–19).

In their book *Empire* (2000), Michael Hardt and Antonio Negri do not even posit an identifiable hegemon at the centre of the world order, but rather argue that there is a fundamental power shift in the establishment of a new sovereignty without spatial and temporal boundaries. Empire, a totalising management network that is, at the same time, 'a *decentred* and *deterritorializing* apparatus of rule' (Hardt and Negri 2000, xii, original emphasis) is the result of a world market that strives for the instantiation of 'a properly capitalist order' (Hardt and Negri 2000, 9). It does not operate from a centre, but through biopolitics as a 'form of power that regulates social life from its interior . . . [or] as a control that extends throughout the depths of the consciousnesses and bodies of the population' (Hardt and Negri 2000, 23). In this totalising and all-consuming Empire, resistance can only come from the inside: the 'creative forces of the multitude that sustain Empire are also capable of autonomously constructing a counter-Empire . . . that will one day take us through and beyond Empire' (Hardt and Negri 2000, xv). 'Counter-hegemonic struggles', as can be observed in what is often called the global periphery, for instance, are already an indicator of the absence of hegemony and the necessity of dominance (Pasha 2005, 555). In this sense, the dystopian take on Western hegemony sees liberalism's universalising logic as threatening and totalising. It deconstructs the normality of Western modernity and points to the existence of multiple pathways to and manifestations of modernity (Eisenstadt 2000a). While Western hegemony is relatively stable, not least because its workings are often invisible and intangible, its critics nonetheless call for forms of political and academic resistance and counterhegemonic practices.

Pluriverse

In contrast, proponents of the pluriverse believe that Western dominance is in its endgame – and that this is a development to be welcomed. They contrast what is perceived as a normatively flawed monocivilisational model with a pluralism of civilisations. While the term 'civilisations' is notorious for implying colonial superiority, it can be observed 'that nonstate actors, states, and international organizations are increasingly talking and acting *as if* civilizations . . . exist and . . . relations between them mattered in world politics' (Bettiza 2014, 2, original emphasis). A strand of world order research has therefore reclaimed the term, stripping it from the 'liberal presumption that universalistic secular liberal norms are inherently superior to all others' (Katzenstein 2010, 2) and constructing it, from the outset, in the plural – that is, as a plurality of civilisations or imagined civilisational communities, depending on the ontological status ascribed to civilisations.

As civilisations become the object and unit of analysis, their interactions in the form of 'transcivilizational engagements, intercivilizational encounters, and civilizational conflicts' come into view (Katzenstein 2010, 8) and ethical programmes can be designed with the aim of transforming them (Bettiza 2014). One example is the notion of a 'dialogue of civilisations'. This is proposed as an antidote to and serves as a counterdiscourse against the clash of civilisations, which is seen 'as a dangerous possibility . . . resulting from wrong policies that need to be opposed' (Petito 2009, 49). The underlying demand is for the normative structure of the world order to be renegotiated. The premise for finding a universal order that is truly worthy of the name is to recognise the plurality of cultures and civilisations, as well as to allow them to participate in building it. In this way, instead of imposing a 'Western-centric and liberal global order[,] . . . a multicultural and peaceful world order' can be constructed (Petito 2009, 51). As Fred Dallmayr (2009, 30, 37) put it, the monologue as a mode of communication through which 'a hegemonic or imperial power reduces all other agents to irrelevance and silence' needs to be replaced by what he calls 'ethical-hermeneutical dialogue' which would 'render concrete life-worlds mutually accessible as a touchstone of ethical sensibility'.

An obvious question to be asked of these normative approaches is how they take power relations into account (Dallmayr 2009, 38). Authors emphasise that, in contrast to the conventional wisdom provided by neo-realism, multipolarity should be considered an opportunity for a peaceful world order rather than a threat to stability (Petito 2009, 52–5). Some make the case that a plurality of political orders, embedded in a 'dialogically constituted normative order' (Petito 2009, 62), provides better prospects for stable and peaceful global relations than other orders. Mouffe, for instance, advocates a 'pluralisation of hegemonies . . . organised around several big regional units with their different cultures and values' (Mouffe 2009, 553). Not only does this preserve the possibility for legitimate opposition and agonistic forms of politics within the world order, as discussed in the section on agonistic legitimacy above, but it also allows for a decoupling of the democratic ideal and liberalism, and makes culturally imprinted forms of democracy in regional orders conceivable. In such a pluriverse, Mouffe goes on to argue, 'diversity of political forms of organisation will be more conducive to peace and stability than the enforcement of a universal model' (Mouffe 2009, 561).

An empirical anchor for these normative considerations can be found in the debate on new regionalism and, more specifically, in what Amitav Acharya (2014) calls the regional world perspective. The growing number and functions of regional institutions, as well as the importance of interregionalism, point to this alternative multiplex world order in which 'regions are becoming crucial sites of conflict and cooperation in world politics' (Acharya 2014, 118). This order is different from the multipolar world prior to World War II in terms of the multiplicity of actors, the density and scope of both economic interdependence and regional and international institutions, and the complexity of conflicts which have replaced the 'traditional challenge to world order, interstate conflict' (Acharya 2017, 277). The multiplex order is also 'not a singular global order, liberal or otherwise, but a complex of crosscutting, if not competing, international orders and globalisms' (Acharya 2017, 277). The pluriverse is thus the utopian version of a world composed of a plurality of civilisations and/or regions. The latter serve as building blocks in or can even become an alternative to the architecture of global institutions (Hurrell 2007, 247–61). Pluralism and the coexistence of competing political orders are considered conducive to peace and more inclusive global politics, rather than a source of instability or conflict.

Clash of Civilisations

The final teleology shares the previous paradigm's concern with cultural difference and the division of the world into civilisations without, however, seeing this state of affairs as benign. The approaches in this paradigm either posit an essentialised understanding of identities and predict that civilisational encounters will lead to virtually unavoidable clashes, or they claim that identities do not matter at all. In the latter case, the anarchical structure of the international system combined with multipolarity is marked by instability and is prone to violent conflict. Both versions of the clash-of-civilisations dystopia view international relations as having a conflictual nature.

A case of this paradigm par excellence, infamous though it may be, is Samuel P. Huntington's thought. For him, the 'fault lines between civilizations will be the battle lines of the future' and the 'clash of civilizations will dominate global politics' (Huntington 1993, 22). The process of modernisation, Huntington claims, will lead to a weakening of the nation-state as a source of identity, which will strengthen religious identities that unite civilisations. Religion is the most important dividing factor between civilisations and it makes civilisational identities particularly resistant to change. As interactions between civilisations intensify, the awareness of civilisational difference increases and civilisational conflict, as the most violent form, erupts. Huntington sees the primary fault line as residing between the 'West and the rest' (Huntington 1993, 39). Western dominance and claims to the universality of Western values, on the one hand, and the minimal resonance these ideas find in other cultures, on the other, stir up this type of conflict, the most dangerous being the one between the West and what he calls the 'Confucian-Islamic military connection' (Huntington 1993, 47).

To Huntington, the 'differences between civilizations are real and important . . . [and] will supplant ideological and other forms of conflict as the dominant global form of conflict' (Huntington 1993, 48). Similar argumentations are put forward by cultural and area specialists whose works on the history and characteristics of civilisations partly inspired Huntington's theses. These include figures such as the Orientalist Bernard Lewis, who originally coined the idea of a 'clash of civilisations' (Lewis 1990, 55–60). To these authors, civilisations have a recognisable essence that is neither easily changeable nor reconcilable with other civilisations, and that is the root cause of severe, intractable conflicts. In Peter Katzenstein's interpretation, Huntington's approach is an adapted version of realism which replaces the nation-state with civilisation as a 'kind of mega nation-state' (Katzenstein 2010, 8) but keeps the idea of a purely anarchical international system. A world society, let alone a global community, is inconceivable in such an account of civilisations. Huntington also seems to deny the existence of a common background culture in which civilisational conflicts are embedded in the first place. This makes it hard to explain how constant civilisational identities can lead to both peaceful encounters and conflict. Understanding civilisations as constructs that may be reified and become primordial at a certain point in time, which may but do not have to lead to conflict, might be a way to think about civilisational conflict more academically (Katzenstein 2010, 12).

Approaches that do not attach any importance to identity eventually make similar arguments about the inevitable conflict-proneness of the international system. Rather than the incompatibility of cultural features, however, they identify 'unbalanced multipolarity' (Mearsheimer 2001, 130) as the cause of conflict. Similar to the Western hegemony paradigm, these approaches view unipolar international systems as unstable and merely as a transitional state from a bipolar to a multipolar system (Layne 1993). They predict the decline of the American world order, as well as a conflictual process towards the establishment of a conflict-prone multipolar system (Kagan 2012). The dystopia of a clash of civilisations thus predicts the demise of the unipolar world order and its replacement by a multipolar system prone to conflict, due to either the logics of balancing or insurmountable cultural differences.

Studying how Islamists Relate to Western World Order Discourse

The three sections that presented the four paradigms of sovereignty, legitimacy and *teloi* span the Western world order discourse as represented in academic debate. Admittedly, as this is not the result of a discourse analysis in its own right, I do not claim to have captured all strands, to be in a position to weigh the various argumentative paradigms against each other or to have delineated the subtleties and inner workings of any of the three discursive fields. Rather, the discursive space sketched out in the sections and summarised in Table 2.1 should be read as an approximation of the plural, multivocal,

Table 2.1 Western world order discourses

	Sovereignty	Legitimacy	*Teloi*
1	Absolute	Individual-based	Liberal convergence
2	Popular	Community-based	Western hegemony
3	Conditional	Deliberative	Pluriverse
4	Shared	Agonistic	Clash of civilisations

sometimes contradictory nature of 'the' Western world order. This approximation fulfils three methodological functions. First, it is meant to counter the imaginary of a unitary Western world order or a consensus on its meaning. Second, if the approximation is plausible enough, it becomes possible to operationalise the notion that a specific discourse or actor is radically different from or indeed the ultimate Other of the Western world order. This would mean that there is no overlap between the Western discursive space and the discourse under investigation whatsoever. Finally, this allows for an empirical investigation of the relationship between a de-essentialised Western and any other world order discourse and an appraisal of grades and shades of difference and identity. In this book, the discursive strategies of two Islamist actors will be scrutinised in this way. However, in principle, any actor's communication could be subjected to such an analysis, including Western parties or states that would end up at a rather specific point in the discursive space spanned by the three axes of sovereignty, legitimacy and *teloi*.

How, then, should such an empirical investigation proceed? First, in terms of material, natural data – that is, data produced by the actors under investigation themselves and documenting 'discursive encounters' (Hansen 2006, 76) or, possibly, a 'clash of discourses' (Dryzek 2006, 155) – is preferred to data produced by the researcher, such as interviews. Typically, such data includes oral or written communications, but also videos and other visuals, websites and online posts, and so on. What specific artefacts and modes of communication are analysed depends on the actor's communicative preferences. The documents should also address or at least be accessible to an international and transnational audience, the 'fellow constructors' of world order or the global discursive space in which the actor under investigation struggles with others over meaning. This reduces useful data to elite utterances deliberately disseminated by the actors themselves beyond their local communities or constituencies.

Second, given the interest in relating specific discourses to a larger discursive space referred to as the Western world order, the analysis proceeds both deductively and inductively. In order to combine these two strategies, to proceed as systematically as possible and to process large quantities of text, the empirical study in this book employed a qualitative content analysis (QCA) using the version developed by Margit Schreier (2012) and, as a concrete analytical instrument, put it into the service of the discourse analytical methodology (see also Schreier 2012, 49). The deductive part concerns, on the one hand, the specification of discursive fields, operationalised as main categories (Schreier 2012, 59–78), which are identified as constitutive of a world order discourse – but could have been selected differently. On the other hand, the four paradigmatic arguments identified in Western discourse for each of the fields are a deductive starting point which serves as the standard from which the discourse subjected to empirical analysis may deviate to a greater or lesser extent. In the terminology of QCA, these strandsof discourse represent deductive categories which, in the course of the analysis, are inductively modified, completed or dropped. Critics may object that such an empirical strategy reproduces Western categories – and it is precisely this point the approach in this book capitalises on. My argumentation starts from a multifaceted yet hegemonic Western discourse to which any other articulation of world order has to relate. Over the course of the analysis, it will become visible whether, how and to what extent this hegemonic discourse is reproduced, modified and transcended by the two Islamist groups under investigation here.

QCA also makes it possible to quantitatively assess the importance of certain themes and tropes, and to track changes in discourse over time. We should treat this type of 'measuring' with care or even a healthy dose of suspicion, as the most important and accepted, almost self-evident, pieces of knowledge, concepts and arguments are precisely those that do not have to be mentioned anymore. This is why the frequency of certain coded categories is more a proxy for the need to establish certain (moral or truth) claims or framings – and, thus, also an indicator of the level of contestation of a theme or trope rather than its absolute importance in the discursive construction of world order.

Besides equating the frequency of a code or category with importance, another risk we face when conducting QCA is being too rigid in 'forcing' the deductive coding frame on the empirical material. We must take care that the analysis is open enough for conceptions of sovereignty, legitimacy and teleologies that go beyond or are located outside the discursive space outlined in this chapter, that is, open for discursive innovation. This requires text sensitivity and contextualisation.

This is why, third, the discourse analytical posture should be maintained throughout and additional steps of analysis, firmly rooted in the epistemological and methodological frame of this book, are necessary. As Chapters 1 and 2 clarified, discourse is understood as a knowledge–power nexus and the focus is on agents (rather than structures) who try to find discursive strategies to 'impose their view of reality' (Holzscheiter 2014, 151) rather than striving for consensus through conviction and the better argument. This does not mean, however, that we should deny the structural side of discourse, which creates the (unequal) positions that speakers can adopt in the first place. But the core empirical interest is to understand how actors construct world order in and through discourse, purposefully (when they explicitly try to offer alternative interpretations), provocatively (when they transgress what are considered the boundaries of Western world order discourse) or unconsciously (when they discursively reproduce certain arguments or do not feel inclined to address a particular aspect of order). This book sees agents (here: Islamist actors) 'as the authors of narratives and, consequently, as active and deliberative constructors of social reality' (Holzscheiter 2014, 153).

In order to do justice to the social, temporal and spatial situatedness of these actors, a thorough analysis of the proximate and distal context of the texts examined (Phillips and Hardy 2002, 18–38) and an investigation of the constructions of the Self and the Other (or rather, mulitple Selves and more or less different Others; Hansen 2006, 33–48) are useful additional steps. Proximate context refers to the circumstances in which a specific text is produced, such as the situation of interaction or occasion, or the specific discourse practices. Concretely, this comprises the production, dissemination and consumption of a text, but also intertextuality and interdiscursivity (Bergström, Ekström and Boréus 2017, 222–4). Besides a detailed description of the material analysed and the audiences addressed by the texts, as well as the material that the actor under investigation produces that is not directly subjected to analysis, such a contextualisation requires reflection on what biases and blind spots these discursive practices imply, including an interpretation of what (may have) remained unarticulated and for what reasons (opportunistic, commonsensical, strategic etc.). A variety of data can help with this contextualisation, including participant observation of speech events, (expert) interviews, focus groups with target communities or online ethnography of audiences. Distal context refers to the broader social context, such as the social, ethnic and regional allegiances of discourse participants or their institutional context or social practices. The analysis of the distal context requires reflecting on the order of discourse – does a text reproduce or challenge hegemonic discourses, does it have an effect on power relations, and so on (Lindekilde 2015, 204–6)? In this book, the most important distal context is the Western world order discourse and how the discourses of the two actors are related to this in terms of recognition and resistance. In a narrower sense, distal context also refers to the order of regional and local discourse in which the text analysis has to be embedded. For this purpose, secondary literature, newspapers and possibly interviews with the actors themselves, as well as with experts or political competitors, can be analysed. In this book, a thorough analysis of secondary literature, observations from field visits and interviews that I conducted between 2014 and 2017 with important figures in the parties analysed as well as experts on the two groups (in Lebanon and Tunisia) were used to investigate proximate and distal context.

Scrutinising constructions of the Self and the Other is important not only because, as argued here and in the previous chapter, any discourse on order comes with a proviso on who is (not) and can(not) be included in it, as well as a notion of what this order is meant to overcome and against whom it is positioned. It also facilitates an understanding of the position and point of view from which an actor formulates their contributions to the global discourse on world order. An actor's construction of and self-positioning within a 'web of identities' (Hansen 2006, 40) may involve identities that cut across those produced by hegemonic discourse and may be an entry point for recasting both reified conflict lines and ways of thinking about world order. The construction of identity does not usually involve 'a single Self–Other dichotomy but a series of related yet slightly different juxtapositions that can be theorized as constituting processes of linking and differentiation' (Hansen 2006, 37). Selves are not always unequivocal, Others not always radically different; one side may reproduce or construct enmities in less antagonistic terms than the other. Such constructions of identity and difference are best analysed by coding the primary material in a way that preserves the original wording, then by looking at how linking and juxtaposing creates relationships of sameness and difference. Again, tacit agreement on certain identity constructions may lead to these no longer being articulated at all. Dimensions to be considered in the analysis of Selves and Others are spatiality (boundary-drawing), temporality (for example, potential for transformation or stasis) and ethicality (morality, responsibility) in relation to identity (Hansen 2006, 42–5).

While the empirical parts of this book (Chapters 4–6) will demonstrate how Ennahda and Hezbollah discursively construct Selves and Others, identity and difference, in their respective environments, the next chapter reflects on what it means to interpret these two parties as Selves in a study on a global world order discourse on unequal footing. Who are these speakers and from what position in their domestic, regional and global context do they articulate their conceptions of world order? What is their history, whom do they (claim to) represent and to whom are their utterances addressed?

Notes

1. As Wojczewski (2018, 8–9) argues, hegemonic discourse is also 'increasingly struggling to fix meanings and identities and thus to reproduce a particular representation of world order because of a shift in self–other relationships'.
2. For instance, I do not explicitly consider economic orders but rather focus on political ones. Economic aspects do, however, play a role in conceptions of legitimacy, as the empirical part of the book will show.
3. Given that the authors quoted 'never did identify themselves with the communitarian movement' (Bell 2023), I will refrain from using the label 'communitarianism' here.
4. Mouffe claims that the basic idea of deliberation 'has accompanied democracy since its birth in fifth-century [BCE] Athens' but explains that it has experienced a revival with Rawls's theory of justice as the birth hour of 'a new wave of normative political theory', which is described as a 'deliberative model', as opposed to the previously dominant aggregative model (Mouffe 2000, 81–2). Therefore, while acknowledging the differences in their theories, Mouffe considers the concepts of

liberal democracy developed by Rawls and Habermas and their respective disciples to belong to the same family of deliberative political theories.

5. https://blog.politics.ox.ac.uk/the-optimistic-agonist-an-interview-with-bonnie -honig/ (accessed 10 October 2023).

6. Most scholars propose a Foucauldian reading of Said, but, increasingly, authors are also identifying the Gramscian legacies in Orientalism (see, for example, Vandeviver 2019). Said himself mentions both authors.

PART II

DISCURSIVE STRUGGLES OVER WORLD ORDER: TUNISIAN ENNAHDA AND LEBANESE HEZBOLLAH

3

ENNAHDA AND HEZBOLLAH: ISLAMIST ACTORS IN THE CONTEXT OF THE ARAB UPRISINGS

Despite recent calls for Shi'a as the 'other Islamists' (Valbjørn and Gunning 2021) to be studied together with Sunni Islamism and Salafism, which have so far dominated the debate, treating Ennahda and Hezbollah in one book may seem odd at first glance. The two groups belong to different sects and Islamist schools of thought. The former has spent several decades renouncing violence, whereas the latter is one of the most active ANSAs in the region. The diverging repertoires of political activity also have consequences for their internal organisational structures. The domestic contexts in which the two operate are quite different, with regard to both societal composition and political system, as are the conditions under which the two movements emerged. Ennahda's activism was primarily directed against domestic repression, whereas Hezbollah became active in the context of a civil war and, notably, foreign intervention and occupation by Israel, against which it called for resistance.

But the two groups have a lot in common, too. Both can be classified as statist Islamists or as movements that at some point started participating in domestic politics (Volpi and Stein 2015, see also Chapter 1). Besides their statist orientation, they share a hybrid quality typical of many Islamists in that they are both a movement and a party. Importantly for the argument of this book, both Ennahda and Hezbollah have been and are still being met with 'misrecognition' (Clément, Geis and Pfeifer 2021) by the Western world for being 'Islamist' (see Chapter 1). As the empirical part of this book (Chapters 4–6) will demonstrate, both actors struggle with their 'Islamist' legacy and the suspicion this label brings with it. At the same time, both parties have been exposed to the Western world order by virtue of having belonged to coalition governments in their respective countries over the whole period studied in this book. As the specific research interest and question are what makes certain phenomena appealing for a study (Philbrick Yadav 2013, 9), Ennahda and Hezbollah can be considered 'politically and analytically pregnant' (Hansen 2006, 76) for the question of the struggle over world order between 'the West' and 'the Islamists'. Admittedly, both are small parties in very small countries, even within the Arab-speaking 'Middle East' and North Africa. But for different reasons, Ennahda and Hezbollah can be considered highly influential in the 2010s, that is, the post-Arab uprisings era, under investigation in this book.

Ennahda's president Rached al-Ghannouchi is one of the foremost influential Muslim intellectuals and political thinkers of our time (March 2019, 153). Until Tunisia's clear deviation from its bumpy democratisation path in 2021, Ennahda was often seen as a potential model for other Islamist groups in the Maghreb and also in the Mashreq – not only for its ideological orientation but also for its practical achievements in the Tunisian transition process (Cavatorta and Merone 2015, Stepan 2012a). Hezbollah shaped the period between 2011 and 2016, too, but for other reasons. Even before this time, it had acquired a certain reputation and popularity beyond Lebanon for being the first and only actor to have 'defeated' Israel twice: in 2000 when it forced Israel as an occupying force out of Lebanon and in the July War of 2006 (Salem 2019, 517, Darwich 2021b, 5). Although it is questionable whether these were clear instances of military victory, they were perceived as a defeat in Israel and celebrated by Hezbollah. The militia had at least managed to demystify Israel and expose its vulnerability (Saade 2016, 110). Hezbollah has cultivated the image of a military force to be reckoned with ever since and expanded its activities after 2010, officially launching an intervention in the Syrian Civil War in support of the Assad regime in 2013. It also started creating its own 'proxies' in Syria, which it co-sponsors with Iraqi non-state actors and Iran (Leenders and Giustozzi 2022). Moreover, it is has been active in Yemen and Iraq, training Shi'i militias (Daher 2016, 159, 197) and deploying fighters to help Ansar Allah militants, also known as Houthis (Cafiero and Krieg 2019). While most of the militias in other countries do not belong to the Twelver Shi'a, some still claim that the presence of Hezbollah may influence the worldviews held by local actors in Iraq or Yemen (Shanahan 2017). Be that as it may, it is clear that both Ennahda and Hezbollah have shaped the post-Arab-uprisings era, the regional dynamics and the global perception of the prevailing conflicts – notably sectarianism and the Islamist–secular divide, as the following chapters will show.

In terms of influence, other groups come to mind as candidates for the study. Arguably, the Egyptian Muslim Brotherhood (or al-Ikhwan al-Muslimun) and ISIS can be considered even more important in terms of size and regional political influence. The former is a statist Islamist organisation, like Ennahda and Hezbollah, whereas the latter is a Salafi-jihadist group. The Muslim Brotherhood was not chosen as a case here. This is not primarily related to the warnings against 'Egyptocentrism' and 'an overreliance on Egypt as a focal point in understanding Islamism . . . in other contexts' (Philbrick Yadav 2014, 56). Rather, the period of rule under al-Ikhwan al-Muslimun after the Egyptian revolution in 2011 was too short to yield relevant results with regard to the question of world order. It lasted from 2012 until the military coup in 2013. In that same year, the Muslim Brotherhood was banned and even listed as a terrorist organisation by the new regime under Abdel Fattah as-Sisi (Ranko and Sabra 2015). While this does not mean that the Brotherhood should be considered marginal, its minimal exposure to the international environment as a governing party makes it less relevant when it comes to studying its relationship with the Western world order – it did not have to enter the global 'clash of discourses' (Dryzek 2006, 155) or 'discursive encounters' (Hansen 2006, 76) with regard to global order. The same holds true for ISIS, but for other reasons (see Chapter 1). As a Salafi-jihadist group, ISIS does not discursively 'work through' its relationship with the Western world order but can, more or less from an outside position, reject the system as a whole (Maher 2016). One would also expect fewer nuances and ambivalences in this case because ISIS was not subjected to, or rather set out to eliminate, societal difference and political pluralism. It therefore did not need to negotiate or seek compromise with either local or global competitors. Rather than rendering the simplistic image of a binary 'Islamist–Western' opposition more complicated, studying ISIS would in fact reiterate and reify the well-known narrative of incommensurateness, thus adding nothing new to the state of research.[1]

Finally, ruling Islamists, such as the Turkish AKP and the Saudi or Iranian regime, could also have been considered for selection. But their contexts are quite different from Ennahda's and Hezbollah's. The AKP has been in power for a long time in a state that is relatively deeply integrated into the Western security community. While there has been more lively debate on the Islamist character of the party since Recep Tayyip Erdoğan began pushing for ever more conservative reforms and 'upgraded' (Heydemann 2007) the authoritarian traits of the Turkish system (Bayulgen, Arbatli, and Canbolat 2018), subjecting Turkey's Islamists to 'Othering' has been limited: Turkey is still a member of the North Atlantic Treaty Organization (NATO) and a close partner (and candidate country) of the EU. As for the two Islamic states, their respective standings in the Western-dominated order could not be more different. Saudi Arabia is a key strategic partner first and foremost to the US, but also to other Western states. In contrast, Iran is one of the 'rogue states', a concept invented by George W. Bush in the 'global war on terror'. What they share, though, is that they can no longer be called Islamist parties or movements – or non-state actors. Until recently,[2] this meant that the two enjoyed the international privileges and protections that come with statehood. Non-state actors and their practices are regularly under more pressure to legitimise themselves and their actions, especially if they are transnationally active and involved in armed conflict (Pfeifer forthcoming). Moreover, neither system is marked by internal pluralism – Saudi Arabia less so than Iran – in particular regarding fundamental questions of ordering. None of this means, however, that the AKP, the Saudi or the Iranian regime could not be studied with regard to their discursive construction of world order and how it relates to Western discourse.

The remainder of this chapter introduces Ennahda and Hezbollah as two 'Selves' that articulate their conceptions of sovereignty, legitimacy and *teloi* towards the co-producers of, and while struggling with, the Western-dominated world order. It recounts the history of their emergence as what academics would call Islamist movements and positions this development in the evolution of Islamism more globally. It then zooms in on the post-Arab-uprisings era in Tunisia and Lebanon, revealing an image of the (partially shared) context of the two parties in a political landscape in turmoil. They were subjected both to the pluralist, more or less democratic game of domestic politics, which saw the rise of new political forces, and to various forms of political violence, from terrorism to civil war, in the Arab MENA. The detailed reconstruction of events in Tunisia and Lebanon, as well as in the wider region, between 2011 and 2016 allows for a contextual understanding of Ennahda's and Hezbollah's discourse as analysed in the remainder of this study (Chapters 4–6). The conclusion of this book will then look beyond the narrow period of empirical investigation, providing an outlook on the unfolding of events after 2016. This allows for an appraisal of Ennahda's and Hezbollah's (discursive) practices of the early 2010s in a broader temporal context and a rough assessment of the consequences they had for Tunisia's and Lebanon's futures.

Who Is Speaking? Ennahda and Hezbollah as 'Selves' or 'Cases' of Islamism

One peculiarity of the study of political Islam is that the actors dubbed 'Islamists' do not refer to themselves using this term. However, it is not unusual for actors to be labelled by others differently than the labels they use for themselves, nor is such naming innocent. Rather, it carries with it implications of varying degrees of subtlety about the characteristics of the named actor, about the relationship between the party doing the naming and the one being named and, when the two are involved in a conflict, about the nature of their struggle and the legitimacy of the goals and means employed in it (Pfeifer, Geis and Clément 2022, Pfeifer forthcoming). As Martin Kramer (2003) aptly identifies, the term 'Islamism' entered the French language in the eighteenth century to refer to the religion practised by Muslims and, with this meaning, travelled to the English-speaking world in the nineteenth century. The meaning of the term was not changed until the 1970s and 1980s in the context of the French debate on new Islamic movements. The by then already dominant American (academic) debate called these movements 'fundamentalist', applying a term which had originally referred to Protestant Christian movements to the Islamic context. The French reintroduced *islamisme* into the semantic repertoire, which then travelled back to the US debate and eventually gained currency – by then carrying a connotation of threat and extremism. As Kramer puts it, the

> entry of Islamism into common English usage had not improved the image of these movements and paradoxically made it easier to categorize them as threats of the first order . . . As the Muslim equivalent of fascists or bolshevists, they were clearly marked as the enemies of democracy and freedom. (Kramer 2003)

Ennahda and Hezbollah are among the movements that gained international attention in the 1970s and 1980s but never identified as Islamists. Ennahda emanated from a Tunisian Islamic movement that formed in the 1960s and 1970s. Hmida Ennaifer, Rached al-Ghannouchi and Abdelfattah Mourou founded al-Jama'a al-Islamiyya (the Islamic Group) in the early 1970s. It was joined by the Islamic trend in the neo-Destour, an anti-colonial movement founded by Habib Bourguiba (later a long-standing Tunisian president) in 1934. The movement grew and was influenced by the writings of the Egyptian Muslim Brotherhood that were circulated among Tunisians. After violent clashes with leftist university students, the Islamic Group split. One strand advocated non-violent political activism against the Bourguiba regime and, after a congress in 1979, founded the Mouvement de la Tendance Islamique (MTI, Harakat al-Ittijah al-Islami). Inspired by the Islamic Revolution in Iran in the same year, the MTI committed to a politico-economic agenda rather than working on the level of individual piety like the Islamic Group had originally done (Wolf 2017, 27–51, Yıldırım 2017). After a failed attempt at achieving recognition under the Bourguiba regime in 1981, which ended in mass imprisonment of its members, the MTI changed its name to Harakat al-Nahdha (Renaissance Movement, hereafter Ennahda) in 1989 (Hamdi 1998, 41–74). The new name was reminiscent of a school of thought which had emerged in the second half of the nineteenth century, the Islamic reformist movement or Salafiyya, which advocated a return to the pious ancestors in the age of renaissance (*'asr al-nahda*) (Jung 2012, 155, Mura 2015, 38). The reformist movement challenged the authority of religious scholars (*'ulama'*) and established legal schools (*madhāhib*) in the Islamic tradition, calling for a new interpretation (*ijtihād*) of the Qur'an and the *sunna*.[3] The movement opened up the discursive space to examine the meaning of Islam in modern times and called for renewal (*tajdīd*). As a consequence, it became an intellectual source for many of the contemporary movements (Roy 1994, 33–4) – including both today's Salafist groups and those classified as Islamists.

But Ennahda's version of Islamism is a derivative of the Egyptian Muslim Brotherhood's brand, which developed at the beginning of the twentieth century and constituted both a break with and a continuation of the Salafiyya. Importantly, its call 'to leave the mosque' (Roy 1994, 35) made the Brotherhood's Islamism a genuinely political project with the aim of establishing an Islamic state. At its inception, Ennahda 'subscribed to the creation of an Islamic state whereby the application of sharia law for the whole society reflected the unitary vision embodied in the principle of *tawhid*' (Cavatorta and Merone 2013, 860), the unity of or perfect overlap between the state and religion. Ennahda also had an Arab Islamic outlook on political order rather than a Tunisian one, for it subscribed to 'the idea that nation-states are historical contingencies that would one day give way to a pan-Islamic state' (Kubicek 2015, 288). What shaped the Islamist movement at least as much as its intellectual heritage from the nineteenth century was the very practical quest to free the Muslim world from colonial rule and foreign domination. It was 'out of the colonial experience [that] . . . the question of the Islamic concept of jihad with "striving" and "struggle" for freedom and independence in the modern political sense [emerged]' (Ayoob 2008, 8). The anti-colonial impetus of historical Islamism should not be underestimated, for it persists, sometimes translated into anti-imperialism, in contemporary versions of Islamism.

This is true not only for Ennahda but also for Hezbollah, which identifies as an Islamic resistance against occupation, imperialism and foreign rule. In the narrowest sense, resistance refers to the liberation of Lebanon and Palestine from Israeli occupation. More broadly, however, and as this book will demonstrate, it is directed against any oppressive scheme devised by foreign powers for the MENA region (see Chapter 6). As a Shi'i group, Hezbollah (or the Party of God) also emerged from a larger social movement that formed in Lebanon in the 1970s. As a politically and socially marginalised minority, albeit a large one, the Shi'i community primarily inhabited the Lebanese south and the Bekaa Valley in eastern Lebanon and lived from agriculture. With growing modernisation and urbanisation, however, many Shi'a moved to the southern suburbs of Beirut, the Dahieh, where a new middle class emerged. This spurred demands for more political rights in the sect-based Lebanese political system. This politicisation was reinforced by Shi'i clerics who had been sent to ḥawzāt (Shi'i seminaries) in Najaf (Iraq) and Qom (Iran) and brought an activist, revolutionary spirit to the movement. One of the clerics, Musa al-Sadr, founded the Movement of the Deprived (Harakat al-Mahrumin) in the early 1970s. When the Lebanese Civil War broke out in 1975, Amal (Hope) was created as a military wing of the movement. Having been expelled from Jordan, members of the Palestine Liberation Organization (PLO) had moved to southern Lebanon, establishing their operating base there and prompting the first Israeli invasion of 1978 (Operation Litani). The losses and suffering of the Shi'a in the south contributed to strengthening the militant trend. The suspicion that the Libyan regime was involved in Sadr's disappearance in 1978 had already led to some distancing between the Lebanese Shi'a and Palestinian factions that were supported by Muammar el Qaddafi. Amal's relationship with the Palestinians quickly deteriorated after the Israeli invasion, which had been prompted by the PLO presence but inflicted more damage on southern Lebanese villages than Palestinian camps. This resulted in clashes and, at the beginning of the 1980s, outright battles between the PLO and Amal. Importantly, an Islamic strand formed within the movement. Following the Islamic Revolution in Iran in 1979, a few hundred Iranian Revolutionary Guards were sent to Lebanon in order to support the emerging Islamic militants in their fight against Israel and spread the teachings of the revolution. Following the teachings of Hossein Fadlallah, a new group formed and officially founded Hezbollah in 1982, the year of the second Israeli invasion (Azani 2009, 47–74, Norton 2014, 9–26, Pfeifer 2021, 150–3).

While the Islamic Revolution in Iran gave a boost to many Islamist movements working to establish an Islamic political order, it was of particular significance to Hezbollah. Ayatollah Khomeini's revolutionary thought was founded on Shi'i theology. At the core of his theory of velāyat-e faqīh or, in Arabic, wilāyat al-faqīh (the guardianship of the Islamic jurist) is the story of the disappearance of the twelfth imam, al-Mahdi, in the ninth century. Twelver Shi'a believe that al-Mahdi was the legitimate ruler in the line of succession after the Prophet and that he returned to earth to establish just rule as a messianic figure. His absence, however, meant that Islamic authority could not be legitimately established. Khomeini's theory allowed for a temporary but legitimate rule by a 'just, knowledgeable, and faithful *faqih* . . . obliged to exercise both religious and political power' (Mahdavi 2013, 184) until the return of al-Mahdi. Hezbollah subscribes to *wilāyat al-faqīh* as one pillar of its programme. In the absence of the last infallible imam, it is the jurist-theologian's task to reveal 'Sharia's verdicts and judgments, becoming the spiritual authority of last resort' (Qassem 2010, 113); he is the source of authority and the leader of the Islamic *umma*. As a consequence, establishing a state based on the Iranian example was among Hezbollah's objectives at its inception.

The famous 'Open Letter Addressed to the Oppressed in Lebanon and the World', released in 1985, was the party's first programmatic document. It contained three goals: 'first, the expulsion of all foreigners from Lebanon; second, the liberation of Jerusalem; and third, the establishment of an Islamic regime in Lebanon' (Azani 2009, 63). It is noteworthy that the document was addressed to the oppressed of the world 'irrespective of their color, race, or religion', simultaneously emphasising that 'this usage conveys and is in conformity with its identity as an Islamic jihadi movement struggling to address and redress the injustices that the oppressed suffer' (Alagha 2011, 16). There has thus been a strong anti-imperialist element in Hezbollah's platform from the very start, at the time directed against the USA and the Union of Soviet Socialist Republics (USSR). More concretely, Hezbollah railed against the foreign presence in Lebanon in the 1980s, especially – but not only – against the Israeli Defence Forces (IDF), even engaging in armed struggle against them. The year of the Israeli invasion, 1982, is also the foundational year of Hezbollah's Islamic Resistance (al-Muqawama al-Islamiyya) project, which is at the very core of the group. Between 1985 and 1987, an organisational unit called the Islamic Resistance was created to mobilise fighters and serve as the armed wing of Hezbollah (Azani 2009, 67–8). But the project of resistance is much broader than this. Resistance is constitutive of Hezbollah's identity, its version of Islamism is geared towards military resistance, and resistance serves as a prism for its endeavour to build a Lebanese nation and society (Saade 2016).

In 1989 and 1992 respectively, Ennahda and Hezbollah ran in their first national elections. This was a rather typical development for the 'second generation of post-colonial Islamist activists [who] conceived of Islamism in a more overt political competition' (Boubekeur and Roy 2012a, 4). It was around the same time that Olivier Roy formulated his diagnosis of the – somewhat misleadingly termed – 'failure of political Islam' (Roy 1994). He held that the Islamist revolutionary programme, which aimed to profoundly transform politics through Islam, had not achieved its goals. Some parties faced state repression, while others failed to provide a truly alternative order rooted in Islam. The prognosis, then, was that Islamism, in this narrow sense, would be replaced by neofundamentalism or a conservative movement that focused on the social rather than the political realm. The other trajectory for the old Islamists would be a transformation into conservative parties as part of a post-Islamist trend (Roy 2012b, 9). The fact that both Ennahda and Hezbollah gave up on the project of establishing an Islamic state or Islamising 'society through the state' (Roy 2012a, 18) places them in this latter group, even though the 'boundaries between Islamism and post-Islamism are fluid and interconnected, bound by deep historical continuities and not by sharp ruptures' (Boubekeur and Roy 2012a, 6).

The term 'statist Islamists', indicating 'the close connection between national structures of governance and the strategies of activists in their particular socio-cultural and socio-economic circumstances' (Volpi and Stein 2015, 277), is more fitting in the context of this book. For Ennahda and Hezbollah continued to participate in their respective political systems. Ennahda faced severe repression at the hands of President Zine el Abidine Ben Ali's regime and his Rassemblement Constitutionnel Démocratique (RCD) party. After significant gains in the 1989 elections, 20,000 Nahdawis (Ennahda members) were imprisoned and a further 10,000 were exiled (Stepan 2012b). While creating and promoting a version of Islam that served its legitimation (Cesari 2014, 43), the Ben Ali regime systematically discredited and dismantled the Islamic movement and presented it as an Islamist threat. Ghannouchi and other leaders tried to keep Ennahda in exile throughout the 1990s. But the movement was weak, disconnected from the imprisoned Tunis leadership, and suffering from an ideological split between advocates of violent and non-violent means (Wolf 2017, 87–98). The 2000s seemed to bring a change in the dynamics, with Ennahda reaching out to the secular opposition, which had come to face similar repression to the Islamists by dint of an increasingly closed authoritarian system. Several opposition groups, Ennahda among them, formed the 18 October Movement in 2005, initiated a hunger strike demanding the respect of human rights in Tunisia and developed a vision for a new democratic Tunisia (Boubekeur 2016, 110, Cavatorta and Merone 2013, 870). In 2004 and 2006 respectively, Ali Laarayedh and Hamadi Jebali, two of Ennahda's leading figures, were released from prison. And finally, a student movement with ties to Ennahda emerged in the mid-2000s, but did not reveal its allegiance until the Arab uprisings.

Hezbollah's trajectory of the 1990s was marked by the legacies of the Lebanese Civil War. The 1989 Taif Agreement did not put an immediate end to the war, which lasted until 1990. But it contained provisions for post-conflict Lebanon, including reforms of the ratios of sectarian representation for the multireligious Lebanese society with its eighteen recognised sects (Norton 2014, 12). Moreover, the agreement stated that all non-state militias must be disarmed – except for Hezbollah. This was an achievement of the Syrian negotiators, who had argued that Hezbollah was a resistance movement rather than a militia and needed to retain its arms to end Israeli occupation (Salem 2019, 515). Finally, the Taif Agreement also stipulated an immediate and full withdrawal of Israeli troops, with the help of the United Nations Interim Force in Lebanon (UNIFIL). As for Syria, the document stipulated that the two governments find an agreement to determine the duration of the Syrian presence. The two states did not withdraw until 2000 (Israeli withdrawal) and 2005 (the Cedar Revolution against Syrian occupation). In 1992, Hezbollah's leader, Abbas al-Musawi, and his family were killed in a targeted assassination by Israel. Just a month earlier, Hezbollah had declared its willingness to participate in the upcoming parliamentary elections. This process of opening up towards the Lebanese public and integrating into the Lebanese political system came to be known as the *infitāḥ* (opening-up) policy and the Lebanonisation of Hezbollah (Worrall, Mabon and Clubb 2015, Saouli 2018, critically Saade 2016, 37).

Under Hassan Nasrallah, Musawi's successor as secretary general, the party continued its path of inclusion. In the run-up to its first elections, Hezbollah showcased its Lebanese roots and identity, emphasising that the resistance against Israel was its priority. Well prepared, the party won eight seats in parliament – a huge success for a first-time runner in the sect-based Lebanese system. Hezbollah's new political activities required a change to its internal structure. It established a political council, a jihad council and 'the Loyalty to the Resistance parliamentary bloc to meet the demands of involvement in government' (Azani 2013, 904). It continued its armed struggle against Israel in southern Lebanon until the IDF started withdrawing in 2000. Under Israel's newly elected prime minister, Ehud Barak, the Israeli occupation came to an end – with the exception of the Shebʿa Farms, a piece of land in the Golan Heights that Lebanon claims as its national territory and that is under Israeli control to this day (Norton 2014, 79–94). To the Lebanese public, this served as an important justification for Hezbollah to keep its arms and continue its militant activity. Meanwhile, the conflict over the continued presence of the Syrian occupation forces in Lebanon intensified. It escalated when the then Lebanese prime minister, Rafiq al-Hariri, was killed along with more than twenty others in a massive car bomb explosion in the middle of Beirut on 14 February 2005. Many Lebanese immediately suspected the direct involvement of the Syrian regime. On 14 March, more than one million people came together in Beirut's Martyrs' Square to demonstrate against the Syrian occupation of Lebanon. Six days earlier, on 8 March, Hezbollah and allied groups had organised a protest supporting continued Syrian presence in Lebanon. Nevertheless, under Lebanese and international pressure, the Syrians withdrew (Salem 2019).

The so-called Cedar Revolution reconfigured the Lebanese political landscape, which had previously been defined by sectarian cleavages. Now, the polarisation between two newly formed blocs, the March 8 and the March 14 alliances, dominated (Nagle 2016). The latter was a coalition of several Christian parties and the Sunni Future Movement led by Rafiq al-Hariri's son, Saad al-Hariri. The former combined the two Shiʿi parties, Hezbollah and Amal, and the largest Christian party, the Free Patriotic Movement led by Michel Aoun, who served as president of Lebanon until October 2022; the Druze Lebanese Democratic Party would join the alliance later. These camps cut across sectarian boundaries between Muslims and Christians, but created new tensions between Sunnis and Shiʿa. This antagonism was reinforced by the regional support for both groups, with Saudi Arabia assisting the Sunni Future Movement and Iran backing Hezbollah.

A year after the Syrian withdrawal, the conflict between Hezbollah and Israel escalated yet again. In July 2006, Hezbollah militants attacked Israeli soldiers on a routine patrol, killing three and taking two captive. In an attempt to capture the attackers, who fled to Lebanon, five more IDF soldiers were killed. Israel's reactions were much more severe than Hezbollah had anticipated: the IDF launched what came to be known as the July War. In total, over 1,100 Lebanese and more than forty Israeli civilians were killed during the war and several hundreds of thousands of people were displaced in both countries. The Lebanese south as well as the Dahieh were devastated (Norton 2014, 132–43). Yet Hezbollah still celebrated the withdrawal of Israeli forces as a success and claimed victory.

In 2009, Hezbollah issued a new manifesto. While there are continuities with the 'Open Letter', the manifesto also features some important changes. It suggests a more nuanced stance on European countries and warns the latter against complicity with US hegemonic plans and submitting to an '"Atlantic drift" (NATO) of colonial backgrounds' (quoted in Alagha 2011, 31). Moreover, this document already contains a call for recognition or, rather, an appeal to end Hezbollah's misrecognition as a terrorist organisation (Pfeifer 2021) – a plea that would become more urgent when Hezbollah began fighting against ISIS in Syria, as the analysis in the following chapters will demonstrate. Hezbollah's demand for recognition was addressed to European nations and embedded in the invocation of their collective memory: through their history, Europeans were familiar with the fight against oppression. Finally, and most importantly, Hezbollah officially revoked its goal of a Lebanese Islamic state. Instead, it advocated a strong Lebanese state that would abolish the sectarian system (Alagha 2011, 32).

Talking about a Revolution: Ennahda and Hezbollah during and after the Arab Uprisings (2011–16)

So many accounts of the Arab uprisings start with the horrific story of Mohamed Bouazizi's self-immolation in the Tunisian city of Sidi Bouzid in December 2010. The 26-year-old street vendor not only found himself in a desperate economic situation but had also suffered several instances of police harassment. On 17 December 2010, Bouazizi's produce and weighing scales were confiscated by a female police officer, Faida Hamdi, on the grounds that he allegedly did not have the correct permit to sell his wares. When he tried to circumvent the confiscation and take back his apples, the policewoman allegedly slapped and insulted the vendor. Turning to the governor's office (or, according to some reports, the provincial headquarters) to complain and retrieve the scales taken from him, officials refused to meet him. 'If you don't see me, I'll burn myself,' Bouazizi is quoted as saying. A short time later, he returned to the site and set himself on fire, dying in hospital two weeks later due to the severity of his injuries (H. Hussain 2018, Ammar 2022).

This drastic act triggered a massive wave of protest in Tunisia, first in the marginalised areas in the south, then all over the country. The Ben Ali regime reacted with brutal repression and by mid-January, more than thirty Tunisians had died. Soon, however, civil society organisations, labour unions, notably the powerful Union Générale des Travailleurs Tunisiens (UGTT), student organisations and professional bodies joined the protests. Realising the scale of the demonstrations, Ben Ali tried to make concessions. But they came too late to stop the protests. When the president ordered the military to shoot at the protestors, the chief of staff refused. On 14 January 2011, Ben Ali fled the country (Esposito, Sonn and Voll 2016, 174–5). His Egyptian counterpart, long-term president Hosni Mubarak, would be ousted just a month later, after millions protested under the slogan '*al-Sha'b yurīd isqāṭ al-niẓām*' ('The people want to topple the regime'). With breathtaking speed, protests spread across the region, hitting virtually all authoritarian Arab republics (Schumann 2013): 'Bread, freedom, social justice, and human dignity (*al-karama*) were the rallying cries that echoed from *mayadeen al-tahrir* (liberation squares) in Tunisia, Egypt, Libya, Yemen, Bahrain, Syria, and elsewhere' (Gerges 2014, 3).

Tunisia's Revolution and Post-revolutionary Phase (2011–16)

After Ben Ali was forced to leave office in January 2011, an interim government was installed in the same month. The government consisted mainly of old elites and some representatives of opposition parties. This state of affairs prompted new protests by leftist parties and UGTT members. Under the pressure of the Kasbah sit-ins,[4] interim prime minister Mohamed Ghannouchi – not to be confused with Rashed al-Ghannouchi – from Ben Ali's party, the RCD, created the Haute Instance pour la Réalisation des Objectifs de la Révolution, des Réformes Politiques et de la Transition Démocratique (HIROR). This body was supposed to facilitate the transition process. While many members of the opposition rejected the institution, Ennahda agreed to accept HIROR despite

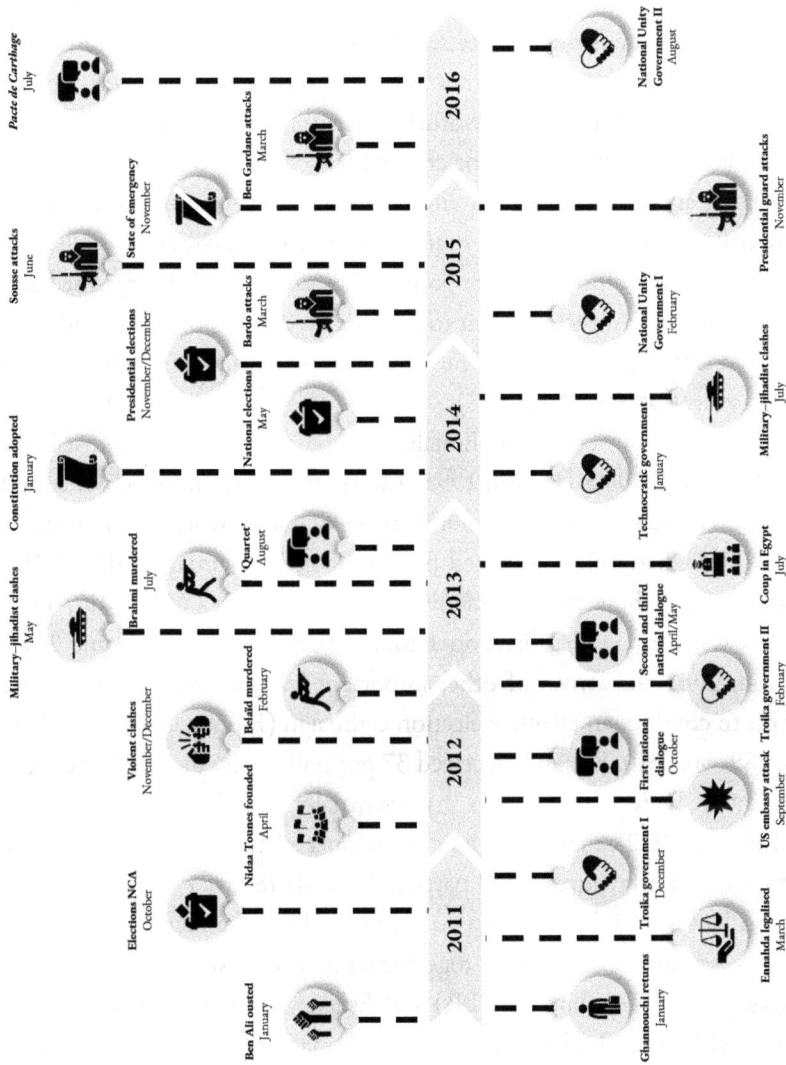

Figure 3.1 Political events in Tunisia and the wider region, 2011–16

its connection to the old regime and the nomination of Beji Caid Essebsi as head of the new interim government. Essebsi had been a leading political figure under both the Bourguiba and Ben Ali regimes. However, Tunisians still took to the streets against the HIROR and the interim government (Boubekeur 2016). After several rounds of expanding the membership of HIROR in order to satisfy the demands of the streets, the institution was tasked with outlining post-revolution trajectories. Interim head of state Fouad Mebazaa decided that elections for a National Constituent Assembly (NCA) would be held in the same year. The NCA would be charged with drafting a new constitution and electing an interim president and prime minister. The old constitution was partially suspended. HIROR drafted a new electoral law and installed the Instance Supérieure Indépendante pour les Élections (ISIE). It organised and supervised the NCA elections that took place on 23 October 2011 and were considered largely free and fair. The NCA was inaugurated in November of the same year (Carter Center 2015).

Despite the restrictions on Ennahda's activity and its quasi-invisibility in the 1990s and 2000s (Hamdi 1998, 72–3), its underground activities and structures allowed for a quick mobilisation of its networks in Tunisia in 2011. When Ghannouchi returned from exile in late January 2011, 10,000 supporters were there to welcome him back to Tunisia (Wolf 2017, 131). Ennahda was formally legalised on 1 March (Cavatorta and Merone 2013, 857) and, upon the arrival of other important leaders, organised itself and went on to conduct an effective election campaign (Esposito, Sonn and Voll 2016, 189–90, 250). Ennahda received 37 per cent of all votes or 54 per cent of the votes cast for those parties that eventually gained a seat in the NCA (Donker 2013, 222), making it the clear winner of the 2011 elections. Due to a formula that favoured small parties, Ennahda received 'only' 90 of 217 seats and had to build a coalition government. In December 2011, the first 'Troika' government was formed together with two leftist secular parties, the Congrès pour la République (CPR) and Ettakatol (Democratic Forum for Labour and Liberties). Hamadi Jebali from Ennahda became prime minister and Moncef Marzouki (CPR) president of the republic, while Mustafa Ben Jafar (Ettakatol) took over as president of the NCA. The Troika I coalition lasted until February 2013 but witnessed many conflicts (Filiu 2015). These mainly revolved around Ennahda's reputed dominance in government, the lack of transparency in the distribution of public sector posts and ministerial positions, the alleged distribution of subsidies among Ennahda members and the question of how to deal with former RCD members. Since the latter had been involved in regime repression, Ennahda had initially taken a firm stance against their inclusion in the new political system. But Ennahda still used informal channels to negotiate with the former RCD members as a bargaining move so as to ensure its survival should the cadres of the old regime undergo a resurgence (Boubekeur 2016).

What was more, there was discord in the government about the role of Islam in a future constitution – and the same applied to the Tunisian population. Some Tunisians suspected Ennahda of planning to make shari'a an integral part of the new constitution and to abandon the Personal Status Code, established in 1956, which had been an important step in Tunisian women's emancipation (Wolf 2017, 4, 28). In April 2012, Essebsi founded a new party called Nidaa Tounes (Call for Tunisia) which mainly comprised old RCD cadres and was intended as a counterweight to Ennahda. Several members of the CPR and Ettakatol left their parties and the government, some of them joining the new party. Delays in implementing transitional justice measures, economic reforms and the constitution-drafting process added to the tensions. As discontent with Ennahda and the Troika government grew stronger and the political process seemed to have reached an impasse, the UGTT launched an initiative for a national dialogue, which was meant to put an end to the political deadlock. But Ennahda and the CPR refused to take up the UGTT's invitation to enter into dialogue in October 2012 as they would have been forced to sit at the same table as Nidaa Tounes.

This phase was also marked by instances of political violence. In September 2012, a film on the Prophet made in the US and perceived as deeply offensive to Muslims provoked a demonstration by Islamists and Salafists. The US embassy in Tunis was stormed by protestors, leaving two people dead (S. Chayes 2014). There were violent clashes between anti-government protestors and the police in April and November in Tunis and Siliana respectively. The potentially excessive response of the security forces was considered by many not to have been properly investigated. In December 2012, there were violent clashes between the UGTT and the Ligue de Protection de la Révolution. The latter was a political movement that had formed in the vacuum after the revolution to 'provide' public security and was mainly composed of Ennahda supporters, despite not being formally affiliated with the party. Finally, in February 2013, the human rights activist and leftist politician Chokri Belaïd of the Front Populaire was shot dead (Boubekeur 2016, Hemkemeyer 2016).

The events described above put the Ennahda-led government under even more pressure. They were now accused of not being able to handle escalating political violence or even of protecting the perpetrators. All this culminated in the resignation of Jebali as prime minister and a significant cabinet reshuffle. Ali Laarayedh (Ennahda) replaced Jebali and was able to obtain the NCA's vote of confidence. Despite these changes, Tunisian society was polarised after the spate of violence. In this atmosphere, President Marzouki tried to launch a government-initiated dialogue round in April 2013. While it managed to bring Ennahda and Nidaa Tounes to the table, this time the dialogue was boycotted by the UGTT and some of the opposition parties. Nonetheless, the forum was able to solve some of the contentious issues regarding the constitution. A month later, the UGTT agreed to launch a third round of national dialogue, which would focus on social and economic issues as well as the security situation. The latter had deteriorated yet again. Troops that had been deployed to Jebel ech Chambi, a mountain close to the Algerian border, violently clashed with militant Salafist groups that had created a stronghold there (Carter Center 2015). In July, yet another political murder was committed against a high-ranking member of the Front Populaire, Mohamed Brahmi. In the same month, the Egyptian military initiated a putsch against the elected president, Mohamed Morsi, a member of the Muslim Brotherhood who had been in office since 2012. Officer Abdel Fattah as-Sisi declared himself the new president of Egypt. In August 2013, the new regime committed a massacre against civilians demonstrating against the putsch in Cairo. Up to 1,000 protestors were killed. Ennahda was in shock over the events. Many Nahdawis showed their solidarity with the Brotherhood and the victims by taking to the streets in Tunisia. Against the backdrop of a polarised society, Ennahda's fears that it might face a similar fate to its Egyptian counterpart grew (Marks 2015).

Following the second political assassination in one year, the Front Populaire and Nidaa Tounes had organised street protests, directed in particular against Ennahda and demanding the dissolution of the NCA and the end of the Troika government. This 'soft coup attempt' (Marks 2017, 103) further reified the secular-versus-Islamist cleavage among the Tunisian public. Moreover, seventy deputies withdrew from the NCA. In a unilateral decision, the NCA president, Ben Jafar, suspended the assembly's activities on 6 August 2013. In the same month, a secret meeting between Ghannouchi and Essebsi took place in Paris. Moreover, the UGTT, together with the Tunisian Confederation of Industry, Trade and Handicrafts (Union Tunisienne de l'Industrie, du Commerce et de l'Artisanat), the Tunisian Human Rights League (Ligue Tunisienne pour la Défense des Droits de l'Homme) and the Tunisian Order of Lawyers (Ordre National des Avocats de Tunisie) formed the so-called 'Quartet', which would go on to win the Nobel Peace Prize in 2015. Although it had set out to mediate between the rivalling political parties, it soon established itself as a moderator in the transition process. It developed a roadmap that consisted of three tracks. First, the ISIE should appoint new commissioners and subsequently organise the elections under a new electoral law to be voted on in the NCA. Second, an independent government should replace the second Troika government. Third, the final draft of the constitution should be voted on in the NCA (Boubekeur 2016, Carter Center 2015).

The constitution was indeed adopted in January 2014. Moreover, an independent government took over in the same month under the leadership of Mehdi Jomaa. In May 2014, the first parliamentary elections in the new Tunisian political system took place. Nidaa Tounes won almost 40 per cent of the seats in the Assembly of the Representatives of the People, while Ennahda received a mere 32 per cent. First Nidaa Tounes tried to establish a minority government, but then the two parties came together in a broad coalition, also referred to as the 'National Unity Government', under the leadership of Habib Essid, an independent prime minister. The new government took office in February 2015. Presidential elections had been held in November 2014, in which Ennahda decided not to field its own candidate. In December 2014, Nidaa Tounes's leader Essebsi had become president of the republic (Quamar 2015).

Meanwhile, the tensions in Jebel ech Chambi had intensified again. The operations by the militants increased until their attack on the Tunisian armed forces in July 2014 that left fifteen soldiers dead (Gartenstein-Ross, Moreng and Soucy 2014, 7–9). The following year would be a traumatic one for Tunisian society with several large-scale terrorist attacks. In March, terrorists attacked the Bardo National Museum, next to the Assembly of the Representatives of the People, killing twenty-one. Just three months later, a man shot thirty-eight people dead in the tourist area of Port El Kantaoui near Sousse. Later, ISIS claimed responsibility for both attacks, which had mainly killed Western tourists (Quamar 2015). After the attacks in Sousse, President Essebsi declared a state of emergency for one month. In November 2015, a car bomb killed twelve members of the Presidential Guard on one of the main roads of the Tunisian capital. As a consequence, Essebsi imposed another state of emergency which has been in place ever since and would be adapted by President Kais Saied six years later and used to systematically dismantle Tunisia's hard-earned democratic institutions (Ben Hamadi 2021).

In March 2016, ISIS carried out a raid on Ben Gardane, a city near the Libyan border. In a suspected attempt to capture the city, militants attacked a military post, killing twelve officers and civilians. The Tunisian military gained control over the situation and killed thirty-six of the attackers (Amara and Markey 2016). Besides security, the government's biggest concern in this phase was the dire economic and social situation of many Tunisians. In July 2016, the parliament voted to dismiss Prime Minister Essid in a vote of no confidence after he had failed to implement major reforms (Al Jazeera 2016b). In the same month, President Essebsi initiated the so-called *Pacte de Carthage*. This brought together nine political parties and three major civil society organisations with the aim of developing a common plan to tackle the country's economic, social and security challenges (HuffPost Tunisie 2016). At the end of August, the president named Youssef Chahed (Nidaa Tounes) head of a new 'National Unity Government', and Ennahda retained one cabinet minister (Al Jazeera 2016c).

Lebanon During and After the Arab Uprisings (2011–16)

While deemed 'notoriously unstable' (Wählisch and Felsch 2016, 1), pertinent indices had classified Lebanon as at least a partly free democracy since 2005,[5] and the country did not witness any uprisings of comparable scope and intensity to the protests in other Arab countries. The dynamics of the events unfolding in Lebanon's neighbourhood reinforced the regional orientation of Hezbollah's discourse, which is, however, mostly an effect of its identity as a transnational resistance. At the same time, the various governments between

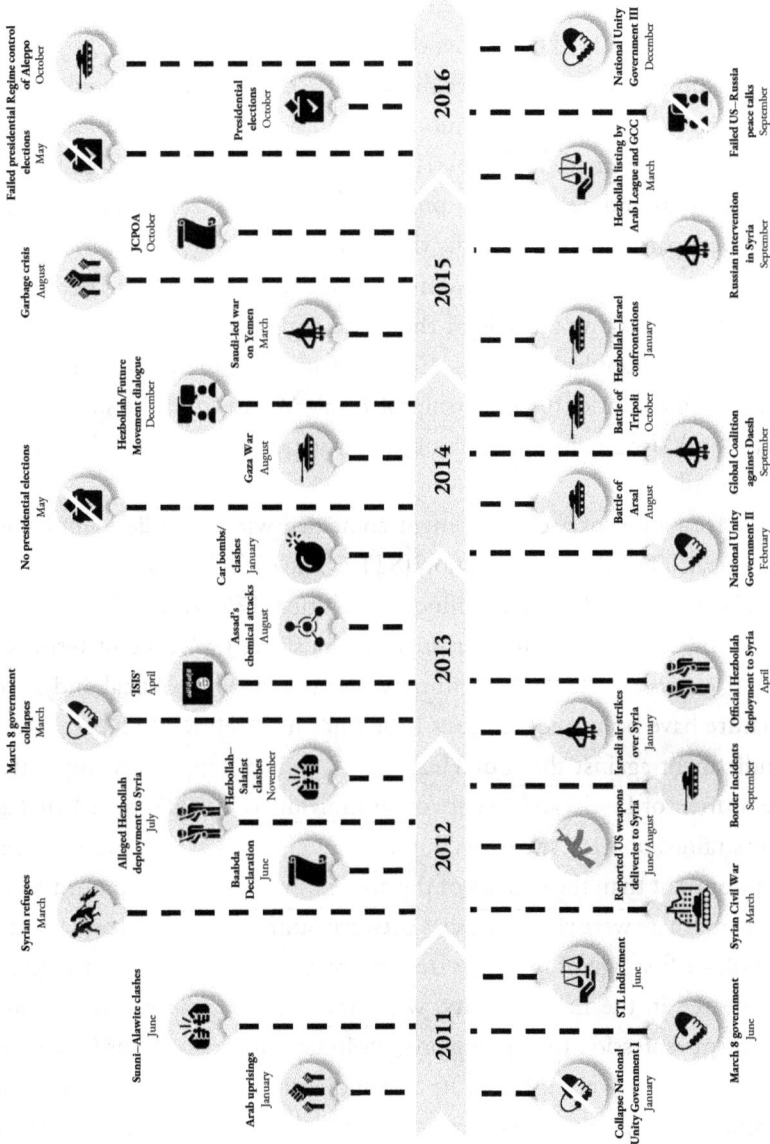

Figure 3.2 Political events in Lebanon and the wider region, 2011–16

2011 and 2016, all of which Hezbollah was part of, faced several crises and the Arab uprisings took their toll on Lebanese domestic politics.

In January 2011, eleven ministers from the March 8 Alliance resigned from the National Unity Government under Saad al-Hariri's (Future Movement) leadership. The cabinet collapsed and this was followed by a five-month vacuum in government (Fakhoury 2016). At the same time the Arab uprisings started, sparking revolutions in Tunisia and Egypt and leading to mass protests in Yemen, Libya, Syria and Bahrain. Due to the close historical connections and geographical proximity of the two countries, Lebanese politics were particularly affected by the events in Syria. As protests there grew stronger, the divide between the March 8 and the March 14 blocs deepened, with the former taking the side of the Assad regime and the latter fervently supporting the popular uprisings. Consequently, in June 2011, a new government formed under the leadership of Najib Mikati from the small Sunni Majd (Glory) Movement and without the participation of any members of the March 14 Alliance.

The formation of the government coincided with an indictment issued by the Special Tribunal for Lebanon (STL). The court had been established as stipulated by UN Security Council Resolution 1757 of 2007 and tasked with investigating the Hariri assassination, considered a 'crime of terrorism in times of peace'.[6] While its legitimacy and potentially political and selective nature have been a contentious issue since its inception (Tolbert 2014), the indictment against the four Hezbollah members supposedly implicated in the murder of Hariri and twenty other individuals in 2005 exacerbated an already strained political situation. But the events in Syria at the time were even more important than the legacies of the occupation. In the same month as the indictment, there were violent clashes between Sunnis and 'Alawites in the city of Tripoli – a first sign of spillovers from the Syrian conflict. Armed insurgents had appeared in the Lebanese city, while the Assad regime was responding with violent repression to ongoing protests in several Syrian towns (Fakhoury 2016, Di Peri and Meier 2017). The Syrian question divided Lebanese politicians and the public alike. In order not to exacerbate these domestic tensions, Lebanon's permanent representative to the UN Security Council abstained in the vote on the resolution which condemned the violence in Syria in August 2011 (Wählisch and Felsch 2016).

As violence escalated in 2012, more and more Syrian refugees arrived in Lebanon. In particular, heavy fighting in Homs, a city about 50 kilometres from the Lebanese border, in March 2012 caused an increase in the number of Syrians seeking refuge in Lebanon (Van Vliet 2016, 94). The conflict had now become a fully fledged civil war. This was not without consequences for Lebanon. There, too, levels of political violence rose. In May 2012, there were new clashes in the city of Tripoli, again between Assad supporters, mainly 'Alawites, and Sunnis (BBC News 2012). In the same month, a group of Shi'i pilgrims returning from Iran were abducted in Syria by opposition forces (Associated Press 2012). In October, a car bomb killed Wissam al-Hassan in Beirut. Hassan was a close ally of the Hariri family and head of the Internal Security Forces (ISF) intelligence unit. The assassination was supposedly connected to both the ongoing trial at the STL and Hassan's opposition to the Syrian regime. In Saida, the Palestinian refugee camp Ain al-Hilweh increasingly became a 'hotbed for jihadi recruitment' (Zelin 2016, 52) under the influence of cleric Ahmed al-Assir. Violent clashes between Hezbollah supporters and Assir's 'resistance brigades' in November led to a number of deaths among the former. What was more, several border incidents had occurred in autumn 2012, among them the bombing of Lebanese territory by the Syrian regime forces and the penetration of the Lebanese border by the Free Syrian Army (FSA) and, allegedly, jihadists who were confronted by the Lebanese army (Wählisch and Felsch 2016).

Realising that the Syrian war would threaten social peace in Lebanon too, the government had already decided to embrace a 'policy of dissociation' in June 2012. The Baabda Declaration stipulated that the Lebanese government would maintain a neutral foreign policy regarding the Syrian and other regional conflicts and commit to non-interference. While the document was claimed to be based on a consensus, Hezbollah stated that it had not agreed to it. Allegedly, just one month after the agreement, Hezbollah started to send advisors and military cadres to Syria to support the Assad regime (Ranstorp 2016). At around the same time, the first reports appeared bringing to light the intelligence and (indirect) arms support that the US had provided for the Syrian opposition (Hosenball 2012, E. Schmitt 2012). The significant financial support and supply of non-lethal and light weapons were channelled through Saudi Arabia and Qatar and, as reports suggested, often reached jihadist rather than secular opposition groups in Syria (Sanger 2012). In December 2012, it became clear that the French financial support for rebels had been used for arms purchases, too (Chulov 2012). Meanwhile, the division over the Syrian conflict and the increasingly 'sectarianised' (Hashemi and Postel 2017) violence in Lebanon caused yet another government to collapse. After Prime Minister Mikati's resignation, the March 8 government was dissolved in March 2013 (Fakhoury 2016, 25, Knudsen 2017, 140).

At this point, the Syrian war was already highly internationalised but the role of external support and intervention would become even more important over the years that followed. In January 2013, the Israeli army conducted its first air strike in Syria's Rif Dimashq governorate, allegedly to stop a weapons delivery sent to Hezbollah via Syrian territory. After renewed strikes in May, Bashar al-Assad declared the Golan Heights a frontline of popular resistance. Public militias, including Palestinian resistance factions, were now officially allowed to fight Israel there. Hezbollah immediately declared solidarity with these operations (MEMRI 2013). The month of April 2013 was of particular importance for the dynamics of the Syrian conflict. First, Hassan Nasrallah publicly admitted having provided military support for the Syrian regime. From then on Hezbollah's involvement in the Syrian conflict on the side of the regime became a crucial factor in the civil war. Over the next couple of months, the Syrian army and Hezbollah forces fought against Syrian rebel groups, among them the FSA and Jabhat al-Nusra (JN), and 'Hizbullah's involvement and combat role not only deepened but was viewed as an integral part of the overall Syrian military effort' (Ranstorp 2016, 39). Second, Abu Bakr al-Baghdadi declared that the 'Islamic State of Iraq', which had previously fought side by side with JN, would now operate on its own under the name of the 'Islamic State in Iraq and Syria' (ISIS) (Gerges 2016, 16, 180).[7] In the months after its split from JN and al-Qa'ida, ISIS would be able to make substantial territorial gains, controlling an area of 95,000 square kilometres in Iraq and Syria by August 2014 (Bamber-Zryd 2022, 1327). Starting in November 2013, alongside the Syrian regime, Hezbollah conducted military operations in the Syrian Qalamoun region close to the Lebanese border where ISIS and JN had several strongholds (Ranstorp 2016, 40). After the EU had lifted its arms embargo on Syria in June 2013, more Western military aid floated into the country in support of the opposition and rebel groups (Sengupta 2013).[8]

Hezbollah's engagement in Syria heightened the conflicts in Lebanon. Between July 2013 and February 2014, six car bombs were detonated in Hezbollah areas in the Dahieh, 'including a double suicide bombing in front of the Iranian embassy' (Wählisch and Felsch 2016, 6). In December 2013, Hezbollah commander Hassan al-Laqqis became the victim of a targeted killing (Ranstorp 2016, 39). Violence in Saida re-erupted, this time between Assir supporters and both Hezbollah and the Lebanese army, leaving eighteen soldiers dead. By then, Hezbollah was facing criticism for its involvement in the Syrian war from both Shi'i and non-Shi'i groups in Lebanon. In August 2013, the Syrian regime carried out a large-scale chemical weapons attack in Ghouta which killed more than 1,400 of its own citizens, over 400 of whom were children (Blake and Mahmud 2013). Hezbollah was accused of one-sided condemnation of jihadi violence, while remaining silent about the Assad regime's atrocities and continuing to support it (Wieland 2016, 177).

Despite their diametrically opposed positions on the Syrian war, the March 8 and March 14 alliances eventually found a common interest in averting the looming threat of a further destabilisation of the security situation in Lebanon. Both the government and parliament found themselves in a deadlock. The former had continued to prolong its own mandate as it could not decide on how to reform Lebanese electoral law and, therefore, kept postponing elections. As for the latter, it was not until February 2014 that a new National Unity Government under Tammam Salam put an end to ten months of political stalemate. The new government consisted of eight members from the March 14 Alliance, eight from the March 8 Alliance and eight from the centrist bloc (Fakhoury 2016, 25, Wählisch and Felsch 2016, 5). But this did not put an end to the political crisis. In May 2014, the term of President Michel Suleiman officially ended and the Lebanese parliament was supposed to elect a new leader. However, the absence of members from the March 8 Alliance blocked the presidential elections. This meant that, in accordance with the Lebanese constitution, the parliament could no longer act as a legislative body. Until a new president could be found, it would only convene as an electoral assembly.

Even though the government had adopted a security plan to coordinate activities by Hezbollah and the Lebanese military, the Salafi jihadists they both sought to counter increased their attacks (Zelin 2016). In August 2014, the border city of Arsal was overrun by ISIS and JN-affiliated fighters. They took control of the city, which by then hosted over 100,000 Syrian refugees. JN took members of the Lebanese armed forces hostage, subsequently beheading three of them (A. Barnard 2014). On the other side of the Lebanese–Syrian border, Hezbollah also fought side by side with the Syrian army and regained control over important cities from ISIS and JN (Wieland 2016, Zelin 2016). In October 2014, another fierce battle took place in Tripoli between the Lebanese army and jihadis from both ISIS and JN, killing around forty people including militants, soldiers and civilians (A. Barnard 2014, BBC News 2014). Against the backdrop of these new levels of armed conflict on Lebanese territory, in December 2014, the Future Movement and Hezbollah announced they were going to enter into direct dialogue in order to ease intersectarian tensions in the country (Wählisch and Felsch 2016, 7).

At the same time, the internationalisation of the Syrian war progressed. The ISIS organisation's massive territorial gains and atrocities in Syria and Iraq, staged for a global audience, prompted the creation of the broad Global Coalition against Daesh (GCAD) under US leadership. Its military operation Combined Joint Task Force – Operation Inherent Resolve launched its first air strikes against ISIS strongholds in Syria and Iraq in September 2014. Besides the 'usual suspects' from the Western alliance, Arab states also contributed troops and flew sorties, among them Jordan, Qatar, Saudi Arabia and the United Arab Emirates (UAE) (McInnis 2016). The strikes over Syria were particularly contentious with regard to their legality, as there was no mandate until a year later and the regime had not invited an intervention (Scharf 2016). Israel's role in the conflict became more complicated, too. Growing evidence suggested that Israel was treating wounded Syrian rebels, including JN members, in its hospitals in the Golan Heights before moving them to the Shebʻa Farms for redeployment in the conflict (Zelin 2016, 58). Moreover, in August 2014, the IDF began a military operation in the Gaza Strip after three Israeli teenagers had been kidnapped and murdered (Crowcroft 2014, Rudoren and Ghazali 2014). More than 2,000 Palestinians and 64 Israeli soldiers lost their lives in the war.

The escalation of the conflict also repaired Hezbollah's relationship with Hamas, which had been tense since 2012. While the former had decided to back Syrian dictator Assad, Hamas sided with the Syrian opposition. The Gaza war of 2014 provided the opportunity to restore the 'axis of resistance' or the alliance between Iran, Syria, Hezbollah and Hamas which had been suspended due to their discord over the Syrian uprising (Darwich 2021a, Meier 2016). These reconfigurations were followed by more direct confrontations between Hezbollah and Israel at several sites. In January 2015, an Israeli air strike in the Golan Heights killed six Hezbollah fighters, including Jihad Mughniyeh, one of its leading commanders, and an Iranian general. Just ten days later, Hezbollah retaliated by attacking an Israeli tank in the Sheb'a Farms, killing two soldiers. Israel fired back into southern Lebanon, leaving a Spanish UNIFIL peacekeeper dead (BBC News 2015). As these events make clear, Lebanon was repeatedly on the verge of being drawn into sustained armed conflict.

The year 2015 would further escalate the regional situation as additional actors became involved in existing conflicts and new wars began. Under Saudi leadership, the 'Arab Coalition' launched a war against Yemen in March 2015. Claiming the military action was legitimate, Saudi Arabia portrayed the campaign as an 'intervention by invitation' to defend the Yemeni government against would-be foreign-backed aggression. These arguments were more than shaky, given that it was far from clear that the government under Abdrabbuh Mansur Hadi would emerge from the civil strife as a legitimate and recognised authority (Ruys and Ferro 2016). The Saudi regime further implied that Iran was behind the Houthis' plan to overthrow the government – a suggestion which has since proven to be unfounded (Transfeld 2017, Darwich 2018). Some see the Saudi-led war as being connected to the promising negotiations on and, in October 2015, successful conclusion of the nuclear deal with Iran. The Joint Comprehensive Plan of Action (JCPOA) was expected to significantly reconfigure power relations as well as the US strategy in the region. The fear of forfeiting US support, at least in relative terms, and the position of Iran as the common enemy would also increasingly make Saudi and Israeli interests align (Stein 2021, 193–209). In Lebanon, the regional dynamics were mirrored and translated into new tensions between protagonists of the established March 8–March 14 antagonism. The Lebanese Future Movement was quick to express its support for Saudi Arabia and its allies – while Hezbollah immediately and fiercely condemned the coalition's air campaign and subsequently also its ground operations. Meanwhile, the warring parties in Syria gained new sources of external support. After ISIS had captured the Syrian city of Palmyra, watched by the whole world in May 2015 (Pfeifer and Günther 2021), Hezbollah and the Syrian regimes made significant gains in the Idlib province near the Turkish border. With the support of the Gulf states, however, jihadi groups including JN and Ahrar al-Sham regained territory. The tide turned when, after more than three years of providing various forms of external support, Russia began its military intervention in September 2015 with air strikes in western and northwestern Syria. While it had not initially planned to do so, Russia also deployed ground forces later that year (Souleimanov and Dzutsati 2018). In October, a targeted Israeli air strike killed another senior Hezbollah figure, military leader Samir al-Quntar, on the outskirts of Damascus (Hadid and Barnard 2015).

Besides the effects of regional and international involvement in the wars in Syria and Yemen, Lebanon had to wrestle with the protracted governmental and parliamentary crisis. In summer and autumn 2015, the Lebanese took to the streets as a garbage crisis unfolded and the political class failed to deal with it. The crisis sparked some anti-elite mobilisation, calling for the downfall of the sectarian system (*isqāṭ al-niẓām al-ṭā'ifī*) and an end to the collusion between politicians and private companies (AbiYaghi, Catusse and Younes 2017). Although this did not seem to turn into a sustainable social movement at the time, these events fed into what would become mass protests in 2019 (Pfeifer and Weipert-Fenner 2022). The year ended with the surprising endorsement of Sleiman Frangieh, Maronite leader of the Marada Movement and Assad supporter from the March 8 bloc, as a presidential candidate by Saad al-Hariri from the March 14 bloc in November 2015. However, Michel Aoun had already been nominated by his own March 8 bloc. After talks with Samir Geagea from the Lebanese Forces, a competing Maronite party belonging to the March 14 bloc, Aoun was endorsed as presidential candidate in January 2016. Despite the rare agreement between these antagonists, it took another eleven rounds of presidential elections in parliament for Aoun to finally be elected president in October 2016. The end of the presidential vacuum only came about after intense negotiations between the big parties about power-sharing agreements. In a form of deal package, it was decided that Saad al-Hariri would become prime minister again. At the end of December 2016, he formed a new cabinet in another National Unity Government, bringing together thirty ministers from ten parties (Al Jazeera 2016a, Cambanis 2016).

In the midst of all these political conflicts, Hezbollah faced another challenge from an international initiative to push for it to be classified as a terrorist organisation. Due to Hezbollah's engagement in Syria, the US had issued the Hizballah International Financing Prevention Act, signed by President Barack Obama in December 2015. The law aimed at cutting off the flow of financial resources to Hezbollah and its TV station, al-Manar, by denying them access to banks. In addition, the Gulf Cooperation Council (GCC) and the Arab League had decided to list Hezbollah as a terrorist group in March 2016 (Pfeifer 2021). In May 2016, the Lebanese central bank took the decision to apply the US legislation on Hezbollah's financing (Reuters 2016b). In June 2016, a bomb damaged the headquarters of Blom Bank in the Verdun neighbourhood of Beirut. As the bank had closed the accounts of people with alleged ties to Hezbollah, the suspicion was that the militia was behind the attack (Reuters 2016a). The restrictions imposed on Hezbollah did not, however, lead to its withdrawal from Syria. With significant support from Russia and Hezbollah, the Assad regime had managed to win the long battle over Aleppo. Yet, at the end of 2016, the regime had control over less than one-third of Syrian territory (Haid 2016). As negotiations between the US and Russia over how to coordinate a battle plan against ISIS and how to curtail violence in Syria had failed in September 2016, too, there was little hope that the war would come to an end any time soon (Wintour 2016).

Letting Ennahda and Hezbollah Speak: In their Own Context and With their Own Voice

As the accounts of political events in the two countries and the wider region show, Ennahda and Hezbollah faced similar challenges, including Salafi jihadism, civil war and regional order. However, their contexts also differ in important ways. Tunisia was much more self-referential in the period under investigation. While not unaffected by the events in its neighbourhood, including the coup in Egypt, the civil war in Libya and the Syrian war, which attracted Tunisian foreign fighters, the country was preoccupied with domestic affairs and organising a political transition – as well as fighting the struggles related to such a transformation. In Lebanon, by contrast, all regional conflicts seem to manifest themselves and then reappear as a kind of domestic imitation of transnational dynamics. This is not to say that Lebanon's 'homemade' political crises were marginal. On the contrary, in fact: they included a collective failure of political elites to address concrete social problems, a deep entanglement between private interests and the public sector, and regular instigation of sectarianism only to suppress it again once it had served the interests of the powerful. However, the degree to which Lebanon was affected by and implicated in the reconfigurations of regional order after the Arab uprisings is considerable. It suffered from direct spillovers of political violence from the Syrian war, interference in domestic affairs by global and regional powers, and the translation of war dynamics into instances of violence that recalled the traumas and were embedded in the structural legacies of the Lebanese Civil War.

One caveat is that the readings of Tunisia's and Lebanon's most recent history presented above are geared towards the analysis of Ennahda's and Hezbollah's discourse. This means that other events might have been chosen had other actors been analysed. The events recounted above are intended to provide a context in which the two parties' utterances are rendered comprehensible and meaningful. What is more, the two discourses will be assessed based on diverging materials. This aims to take into account the differences in their organisational structure.

Ennahda is very much shaped by the ideas of its leader, Rached al-Ghannouchi. But it is at the same time structured in a democratic manner, allowing for dissent and deliberation. In order to do justice to its – albeit limited – multivocality, Ennahda's discourse was analysed through a variety of documents: party and election programmes, party and press statements, opinion pieces by and interviews with leading Ennahda figures in the international news outlets and manuscripts of speeches by party leaders. What these documents have in common is that the party itself chose to disseminate them, in English or French, to a (potentially) global audience via its social media channels.

As for Hezbollah, its organisation is much more hierarchical and opaque. This is due to its militant activities, which necessitate an effective command structure and discipline, as well as secrecy and confidentiality. Even among themselves, Hezbollah's cadres are often not aware of each other's exact position and function in the organisation. There are also deliberative spaces among groups in the upper leadership ranks. But from there, decisions are communicated top down (Daher 2016). With regard to Hezbollah's ideology and military operations, figures such as deputy secretary general Naim Qassem and Mustafa Badreddine, who served as military chief of the Islamic Resistance until his assassination in Damascus in 2016, are influential. However, Hassan Nasrallah is Hezbollah's military and political leader and is perceived as 'uniquely charismatic' (Matar 2014, 153) and rhetorically gifted – so much so that his speeches and appearances are used in rhetoric training in Lebanon (Interview 6). Given that Nasrallah has been living in an underground hideout since 2006, fearing an Israeli attempt to assassinate him, he only appears in public very rarely. When he does – ten times between 2011 and 2016 – his performance is perceived as 'the return of the revered occluded leader' (Matar 2014, 175). In this sense, his speeches – whether live or recorded – are both momentous and programmatic for Hezbollah. He is the 'voice of Hezbollah' (Noe 2007). The following chapters are, therefore, based on an analysis of Nasrallah's speeches translated into English and disseminated via the website of one of Hezbollah's main media outlets, the newspaper *al-Ahed* ('The Promise').[9]

Notes

1. This is also one of the more important reasons why this book upholds the distinction between Islamists and Salafi jihadists, rather than subsuming the latter under the umbrella term of Islamism, as sometimes happens in the study of civil war (Bamber and Svensson 2023, Walter 2017, Nilsson and Svensson 2021). For a critique of the lack of differentiation *among* Salafi-jihadist groups, see, for example, Schwab (2018, 2023) and Stenersen (2020).
2. For the Iranian case, the distinction between state and non-state actors may have become blurrier since 2020, when the US military under the Trump administration killed Iranian general Qassem Soleimani in a targeted drone strike in Baghdad. Besides being a general in the Iranian military forces, Soleimani was the head of the Islamic Revolutionary Guard Corps' s (IRGC's) Quds Force. The Trump administration put the IRGC on the list of terrorist organisations in April 2019 – which legitimised the targeted killing of a member of Iran's official armed forces (Pfeifer 2021).
3. The term refers to the records of the Prophet's and his companions' deeds.
4. Kasbah is the district in Tunis where the government and ministries reside.
5. https://freedomhouse.org/country/lebanon/freedom-net/2016 (accessed 6 November 2023) http://www.systemicpeace.org/polity/leb2.htm (accessed 11 October 2023).

6. https://www.stl-tsl.org/images/stories/About/STL_Close-up_EN.pdf (accessed 11 October 2023).

7. The Arabic name *al-Dawla al-Islāmiyya fī l-ʿIrāq wa-l-Shām* is usually translated in this way even though 'Shām' refers to the historical Islamic Syria, which covers areas in today's Syria, Jordan, Lebanon, Israel, Palestine and Turkey.

8. https://www.sipri.org/databases/embargoes/eu_arms_embargoes/syria_LAS/eu -embargo-on-Syria (accessed 11 October 2023).

9. See https://english.alahednews.com.lb (accessed 11 October 2023). The newspaper was founded in 1984 and launched its website in 1999. Besides global news, it publishes full speeches, reports on speeches and information on Hassan Nasrallah, Hezbollah's secretary general. Although there is also an Arabic version of the *al-Ahed* website, the main Arabic communication platform used to be moqawama.org, which was operational until April 2023. It reported on the subjects of the resistance and Israel, and regional and international politics, especially events in Iran, Yemen and Syria, as well as the martyrs and military successes of Hezbollah. Since May 2023, the website has been seized by the US government 'for sanctions violations and for being controlled by an entity [. . .] designated as a "Specially Designated National"'. See https://moqawama.org and https:// www.justice.gov/usao-edva/pr/edva-seizes-thirteen-domains-used-lebanese- hizballah-and-its-affiliates (accessed 31 October 2023).

4

SOVEREIGNTY

Ennahda

In his account of a 'genuine intellectual revolution in modern Islamic thought', Andrew March (2019, x) outlines how popular sovereignty entered Sunni Islamic political philosophy. Although some of the most important Islamist thinkers in the twentieth century, Abul A'la Maududi and Sayyid Qutb, are usually associated with rather strict concepts of divine sovereignty, March argues that they also paved the way for the notion of popular sovereignty to develop and culminate in ideas of Islamic democracy. One of today's foremost intellectuals is also the president of the Tunisian Ennahda party, Rached al-Ghannouchi. Not least due to his dual role as a modern political thinker and politician, his 'influence historically and in the present is undeniable' (March 2019, 153) and reaches far beyond the Tunisian context. Ghannouchi's intellectual work has been analysed from the perspective of the history of ideas and political philosophy (Tamimi 2001, March 2019), and it is remarkable that even when Ennahda was part of the Tunisian government, Ghannouchi still published academic works and essays, as he had done during his years in exile (see, for example, Ghannouchi 1993a, 1993b, 2013, 2016). One of the core concerns he seeks to address in his theoretical work is to solve the tension between divine and popular sovereignty through the invention of an 'Islamic state as a republic of virtue' in which 'the *umma* [is assigned] the sovereign right not only to control secular rulers but also to determine what it means to "apply the *sharī'a*'" (March 2019, 199).

As I will demonstrate in this chapter, Ghannouchi's ideas have had a significant impact on political discourse and the way in which Ennahda communicates its conceptions of order to a Western and potentially global audience. Indeed, an empirical investigation of Ennahda's discourse on sovereignty – rather than an analysis based on the history of ideas or political theory – reveals similar findings in as much as popular sovereignty is by far the most important concept advanced. In contrast to March's findings on Ghannouchi's political theory, however, divine sovereignty is barely alluded to in Ennahda communications. Rather, the question of Islam's place in politics is negotiated in Ennahda's portrayal of legitimacy, as Chapter 5 will show. I will discuss interpretations of this at the end of the chapter but one preliminary methodological remark is of importance here. As March (2019) shows, sovereignty, legitimacy and authority are closely related concepts, which means that this divergence may be a result of coding rather than a significant and substantial difference. The concluding subsection of this section will argue that there are still good reasons to assume that intellectual and political discourse actually follow different lines of argument.

Popular Sovereignty: Self-determination and Popular Will

The concrete political significance of popular sovereignty for Ennahda can be explained in a rather straightforward way. First, Tunisia's history as a former French colony makes popular sovereignty a core claim of a subjugated people against heteronomy. Second, the notion that the people were able to liberate themselves from a decades-long dictatorship and wrested sovereignty from an unjust state was an obvious and prevalent interpretation of the Tunisian revolution of 2011. Ennahda thus argued for both the self-determination of a people and the realisation of the popular will. Tunisia's history can be read as a story of realising popular sovereignty. In this narrative, the toppling of the Ben Ali regime and the subsequent restructuring of the Tunisian political system, notably reflected in the adoption of a new constitution, are the next steps in the process of the Tunisian people's liberation, which had begun with shaking off French colonial rule and achieving independence in 1956.

That said, it was the immediate temporal and spatial context that was most relevant for Ennahda's articulation of popular sovereignty between 2011 and 2016: the old regime's complete loss of legitimacy and the need to build a new system based on popular sovereignty. In the midst of the protests in early 2011, Rashed al-Ghannouchi called on the 'tyrant to leave the people to manage their own affairs' (Ennahda 2013al). The revolution would restore 'the power of the people – a people that has risen, realised its strength and potential and broken the barrier of fear' (Ennahda 2011f). Far from being a coup or a regime change imposed by one group inside or outside the country, the revolution was a manifestation of the popular will (Ennahda 2011r) and 'reassert[ed] people's sovereignty' (Ennahda 2016h).

Elections are of particular relevance for the realisation of popular sovereignty. Ennahda believes in 'establishing the people's full sovereignty through the ballot box' (Ennahda 2014w). It considers the first free elections for the NCA in 2011 to have been a 'symbol of the achievement of free popular will' (Ennahda 2012ak). Popular sovereignty is a *conditio sine qua non* for state authority (Ennahda 2014z), which is why Ennahda pledges to always respect the will of the people and the peaceful alternation of power (Ennahda 2013f). But even between elections, state power can be considered legitimate only in so far as it expresses the will of the people. Ennahda therefore insists that any political decision-making take place within elected institutions that are directly endorsed by the people (Ennahda 2013ae).

While it mostly discusses popular sovereignty in the Tunisian context, Ennahda also attaches a more general, almost universal significance to the concept. For 'a growing part of humanity is demanding dignity, freedom, justice and the right to self-determination, away from foreign hegemony and internal despotism' (Ennahda 2012a). Popular sovereignty was central to the Arab uprisings and Ennahda supports the demand of all Arab peoples that 'their rights to freedom and dignity' (Ennahda 2012i) be acknowledged. Rather typically for Islamist discourse, Ennahda also addressed the Palestinian cause from the perspective of popular sovereignty and frequently alluded to the Palestinian people's demand that 'its legitimate historical rights' (Ennahda 2012b) be respected. Still suffering from occupation and struggling for its liberation, the Palestinian people are striving to 'establish a state with Jerusalem as its capital' (Ennahda 2013q, 2014o), thereby achieving self-determination.

Popular sovereignty became less prominent in Ennahda's discourse after 2014. This indicates that, mistaken as this may seem in hindsight, Ennahda was rather confident about the stability of achievements made with regard to the realisation of popular sovereignty after the successful conclusion of the second round of free elections in 2014 and considered the danger of the people losing their sovereignty to be contained (Ennahda 2014g). For Ennahda, Tunisian popular sovereignty, it seems, increasingly acquired a taken-for-granted status.

Absolute Sovereignty: The Virtues and Vices of a Strong State

Whereas popular sovereignty is an unambiguous core norm in Ennahda's conception of order, matters are more complicated with regard to absolute sovereignty. Regarding the external side of sovereignty, Ennahda has acted as a consistent advocate of the principle of non-interference and sovereign equality (Ennahda 2011r, 2012aj, 2013f, 2014z). As will be discussed in more detail in Chapter 6, Ennahda considers foreign interference and intervention in domestic affairs to be a central problem and root cause of many political and socio-economic grievances and injustices in Tunisia and, more widely, the Arab world. Claiming state sovereignty in international relations, and reinforcing and recognising the norms associated with it in the world order, is therefore a clear endeavour. It is the internal side of sovereignty that has turned out to be the trickier part of absolute sovereignty for Ennahda. It has had to carefully navigate the issue of (the limits to) the monopoly on the use of legitimate force, emphasising and de-emphasising state power depending on the respective context.

Indeed, the further the new Tunisian system evolved, the more importance absolute sovereignty gained in Ennahda's discourse. In 2011 and 2012, any allusions to a strong state would have been perceived as misplaced, if not suspicious, for they could have been read as a legitimation of the old regime and therefore weakened the demands of the revolutionaries. At the same time, Ennahda also had to be careful not to exaggerate its opposition to the state. Rather, it 'stressed the continuity of the Tunisian state which was not dismantled by the revolution as in other countries' (Ennahda 2011q) and praised Tunisians' commitment to the 'preservation of their state' (Ennahda 2013af) in the post-revolutionary phase. Seeing the descent of societies in Tunisia's neighbourhood into violence and, later, outright civil war, Ennahda was convinced that chaos and state failure needed to be avoided and the work of the administration had to be kept up and running (Ennahda 2012i). Witnessing the failure of the Libyan state, its inability to control its borders and the violent struggle over authority not only posed severe problems to Tunisia as an immediate neighbour, but was also perceived as a warning (Ennahda 2015p). Yet Ennahda was also aware of the tension between preserving state sovereignty, on the one hand, and restoring popular sovereignty, on the other: '[H]ow can we maintain the balance of the public administration, achieve the goals of the revolution and sever ties with the previous system of tyranny and corruption?' it wondered (Ennahda 2014b). The existing institutions of the state were largely perceived as illegitimate and needed to be reformed or even replaced by new ones. Accountable institutions, guided by the rule of law, were indispensable for 'supporting state authority' (Ennahda 2014z).

The more time passed and the longer Ennahda was in government, the more assertively it advocated a strong state and absolute sovereignty. Initially, this mirrors the necessities of running a functioning state which is able to generate outputs and maintain public order, in particular with regard to providing security. Ennahda had faced accusations of not responding adequately to the increase in political violence in 2012 and 2013, especially after the political assassinations of two members of the leftist Front Populaire. It reacted by calling for a strong state and military institutions, while insisting that such a state be democratic.

> Un État démocratique, c'est un État fort. Il n'y a pas de contradiction à respecter la loi et à utiliser la force dans les limites de la loi face à ceux qui ont profité de la faiblesse des institutions de l'État ou qui ont pensé que l'État est faible. (Ennahda 2013d)[1]

Ennahda evoked absolute sovereignty and a strong state even more emphatically with the deterioration of the security situation and drastic rise in terrorist attacks in 2015. Ennahda, still in government with one minister at the time, even supported the state of emergency declared by the president after terrorist attacks had occurred in Sousse earlier in the year (Ennahda 2015r). It called upon the 'Tunisian people to rally around state institutions and security and military services' (Ennahda 2015s). The terrorist threat thus triggered similar mechanisms as in Western societies, ranging from a strengthening of security institutions to the transfer of power from legislative to executive branches.

Shared Sovereignty: Dreams of Regional Integration and Steps towards Decentralisation

Ennahda's support for a strong Tunisian central state has to be further unpacked, though. Over the six years after the revolution, the period under investigation in this book, Ennahda developed two ideas of shared sovereignty, one on an international level and one on a substate level. Regarding the former, Ennahda included demands for reviving the Arab Maghreb Union (AMU) as early as 2011 (Ennahda 2011b, 2014z). The AMU had been founded in 1989. Its five member states, Algeria, Libya, Mauritania, Morocco and Tunisia, had set out to pursue the goals of free trade, economic cooperation and political coordination. Due to the conflict between Morocco and Mauritania over Western Sahara, the organisation's activities had stalled. However, the euphoria for the revolutionary moment in various Arab states brought a new vision for the AMU. Ennahda suggested creating 'a joint Maghreb market by activating cooperation and integration among its different countries and considering the potential of expanding it to include Egypt' (Ennahda 2011b), to establish 'free trade zones' (Ennahda 2011b) and to develop common political positions on regional affairs. For instance, Ennahda aimed at concerted support of the Libyan Government of National Accord by the Maghreb states and suggested coordinating policies in order to achieve consensus among different forces in Libya (Ennahda 2016m, 2016n).

However, emphatic as the calls to deepen integration and institutionalise the AMU had been in 2011, over time they became virtually irrelevant. When I addressed this issue in interviews in 2017, Ennahda representatives admitted that the prospects for integration were poor but the idea was still prominent. At the same time, they contended that, in a multipolar world, regions played an increasingly important role. Single countries do not carry enough weight in international negotiations to pursue their interests. Moreover, the representatives cited estimates showing that an integrated market or some other free trade arrangement would increase the gross domestic product (GDP) of the five member countries by 3 per cent (Interviews 1, 2, 4). They compared the Maghreb situation to the early days of the European Economic Community, which aimed for close economic ties, without, however, imposing a single political model on the six distinctly organised member countries.

Ideas of shared sovereignty on the subnational level were evident in Ennahda's agenda to decentralise the Tunisian system of governance, which demanded more authority for regional and local councils (Ennahda 2011b, 2014z). Tunisia had inherited a strongly centralised system from the French colonisers. The system of *tutelle* or administrative oversight had 'developed into a subnational instrument to enforce the rule of the Ministry of Interior and presidential palace' (Bohn and Vollmann 2021, 82). Elected institutions hardly played a role at the subnational level. According to Ennahda, decentralisation would enhance Tunisia's democratic and participatory culture (Ennahda 2014ah, 2015ab, 2016b) and would 'constitute an important gain for the state of law and division of powers' (Ennahda 2016a).

Indeed, the 2014 constitution dedicated a whole chapter to decentralisation, and foreign donors and foundations quickly declared their support for the decentralisation project, too. An ambitious decentralisation law passed in 2018 stipulates the creation of 'strong democratic institutions on levels between the local and national governments with quasi-regional and governorate councils' (Bohn and Vollmann 2021, 83), which have yet to be established. In fact, the sluggish implementation of the law, particularly the failure to set up regional-level institutions, has created new sources of conflict between the national and the local levels, as well as between the ruling parties. Ennahda had good reason to expect favourable results from the local elections, which it deemed 'a critical moment for consolidating participatory democracy and a genuine step towards redistributing power' (Ennahda 2016a). The party's movement structure implied a firm rootedness in society at the local level and Ennahda was the only party that could count on a sufficient number of party affiliates able to run in local elections at all. In contrast, all other parties feared that they would 'not be able to provide party list coverage for subnational elections' (Bohn and Vollmann 2021, 86). And indeed, Ennahda won 131 of 350 mayorships in the local elections of 2018. Almost as many mayorships went to independent candidates. Its grassroot and movement structures thus give Ennahda a comparative advantage over other parties and explain its firm commitment to shared sovereignty in the form of decentralisation.

Discussion

In Ennahda's discourse, popular sovereignty is the most prominent concept. In line with findings on Ghannouchi's political philosophy (March 2019), the question of how to best assure that the people remain in charge of their own destiny and brace themselves against assaults on their sovereignty from both heteronomy and dictatorship is a concern for Ennahda – as it is for many other political actors in formerly colonised societies. But Ennahda's sovereignty discourse also has a more pragmatic trait. Having been in charge of state affairs for several years and faced several security crises, Ennahda advocated a strong state, including security institutions, and emphasised its monopoly on the legitimate use of force in phases of violence. As the chapter on legitimacy will demonstrate, Ennahda needed to balance these necessities with precautionary measures to counter any impression that it was interested in state capture and was seeking to build a new Islamist dictatorship. The suggestions for shared sovereignty also seem to relativise any suspicion that the party may have been overcommitted to the notion of a strong state. At the same time, the strategic advantage that Ennahda could expect at the subnational level reveals that its advocacy for decentralisation was more than an idealistic agenda to hedge Tunisia's emerging democratic system against authoritarian temptation.

The fact that there was not a single allusion to the notion of divine sovereignty in Ennahda's discourse between 2011 and 2016 can be read as a precautionary measure against conveying 'the wrong message', too. That said, one should not conclude from this that Ennahda was oblivious to the potential tensions between its pursuit of Islamic ideals and its commitment to a popular will which might not always be in line with these ideals. On the contrary, Ennahda negotiated this issue extensively in the process of creating its model of an Islamic democracy. But this was framed as a problem of legitimacy, or how order should be organised, rather than sovereignty, that is, who the subject and object of global order are. Here, Ennahda communicated a clear commitment to popular sovereignty or the notion of self-rule – instituted in the form of a state with unconditional external and, within limits, internal sovereignty. Ennahda commits to a world order of states, inhabited by free peoples.

Ennahda's communications aimed at the international sphere in the discursive field of sovereignty are thus entirely within the space that Western world order discourse spans. Ennahda not only fully recognises established sovereignty norms but even demands full compliance with them by both its domestic adversaries, especially former regime cadres, and third states in their behaviour towards Tunisia and other countries. As the chapter on *teloi* will further illustrate, the West's lenience when it comes to interventionism is firmly rejected and conditional sovereignty is not a conception that Ennahda could embrace. In fact, comparatively few of Ennahda's communications analysed for this book address the issue of sovereignty at all. This should be interpreted as further evidence in support of the thesis that Ennahda has internalised hegemonic sovereignty norms and does not challenge Western conceptions of order at all, at least as far as sovereignty is concerned. There is no real need to elaborate on this matter, there is tacit consensus about what sovereignty should mean in the world order – Ennahda just highlights dangers to, and the limited realisation of, these ideals.

Hezbollah

One would expect Hezbollah or 'the party of God', with its origins in the Shi'i social movement in Lebanon and the strong influence of Ayatollah Khomeini's revolutionary thought and teachings on its ideological development in the 1980s, to differ significantly from both Western discourse and Ennahda's take on sovereignty. As in the case of Ennahda, one could reconstruct the political theoretical foundations of Hezbollah's sovereignty politics (Pfeifer 2018). The key figure for Hezbollah's political thought, besides Khomeini and Ayatollah Fadlallah, an Iraqi cleric active in Beirut who was known as Hezbollah's spiritual leader until his death in 2010, is Naim Qassem, the party's deputy secretary general. He has written extensively on the question of how *wilāyat al-faqīh* (or the guardianship of the Islamic jurist) is related to political principles and order (Qassem 2010). *A priori*, it seems that the notion of a submission to the jurist-theologian (*wālī al-faqīh*) who is currently the supreme leader of Iran, Ali Khamenei, defies the logic of the nation-state, thus creating a tension with absolute sovereignty. Indeed, *wilāyat al-faqīh* might be interpreted as a form of divine sovereignty (Pfeifer 2018). The question for this book, then, would be to what extent this sovereignty conception, which is clearly located outside the Western discursive realm of world order, also plays a role on the level of political practice in how Hezbollah articulates its interpretation of order towards a global audience. Again, there might be some 'strategic' silence involved, since both divine sovereignty and an overly close connection to Iran, a notorious and recurring problem country in the eyes of the West since the Islamic Revolution of 1979, can be expected to be perceived as alien and suspicious by (significant parts of) the global audience. But that alone may not be enough to deter an actor that has on occasion expressed its indifference towards or even pride in being perceived as a rogue state by the West from articulating dissident ideas on order to the hegemon (Dudouet 2021, 243).

Absolute Sovereignty: Failures of a Weak State

Compared to Ennahda, absolute sovereignty is of greater concern to Hezbollah. Given the Lebanese political context, Hezbollah's emphasis on the right to defend state territory, the principle of non-interference in internal affairs and the need to strengthen the state's capabilities of providing security and stability is not surprising. What makes absolute sovereignty complicated for the Hezbollah case is that the group itself regularly violates these principles and undermines the state's monopoly on the legitimate use of force. Hezbollah legitimises these practices by arguing that, where the state is too weak to exercise its sovereignty, a surrogate must be created in order to maintain external state sovereignty. This surrogate force is the Lebanese resistance.

Hezbollah's articulations of absolute sovereignty have to be viewed primarily in the context of what it understands as the Israeli threat to Lebanon: Israel violates Lebanese borders on a regular basis and, as acknowledged by international law, still occupies parts of Lebanese territory (Hezbollah 2011e, 2011f, 2012c, 2014b). As Lebanese territories and resources are under constant threat through 'the violation of air, land, and sea sovereignty' (Hezbollah 2014a, 2014c, 2015a), the state should switch to a defence mode. However, the Lebanese army is far too weak to tackle these violations by itself:

> All of us want a strong army that can act responsibly and defend the country. But, have the troops been reinforced? Has the army been armed and prepared well enough to deter the enemy from assailing Lebanon? Has the army been made powerful enough in the eyes of our enemy?! No answer. (Hezbollah 2013a)

Hezbollah denounces and despises what it perceives as the naivety of the Lebanese state regarding the Israeli threat. A telling example is its view of the Lebanese state's behaviour concerning the oil and gas reserves off the Lebanese coast. In 2011, Israel had discovered two large undersea gas fields, which saw the dispute over sea borders resurface. The two countries had drawn maps depicting diverging maritime borders, on which the claimed territories overlapped, and, consequently, both voiced claims to the gas fields – a dispute that would not to be settled for more than a decade.[2] At the time, Hassan Nasrallah ironically commented on the bleak prospects of any decisive action by the Lebanese state in the matter, or of a plan to enforce its legitimate right to exploit these resources should the Israelis decide to insist on their version of the maritime boundaries: 'How should we defend ourselves and our oil and gas? With poetry? Banners? Neckties?' (Hezbollah 2011e).

Nasrallah's sarcastic undertone here is rather typical of his assessments of the Lebanese state's capacity to defend its borders, interests and sovereignty, especially with military means. He sees the experience of several wars with Israel as representative of what to expect from the Lebanese state when it is attacked: despite calls to defend the Lebanese south, 'the state did not respond. That was because the state was somewhere else . . . The political authority has always been in another world' (Hezbollah 2012c). The state does not recognise the magnitude of the threat posed to Lebanon by Israel, nor does it understand this enemy and its plans for Lebanon and the region (Hezbollah 2013a). Hezbollah, in contrast, has always been and always will be prepared to defend Lebanese sovereignty.

With the violence in neighbouring Syria escalating into a fully fledged civil war in 2012, Hezbollah identified a second external threat to Lebanon: spillovers from the civil war, especially in the form of what Hezbollah calls 'Takfirist'[3] groups penetrating the border between the two countries. Even though the borders were also violated by the Syrian army, in its discourse, Hezbollah concentrated on ANSAs who entered Lebanese territory or shelled border villages – and on the state's responsibility to address these acts of violence and attacks on Lebanese sovereignty. The army should provide security on a domestic level and protect the Lebanese from 'Takfirist' attacks, including booby-trapped cars and abductions (Hezbollah 2014c). Besides this internal side to sovereignty, the army is also supposed to defend the state's borders against foreign aggression and liberate those towns already occupied by 'Takfirist' groups (Hezbollah 2014e, 2015c, 2015k). Hezbollah not only acts as an advocate of a strong army but also promotes its active support by all Lebanese factions, sects and parties, as they all share an interest in 'preserving security, stability [and] national integrity, and defending the state' (Hezbollah 2014g). Hezbollah was careful to both foreground the threat posed by the 'Takfirists' (among other actors that penetrated the border and committed violence) and display it as a national problem which jeopardises Lebanese society as a whole, thereby framing it as an attack on the country's sovereignty (Hezbollah 2014c, 2015d) and, as Chapter 6 will demonstrate in more detail, a danger for the region as a whole.

This was, on the one hand, an attempt to avoid the impression that spillovers from the civil war were in any form attributable to Hezbollah's activities there. This type of argumentation is well known to Hezbollah from the Israeli wars against Lebanon which were blamed on its provocations at the southern border. On the other hand, Hezbollah's argumentation was also part of the construction of ISIS and other Salafi-jihadist groups as the common enemy, irrespective of sectarian belonging. In this way, Hezbollah tried to avoid treating the problem using reasoning based on intersectarian violence. Again, it held the Lebanese state fully responsible for protecting Lebanese civil peace, preventing domestic (sectarian) violence and preserving national unity (Hezbollah 2011a). It thus agrees with the widespread assessment that the Lebanese army is an important, if not the main, unifying force in Lebanon and the only armed actor or even institution that is not clearly affiliated more or less exclusively to one sect or political faction. Lebanese history had 'proven that after the collapse of everything, the disintegration of everything and the loss of everything, this institution would always be the saving rod' (Hezbollah 2011k). This emphatic declaration of support was complemented by the assertion that 'the Lebanese Army and the security systems have access to all Lebanese territories' (Hezbollah 2013d), countering those analyses that consider Hezbollah to have established a 'state within a state' and no-go areas for the state's security institutions. As the discussion of shared sovereignty in Hezbollah's discourse will show – and as anyone who has tried to visit the Lebanese south will know – the notion that Hezbollah does not challenge the Lebanese state's internal sovereignty in any way is mistaken. The insistence on absolute sovereignty should rather be viewed as a way of immunising Hezbollah against allegations that it enjoyed (or rather, enforced) privileges regarding the use of force and territorial control in Lebanon, aggravated sectarian tensions and caused strife.

For indeed, in the domestic political context, it seems that Hezbollah's goal is to preserve unity in order to, as I will argue later, free up capabilities and extend the room for manoeuvre for its transnational projects. Part of its endeavour to stabilise Lebanese society is also its unequivocal condemnation of third-party interference in domestic affairs. Here, Hezbollah skewers US and French attempts to influence Lebanese politics, which it considers severe breaches of Lebanese sovereignty and independence (Hezbollah 2011j). Importantly, Hezbollah views the Special Tribunal for Lebanon as one of the tools at the disposal of these external forces, pursuing an agenda of changing the Lebanese political game. Again, the Lebanese state had proven to be too weak to prevent the foreign imposition of the tribunal (Hezbollah 2011c). It exhibited the same blind and willing compliance some years later, when the US imposed new sanctions on those affiliated with Hezbollah, freezing their bank accounts, and Lebanese banks, under the leadership of the Lebanese National Bank, followed suit. 'Doesn't this country have any sovereignty? Aren't there any laws? Aren't there courts? Isn't there an authority?' Nasrallah blustered (Hezbollah 2015j, 2016g).

As important as the cases of interference are those relations with third states which are not considered a threat to sovereignty by Hezbollah. While Nasrallah openly admits that Iran and Syria support Hezbollah financially and politically, this is portrayed as unproblematic in so far as the two countries do not ask for anything in return and do not try to pursue their interests by pressuring Hezbollah into a certain kind of behaviour (Hezbollah 2014g). Similarly, Hezbollah's military support of the Syrian regime through active fighting on the ground, which it officially started in 2013, is not considered an infringement of Syrian sovereignty, for it entered the war with 'approval from the Syrian government' (Hezbollah 2014a). This could be read as a confirmation of the intervention-by-invitation norm, which also legitimises the Russian intervention in Syria or the GCAD's Operation Inherent Resolve in Iraq – but not, as Nasrallah reminds us, in Syria. Deploying troops to, or launching air campaigns over, foreign territory without the regime's permission violates a country's external sovereignty (Hezbollah 2014a).

Interestingly, though, Hezbollah concedes that there is potential tension between its actions in Syria and Lebanese sovereignty. This question is 'debatable' (Hezbollah 2014a), however, because it is not the Lebanese state but a non-state actor which became involved in the conflict. Nasrallah justifies this in a similar way to many other cases in which Hezbollah could be perceived or portrayed as a threat to Lebanese sovereignty: rather than undermining the state, Hezbollah complements it where it is too weak to act on its own. In the case of the Syrian war, while Hezbollah had admittedly not 'specifically [asked] the state to get the Lebanese Army deployed on the Syrian territories', Nasrallah blamed the state, declaring that 'no political or diplomatic efforts [had] been made!' (Hezbollah 2013d). In this sense, the deployment of Hezbollah fighters in Syrian territories is legitimated as a form of collective self-defence, including the defence of Lebanon against the dangers creeping across the border from Syria.

Shared Sovereignty: The Army–People–Resistance Formula

Indeed, this last line of argumentation can be seen as exemplary of a rather specific notion of shared sovereignty in Hezbollah's discourse: a shared responsibility (and authority) for the Lebanese people and territory between state institutions, the resistance and the Lebanese people. Nasrallah calls this the 'Army–People–Resistance formula' (Hezbollah 2011f, 2011h, 2011j, 2012a, 2015d, 2016e, 2016k), sometimes also the 'tripartite' (Hezbollah 2014a, 2014d) or 'golden equation' (Hezbollah 2014b). This formula is presented as an antidote against hegemonic projects by external powers in Lebanon and the Arab world more generally. Such a comprehensive form of resistance consists of three components: the military, the organised resistance and the popular resistance, sometimes also referred to as 'will of the people' (Hezbollah 2012a). The resistance project will (and can only) be successful if its three components fight side by side in defence of their country and people, as the Lebanese struggle against Israel has proven. As long as the army, Hezbollah and the people stand together, they will succeed in deterring Israel (Hezbollah 2012c, 2013f, 2015d) and other external enemies, such as the 'Takfirists' (Hezbollah 2014c, 2015e, 2015h). 'This is the formula of victory. This is the deterrence formula' (Hezbollah 2015d). Given its promise and proven success, Hezbollah makes the case for the equation to be applied in other contexts as well. More specifically, Nasrallah names the Iraqi and Yemeni conflicts. The former has proven that 'the army is not enough' to fight against the 'Takfirists', a struggle that needs broad support from resistance by 'the popular masses who must widen to cover everybody including the Sunni and Shia tribes, all the people of Iraq including Kurds and Turkmen, and all the popular forces' (Hezbollah 2015d). As for the latter case, the formula adopted by the Yemenis is 'the Yemeni Army, the popular Yemeni resistance, and the popular Yemeni incubation [who] are standing in face of this (US–Saudi) aggression' (Hezbollah 2015d). As will be explained in Chapter 6, the 'schemes' against which Hezbollah recommends the 'formula' be applied are manifold but, over the period of investigation, were increasingly reduced into one big threat scenario.

Hezbollah uses two main arguments to justify its version of shared sovereignty. First, as the state does not have the effective monopoly on the legitimate use of force and is too weak to take action against external threats, it is dependent on a surrogate power, in the Lebanese case the armed organised resistance. This state of affairs, second, legitimises Hezbollah eluding attempts by the state, or rather its political adversaries who use the state, to stop the organisation from taking the unilateral action it considers necessary, such as deploying fighters to Syria, or to wrest power from Hezbollah in other ways. '[T]hey can't unarm us or confiscate our arms under any resolution!' Nasrallah declared (Hezbollah 2013a). If history is anything to go by,[4] these are not empty words. Hezbollah considers shared sovereignty a necessity or the result of a failure of absolute sovereignty. It deems itself competent and responsible for the external sovereignty of Lebanon. While it does not challenge the monopoly of the state in principle, it does so in practice by undermining Lebanese sovereignty internally in order to preserve the means for assuming the responsibility to defend the state's sovereignty externally – something the military is incapable of doing. In this sense, shared sovereignty is a corollary of the state's failure to perform absolute sovereignty.

Popular Sovereignty: Look Out for Oppressive Schemes

As in Ennahda's discourse, for Hezbollah, too, popular sovereignty carries the biggest normative weight, and the other sovereignty principles derive from and are legitimised by the notion that people have a right to self-determination.

This implies another similarity with the Ennahda case: conceptions of sovereignty are closely linked to considerations of legitimacy. But as Chapter 5 will demonstrate, while insubstantial and abstract allusions of 'the people' or 'popular will' suffice to make the case for self-determination, matters become more complicated when the specific meaning of these terms needs to be spelt out in order to determine the conditions under which authority, order and the resort to violence are justified. Hezbollah defines popular sovereignty *ex negativo*, that is, through what it calls oppressive schemes that infringe upon the self-determination of (Arab) peoples. Such schemes include states of occupation, the (violent) enforcement of an external will on a people and, as in the case of Ennahda, rule by a tyrant who violates the popular will.

For Hezbollah, the most serious violation of popular sovereignty is the Israeli occupation of Palestine. The state of occupation has deprived the Palestinian people of their legitimate rights to self-determination (Hezbollah 2011e, 2015a) and to 'return to their land, decision, homeland and sanctities' (Hezbollah 2011a). This also prevents the eventual establishment of 'an independent Palestinian state . . . on the entire land of Palestine from the Sea to the River' (Hezbollah 2011j), which Nasrallah considers to be the restoration of 'all . . . [the Palestinian] rights' (Hezbollah 2011k). And while he appreciates acts of recognition of a Palestinian state within the 1967 borders, as he expressed when the United Nations Educational, Scientific and Cultural Organization (UNESCO) voted to admit Palestine as a full member in 2011,[5] even this scenario is rendered impossible by the Israeli settlement practices in the West Bank, which seize ever more territories from what would be a Palestinian state. Nasrallah interprets these policies as an attempt to Judaise Palestine and change the composition of the population living in this geographical space (Hezbollah 2011g, 2012f, 2013b). Hezbollah does not recognise Israel's right of existence, as Nasrallah has pointed out on various occasions and often using harsh words: '"Israel" is an illegitimate state and . . . it is a cancerous gland which must be eliminated from the map of existence' (Hezbollah 2012f). Achieving Palestinian popular sovereignty is impossible in an Israeli state that self-identifies as Jewish. In an interview with Julian Assange on Russia Today, Nasrallah made a rare comment on what scenario might be realistic in terms of the future of the conflict. He left no doubt that he considers the status quo illegal and what his ideal vision for

Palestine would be. At the same time, however, he proposed a rather unexpected solution which can only be interpreted as a tribute to what he calls 'political realities':

> [T]he only solution is we don't want to kill anyone, we don't want to treat anyone unjustly, we want justice to be restored . . . and the only solution is the establishment of one state – one state on the land [of] Palestine in which the Muslims and the Jews and the Christians live in peace in a democratic state.[6]

This comment somewhat nuances the uncompromising language Nasrallah uses when he talks about Israel – a word which is always put in inverted commas in the transcripts of his speeches.

The call to support the 'Palestinian cause' (Hezbollah 2016i) remains unequivocal and urgent in Hezbollah's discourse. Although it loses importance over time and cedes its role as the main unifying cause to the 'Takfirist' threat, as Chapter 6 will show, fighting for Palestinian rights is a core concern for non-Palestinians, too. For the occupation is a humiliation of all Muslims (Hezbollah 2011h) and a violation of the 'Palestinian, Arab and Islamic right' (Hezbollah 2012f). Hezbollah's take on popular sovereignty extends the 'nation' to the Arab or Muslim people (Hezbollah 2011l), which could be interpreted as having traces of both the concept of the *umma* and pan-Arabism, but may also express attempts at pragmatic alliance-building and mobilisation. The 'people' whose sovereignty is described oscillates between a specific and a more universal understanding of the nation and, in this way, mirrors how Hezbollah characterises the threat scenario at hand: Israeli and international efforts aiming to break the popular Palestinian and Arab will by both dividing the Palestinian people and separating them from other Arab peoples (Hezbollah 2011g, 2011h). While this project needs to be countered at any price (Hezbollah 2011a), the question of establishing a state and drawing its borders is 'a Palestinian affair which is decided upon by our Palestinian people' (Hezbollah 2011j). Support should therefore not be patronising or an attempt to exercise hegemony over the Palestinian people. There is an unresolved tension between the transnational dimension in Hezbollah's discursive construction of popular sovereignty and its insistence on Palestinian self-determination.

This dual sense of popular sovereignty is also evident in Hezbollah's initial reading of the Arab uprisings as a sign of popular liberation and reconstitution of an encompassing Arab will with the Palestinian cause at its heart – as mistaken as this euphoric interpretation may have turned out to be (Hezbollah 2013b). The mass protests of 2011 and their consequences are the second context in which Hezbollah evokes popular sovereignty. Remarkably, Nasrallah likens the pre-uprising situation of oppression in several countries to the Palestinian experience of occupation, which anticipates the shift to new enemy images that would later be given a similar status to Israel in Hezbollah's world order discourse. Libyan dictator Muammar el Qaddafi was denounced in this way after he began bombing his own people (Hezbollah 2011e). Even more explicitly, Nasrallah compared the Khalifa dynasty's project of replacing the Shi'i population in Bahrain by naturalising Sunni foreigners as

> a scheme similar to the Zionist project; there are settlements, a huge invasion, and an endless rapid-growing act of naturalization . . . Industrious efforts are exerted around the clock to change the identity of the Bahraini people, and a day will come when a people other than the Bahraini people will be residing in Bahrain. (Hezbollah 2015e)

Bahrainis have claimed their 'indisputable legitimate rights' (Hezbollah 2015e) against a regime which in no way respects 'the desires and expectations of this dear people' (Hezbollah 2011g). Similar to this 'popular Intifada' (Hezbollah 2016k) in Bahrain, the Yemeni people's liberation struggle was stopped by the war launched by the so-called Arab Coalition in 2015 under the leadership of Saudi Arabia and the UAE. Hezbollah interprets this as an attempt to 'restore US–Saudi hegemony and guardianship over Yemen after the Yemeni people [had] restored its decision and sovereignty and refused any kind of external hegemony' (Hezbollah 2015l, 2016i). The Saudi regime not only aims at 'breaking the will of the Yemeni people' (Hezbollah 2015l) but generally defies any notion of popular sovereignty, as Nasrallah suggested in an emphatic expression of solidarity for the protesting masses back in 2011:

> There is a problem in the mind which is not recognizing any so-called 'people' – the Tunisian people, the Egyptian people, the Yemeni people, and even the Gulf people, the Saudi people, the Iraqi people, movements of peoples, the will of peoples, and the causes of peoples. So, they might be 'powerful' kings

and rulers; thus, they look to people as their subjects, and consequently, the subjects mustn't have an independent will, an independent cause, nor an independent identity. (Hezbollah 2015i)

Nasrallah comes across as a firm supporter of popular sovereignty, which he describes as 'a divine norm, a natural, divine law' (Hezbollah 2011e). As 'is evident through the history of revolutions, public uprisings, and recent and post resistant acts' (Hezbollah 2011e), eventually it can no longer be suppressed. For Hezbollah, the uprisings in Bahrain, Egypt, Tunisia, Yemen and Libya are 'true, popular revolutions' (Hezbollah 2011e).

But why, then, does Hezbollah support and even fight for the Syrian regime? Nasrallah portrays the Syrian case as fundamentally different. Although he initially still adopted a position of restraint, arguing that the 'Lebanese shouldn't interfere in what is going on in Syria, but rather let the Syrians themselves address their issues as they are able to do that' (Hezbollah 2011l), this changed with Hezbollah's interference in the Syrian war in 2013. Nasrallah declared that Syria was 'no longer a place for a public revolution against a political regime; [it had become a] place for forced implementation of a political US-West-regional puppet regimes-led scheme' (Hezbollah 2013a). This shows that Hezbollah prioritises the defence of peoples against what it identifies as attempts to impose an external will over popular sovereignty interpreted as a republican understanding of democracy or self-determination. For the Lebanese context, too, Hezbollah warns against hegemonic schemes which target the sovereignty of the Lebanese from the outside. Nasrallah denounces the Western hypocrisy manifested in assertions about 'respecting . . . the will of the Lebanese majority' (Hezbollah 2011h), on the one hand, and the meddling in the presidential elections in Lebanon (Hezbollah 2013e) or the composition of the government (Hezbollah 2011l), on the other. His reproach of interference also referred to Saudi Arabia and the pressure it exerted on its ally and the largest Sunni party, the Lebanese Future Movement (Hezbollah 2014g, 2015i). He reminded the other Lebanese parties that '[t]rue sovereignty . . . is when we, the Lebanese people, truly elect a president without receiving a password from any country in the world, whether it is a friendly, regional country, or [an] international country' (Hezbollah 2013e).

Discussion

Compared to Ennahda, more ambivalences and unresolved tensions inhibit Hezbollah's discourse on sovereignty. They arise from either the need to justify applying particular principles in different cases or a divergence of discourse from practice.

While Hezbollah calls for a strong state which performs its sovereignty in external relations and has absolute authority internally, it jeopardises the effectiveness of the state monopoly in both the external and the internal dimension. It assumes responsibility for defending Lebanese borders, as it does not deem the Lebanese state fit to protect its territory. Internally, Hezbollah challenges the state's monopoly on the legitimate use of force. First, it is the only militia to have kept arms after the civil war. It is also prepared to use them against Lebanese adversaries who threaten the survival of the resistance. Besides regular rhetorical assertions, Hezbollah has also proven that it is willing to make use of its power when deemed necessary, as exemplified by its successful defence against the 2008 attempt by the government to abolish Hezbollah's communications system – which Nasrallah is not shy to evoke in moments when the discourse turns against Hezbollah holding arms.[7] While such events tend to be the exception, Hezbollah also has effective control over some of the Lebanese territories, in particular in the south, the Dahieh and the Bekaa. The need to 'supplement' Lebanese state capacity so as to safeguard Lebanese sovereignty is also the justification for Hezbollah's version of shared sovereignty, the army–people–resistance formula.

Similarly, popular sovereignty is vehemently advocated, particularly in the Palestinian context, but also for the Arab peoples oppressed by their own regimes. However, when it comes to the Syrian case, the real popular will dissipates as a standard of popular sovereignty and is overridden by the need to protect Syria and the region against would-be schemes of division and heteronomy, with the protests against Bashar al-Assad being denounced as foreign instigation, representing a minority (and therefore not the popular will) or infiltrated by 'Takfirists'. While there is some consistency in Nasrallah's rejection of non-intervention and non-interference with regard to Western countries and the Gulf states, the same cannot be said about Iranian influence. For instance, financial support for the Lebanese army by Iran is unproblematic, whereas Lebanese security institutions must maintain their independence from Western states. Another example is Hezbollah's intervention by invitation in Syria, which it does not consider a violation of Syrian sovereignty. But it categorically (and, one might add, with good reason; see Ruys and Ferro 2016) rejects the same argument when used by the Saudi regime to justify its intervention in Yemen. Hezbollah does advocate the principles of non-interference in other states' internal affairs and of Arab-Islamic – rather than strictly national – self-determination. But it mainly addresses these demands to the non-Arab and non-Islamic world, as well as to those who are perceived as puppets of Western interests. It argues that peoples should find their own solutions for problems and their own visions of how to coexist in autonomy. But what counts as external interference and what is accepted as the will of the people remains ambiguous.

The discursive processing of these struggles to legitimise what seems like the application of double standards and a failure to 'walk the talk' is clearly observable. But this should not be mistaken as a rejection of what was introduced as Western discourse on world order or a transgression of the boundaries of that discourse. Rather, it indicates, first, a clear awareness of existing norms and, second, a certain degree of acceptance and socialisation into those norms (similarly Dionigi 2014). In contrast to Ennahda, Hezbollah does not actively articulate its recognition of these categories of world order or seek recognition as a member of the normative community that identifies with this order. Rather, it denounces Western hypocrisy and explains – more or less plausibly – the need to diverge from established principles in certain cases and to prioritise some concepts of sovereignty over others, depending on context.

It is noteworthy that absolute and popular sovereignty seem deeply internalised in Hezbollah's normative system and are depicted as 'natural' standards in its order discourse. Indeed, Nasrallah feels that explanation is necessary when Hezbollah's behaviour appears to fall short of meeting those standards. Still, there is one category that clearly challenges and is meant to challenge concepts of sovereignty in Western discourse: the 'golden formula' is a Hezbollah innovation and transforms the meaning of shared sovereignty that prevails in Western discourse. But this should not be interpreted as amounting to a rejection of Western world order. Not only is the formula still of minor importance compared to absolute and popular sovereignty, its normative value is also derived from the latter. Moreover, the context of armed conflict in recent history, the immediate neighbourhood and lingering danger in everyday politics needs to be factored into any assessment of how dissident this innovation is. It should therefore be interpreted as an element of resistance in Hezbollah's discourse, which is otherwise marked by recognition of the Western-dominated world order – despite regular assertions to the contrary and a clear rejection of hegemony. For sovereignty, this apparent contradiction is more than plausible – for the principles of absolute and popular sovereignty are by no means exclusively Western concepts. On the contrary, Western discourse connected them to racial hierarchies and is what made them exclusive to the white and male culture for a long time. In this sense, the recognition and confirmation of both sovereignty concepts by Ennahda and Hezbollah should not be seen as surprising. Rather, it reveals that the two groups originate in an Islamist and therefore anti-colonial movement, making absolute and popular sovereignty a tool against heteronomy and hegemony.

Notes

1. 'A democratic state is a strong state. There is no contradiction between respecting the law and using force within legal limits against those who benefited from the weakness of state institutions or who thought that the state was weak.'
2. See BBC News (2011). It was eventually resolved in October 2022 when, with the help of US diplomacy, a deal was struck and a new line drawn to redefine the two exclusive economic zones (Schaer 2022).
3. 'Takfirist' is a term used for those persons or groups who adhere to the concept and practice of *takfir*, by which individuals or groups are defined as *kuffār* (infidels) or *murtaddūn* (apostates). ISIS's conception of *takfir* differs from how other Salafi-jihadist organisations like al-Qaʿida use the concept. While the two organisations 'follow a similar ideology and the works of Ibn Taymiyya, Ibn Abd al-Wahhab, and Qutb have stimulated both' (Kadivar 2020, 265), they differ with regard to whom they prioritise as targets of violence, justified on the basis of *takfir*, and what means they consider legitimate (Kadivar 2020).
4. A telling example is the violence that erupted over the attempt of the Future Moverment-led government to investigate and potentially deprive Hezbollah of its telecommunication system. The latter connects the Lebanese south to the Bekaa valley and the Dahieh and, thus, three Hezbollah strongholds in Lebanon. The party considers it the 'most importan[t] weapon in the resistance ever' (Hezbollah

2012b). To what it perceived as a threat to this core technology, Hezbollah reacted by blocking the road to the airport and seizing control of West Beirut. Fearing an internal sectarian split, the Lebanese military forces did not intervene in the conflict. A private militia under Saad al-Hariri and the ISF could not defy Hezbollah and the allied armed groups that supported it.

5. https://news.un.org/en/story/2011/10/393562 (accessed 12 October 2023).

6. This is an extract from an interview with Hassan Nasrallah in the first episode of *The Julian Assange Show*, aired on Russia Today in 2012. The transcript can be found here: https://web.archive.org/web/20120425030505/https:/worldtomor row.wikileaks.org/static/pdf/Assange%20Nasrallah%20Broadcast%20Interview .pdf (accessed 6 November 2023).

7. See note 4.

5

LEGITIMACY

Ennahda

To the astonishment of observers, Ennahda's president, Rached al-Ghannouchi, declared after the tenth party congress in 2016: '*Il n'y a plus de justification à l'islam politique en Tunisie. On sort de l'islam politique pour entrer dans la démocratie musulmane. Nous sommes des musulmans démocrates qui ne se réclament plus de l'islam politique*' (Ennahda 2016d).[1] As this chapter will show, Ennahda wrestled with the question of political legitimacy and how to build a political order in post-2011 Tunisia to such an extent that it even recast its own identity as an Islamist party and movement, but also renegotiated the relationship between and altered the meanings of democracy and Islam, just as other Islamists in North Africa have (for the Moroccan case, see Khanani 2021). Ennahda's discourse on legitimacy between 2011 and 2016 is extraordinarily sophisticated and complex, and it testifies to the internal and external struggles it endured after the ousting of Zine el Abidine Ben Ali. This chapter cannot outline all the nuances in Ennahda's understanding of political legitimacy. Instead, it seeks to give an impression of the distinct ideas and core building blocks of Ennahda's very own take on what legitimate political order in Tunisia and the world should look like: a culturally and religiously imbued, consensus-based democracy which is embedded in peaceful, respectful and economically just international relations and a multipolar world marked by the plurality of the orders it embraces.

Another caveat is that Ennahda's legitimacy considerations are introversive in the sense that they focus primarily on the Tunisian context – which is a noteworthy contrast to Hezbollah and telling with regard to differences in the self-conception of the two groups. However, Ennahda is, at the same time, very aware of the necessity to take the global order into account if Tunisia's political system is to have a future – and if Ennahda itself wants to survive. Given the deeply rooted scepticism towards Islamist actors in Western decision-makers' perception of the region, Ennahda has to navigate its suggestions for order as well as its self-representation to the world through international expectations and pressures from its own members and constituency. One normative structure which restrains Ennahda's articulations of order and identity is secularism, which has become a 'standard of recognition of political actors (and orders) as legitimate' (Pfeifer 2019, 479). Ennahda's discourse has to be interpreted with an international 'overhearing audience' (Heritage 1985) in mind which tends to fear and distrust Islamists. This also means that there may be some strategic choices involved when it comes to choosing what (not) to say in statements that are intended to or at least might reach this audience. This might be one explanation for the quantitative importance of certain claims about legitimacy and the relatively low prevalence or absence of others.[2]

In a nutshell, Ennahda attempted to mark a clear break with the old regime while simultaneously avoiding the risk of being banned by secular political forces which had emerged from old cadres; to introduce Islam into the nascent democratic system without nourishing the fear that it, like other Islamists, had a hidden agenda and intended to capture the state (Netterstrøm 2015); to signal and seek consensus and recognition without sacrificing core parts of its platform; and to solicit international support while simultaneously claiming Tunisian autonomy. The following portrayal of Ennahda's legitimacy discourse mirrors these discursive strategies and struggles.

Individual-based Legitimacy: Elections, Institutions, (Women's) Rights

An important part of Ennahda's legitimacy discourse is dedicated to what could be called the fundamental institutions of a democracy which are justified by referring to the individual – if only implicitly, by following an individualist and aggregative logic of reasoning. These institutions constitute the bones of what Ennahda envisions as a post-Ben Ali political system in Tunisia and were particularly present in Ennahda's discourse from the immediate aftermath of the revolution to the conclusion of the constitutional process in 2014. For Ennahda, elections as well as institutions that are legitimated by elections and follow the logic of the separation of powers, thereby protecting the individual against the state, and equal individual rights and freedoms are at the core of Tunisia's political transition. These institutions fulfil one of the revolutionaries' central demands, the demand for (political) freedom.[3] In this sense, elections, accountable institutions and individual rights and freedoms are priorities for Ennahda, not least because the old regime had provided none of them.

Elections grant immediate legitimacy (Ennahda 2011f) by consolidating individual wills in the will of the people. Elections are seen as a matter of priority because they can bestow legitimacy upon other institutions and are a *conditio sine qua non* for legitimate rule (Ennahda 2011f, 2011o, 2012z, 2012ak). Through competitive elections, people should 'engage positively and go to the ballot box in order to choose those most able, truthful, competent, and trustworthy to represent [them]' (Ennahda 2014e). Moreover, a considerable symbolic power inheres in elections, as they marked the end of dictatorship in 2011 (Ennahda 2011m, 2011n, 2012s) and, with the second legislative and presidential elections in 2014 which put in place the first 'full-term democratically elected government' (Ennahda 2014f), concluded Tunisia's democratic transition (Ennahda 2014p). Although Ennahda initially rigorously rejected participation by successors of the old regime (Ennahda 2012ad), it eventually agreed to letting Nidaa Tounes run in the elections of 2014. The meeting between the two party leaders, Ghannouchi and Essebsi, in Paris seems to have contributed significantly to this decision (Interview 3).

Ennahda foregrounded the normative quality of elections especially when it was attacked for having created an Islamist-dominated cabinet. This was particularly pronounced in the phase of the Ennahda-led Troika governments between 2011 and 2013. The discontent with the Troika culminated in two events. First, in mid-2012, Nidaa Tounes was founded as an umbrella organisation for disillusioned members of the NCA and old regime cadres. As some delegates from the NCA joined the new anti-Islamist party, this led to the peculiar situation that Nidaa Tounes had seats in the NCA, even though it had not run in the 2011 elections. Second, the pressure of street politics and the increasing escalation of conflicts between the opposition and the government – or rather Ennahda – led NCA president Mustafa Ben Jafar to unilaterally suspend the assembly's activity. The only elected Tunisian body was further sidelined when civil society organisations, in particular the UGTT, pushed for a process of 'national dialogue' and then, in 2013, formed the 'Quartet', a consortium of trade unions and NGOs in the field of human rights and law that mediated between conflicting political parties and moderated the transition process.

Ennahda insisted that elected bodies were the only ones with 'democratic legitimacy' (Ennahda 2014p), thereby initially questioning the initiatives that emerged from society. But the further the transition advanced, the less pronounced Ennahda's references to the legitimising power of elections were. For the majority that a party gains in elections can never produce a sufficient amount of legitimacy in times of transition and laying the foundations of a political system: 'We chose to strengthen the transition by building it on a higher level of legitimacy – one based on consensus, not majority,' the party argued in early 2014 (Ennahda 2014f) – and thus at a time when it still had the clear majority in the NCA and was the dominant party in the government. Ennahda deems elections an indispensable mechanism for 'the peaceful alternation of power' (Ennahda 2011b, 2012aj), but there are limits to the importance it attaches to them, even if it is the winner. After its landslide victory in 2011, for instance, it immediately chose to form a coalition government with two secular parties and made considerable concessions during its time in government. This indicates that Ennahda was aware of the precarious nature of its incumbency and, even more importantly, of its survival as a party should it give an impression of Islamist domination. Ennahda had learnt a painful lesson from the Muslim Brotherhood's fate in Egypt, where the military coup against President Morsi brought an abrupt end to the experiment of Islamists in government. It is in this context that Ennahda re-emphasised that elections are the single most important mechanism to organise a legitimate transition of power (Ennahda 2013s, 2013t, 2013aa). Ennahda also reminded the Western powers of their responsibility to recognise election results, which they had done in 2011 but failed to do on various occasions before that when they had been displeased with the results (Ennahda 2012d, 2016j). The narrative of the dangerous Islamists who, through winning elections, would capture and monopolise state power and dissolve democratic institutions had often served as an argument against free and fair elections in Middle Eastern countries (Ennahda 2013f).

Besides elections, according to Ennahda, the establishment of accountable institutions is of utmost importance to prevent any backsliding to authoritarianism (Ennahda 2011c). The fear of concentrating too much power in the hands of a single person was behind both Ennahda's calls for nurturing a thriving civil society and its promotion of a parliamentary system, rather than the presidential system favoured by Nidaa Tounes. With regard to its support for a strong civil society, Ennahda explained that a 'balance between state and society' (Ennahda 2011i) can only be achieved through mutual independence: NGOs, unions and other civil society actors must be protected against an invasive state. Conversely, civil society has to accept the primacy of political institutions when it comes to the democratic organisation of public life. Ennahda envisioned the development of 'a new political culture clarifying and distinguishing the roles and functions of all public space stakeholders, in a spirit of cooperation and distinction' (Ennahda 2012y). This included 'professional, credible, constructive, unbiased' media (Ennahda 2012v), Ennahda claimed, though it simultaneously faced allegations of opaque media and funding practices, including '"Qatari-inspired influence" in both private and public broadcasting media' (Kausch 2013, 7). As for the question of the political system, the NCA eventually opted for a semi-presidential system, with a directly elected president and an indirectly elected prime minister, both with significant powers. During the transition phase, Ennahda considered the NCA an exemplary institution. Calls for dissolving it grew louder in 2013, when the security situation deteriorated, two members of the Front Populaire were assassinated and members of the NCA and the government began to withdraw from office. But Ennahda maintained its unflinching commitment 'to the constituent assembly as the cornerstone of [Tunisia's] emerging democracy' in the face of 'anarchist calls for its dissolution' (Ennahda 2013aj).

Ennahda was wary of any demands to suspend or abolish state institutions, attributing them to counterrevolutionary forces. It was of the view that both anarchists and former regime cadres were trying to 'topple democratic legitimacy' (Ennahda 2013k) and imitate the Egyptian military coup (Ennahda

2013a). The party continually praised the Tunisian military for its tradition of neutrality and the civil state as a cornerstone of democracy. Legal institutions gained importance in Ennahda's discourse when political violence escalated in 2012 and 2013. The party was confronted with allegations that it turned a blind eye to the Salafist motivation behind, or was even implicated in, the attacks on the US embassy in September 2012 and the assassination of Chokri Belaïd, the human rights activist and leftist politician of the Front Populaire in February 2013. Being part of the incumbent government, Ennahda was expected to demonstrate that it could handle Tunisia's security problems. At the same time, however, it did not want to alienate its constituency, which at least partly sympathised with the Salafists. In its discourse, this manifested, on the one hand, in strong advocacy for the neutral and rigorous investigation of all incidents of political violence, irrespective of the suspected political background (Ennahda 2012y, 2013f): the 'law applies to anyone violating it, and . . . no one is above the law,' Ennahda asserted (Ennahda 2013f, 2013g). On the other hand, it also invested in discourse to counter a collective demonisation of Tunisian Salafists. No one, Ennahda claimed, should be judged or persecuted for their convictions – but if, and only if, they committed crimes, Salafists were to subject to prosecution like anyone else (Ennahda 2012e, 2013f).

An independent judiciary was also extremely important in the context of the transitional justice process (see also Salehi 2022). The latter involved, among other things, trials against those who committed crimes, in particular human rights violations and the misappropriation of public funds. Ennahda was careful not to create the impression that the trials were politicised and arbitrarily targeting old regime members. At the same time, the population had high expectations that justice would be done, and Ennahda wanted to avoid any forms of vigilantism, revenge or collective punishment (Ennahda 2011a). Again, Ennahda opted for the creation of institutions. Under the Troika government, the Truth and Dignity Commission was established in order to provide 'a judicial process guided by human rights and rule of law to help us turn the page on the past' (Ennahda 2014i) and formally started work in June 2014.

Finally, Ennahda made it an 'utmost priority . . . to guarantee freedoms: personal freedoms, social freedoms, and women's rights' (Ennahda 2011c, 2012c) and declared the realisation of individual liberties and rights for all Tunisians, 'regardless of their religion, sex, or any other consideration'

(Ennahda 2012ag, 2013i, 2014k), as the primary goal of the constitution. Despite this emphasis on equal rights, one group stands out in Ennahda's individualist legitimacy claims: women. What is even more remarkable than the importance of women in Ennahda's discourse is the party's gender quotas compared to other Tunisian parties and Arab (or, for that matter, non-Arab) countries and parties. Of forty-nine female representatives elected to the NCA in 2011, a total of forty-two were from Ennahda. Not only did female Islamists account for 40 per cent of the party's MPs in 2016, Ennahda was also the only party to nominate women to executive and leadership positions, such as Meherzia Labidi as vice president of the NCA (Ennahda 2016g). There are two main explanations for the pronounced role women play for Ennahda. First, women's rights are an important discursive field for delegitimising and marking a break with the old regime. For a long time, the feminist movement in Tunisia had been divided between Islamists and secularists. The latter accused the former that their feminism was a reproduction of Islamic conservatism and that many of them did not really accept women's rights as an integral part of human rights. Conversely, Islamists condemned the closeness of the secularist feminists to the old regime, denouncing it as a form of exclusive and repressive state feminism (Jünemann 2017). One reason for Ennahda's commitment to women's rights is therefore that it is almost a traditional cleavage constituting the Islamist and secular identities in Tunisia. According to Ennahda, the old regime presented itself as a defender of women, while, in fact, the latter remained in a precarious and often marginalised situation, deprived of equal rights (Ennahda 2011j). One example of the authoritarian version of laicism as practised under the Ben Ali regime is the question of the headscarf. The regime had stripped women of their right to wear a headscarf in public institutions (Ennahda 2014c), thereby denying them religious freedom. Women should neither be forced to wear a headscarf nor prevented from doing so, and Ennahda's female politicians are leading by example in this regard (Ennahda 2011r).

Second, however, it was precisely such attempts to reconfigure gender politics that made Tunisian adversaries and international observers distrustful of Ennahda's intentions. In this sense, the overhearing audience determines Ennahda's discursive priorities yet again – and it is probably one of the (Western) clichés about Islamists that they undermine gender equality and deprive women of their rights. On several occasions, Ennahda actively fought what it perceived as a misrepresentation of its policies and views on women by Western media, asking them to officially apologise and put more effort into their investigations and reporting (Ennahda 2012h, 2014u). It maintained its commitment to the Tunisian Personal Status Code when accused of planning to abolish the very same policy, reintroduce polygamy or force women to wear headscarves (Ennahda 2011r, 2012g). And yet, some of Ennahda's ideas continued to be seen as ambivalent. For instance, it suggested including an article on the complementarity of man and woman in the constitution, arguing that it would 'not contradict the concept of equality, [but rather constitute] a reflection of equality. Complementarity means that women complement men, and men complement women. Because they need one another, they supplement each other' (Ennahda 2013w). Ennahda's critics saw this as a thinly veiled attempt to reintroduce legal inequality through the back door.

As for its take on women's rights, Ennahda not only claimed compatibility between individual rights and Islam but even argued that the former were directly derived from the latter: 'Islam was revealed to establish human rights. This is the very essence of Islam' (Ennahda 2011f, 2011r). At the same time, it was careful to showcase its advocacy for religious freedom and freedom of conscience, for 'people are completely free in their belief . . . and there is a verse in Koran that says there is no compulsion in religion' (Ennahda 2011r, 2012ag). On various occasions, the party has emphasised the need to protect religious minorities, especially the old Jewish community in Tunisia (Ennahda 2012j, 2012ah). Again, Ennahda's discursive commitments did not remain without tensions. When Salafist groups organised – partly violent – demonstrations against films and artworks because of their 'blasphemous' quality in 2011 and 2012, Ennahda issued a statement which advocated the 'freedom of expression and creativity within the values of co-existence' (Ennahda 2012a). The latter refers to the offence potentially taken by believers who perceive media and art as hostile towards Islam. Ennahda was heavily criticised for its stance on the issue by some of its own members and religious authorities such as Houcine Laabidi, the chairman of the Zaytouna Mosque. The latter strongly condemned the artworks as sacrilegious, even 'calling for the death of the artists for their blasphemous work' (Cesari 2014, 250). Ennahda responded by issuing a statement in defence of the Salafists' 'right to freely express their views and all their rights' (Ennahda 2012f). But this clashed with the expectations of its secular counterparts in government and opposition. They wanted Ennahda to clearly position itself in favour of freedom of expression and to defend it against calls for restrictions based on blasphemy claims. Ennahda's discursive ambivalence remained restricted, which may indicate both that it considered certain matters settled with the adoption of the constitution in 2014 and that it had experience of navigating through the troubled waters of the religion/ politics question. To achieve the former, its politics of consensus was crucial, whereas the latter was the result of its sophisticated conception of Islamic democracy. Both will be discussed in the following two subsections.

Community-based Legitimacy: Islamic Democracy

If what was presented as individualist elements in Ennahda's discourse of legitimacy constitutes the bones of the party's ideas of legitimate authority, its vision of an Islamic democracy puts flesh on those bones. At the same time, it also represents Ennahda's take on community-based legitimacy, which consists of two interdependent dimensions: Islamic/cultural democracy and state neutrality. These are held together by one argument: democracy needs to be adapted to the society for which it is built. There is no single, abstract model of democracy that could serve as a blueprint for all societies. While Ennahda does acknowledge some degree of (global) norm convergence, it still holds that every country, society and world region, each with its own history, deserves its own model of democracy. The quality and detail of the arguments Ennahda presented in its elaborations on Islamic democracy are remarkable, which is a direct result of Ghannouchi's influence as a political theorist. In terms of prevalence, however, the topic is less present in Ennahda's discourse than others. Again, this may be due to not wanting to overemphasise Islam to an international public (and domestic opponents), which in fact culminated in Ennahda's outright renunciation of its Islamist identity in 2016. But there is also a more practical reason for the relatively marginal position of this topic: it may simply be too abstract to guide everyday political action.

Similar to its individual legitimacy claims, Ennahda's story of an Islamic democracy starts, first, with the failures of the old regime which had deprived Tunisia of its cultural heritage and Islamic identity. Ennahda believes in the 'validity of Islam and its heritage as a value and cultural reference and a basis for [Tunisia's] project of reform and modernisation through *ijtihad* (creative interpretation) [and] *tajdid* (renewal)' (Ennahda 2011b). The new political system should be informed by 'values stemming from the cultural and civilizational heritage and Arab Islamic identity of Tunisian society' (Ennahda 2011b). Ennahda claims that this identity is unequivocal among Tunisians: '*Notre identité ne fait pas débat parmi les Tunisiens. Nous sommes un pays arabo-musulman: c'est un fait partagé par tous*' (Ennahda 2011d).[4] Of course, this glosses over important differences. Besides ignoring religious and ethnic minorities, such as Christians, Jews and Amazigh, this representation downplays the affectively laden quality of both religious and secular identities. In Tunisia, the secular–Islamist divide was probably the most important cleavage in the post-authoritarian era (Pfeifer 2017) and clearly a manifestation of profound identity conflicts. Nevertheless, Ennahda presented the supposed homogeneity of Tunisia's Arab-Muslim society as an asset compared to other transitioning societies in the neighbourhood that had to cope with sectarian and ethnic difference (Ennahda 2012d). As will be discussed in the next subsection on the politics of consensus, Ennahda's assessment that Tunisian identity was non-controversial among political parties turned out to be wrong and led to some surprises during the constitution-making process (Cesari 2014, 243–7).

Second, another known motive is Ennahda's rejection of misrepresentations of Islam. Muslims have often been portrayed 'as unworthy of democracy, or their political culture as rooted in the philosophy of "oriental despotism"' (Ennahda 2014i, 2014ae), and 'Islamic democracy' (Ennahda 2011e) tends to be seen as a contradiction in terms. But Ennahda considers them to be natural allies: 'Democracy thrives with Islam and Islam thrives with democracy. They . . . are intimate and co-existent couples and friends' (Ennahda 2012f). Democratic principles 'reflect the Islamic principles of consultation, justice and accountability' (Ennahda 2011i), of consensus and of the rejection of tyranny (Ennahda 2012aj). In the aftermath of the revolution, Ennahda frequently referenced the Turkish AKP as an exemplary model of a Muslim democratic agenda. Conversely, Ennahda claimed that many Turks were inspired by Ghannouchi's political thought. But with growing political tensions between Recep Tayyip Erdoğan and his European counterparts, revolving, among others, around state violence in response to the Gezi Park protests in 2013 and the government reactions to the coup attempt in 2016, the reference lost appeal or even did a disservice to Ennahda, as it seemed to confirm all suspicions about Islamists (Marks 2017).

For Ennahda, the model of Islamic democracy is distinct from the Western model of democracy. The latter is based on individualism and treats 'members of society like separate islands, all living separately with no . . . solidarity between them' (Ennahda 2012g). Moreover, it bears the traces of a specific European history with distinctive problems and responses to them. One of these legacies is secularism (Ennahda 2012ag). The distinct nature of the European experience means that Western secularism cannot simply be transferred to Muslim contexts. 'Islam, since its inception, has always combined religion with politics, religion [with] state' (Ennahda 2012ag). What is more, secular settlements in the West are by no means unitary – and often less secular than they seem. Religion informs politics in the US (Ennahda 2012ac, 2012ag) and the Christian Democratic Union rules in Germany – but 'when we speak of Islam and democracy, it's [considered] blasphemy' (Ennahda 2015ab). Ennahda constructs French laicism or 'comprehensive secularity' (Ennahda 2012ac), with its total exclusion of religion from public life, as a form of secular extremism and the antipode to its own ideas of legitimate order. It hollows politics out and strips it of ethics, giving way to fierce and raw capitalism:

> [The] total stripping of the state from religion would turn the state into a mafia, and the world economic system into an exercise in plundering, and politics into deception and hypocrisy. And this is exactly what happened in the Western experience . . . International politics became the preserve of a few financial brokers owning the biggest share of capital and by extension the media, through which they ultimately control politicians. (Ennahda 2012ag)

Ennahda considers religion to be a fundamental moral source of political life and the state – it is the ethical foundation of politics and gives the state and politics a normative purpose by providing answers to

> the big question[s] . . . those relating to our existence, origins, destiny, and the purpose for which we were created, and [by] provid[ing] us with a system of values and principles that would guide our thinking, behaviour, and the regulations of the state to which we aspire. (Ennahda 2012ag)

The challenge, then, is that Islam is not univocal, nor does it possess an authoritative interpretation or an interpretative authority that could create one, like an equivalent to the church (Ennahda 2012ah). Islam needs to be put into practice through laws made according to 'Islamic values as understood at [a] particular time and place' (Ennahda 2012ag) and through 'the democratic mechanism [as] the best embodiment of the Shura (consultation) value in Islam' (Ennahda 2012ag). In practical terms, in a democracy this implies that deliberation determines what Islamic teachings mean and that the parliament 'translate(s) the Arabic Islamic identity' (Ennahda 2012ah) into laws.

In Ennahda's model of democracy, passing on Islamic values and education more generally occupy a prominent place. Children and migrants should be socialised into 'Arab and Islamic values' (Ennahda 2011b, 2012a, 2014e) and politicians need to be familiarised with the teachings of Islam (Ennahda 2012ag). Ennahda argues that a 'balanced identity provides democracy with the foundations it needs to exist and flourish, and protects society from extremism and radicalism' (Ennahda 2014z). Institutions like the Zaytouna Mosque and its reformist tradition of thought are at the centre of an educational project aimed at attaining such a balanced identity (Ennahda 2012a). Excluding religion from the public sphere, in contrast, only feeds extremism (Ennahda 2014g). It is Ennahda's core belief that '"[d]emocratic Islam" is the antidote and alternative to all forms of terrorism' (Ennahda 2014ae, 2014af, 2016j). Showing that 'prosperity and democracy can emerge and develop within our own culture and are not unattainable nor do they have to be imposed by external intervention' (Ennahda 2011f) is the best argument against terrorism. It demonstrates that the 'apparent choice between Islam and democracy that ISIS insists Muslims must make is just . . . false' (Ennahda 2016h). According to Ennahda, extremism results from a lack of real knowledge about Islam. It presents religion as incompatible with modernity and democracy, thereby destroying Islam's true image (Ennahda 2014aa, 2014af, 2014ah, 2015n). There are, therefore, limits to what Ennahda considers to be reasonable and legitimate interpretations of Islam. While the party rejects state control of mosques and imams in principle, it contends 'that extremists took advantage of the security vacuum [after the revolution] to take over 20 percent of the country's mosques' (Ennahda 2015i). This is why, when it was in government with the Troika coalition, Ennahda tried to bring 'nearly 1,000 mosques back under the control of moderate clerics' (Ennahda 2015i).

There is a certain tension between these policies and state neutrality, the second pillar of Ennahda's Islamic democracy (see also Donker and Netterstrøm 2017). Whereas state neutrality is associated with the state's independence from the church (Taylor 2011), Ennahda proposes a more comprehensive under-standing: the state needs to be protected against both Islamist and secular extremism. The former 'would like to impose [a single] understanding of Islam from above using state tools and apparatuses . . . [whereas the latter] aspires to strip the state, educational curricula, and national culture of all Islamic influ-ences' (Ennahda 2012ag). The state should enforce neither one single model of religion nor strict secularism – this is the lesson to be learnt from the history of Muslim societies, which diverges from the European experience.

> While the problematique in the west revolved around ways of liberating the state from religion and led to destructive wars, in our context the problem is one of liberating religion from the state and preventing it from dominating religion, and keeping the latter in the societal realm . . . (Ennahda 2012ag)

While a separation of religion and politics is alien to the Islamic tradition, according to Ennahda, it has distinguished between the religious and the polit-ical since its inception. Ennahda alludes to the *ṣaḥīfa*, sometimes referred to as the Constitution of Medina and implemented after the Prophet Mohamed's *hijra* from Mecca to Yathrib (subsequently known as Medina) in 622 (Arjomand 2009). The document regulated relations between two religious nations, the Muslims and the Jews of Medina, which constituted a political nation (*umma*) under one constitution.[5] According to Ennahda, two spheres can be distinguished: the 'system of transactions/dealings (*Mu'amalat*)' is the 'domain of searching for the general interest' and demands practical reason to interpret Islam's teachings in light of political and societal circumstances (Ennahda 2012ag). In contrast, the system of 'worship (*'Ibadat*)' is 'the domain of constancy and observance' in which 'reason cannot reach the truth' (Ennahda 2012ag). Democratic politics are a method for handling the plural-ity of interpretations in the first of these two domains (Ennahda 2012ah).

One implication of state neutrality is the realisation of certain individual rights, such as freedom of conscience and religion, which notably includes

the free practice of religion without any restrictions in the name of secularism (Ennahda 2011i, 2011r). But it also proscribes the imposition of a 'single
all-powerful interpretation of Islam' (Ennahda 2011e, 2011f, 2014ah) by
the state. Such a religious state would seriously harm the principle of popular sovereignty (Ennahda 2012g), as discussed in Chapter 4. In a democracy,
'[w]e don't want a theocracy on top of parliament,' Ennahda affirmed (2013i).
Conversely, the state should leave it to religious scholars to interpret Islam and
it is not supposed to interfere with religious institutions, for example, by training imams or controlling mosques (Ennahda 2015u).

As the need to react to religious extremism and terrorism shows, however, Ennahda's principles have sometimes been challenged by the practical
needs of running a country. Besides, Ennahda's version of Islamic democracy
of course also faced principled opposition in Tunisia, and Ennahda had to
walk the line between Islamist identity and the compatibility of its suggestions
with the views of the masses several times, sometimes slipping to one side or
the other. One such glitch occurred briefly after the NCA elections in 2011.
Hamadi Jebali, then designated prime minister, gave a talk in Sousse where he
evoked the notion of a 'sixth caliphate' in Tunisia. This statement unsettled
Tunisians and notably Ennahda's coalition partner at the time, Ettakatol. But
Ennahda was quick to respond to this debate and remove the 'ambiguities'
from Jebali's speech: '[L']allusion à la "khilafa arrachida" visait simplement
à s'inspirer de nos valeurs et notre patrimoine politique et de l'héritage civili-
sationnel de la société tunisienne à laquelle nous sommes fiers d'appartenir,'[6]
it declared (Ennahda 2011o). Ennahda's ideas faced another important test
when the question of whether or not to introduce the shari'a into the constitution was on the table. Ennahda had officially taken a position against this. But
'after the elections [of 2011], [some] Ennahda leaders voiced different stances
on the issue' (Cesari 2014, 245), partly due to the pressure exerted on the party
by Salafists to adhere to clearly Islamic positions. Again, Ennahda found an
argumentative workaround, stating that 'Tunisian law [was already] largely
based on Sharia. Sharia never left our country – hence it does not need to be
"returned"' (Ennahda 2012ac).

In an attempt both to put an end to what seemed like interminable allegations and distrust against the party and to consolidate the image of being
a firm champion of Tunisian democracy, Ennahda surprised observers at its

tenth party congress in May 2016 when it officially renounced its Islamist identity. From then on, it wanted to be known as a party of Muslim democrats (Ennahda 2016a) or 'a democratic party inspired by an Islamic reference' (Ennahda 2016a). The relabelling went hand in hand with more pronounced advocacy for a stronger separation and differentiation of societal spheres. Drawing a sharper distinction between the state and society would allow for more specialisation and free 'those working [in societal fields such as religion] from obstruction and from dependence on political changes' (Ennahda 2016a), thereby making society as a whole stronger. Religion would then be able to reassume 'its role of unification rather than division' (Ennahda 2016p). In a similar vein, Ennahda itself would specialise in political action as the most important aspect of the party's work (Ennahda 2016c).

What seemed like a drastic change in Ennahda's identity and platform provoked a raft of international reactions. The American news channel Cable News Network (CNN) claimed that Tunisia was 'now in the middle of another historic shift: the separation of Islam and politics' and deemed this a 'dramatic and democratic turn' in Tunisian politics.[7] In an interview, Ghannouchi explained that it was high time for the party to take this step of specialisation within the framework of a modern constitution, but quickly added that no one was asking Muslims to separate their beliefs from politics in their minds. His statement seemed to confirm the impression of a radical break. Yet the above analysis questions the extent to which a change of label is also a change in substance. As Monica Marks argues, Ennahda's public statement that it was changing from an Islamist to a Muslim democratic actor was not a U-turn in the party's history but a logical step in its ideological development: '[Adopting] the term "Muslim democrat" indicates less a shift in how nahdawis see themselves . . . than an effort to help media and outside actors understand the party on its own terms' (Marks 2016, 5–6). Ghannouchi's speech at the party congress in 2016 casts a soupçon of doubt on Marks's assessment that Ennahda leaving political Islam behind adds to a more or less coherent picture of a party coming of age. He ended it very emotionally, crying in front of thousands of Nahdawis gathered for the occasion. As with other instances of Ennahda's discourse, the recasting of its identity could be interpreted as one of the more painful concessions to (transnational) normative structures and sceptics of the party, including Tunisian adversaries and

Western political actors reluctant to interact with Ennahda on an equal footing (Pfeifer 2019). Ennahda was very aware, it seems, that the 'Islamist' label
would always associate it with threat images in the Western mind, which tends
to lump Islamism, jihadism and terrorism together (see Chapter 1). Giving
up political Islam, then, was a bitter pill to swallow for the sake of building
consensus in Tunisia, improving the prospects of finding partners outside the
country and thereby, not least, securing the party's survival.

Outbidding Deliberative Legitimacy: Politics of Consensus

If Ennahda's method were to be summarised in one phrase, it would be
'consensus-building'. Indeed, while the aforementioned bones and flesh are the
substance of its political vision, the politics of consensus became its core strategy for political action and party survival. Behind this method are substantial
fears for the fate of Tunisia and Ennahda itself. Ennahda considers transitional
phases a very sensitive time for a country and society. The risk of irreconcilable
polarisation among different political and societal actors is heightened and,
in the worst case, transitional societies might drift into violence. Ennahda's
consensus-seeking was particularly pronounced in the run-up to the adoption
of the Tunisian constitution in 2014 but also remained its signature move
afterwards – and the language became even stronger. While Ennahda had
advocated cooperation and dialogue and clarified the need for concessions and
reasonable arguments when it led the Troika governments between 2011 and
2013, it shifted to a rhetoric of consensus from 2014 onwards. The 2014 elections relegated the party to second place after Nidaa Tounes, reviving fears of
Ennahda being excluded again from the government or, worse still, the entire
political system. Ennahda was also aware that, after the conclusion of the political transition, painful processes of economic transformation would have to be
tackled next. For this, it considered a broad consensus indispensable.

    Ennahda publicly declared its shift towards dialogue and cooperation
immediately after the Tunisian elections of 2011, seeking a coalition that
would resolutely bridge the dominant cleavage between Islamists and secularists (Ennahda 2011a, 2012l, 2013e). Mere coexistence of the two trends
would not be enough. Rather, power-sharing and substantial cooperation
were to be sought, and 'Islamists [had] to work with others' (Ennahda 2011a,
2011e, 2013al). In this respect, Ennahda considered the Troika a resounding

success and an 'inspiring example of Islamic–secular co-operation for the greater national interest' (Ennahda 2011i). The only *conditio sine qua non* for any such cooperation was a commitment to breaking with the dictatorship (Ennahda 2012i, 2012o, 2013ad).

The modus operandi for cooperation is dialogue – a form of communication in which Ennahda is particularly skilled due to its internal culture of and profound appreciation for pluralism, difference and self-criticism (Ennahda 2011j, 2011m, 2012a, 2012ab, 2012ai, 2013f, 2013ae, 2016e). Dialogue is the 'language of reason' (Ennahda 2012u), the only civil method of processing conflict (Ennahda 2012t), and has the potential to prevent violent means of dealing with difference (Ennahda 2012v, 2013ad). Ennahda insists that, rather than demonising them, dialogue should be pursued with Salafists, too (Ennahda 2012v, 2013ai). For they can change their convictions and be persuaded to abandon the path of violence (Ennahda 2012d). Ennahda, it seems, firmly believes in 'the unforced force of the better argument' (Habermas 1996, 306), and dialogue can be considered Ennahda's default response to crisis (Ennahda 2013af, 2015z).

The party identifies certain ethical standards of deliberation (Ennahda 2012a) which a dialogue must meet in order to work as a mode of interaction. These standards were evident when the first rounds of national dialogue were initiated in late 2012 and early 2013. First, dialogues must not *a priori* exclude anyone – participation in dialogue should not be premised on the acceptance of certain outcomes (Ennahda 2013j). Second, though, Ennahda itself refused to participate in the first national dialogue because Nidaa Tounes had been invited (Ennahda 2012w) – a party Ennahda initially asserted was the immediate successor organisation of the old regime and suspected of organising a counterrevolution. But even in respect of this opponent, Ennahda eventually yielded and prioritised being 'under the same tent, . . . the tent of national dialogue' (Ennahda 2013e). Third, Ennahda insists that political stances be reasonable (Ennahda 2012a) and claims made be supported by arguments and proof (Ennahda 2012ag). This means that actors must adopt a non-ideological attitude, must refrain from instigation of and provocation with political or partisan motives and must not give in to the temptation of violent means (Ennahda 2011k, 2012n, 2012q, 2012r). In this context, Ennahda accused the UGTT of irresponsible behaviour, blaming it of deliberately pushing for confrontation (Ennahda 2012n, 2012y, 2012ae) and concealing political strategy behind would-be advocacy for workers' interests (Ennahda 2013ai). Similarly, it condemned attempts by some parties to exploit political events and terrorist attacks for their own partisan interests (Ennahda 2013g), a behaviour the party considered 'a crime against the country and a service to the aims of terrorists' (Ennahda 2014s).

Besides dialogue, cooperation requires concessions and compromise, as well as a commitment to the democratic transition as a matter of national interest rather than submission to 'narrow partisan or group-specific considerations' (Ennahda 2011k, 2013o) and fantasies of monopolising or clinging to power (Ennahda 2014c). Other parties should follow Ennahda's example. The party had even agreed to step down and be replaced by an independent government for the sake of the national interest (Ennahda 2013e, 2013v). On the occasion of his resignation in 2014, Ali Laarayedh emphatically stated that he was taking this step 'out of love for Tunisia, as a contribution to the success of its revolution, in fulfilment of pledges made, and within the context of affirming our Tunisian model in managing the democratic transition' (Ennahda 2014ab). As the biggest party in the NCA and in government, Ennahda could have '[clung] to the government and confront[ed] the street crowds with bigger street crowds' (Ennahda 2014b). But it chose to adopt an attitude of 'radical moderation' (Ennahda 2016j) and act accordingly, for its sacrifices were a 'small price to pay for national unity' (Ennahda 2014i).

Not all Nahdawis were in favour of this compromise position, however. When facing internal criticism, Ghannouchi complimented his followers for protecting the revolution and thanked them for their readiness to engage in dialogue and embrace an attitude of moderation (Ennahda 2013e). But such praise of the base would certainly not have been enough to preserve party coherence. Rather, 'radical moderation' became a survival strategy for a party that was painfully aware of the fate it might have to face when opting for an overly confident political attitude. The 2013 military putsch against the Muslim Brotherhood in Egypt had shown Ennahda how quickly a position of power could turn into one of weakness and even violent suppression. It knew that it had to avoid giving the impression that it fulfilled the Islamist cliché and aimed to monopolise state power. The value of this strategy became increasingly evident as crises in the rest of the Arab world deepened (Ennahda 2016j).

In contrast to its chaotic neighbourhood, Tunisians had brought about a 'victory of the middle . . . [as the] fruit of an important, but difficult, co-existence between Islamists and secularists in power' (Ennahda 2014ag).

Over the course of the post-revolution years, and especially during the struggle over the constitution and the phases of increased violence, Ennahda's radical moderation slowly transformed into an attitude which dismissed difference, shied away from confrontation and was positively depoliticising. It now promoted a 'model of consensual democracy' (Ennahda 2014f), the 'culture' or 'art of consensus' (Ennahda 2014z) or the 'spirit and methodology of consensus-building' (Ennahda 2012ai, 2014z). A constitution, Ennahda claimed, '*ne peut être bâtie sur une majorité de 51% mais sur le consensus. Elle doit porter des idées claires avec lesquelles tout le monde est d'accord*' (Ennahda 2012e).[8] Consequently, Ennahda agreed to omitting any reference to shari'a in the constitution. 'People don't agree on sharia, so we should leave it out,' it declared succinctly (Ennahda 2013i). Initially, Ennahda had warned against the danger of a consensus that neutralises politics (Ennahda 2013l) but this caveat eventually gave way to the notion of an all-encompassing consensus and radical inclusion of 'all Tunisians – Islamists, secularists, liberals, communists' (Ennahda 2014r), which did not even stop at Nidaa Tounes. Ennahda linked this politics of consensus to Tunisia's transitional justice and reconciliation process. Tunisians should not fall prey to 'a logic of revenge' (Ennahda 2014b, 2014ag). Confronted with the dangers of polarisation, extremism and terrorism, Tunisians should *a fortiori* rely on solidarity and national unity and 'unite their ranks' (Ennahda 2013r). In line with this idea of consensus, inclusion and unity, Ennahda committed itself to the idea of a National Unity Government, which was ultimately installed in February 2015 under the leadership of the 'independent' prime minister Habib Essid.[9] A second incarnation was set up under the leadership of Youssef Chahed from Nidaa Tounes in summer 2016, after terrorist violence had devastated Tunisia in 2015.

Discussion

One could be inclined to claim that Ennahda replaced the old slogan attributed to Islamists, 'Islam is the solution', with 'consensus is the solution'. As we now know (see also Chapter 3), Ennahda's methodology of consensus eventually averted neither Tunisia's authoritarian relapse nor the party's marginalisation in politics. Indeed, at the time of writing in autumn 2023, the Court of Appeal in Tunis has just sentenced Rached al-Ghannouchi to fifteen months in prison for supporting terrorism and inciting hatred. He had been arrested and jailed ahead of his trial in April 2023, after having appeared before a 'counterterrorism court' several times in the preceding months (Associated Press 2023, Middle East Eye 2023a, 2023b). The 'art of consensus' (Ennahda 2014z) was a tactical move at first but later turned into a strategic choice or 'ideological rationale' (Netterstrøm 2015, 120). It had grown out of Ennahda's decades-long experience of exclusion, imprisonment and state violence. Some argue that it is through exclusion that Ennahda may have learnt to value political freedoms and checks and balances (Cavatorta and Merone 2013), making the party a counterexample to the 'inclusion-moderation hypothesis' (Schwedler 2011). What is certain is that Ennahda sought ways to prevent secularists from capturing the state and (re)gaining a kind of hegemony that could become fatal for the party, knowing that the 'very worst repression of competing identities has often come from actors' struggling to secure their hold over the state, and the state's hold over society' (Dryzek 2005, 226).

Consequently, as I showed in the first section of this chapter, Ennahda initially prioritised the institutional and constitutional process, which the party considered the backbone of a new democratic polity. In order to achieve this in a polarised society, seeking consensus and making major concessions seemed like the only modus operandi that would avert both the danger of a stalled transition and of Ennahda being marginalised again. But, as theorists of agonistic legitimacy warn (Mouffe 2000), the pursuit of consensus may come at a price: attempts to make difference disappear simultaneously kill the political. Before that happens, though, positions of difference which can no longer be channelled through regular political processes find other forms of articulation. In the case of Tunisia and Ennahda, several such instances have been observed. First, post-revolutionary Tunisia experienced a revival of street politics (McCarthy 2019, Merone 2015). Second, Ennahda lost some of its supporters who felt that the party had given up too easily and quickly on cornerstones of an Islamist agenda. Disappointed Nahdawis sometimes turned to Salafist alternatives (Marks 2014). Besides blurring its Islamist platform, Ennahda also contributed to Salafist sidelining and its displacement from the institutional political realm. Although it engaged in a dialogue with Tunisian

Salafists at first and encouraged them to channel their claims through political parties, Ennahda abandoned this mode of interaction when political violence grew and it was expected to improve the security situation. Although Tunisian Salafists had considered the political path after the revolution, this changed after 'the political crackdown of 2013 . . . The combination of state repression and failed strategic choices made the space of contention move from the local to the regional and from political-institutional to confrontational-violent' (Merone 2017, 73). Not only did Salafists start to pursue the (international) jihadist path, Tunisians were overrepresented among the foreign fighters who joined the ISIS organisation. As socio-economically marginalised Tunisians were key supporters, Salafists' disappearance from institutional politics also implied a further exclusion of disenfranchised groups. Ennahda, then, continued on its trajectory to becoming a representative of a moderate middle class (Merone 2015).

In hindsight, what was even more problematic was that Ennahda's strategic choice does not seem to have prevented its marginalisation and even persecution. The politics of consensus went hand in hand with a discursive reiteration, reproduction and reification of the secular–Islamist divide as a core fault line and marker of identity and difference in Tunisian politics – in both Ennahda and the successor parties of the old regime (Boubekeur 2016). While it temporarily froze polarisation and allowed for a '"historic consensus"' (McCarthy 2019, 261) in the form of a new power-sharing agreement and the 2014 constitution, it did not manage to transform the antagonistic relations between Islamists and secularists. The pursuit of consensus also came at the cost of 'a sharp decline in trust towards political institutions' (McCarthy 2019, 261), which manifested in notoriously low levels of trust in the central government, parliament and especially political parties. As for Ennahda, the search for unity aimed to bridge the – certainly significant but also politically rendered – rift between Islamists and secularists and Ennahda's – publicly staged and potentially exaggerated – metamorphosis from a persecuted and repressed Islamist movement to a modern, Muslim democratic party. It consumed a good part of Ennahda's resources between 2011 and 2016 but, from today's perspective, has to be considered a failure.

Some suggest that the struggles framed in terms of identity politics may, at a certain point, also have become a welcome battlefield which could plausibly be prioritised over but also serve as a distraction from other arguably more pressing questions. Tunisian political elites opted for a conservative transition pathway which avoided 'costly and potentially explosive issues, such as structural economic reform and transitional justice' (Boubekeur 2016, 109). In 2014, the World Bank stated that, while Tunisia acted as a 'role model for other developing countries' until 2010, the revolution had revealed that 'the Tunisian model had serious flaws' (World Bank 2014, 26). Many of Tunisia's economic deficits came to light only after the ousting of the Ben Ali regime. And while the dramatic development of pertinent indicators post-2010 revealed the seriousness of the country's socio-economic situation,[10] this was neglected by political elites in Tunisia (just as it was in other post-Arab-uprising countries), who 'asked for patience, since economic recovery [would] take time and [needed], in particular, political stability' (Weipert-Fenner and Wolff 2015, 1).

Yet it would be too easy to conclude that Ennahda simply ignored social and economic questions. The dire economic situation and social hardship experienced by many Tunisians could, of course, not be glossed over forever and Ennahda was aware of that. During the period under analysis, the party did make proposals for economic policies and social justice but these were mainly confined to the 2011 and 2014 electoral campaigns rather than being systematically integrated into day-to-day politics. The party calls its economic model 'social capitalism' (Ennahda 2014a, 2014e) and, in particular, emphasised the need to strengthen the private sector in order to move away 'from a rentier economy to a genuine competitive economy through a definitive break with nepotism, clientelism and instrumentalisation of political relations in the economic field' (Ennahda 2014z). Moreover, Ennahda tried to position Tunisia as a trade partner in the international arena, placing an emphasis on building trade relations and gaining access to European markets, in particular by achieving the status of a privileged partner with the EU (Ennahda 2011b). Here, it insisted that any 'external relations with friends [must be built] on the basis of partnership and equality to serve the interests of the Tunisian people' (Ennahda 2012s), rejecting the idea of conditional aid and Tunisia's international relations having any kind of postcolonial configuration. It also proposed that Tunisia become a metaphorical bridge between Europe and Africa with all the economic potential that would bring (Ennahda 2011i, 2015i,

Interview 2). However, with an increase in terrorism in Tunisia and Europe and the worsening of the Tunisian socio-economic situation around 2015 and 2016, Ennahda changed its 'pitch' towards the Europeans, asserting that they should have an interest in preserving the Tunisian model as the only remaining democracy in the region through 'greater investment and [economic] support' so as to enable the government to 'address the needs of young people, provide an alternative to ISIS, and build a prosperous society on sustainable foundations that can be a model for the region' (Ennahda 2015e). Thus, the argument was that democracy needed to be nourished by socio-economic development – otherwise, desperate young men would turn to violence.

Besides these (rare) direct allusions to a more just international economic order and the need to cooperate in the fight against terrorism, Ennahda's legitimacy discourse does not make the international order itself its core subject. However, the overhearing global audience does play a significant role for a party that is eager to demonstrate its commitment to democracy and, indeed, liberal values while simultaneously promoting the compatibility of its version of Islamic democracy with widely accepted standards of legitimacy. To put it in a nutshell, Ennahda sought recognition for both the party's identity as Muslim democrats who are 'freedom loving people' (Ennahda 2014t) and the Tunisian model of democracy – and it did so by demonstrating that its ideas on legitimacy were entirely compatible with Western standards of order. For this dual recognition project, first, Ennahda presented itself as a pragmatic and problem-oriented political actor that understood the Tunisian zeitgeist: 'Les gens [veulent] un parti qui parle des problèmes quotidiens, de la vie des familles et des personnes, et non pas un parti qui leur parle du jugement dernier, du paradis, etc.' (Ennahda 2016d).[11] Accordingly, Ennahda transformed itself from an Islamist movement into a professional party, a Tunisian version of the 'Christian Democrats in Germany[, who] are a good model for us [regarding the question of] how religious values can be the basis of political action without ever becoming an end in themselves' (Ennahda 2016k).[12] Second, Ennahda made abundantly clear that it accepts the universality of certain values. It accepts the framework of international law, including human rights; it holds actors responsible for acting in accordance with these norms, as demonstrated by the party's outspoken support of popular revolutions against dictatorships in its neighbourhood and its public denouncement of human rights violations (see, for example, Ennahda 2012m, 2013m, 2015q). Beyond these core values and institutions – of both the Tunisian and the world order – there are particularist elements which need to be mirrored in the specific political order a society chooses. Different societies have different histories and consequently cannot be subjected to one normative model of democracy. As such, an Arab Islamic version of a democratic political order needs to be found for Tunisia. In this regard, parts of Ennahda's proposal are surprisingly similar to concepts of a postsecular society as seen in Western discourse (Habermas 2009). Finally, and this is where Ennahda's view converges with agonistic views on international relations (Mouffe 2009, 2013), such a plurality of community-based orders can only exist in a world order which is based on sovereign equality (see Chapter 4), accommodates difference and does not strive towards hegemony (Interview 4). Accordingly, and as Chapter 6 will show, Ennahda's utopia for the world order is a story of liberation not only from dictatorship but also from colonial and postcolonial domination.

Hezbollah

In a speech delivered in March 2016, Hezbollah's secretary general, Hassan Nasrallah, denounced what he perceived as hypocritical stigmatisation of his organisation. Referring to Hezbollah's military activities to combat the ISIS organisation in Syria, Nasrallah exclaimed: '[W]e are fighting the terrorist organization which is labeled by the world as a terrorist organization. How come we are labeled as terrorists? How come we are condemned? How come our martyrs are condemned?' (Hezbollah 2016k, 2016n). His irritation, it seems, was not only caused by the perceived misrecognition of being classified as a terrorist organisation (Pfeifer 2021) but also by Hezbollah being placed on the same level as ISIS. Nasrallah's words certainly express some indignation at the West's failure to recognise the differences in the resort to violence and its legitimacy. And indeed, the distinction between legitimate and illegitimate violence is the dominating topic in Hezbollah's discourse on legitimacy. This is due not only to the nature of Hezbollah's activities, often referred to as a 'hybrid' between political and military activity (Azani 2013), but also to the context in which Hezbollah operates. It is regularly involved in armed conflict, ranging from military skirmishes on the Lebanese–Israeli border to active fighting over several years in the Syrian Civil War. The focus on violence is therefore not surprising.

What may be more remarkable is the lack of ideas on political legitimacy and authority, as well as their comprehensive justification, in Hezbollah's discourse – especially since the party was part of all the governments active in the period under investigation in this book (2011–16). From Nasrallah's speeches alone, one would be hard pressed to gain a picture of Hezbollah's plans for designing political order and concrete policies in Lebanon. Indeed, this is one finding of the analysis. It is not a priority for the party to shape domestic policymaking or find solutions to economic, social, environmental and political problems. Rather, Hezbollah's goal is to maintain societal peace in Lebanon's domestic politics, at least to such an extent that domestic politics does not interfere with its core project: resistance. Hezbollah draws a line between the realms of domestic and regional/international politics. The former is a sphere in which peaceful means of solving conflict and organising political and social life have to be found. While Hezbollah proposes some institutional and output-oriented methods of achieving this, this chapter will focus on its ideas on community-based and dialogue-based legitimacy, which are more prominent and important in its discourse. As for regional/international politics, Hezbollah perceives Lebanon's regional and international environment as downright hostile. The logic of conflict which determines these realms dictates the use of violent means within certain limits. In what Hezbollah considers legitimate and illegitimate violence, its self-identification as a resistance and 'jihadist' group plays an important role.[13] This section will focus on what Hezbollah considers legitimate violence, which essentially comprises different versions of resistance. The threat scenarios which make resistance necessary in the first place and, thus, a more detailed account of how Hezbollah characterises the conflictual international environment will be presented in Chapter 6.

Community-based Legitimacy: Form Follows Identity

Hezbollah's version of community-based legitimacy is not a unitary concept but rather illustrates the need to disaggregate the term 'community'. For Hezbollah makes suggestions about legitimate political order to and claims to speak for at least three groups. The audiences the party addresses and communities it purportedly represents correspond to different layers in Hezbollah's social identity: its Shi'i, Lebanese and Arab-Muslim aspects. What links these three layers is Hezbollah's core identity as a resistance group. Where its legitimacy claims are on the verge of becoming self-contradictory or being traded off against each other, resistance, exalted as a noble cause, serves as the crucial normative criterion for choosing one claim over the other.

Hezbollah's ideas of a legitimate political order for the Lebanese community could be described as a pragmatic concession to the reality and inescapability of religious difference in the country. It considers politics on the basis of sectarianism as counterproductive and seeks to eventually transcend it as the foundation of the Lebanese political system. But it still accepts this status quo of Lebanese political life and deems it necessary to take the fears and interests of every community into account: 'Well we have this mentality . . . [T]his is our country. The people are our people. All the sects are our people whether Shi'a, Sunnites, Druze or Christians in all regions. We are a people who want to live together' (Hezbollah 2011i). It sometimes even seems as if Hezbollah not only recognises but even appreciates religious pluralism. And while it considers the 1989 Taif Agreement, concluded one year before the end of the Lebanese Civil War and regulating the representation of sects in the post-war political order, the product of a suboptimal settlement and in serious need of reform, Hezbollah also acknowledges the risks involved in changing the precarious modus vivendi. It therefore stands behind the agreement (Hezbollah 2011a, 2013c) and only advocates reforms that give due consideration to the fears of sects. One reform Hezbollah supports is the establishment of a proportional electoral system (Hezbollah 2012b, 2013f). At the same time, the party understands why Christians in Lebanon are afraid of losing their influence, given the crimes perpetrated against their fellow believers in the Middle East (Hezbollah 2013c, 2013f), and argues that these fears must be taken into account in any reform.

Sectarianism and the real-life experience thereof thus determine the general condition of the whole country. If relations are good, a culture of cooperation can be developed; if they are bad, 'nothing in this country may move forward properly or be reformed' (Hezbollah 2011i). This is also why religious moderation and interreligious dialogue have to be practised, violence must be condemned irrespective of the sectarian affiliation of the group against which it is directed, and movies, cartoons and books that deliberately offend one religious community are dangerous (Hezbollah 2011g, 2013f, 2014g). The sectarian composition of society may not be abused for political purposes, sects should not be played off against one another and conflicts should not be declared sectarian in nature when they are about something else. According to Nasrallah, none of the contemporary conflicts and wars are fought due to sectarian difference, but are rather a result of political disagreement or attempts to seize power (Hezbollah 2013d, 2013f, 2014g).

Despite sectarian differences, one of Hezbollah's declared goals is to build a unified Lebanese 'community and . . . a nation as a prelude for building a state for it later on' (Hezbollah 2011h, 2016m). Besides, building a Lebanese nation will also bring about broad solidarity with the resistance (Hezbollah 2013f, 2014a, 2015k, 2016m). This does not mean that everyone has to fight. But the Lebanese should support the resistance morally and make it their own cause (Hezbollah 2013b). Nasrallah proudly reports on the significant amount of solidarity Hezbollah experiences among the families of the martyrs within the Shi'i community (Hezbollah 2016c). Yet, the victories of the resistance were for all the Lebanese people and not just for one sect. They are a national achievement (Hezbollah 2011e, 2011i, 2012c). The resistance should be honoured in a similar way to the Lebanese army, for both consist of 'men of our Lebanese nation and patriotic culture' (Hezbollah 2013a) and both make sacrifices for all the people of Lebanon, irrespective of their sect (Hezbollah 2011b, 2014b, 2014g). And indeed, the majority of the Lebanese population support the resistance in spite of all the wicked attempts to break it (Hezbollah 2011i, 2011j) – or so Hezbollah claims. While, following the 2006 July War, support for the resistance was very high among the non-Shi'i Lebanese, this has fallen since Hezbollah became involved in the Syrian conflict.

When speaking to his fellow Lebanese citizens, Nasrallah gives his assurance that Hezbollah no longer has an interest in building an Islamic state in Lebanon. 'True in our early days back in 1982 and 1983, there were a group of brethrens [sic] . . . who made speeches and talked about the choice of the Islamic Republic in Lebanon . . . Now [these] young men in Hizbullah are a bit [grey]-haired,' Nasrallah has explained, reassuring his audience that Hezbollah has now 'entered deeper into the Lebanese status quo' (Hezbollah 2011h). However, the party still accepts the authority of *walī al-faqīh*, the supreme jurist or jurist-theologian, and 'clerical custodianship' (Qassem 2010, 119). In Nasrallah's speeches, the topic is hardly evoked. The only context in which this allegiance plays a role is when Nasrallah refers to fatwas Hezbollah had requested from clerics in Iran or Iraq on specific matters, for example regarding the use of weapons (Hezbollah 2013g). Besides, Nasrallah states that he seeks legal authorisation for basic political decisions. For instance, Hezbollah would not have taken the decision to participate in democratic elections without 'the religious and legitimate justification from the senior scholars' (Hezbollah 2011h). But this does not mean, Nasrallah assures his audience, that Hezbollah has

> no political choice other than establishing an Islamic country in Lebanon . . . In fact, one of the aspects of Islam's greatness, flexibility and vitality as a religion, doctrine and legislation is that any Muslim group in any country with special conditions would enjoy special guidance. Things are not closed at all. (Hezbollah 2011h)

Rather, clerics interpret Islamic principles for the specific context in which Hezbollah operates and formulate their guidance accordingly. This is also why Nasrallah categorically rejects the notion that Iran seeks hegemony over Lebanon or forces others to make certain decisions (Hezbollah 2015i).

That said, Nasrallah still has a lot of praise for the Islamic Republic of Iran as an example from which others can learn. It is a 'modern state which joins originality and modernity' (Hezbollah 2012e) and which is 'based on the views and the will of this people besides the civilization, culture and religion of this people' (Hezbollah 2011a). In this sense, it is also the right system for Iranian society, according to Hezbollah. While the supreme jurist is qualified for his position by virtue of his merits as a 'first-class man of law' (Hezbollah 2011a), as determined by an elected group of expert scholars, 'all the primary authorities in Iran are subject to popular elections' (Hezbollah 2011a). It is therefore beyond doubt that the Iranian political regime acknowledges the Iranian popular will – and in a much more reliable way than is the case in Lebanon. Hezbollah 'hopes that similar democratic events (as in Iran) would happen in the Arab and Muslim worlds' (Hezbollah 2013g). However biased Nasrallah's assessment of the Iranian political system may be, it demonstrates that he needs to justify the system's worth by referring to its democratic qualities and suitability for the Iranian people rather than to religious principles and doctrine.

Finally, Nasrallah elaborates on legitimate orders for the region and the Arab and Muslim people living in it. In his view, two resistance projects are necessary to build a legitimate political order. The first is the Palestinian cause. Nasrallah believes 'that every Palestinian, Arab, Muslim, and Christian has a national, popular, religious, convictional and ethical responsibility towards al-Quds and its future, identity and destiny' (Hezbollah 2012f). Arabs and Muslims cannot accept 'that Palestine is "Jewish"' (Hezbollah 2013b) and they have to refrain from a naturalisation of Palestinian refugees in third countries and from any acts of recognition or normalisation towards the Israeli state (Hezbollah 2012f, 2016k). No situation 'justifies giving in to the enemy, recognizing the legitimacy of the enemy, accepting the enemy, and agreeing to give the land to the enemy, besides . . . making commercial, diplomatic, and security relations with this enemy' (Hezbollah 2016l). Negotiations are no longer an adequate means of interaction. For past experience has shown that Israeli promises of talks were accompanied by actions to the contrary, such as the building of new settlements (Hezbollah 2011j, 2014e). Moreover, Israel has made the status of Jerusalem a non-negotiable item, which renders further talks futile (Hezbollah 2011l, 2012f). Any so-called peace agreement would actually be a settlement according to conditions laid down by the Israelis, especially when negotiated with the help of supposedly neutral mediators, such as US presidents or the UN, both of whom Hezbollah considers clearly biased (Hezbollah 2012c, 2013b, 2013c, 2014c).

This makes resistance the only remaining legitimate choice for Arab and Muslim peoples and countries. Any action must be evaluated according to its contribution to the Palestinian cause, the 'ruling norm in this time' (Hezbollah 2012d). The only countries that have credibly committed to this cause, by showing solidarity with the transnational resistance, providing unconditional and generous (financial) support and delivering weapons, are Iran and Syria (Hezbollah 2011h, 2012b, 2012c, 2013b, 2013c, 2014d, 2014e, 2015i, 2016c). Their contribution was critical to the success of the resistance in Lebanon and Palestine. Those Arabs and Muslims who are not capable of providing the resistance with active support and fulfilling their 'direct jihadi obligations' (Hezbollah 2011j) should stand by the Palestinians financially and morally (Hezbollah 2011j, 2012b, 2014d, 2015b). In reality, however, many Arab states acted like 'submissive tails' (Hezbollah 2011e) of the US and Israel instead and sold out the Palestinian cause for their own advantage, thereby destroying the nation's hope of ever triumphing over Israel (Hezbollah 2012d, 2014d, 2015i, 2016l). The Gulf states in particular traded US support for their regimes and 'the guarantee for [their] thrones . . . [for] defending "Israel", protecting "Israel", and not harming the existence of "Israel", the entity of "Israel", and the persistence of "Israel"' (Hezbollah 2016k). They did not even try to hide their relations with Israel anymore (Hezbollah 2016c), offering 'gains . . . for free to the "Israelis"' (Hezbollah 2016e). Here, Nasrallah was referring to instances of alignment between Israeli and Saudi positions which started in 2015 with their common opposition to the nuclear deal with Iran (JCPOA) and continued throughout 2016 with the visit of a Saudi delegation to the Israeli foreign minister and Knesset members in Jerusalem. These rapprochements between Saudi Arabia and its allies and Israel anticipated the 2020 Abraham Accords signed by Israel, Bahrain and the UAE, as well as Morocco and Sudan, and backed by the Saudis.

The second resistance project is that of the Arab peoples against their rulers as manifested in the mass protests and revolutions in the context of the Arab uprisings. It is important to note that this project is secondary to the people's duties towards Palestine. When judging a political regime, there are

> two angles. The first angle is the stance of that Arab regime [on] . . . the Arab–'Israeli' conflict . . . The second angle is the absence of any hope for reform at the domestic level – when the regime is closed to all doors, windows or even small gaps for reform for the benefit of the peoples of these countries. (Hezbollah 2011l, 2012d, 2015e)

Only if a regime neither supported the Palestinian cause nor showed a willingness to make concessions to the protesting masses did Hezbollah consider a revolution legitimate. And indeed, it welcomed the protests in Tunisia, Egypt, Bahrain, Yemen and Libya, calling for solidarity with the people in the streets and descrying a window of opportunity to free the region from a number of regimes that were submissive to Israel and the US (Hezbollah 2011e, 2011j). While cautioning against attempts by foreign powers to 'confiscate' these revolutions, Nasrallah considered them genuinely popular rebellions that might work in favour of the resistance and help 'Iran and Syria . . . gain new allies, advocates and members in [the] axis [of resistance]' (Hezbollah 2011k). After the initial euphoria faded, Hezbollah realised with regret that the issue was of little relevance to the new and resurgent old regimes (Hezbollah 2013b). Even worse, some societies in the region were dragged into civil war. '[W]hat we are experiencing today as a nation and as an *Ummah* is the most dangerous situation ever since the occupation of Palestine due to the systematic destruction that took place in our region,' Nasrallah wearily announced (Hezbollah 2014d).

With all the enthusiastic support given to the protesting masses in virtually every country except Syria, how did Hezbollah legitimise its intervention on the side of the Assad regime? In 2011 and 2012, Nasrallah conceded that the Syrian system was in need of reform and that a political dialogue among different groups had to be initiated – a position which, he claimed, Hezbollah shared with the Assad regime (Hezbollah 2011h, 2011l, 2012d, 2013a). Yet, he continued, the constellation of international interests had rendered both impossible. A Western–Israeli-led and Gulf-supported coalition had decided to try and topple the Syrian regime. In such a situation of threat to the incumbent regime, negotiations were no longer an option and, thus, war was imposed on the Syrians (Hezbollah 2011l, 2012d, 2013a, 2014a). According to Nasrallah, the outbreak of the war only strengthened the popular support for the regime which had always existed (Hezbollah 2011h, 2014c, 2014h). What had initially seemed like an opposition camp in a divided society (Hezbollah 2013g) turned out to be militant groups which did not represent the people (Hezbollah 2011h, 2012b). Further, Hezbollah's support for the Assad regime relied on the assertion of Assad's merits with regard to the Palestinian cause: 'Syria has been the cherisher of the Resistance, so the Resistance can't stand still while that cherisher is being ruined' (Hezbollah 2013a, 2013b). Syria was of strategic importance to Palestine and consequently also to the 'Arab nation' (Hezbollah 2011l, 2013a, 2014c).

As can be seen from this discussion, Hezbollah's gold standard for evaluating the legitimacy of rule and political action is whether or not it advances the cause of resistance. But the regional conflict dynamics brought a change in Hezbollah's priorities, as Chapter 6 will elaborate in more detail. Nasrallah now tried to rally Arabs and Muslims of the region around the common fight against 'Takfirism', which, according to Hezbollah, dominated the Syrian opposition by 2014 at the latest (Hezbollah 2014a). But the reaction of the neighbouring regimes was yet another blow to what Hezbollah perceived as the project of building an Arab and Muslim nation, instilling the community with solidarity (Hezbollah 2014e, 2015c, 2015f) and uniting it against the 'Takfirists' and their backers. 'It is time for Muslims, Arabs, and the Islamic world to tell the Arab Kingdom of Saudi Arabia: That's enough, and enough is enough,' Nasrallah canvassed (Hezbollah 2015l). For the 'region has one destiny, one history, one future, and one present. Our children, our grandchildren, and our great grandchildren will remain living in suffering if we [do] not assume [this] responsibility' (Hezbollah 2015d, 2015g). The fact that so many did not follow his calls to offer help in Palestine, Syria, Iraq and Yemen was a sign of their cowardice and showed that they had 'nothing to do with Arabs, Arab identity, Arab chivalry, and Arab dignity' (Hezbollah 2016k).

Legitimate and Illegitimate Violence: The Heart of the Matter

It is remarkable how strongly Nasrallah links legitimacy to the resort to violence, even when he is not explicitly dealing with the question of legitimate violence. Where he does address this issue, however, a complex normative structure becomes visible, which makes a clear distinction between necessary and unacceptable forms of violence and sometimes resembles the ethics of just-war theory (Kızılkaya 2017). The overrepresentation of claims to (il)legitimate violence in Hezbollah's discourse are, on the one hand, indicative of the intensity of the regional transformations the 'Middle East' witnessed after the Arab uprisings. This was a phase which consisted of changing alliances among states and non-state actors (Darwich 2021a), as well as the internationalisation and military escalation of conflicts in Libya, Syria, Iraq and Yemen (Ahram 2020). As Hezbollah considered its core interests to be jeopardised by some of the developments during this period, and notably anticipated further damage to the 'axis of resistance' (see Chapter 6), the delegitimation of some forms of violence and simultaneous legitimation of others was part of offering, or trying to discursively impose, a 'compass' of interpretation for the political developments in the region to a regional audience. On the other hand, it also specifically addressed the Shiʿi community in Lebanon. Here, it was not only about Hezbollah selling its own version of the story and safeguarding abstract support. Rather, the party had to make it palatable to its constituency that families should still send their fathers, husbands and sons to fight for the

'Islamic resistance' – which used to be a militant project against Israel and for the liberation of Palestine (Malmvig 2021). How, then, did it transpire that Lebanese fighters were now being deployed to Syria to engage in combat against fellow Muslims and Arabs, rather than Israelis?

Hezbollah regularly alludes to its foundation and military victories against Israel in an almost mythological fashion (Hezbollah 2011i, 2011k, 2014e), claiming legitimacy for its resort to force against an external enemy to defend the Lebanese people – a task which neither the Lebanese army nor UNIFIL had proven capable of in the past (Hezbollah 2012c, 2014e). Hezbollah sometimes emphasises the Islamic resistance in this context, especially when denouncing the Christian collaborators who had formed a militia (the South Lebanon Army) to support the Israeli occupation of Lebanon during and after the civil war (Hezbollah 2014b). And even though there is a multiconfessional brigade within the Lebanese resistance (Alagha 2011, 160, 188–9), foregrounding the Islamic character of the resistance provides Hezbollah with additional religious sources of legitimation. Becoming a martyr when standing up to oppression is not only an honour but a religious duty. Living under a system of injustice or in a state of oppression is unacceptable and leaves only two options: 'either victory or martyrdom' (Hezbollah 2011g).

It is here that Shi'i history and symbolism come to bear in Hezbollah's discourse. The most important reference is to the martyrdom of Imam Husayn ibn 'Ali at the Battle of Karbala, which is commemorated every year on 'Ashura' Day, the tenth night of Muharram, which is the first month of the Islamic calendar. At the Battle of Karbala in Iraq in 680, Husayn and his followers fought the caliph Yazid. The latter had been appointed caliph by his father Mu'awiya, the first caliph after the four *rāshidūn* or 'rightly guided' caliphs. However, Hassan – grandson of the prophet and son of 'Ali, the fourth caliph, as well as Husayn's brother – had claimed succession to 'Ali. He eventually agreed with Mu'awiya that the latter would not appoint a new caliph but let the Muslim world choose one. As he considered this treaty to have been broken and, therefore, the rule of Yazid to be illegitimate, Husayn refused to pledge allegiance to the newly appointed caliph. For him and his followers, only descent from the Prophet (*ahl al-bayt*, followers of the House of the Prophet) qualified a person to be the rightful successor and guide for the people. In reaction to this opposition, Yazid attacked Husayn's caravan, killing him and his companions.

This incident was more than just murder (Jafri 2000, 130–222). 'It was also an ideological battle between a group of principled individuals and a militarily powerful political administration, making Husayn the ultimate tragic hero figure' (A. J. Hussain 2005, 79).

The story of Husayn and his family plays an important role in Hezbollah's idea of legitimate violence. Husayn's words and actions are emphatically cited whenever steadfastness and commitment to the resistance are demanded from Hezbollah's constituency, its fighters and their families. For instance, Nasrallah quotes Husayn's words when facing Yazid:

> 'The bastard son of a bastard has put us before two choices: war or humiliation. Humiliation, how remote! Allah does not accept that to befall us, neither his Prophet, the believers nor the zealous and haughty souls. They don't accept that we favor the obedience of the ignoble to the death of the noble.' (Hezbollah 2011g, 2012d, 2014f)

Resistance is a jihadi duty (Hezbollah 2015f, 2016a, 2016m) and is described not as a project of war but an attempt to bring calm to Lebanon and the region (Hezbollah 2011f, 2014a, 2015a). It is a project of self-defence. Of course, in order to understand what it is that should be resisted, the state of injustice and those who orchestrate it have to be identified first. Similarly, the community being defended also has to be specified. Indeed, several hegemonic schemes were all devised for the region at the same time, schemes which, however, turned out over time to be manifestations of one big plan – at least that is how Nasrallah reconstructed the events over the course of the years, as Chapter 6 will demonstrate. The corresponding resistance projects are legitimate – as long as they follow certain norms.

A first and second norm could be described as the proportionality and rationality of violence. 'Everything is being tackled relatively and in a proportional way. The resistance has courage, capability, and wisdom, too. It considers precisely what it can do to prevent this status quo that the enemy seeks to consolidate at the border' (Hezbollah 2014b, 2014e). The resistance thus needs to adapt to the respective context and adopt different forms depending on the (stage of) conflict. With regard to relations with Israel in the 2010s, such a rational use of force consisted in maintaining a balance of power or mutual deterrence in southern Lebanon (Hezbollah 2015a). While Hezbollah claims that it has a right to retaliation, not every provocation calls for a reaction. Where they are necessary, acts of retaliation have to be measured and precise operations with specific goals. An example of this is the counterattack against the Israelis in the Sheb'a Farms after they had targeted a Hezbollah vehicle in the Golan in January 2015 (Hezbollah 2015a). Furthermore, retaliation has to follow the principle of 'paying back in kind'. For example, Hezbollah claims that it would never kill a civilian, diplomat or recruit in revenge for the death of one of its fighters (Hezbollah 2012d, 2015j, 2016h). This could be seen as alluding to another norm, the protection of civilians. That said, whereas Hezbollah's commitment to this norm on a discursive and practical level has existed since 1996 (Dionigi 2014, 111, 157), upholding it, even rhetorically, proved difficult in the context of the cruelty and atrocities committed against civilians by the Assad regime.

The question of civilian protection was not the problem when it came to Hezbollah's military involvement in the Syrian conflict. When Hezbollah resorted to acts of retaliation, the aim was to show Israel that the armed group's power and vigilance with respect to 'the enemy' had not been diminished by its activities in the Syrian war. At the same time, such a demonstration of force had to be measured so that it would not provoke acts of Israeli revenge and endanger the Lebanese people. Indeed, Hezbollah tried to avert two military constellations. First, it was wary of miscalculations similar to the one that had occurred in the 2006 July War, when Israel reacted to a Hezbollah attack on a border patrol by launching large-scale operations (Norton 2014, 136). Second, it wanted to avoid actually getting caught up in a two-front war in Syria and against Israel (Ranstorp 2016, 46) – while maintaining the credibility of its deterrents vis-à-vis Israel and reassuring its constituency, in particular the southern Lebanese, that any Israeli attack would be prioritised. This balancing act rendered the relative calm between Israel and Hezbollah precarious, at some moments more than at others (Noe 2017).

It also entailed complicated rhetorical manoeuvres on the part of Hezbollah's leadership, which tried to convince the Lebanese Shi'i community that the group's engagement in Syria, too, was an act of self-defence – and that it would not only not harm but rather constituted a core part of the resistance project. This proved particularly difficult at the start of Hezbollah's activities in Syria in 2013, when neither the 'Takfirist' threat nor Israeli involvement had become significant enough to dominate the regional and global public debate. While the international concern about Salafi-jihadist groups only started growing with ISIS's significant territorial gains and its active dissemination of media coverage depicting the atrocities it committed (Pfeifer and Günther 2021), Hezbollah cited the 'Takfirist' threat as the reason for its military engagement in Syria from the beginning: 'Obviously, the Takfiri current is dominant among the Syrian opposition,' Nasrallah declared in May 2013 (Hezbollah 2013a). It may, therefore, not be a coincidence that Hezbollah officially announced its military support for Assad when ISIS split from Jabhat al-Nusra in spring 2013, which indicated a diversification of the Salafi-jihadist spectrum and could be read as anticipating a potential radicalisation and escalation of violence. But other evidence suggests that the decision to deploy fighters was related to other events in 2013: rebel attacks on Lebanese Shi'i villages in Syria, the extension of fighting to the area of Sayyida Zeynab's shrine[14] in Rif Dimashq governorate and an assault on an armed Hezbollah convoy (Hashem 2013).

In its public discourse, Hezbollah legitimised its military engagement in Syria by means of several arguments, combining the right to self-defence with the resistance culture and, later on, the religious duty to fight 'Takfirism'. It seems that this last argument on its own was simply not enough to convince the Lebanese audience. It was therefore linked to the construction of an imminent double threat to Lebanon and all Lebanese people, irrespective of their sect, posed by Israel and the 'Takfirists' (Hezbollah 2013a, 2014b, 2014c, 2014e, 2015b, 2016l, see also Chapter 4): 'Yes, we have engaged in combat to defend Syria and Lebanon's people, territories, and economy,' Nasrallah elaborated (Hezbollah 2013g). Fighting in Israeli-occupied Golan was already very much in keeping with the resistance narrative (Hezbollah 2013b). But Hezbollah went further: 'The battle over Syria must be understood not as a battle of existence for us as Hizbullah only, but also a battle of existence for Lebanon, Syria, Palestine, the Palestinian cause, and the entire resistance project in the region' (Hezbollah 2013e). Defending the Syrian regime became an imperative for the resistance project 'because if Syria [were to be] lost, Palestine would be lost too' (Hezbollah 2015b). While this line of argumentation may only have convinced the hard core of Hezbollah's supporters, the party could also reference several violent incidents at the Lebanese–Syrian border to make the case that Lebanese sovereignty was jeopardised (Hezbollah 2014e, 2015a). 'It is our right and the right of the people of Bekaa and especially Baalbeck-Hermel to look for a day in which our barren areas, borders, and the gates of our villages and towns do not have terrorist groups,' Nasrallah declared (Hezbollah 2015h).

Hezbollah's critics, however, told a different story. Their view was that it was Hezbollah's activities that had provoked the attacks by Salafi jihadists in the first place. Politicians from different parties were angry and asserted, almost regretfully, that the resistance, once so dear to any Lebanese citizen and accepted by all parties, had lost all credibility since Hezbollah started fighting in the Syrian war (Wieland 2016, 176–7, Zelin 2016, 54–6). Nasrallah attempted to frame Hezbollah's mission as being an act of collective self-defence against a 'Takfirist' project that threatened the whole region and the *umma*: 'Fighting in defense of Aleppo is fighting in defense of the rest of Syria and in defense of Damascus. It is also fighting in defense of Lebanon, Iraq, and Jordan' (Hezbollah 2016g, 2016h). The religious line of Nasrallah's argumentation gained importance when the Shi'i religious authorities in Najaf issued a fatwa which 'called for defensive Jihad and for confronting Daesh' (Hezbollah 2015g) in mid-2015, encouraging every Muslim to fight 'Takfirism' with or without arms and calling for the protection of the Muslim *umma* and its symbols (Hezbollah 2015c, 2016k). This is when Hezbollah self-reportedly decided to extend its operations to Iraq and support the country's government in its struggle against ISIS, too (Hezbollah 2016k). It called upon Arab countries and the Muslim *umma* to assume their responsibility and join Hezbollah in the battles in Syria and Iraq. For the 'Takfirist' project would have disastrous consequences for the region (Hezbollah 2015c, 2015d, 2015h). Nasrallah even went so far as to predict that 'Takfirism' would create 'a new Nakba which is greater and more dangerous [than the first one]' (Hezbollah 2015g, 2015h).[15] Referencing the foundation of the state of Israel and the mass displacement of Palestinians, and, thus, what Hezbollah considers the root cause of the resistance project, illustrates how vigorously the party tried to mobilise support for its actions in Syria.

Besides presenting the fight against ISIS and similar Salafi-jihadist groups as a necessity, the party also never tired of emphasising that it did not seek war but rather considered it as a last resort, which is the third norm of legitimate violence (Hezbollah 2013g). The best proof of this, Hezbollah claimed, was that it assumed a responsibility that actually lay with the Arab states and their militaries even though its core project was the resistance against Israel (Hezbollah 2015d, 2015f). The norm of last resort is closely connected to proportionality and rationality: Hezbollah did not take the decision lightly to become involved in Syria but evaluated the situation carefully, in particular with regard to the identities of the rebels, collected evidence and made a rational choice (Hezbollah 2013e, 2013g, 2014a, 2014b, 2016k). Having taken a political stance on the Syrian situation, Hezbollah saw, at some point, that dialogue was not leading anywhere and political solutions were no longer an option (Hezbollah 2013a, 2016g, 2016k), which meant that non-violent means had been exhausted. Upon the invitation of the Syrian regime, it began its engagement in the civil war. Hezbollah then reacted to developments on the ground. It started with a limited intervention, adapted its goals and strategies, and only slowly increased its activities according to the needs of the battlefield (Hezbollah 2013g, 2014a). 'We got engaged in the battle pursuant to a clear diagnosis which never did change; it was rather asserted by daily evidences,' Nasrallah explained (Hezbollah 2015d, 2015g). Hezbollah's insistence that it had been asked first by the Assad regime (Hezbollah 2013g, 2014a) and then, later, by the Iraqi government to join forces with the former points to another norm: the resort to the use of force needs to be sanctioned by the consent of the respective incumbent regime. This is also why the Turkish invasion of Syria, Israeli operations in Syria and the US-led war in Iraq launched in 2003 are considered illegitimate – they were not interventions by invitation (Hezbollah 2013b, 2014a).

Indeed, Hezbollah's normative compass is completed by those forms of violence that it considers illegitimate. A war can be illegitimate because its cause is unjust or because it resorts to illegitimate means, such as targeting civilians, using certain kinds of weapon or engaging certain types of fighters. Nasrallah's verbal condemnations usually refer to wars waged by Israel, with the support of the US and other Western states, against Arab states and peoples. He accuses Israel of illegal border violations, wars of aggression in Lebanon in 2006 and Gaza in 2008–9 and 2014, which sometimes had no other goal than to make people submit to the Israeli will, the lack of proportionality in its use of violence, the targeting of civilians and the commission of war crimes

(Hezbollah 2011d, 2011f, 2011k, 2012b, 2012c, 2013e, 2014a, 2014b, 2014d, 2014e, 2016l). The virtually exclusive focus on Israel almost entirely disappears from Hezbollah's discourse in 2015, when the Saudi war against Yemen, launched in that year, begins to dominate Nasrallah's normative reflections on state conduct in war. He considers the war on Yemen, launched by a Saudi-led coalition and supported by the US, to be an act of aggression (Hezbollah 2015f, 2015g, 2015h, 2015i, 2015l).

While the Saudis attempt to legitimise their intervention, initially executed through an air campaign and only later followed by ground operations, the reasons given are fabricated, according to Nasrallah. First, the Saudis cannot provide any proof of their claim that their intervention was a pre-emptive war made necessary by the emergence of a new security threat in Yemen (Hezbollah 2015i). Nasrallah emphasised that not only were the Yemenis a very poor people, but their military capabilities were also severely limited (Hezbollah 2015i), making the war a very unequal confrontation between the Saudis with 'more tanks than soldiers . . . and barefoot Yemenis' (Hezbollah 2016n). According to Hezbollah, it was obvious that there was no threat. The second argument presented by Saudi Arabia was that it wanted to restore the rule of the 'legitimate' president, Abdrabbuh Mansur Hadi. To start with, Hezbollah did not consider Hadi the legitimate president of Yemen (Hezbollah 2015i), and indeed this is also a contested question among scholars of international law (Ruys and Ferro 2016). But even if he were, Nasrallah continued to argue, waging a war to restore the power of a president was simply not proportionate (Hezbollah 2015i, 2015l). Finally, the Saudis tried to cast doubt on the 'Arabism' of the Yemeni people, suggesting that Iran secretly held sway over Yemen (Hezbollah 2015l). They even questioned the Islamic identity of the Yemenis, claiming that they were a threat to the holy shrines in Mecca (Hezbollah 2015l, 2016f). To Nasrallah, these allegations were the most ridiculous of all the justifications presented by the Saudis. Not only were Yemenis 'pure Arabs' (Hezbollah 2015i, 2015l), Nasrallah also considered the Saudi challenge to the Muslimness of Yemenis – or rather, the Shi'i minority in Yemen – as an attempt to divert from their own questionable belief: 'The Yemenis do not need a testimony . . . of their Islam. I further say: Those who are aggressing against the Yemeni people are the ones who must search for evidence of their Islam and their Arabism' (Hezbollah 2015l).

Like Israel's wars in its neighbourhood, the Saudi war in Yemen aimed at restoring the kingdom's hegemony and breaking the will of the Yemeni people (Hezbollah 2015i, 2015l, 2016k). These goals already rendered the war illegitimate, but what was more, they could never be achieved through violent means, let alone just a military air campaign (Hezbollah 2015l, 2016n). The war was also not a means of last resort, for there had been no serious attempts at political dialogue and achieving the goals through dialogue (Hezbollah 2016c, 2016g). When Saudi Arabia and its allies realised that they were not making any progress with their air campaign, they launched their ground operations as a mission of revenge (Hezbollah 2015b, 2016i). 'This is not a war for political targets,' Nasrallah concluded. 'This is a war of grudge – the Saudi-Wahhabi grudge' (Hezbollah 2016a). These words were only one instance in what must be considered an escalation of rhetoric towards what Nasrallah ironically called the 'Kingdom of "Benevolence"' (Hezbollah 2015i, 2015l) and especially Mohamad bin Salman, freshly appointed minister of defence and deputy crown prince in 2015 but effectively controlling the Saudi government, as his father, King Salman, had been sick since his enthronement in the same year. He further denounced Saudi cowardice when the kingdom requested troops from other Arab countries (Hezbollah 2015g, 2015i) and called upon governments of the region to

[l]isten to your consciences, religion, mind, and interests. Do you accept that your son's blood be shed for the sake of a self-indulgent prince who lives in luxury to restore his power and control over a prideful, poor, oppressed, struggling and striving people? (Hezbollah 2015i)

The spinelessness of the Saudis also manifested itself in the deliberate targeting of civilians (Hezbollah 2015g, 2015h, 2015l). Besides acts of lethal violence, as happened in 2016 when the coalition bombarded a funeral which left more than 140 Yemenis dead (Hezbollah 2016n), the Saudi aggressors cut off civilians' access to food, water and medical supplies, shelled ports and airports and even blocked humanitarian aid (Hezbollah 2015g, 2015l). Nasrallah claimed that the Saudis were leading a war of total destruction, targeting the same places over and over again and using cluster bombs and other prohibited weapons (Hezbollah 2015g, 2015l, 2016n). Hezbollah considered this war not only to be an immediate catastrophe for the Yemeni population, but also to imply an unprecedented lowering of moral standards with disastrous consequences for future practices in the region and their acceptability (Hezbollah 2015h). 'Yemen is today's version of Karbala. It is a scene of tragedy and sacrifice. It is a scene where chopped bodies of children, women, and men mingle with rubble . . . in Sanaa, and all over Yemeni cities, villages, and neighborhoods' (Hezbollah 2016a). The amount and intensity of Saudi atrocities led Nasrallah to conclude that the kingdom constituted a greater evil even than Israel (Hezbollah 2015h).

In this sense, Saudi Arabia's direct support for 'Takfirist' groups in the armed conflicts of the region was just the peak of what Hezbollah considered repugnant behaviour and, according to the party, should come as no surprise – even less so because groups such as ISIS and JN were children of Wahhabi ideology. Referring to terrorist attacks in Europe, Afghanistan, Iraq and Syria, Nasrallah addressed the Saudis, stating that

> the whole world now knows that this is your Wahhabi culture, and that these are [products of] your schools, and . . . [of] your educational curriculums, and your sheikhs, your media, and your television channels, all of which do Takfiri (label others as infidels and kill them)! (Hezbollah 2016e)

According to Hezbollah, 'Takfirism', or the 'intellect which labels as an unbeliever everyone other than themselves' (Hezbollah 2014e), is in itself an illegitimate practice which is irreconcilable with Islam, even in its Sunni version (Hezbollah 2014e, 2016k). It is 'a mentality that you can never communicate with through dialogue. They know nothing [of] "being flexible", "setting priorities", or "finding common things"' (Hezbollah 2013a, 2014b, 2014h, 2016d, 2016l). 'Takfirists' consider violence justified against anyone who is different or does not share their exact convictions (Hezbollah 2013g, 2014e). They are therefore not simply a conflict party, but rather a terrorist group committing 'a massacre on the human, cultural, intellectual, moral, psychological, and moral levels' (Hezbollah 2014e, 2015d, 2016d). It does not stop at any form of crime. It 'sheds blood, demolishes, kills, rapes, take[s] women as prisoners, slaughters' (Hezbollah 2013g, 2015d, 2016d, 2016k).

While Nasrallah persistently decried Saudi Arabia's conduct in Yemen, more and more war crimes committed by the Syrian regime came to light, including the use of chemical weapons. The regime was also responsible for by far the highest number of civilian casualties. While the exact numbers are contested, several observation centres found that, between 2011 and 2016, the Assad regime was responsible for between 87 and 93 per cent of civilian casualties, amounting to an estimated 94,000–190,000 civilian deaths at the hands of the rulers in this period (SNHR 2016, VDC 2016). Nothing in Nasrallah's speeches gives any indication of these atrocities. Instead, it seems he tried to exaggerate the danger posed by 'Takfirism' to a point where almost any means of defeating it seemed legitimate. In this sense, the creation of a larger-than-life enemy in the form of ISIS also served the purpose of resolving the tensions evident in Hezbollah's normative framework of legitimate violence.

Less than Deliberative Legitimacy: Keeping Lebanon Calm

As belligerent and steeped in violence as Hezbollah's discourse appears with respect to what it deems legitimate behaviour towards the conflict-torn Lebanese environment, it is calm and dialogue oriented when it comes to Lebanese domestic politics. While Hezbollah is far from embracing a Habermasian-style notion of deliberative legitimacy as developed in Chapter 2, its discourse does contain traces of discourse ethics. At the domestic level, authority in Lebanon can only arise from a peaceful and dialogue-oriented interaction between different religious sects, and this interaction must be guided by certain rules and norms. The heavily moralised discourse with which Hezbollah addresses its allies and adversaries in Lebanon can be interpreted as the party's attempt to keep domestic politics as calm as possible, so as to free the party's resources for its actual *raison d'être*: the transnational resistance project (Interview 6). To a considerable degree and in contrast to Ennahda, then, Hezbollah is a transnational actor whose priorities lie in regional and international rather than domestic affairs. This does not imply, however, that Hezbollah is not a Lebanese actor or that it is 'foreign' to Lebanese society – a claim that the party regularly perceives as an act of misrecognition and an attempt by its adversaries to delegitimise its claims (Pfeifer 2021).

Calls for dialogue and cooperation serve Hezbollah's self-presentation as a national Lebanese actor, rather than a sectarian Shi'i group (Matar 2014, 173). It is therefore no coincidence that these calls were particularly pronounced between early 2012 and early 2014, when terrorist attacks hit Lebanon and Hezbollah sought to counter intersectarian tensions and violence with its discourse. It was extremely important for Nasrallah to avoid giving the impression that Hezbollah's judgements were guided by sectarianism. This was made very difficult by what could easily be interpreted as systematic interference in favour of the Shi'a in regional conflicts. 'Alawites, the religious community to which Bashar al-Assad and his family belong, are often considered a Shi'i minority.[16] In contrast, the overwhelming majority of the victims of the Syrian war, including those who died at the hands of the Assad regime and its allies, are Sunnis. Hezbollah also clearly positioned itself on the side of the (majority Shi'i) Bahraini people in their protests against a regime run by a Sunni minority. Finally, although Hezbollah, with good reason (Darwich 2018), worked against this framing, the Saudi-led war on Yemen was also read as an attempt to prevent Iranian hegemony and a victory of the Houthis. The latter also identify as Shi'a – albeit as Zaidis, and therefore following a different tradition again to Iran and Hezbollah. But in spite of this, and even though the Iranian influence on the Houthis tends to be overestimated (Asseburg, Lacher and Transfeld 2018, 49), Hezbollah's supporting the Houthis and positioning itself against the Saudis added to the impression that the party's actions were driven by sectarian considerations (Matar 2014, 178–9).

As a consequence, it became all the more important for Hezbollah to prevent the 'sectarianisation' (Hashemi and Postel 2017) of regional conflicts and politics from spilling over to Lebanon. As in the case of Ennahda, there is a certain ambiguity to Nasrallah's anti-sectarian discourse, for his messages simultaneously reject and reproduce sectarianism as the main dividing line of Lebanese politics (Khatib and Matar 2014, 187). Sectarian discourse played a major role in recruitment strategies for the Syrian war, even though it seems that Hezbollah rejected the kind of overly simplistic sectarian framing pursued by Iranian forces, 'stressing that it was working with militia members of all sects' (Leenders and Giustozzi 2022, 625). With regard to the domestic context, how to manage sectarian identities and avoid civil strife in Lebanon is one of the main issues in Hezbollah's discourse. According to Hezbollah's argumentation, Lebanon's political system and societal composition make political dialogue inevitable. It is the only means by which sectarian conflicts can be eased, relations with other parties developed and differences overcome, especially in the repeated government crises between 2011 and 2016 (Hezbollah 2011a, 2011b, 2011c, 2011k, 2012e, 2013f, 2015c). In times of regional chaos, dialogue needs to sought, even with adversaries, so as to safe-guard domestic stability and the 'civil peace' in Lebanon (Hezbollah 2013f, 2014b). Hezbollah cites the dialogue with the Future Movement in early 2015 as an example (Hezbollah 2015e). Against the backdrop of both a tense security situation due to a spike in attacks by Salafi jihadists on Lebanese soil and the presidential crisis, dialogue allowed the situation to be assuaged and eventually led to the surprising endorsement of presidential candidate Sleiman Frangieh from the March 8 bloc by Saad al-Hariri, then prime minister and leader of the adversarial March 14 bloc. To seek dialogue is both the duty and the responsibility of any political party – and also implies behaving like a rational actor in decision-making processes (Hezbollah 2011a, 2011g, 2014b): 'We work according to what we agree on, and we organize what we disagree on, postpone it, or find a mechanism to continue a dialogue in it. This is what logic and the mind says. Religion, morals, and national interest say so' (Hezbollah 2015e).

This language of virtues and vices is rather typical of Nasrallah's speeches. With regard to what he considers the appropriate mode of Lebanese domestic politics, they are consolidated into his very own version of discourse ethics and, thus, guidelines for legitimate decision-making. Dialogue must, first, be guided by rationality, as well as 'transparency and clarity among those who sit on the table or will sit on the table' (Hezbollah 2011e, 2012d). Second, it should be open in two regards: participation must not be subjected to conditions and there must not be any predetermined outcomes (Hezbollah 2012d). Third, power may not be exerted in ongoing dialogue, for example by imposing choices or opinions on participants (Hezbollah 2012b). Fourth, an actor's decision (not) to participate in a given dialogue may not be used against them or their allies in the form of blackmail or similar practices (Hezbollah 2015f). Finally, dialogue should be a direct and immediate encounter, rather than taking the form of a media battle (Hezbollah 2014g). If these standards are met, Hezbollah is 'open for any discussion that might lead anywhere' (Hezbollah 2013a) – including on the contentious issue of its participation in the Syrian Civil War; at least this is what its secretary general claims (Hezbollah 2013g, 2014e). The only topic which Nasrallah excludes from any agenda is Hezbollah's resistance activity, which includes the party's insistence on keep-ing its arms (Hezbollah 2013c).

It is noteworthy that Nasrallah's call for dialogue is also addressed to conflicting parties in the region (Hezbollah 2012a), be they Iran and Saudi Arabia (Hezbollah 2015l, 2016e), Bahrain and Yemen (Hezbollah 2011e, 2011g, 2012a, 2015d, 2015g, 2015i, 2016c, 2016k), or the warring parties in Syria (Hezbollah 2011g, 2011l, 2012b, 2012c). For 'anyone who pushes for dialogue instead of violence . . . is a friend' (Hezbollah 2011j). But as shown above, in the contexts of the international realm and regional conflicts, the conditions under which dialogue makes sense and can lead to results are far less likely to be met. *A priori* excluding a party from the negotiation table or setting conditions (like Assad's resignation from power) prior to talks makes them futile (Hezbollah 2013a, 2014a). Hezbollah does, however, exempt one actor from any dialogical solution. In view of the war in the neighbouring country, with Syrians tired of fighting and without any prospect of a military solution (Hezbollah 2015b, 2015i), Nasrallah appealed:

> Be realistic in viewing the status quo in Syria. Open the gate for a political solution. Allow the opposition to partake in a settlement. Here, I do not mean the Takfiri opposition which is not allowed to partake in a settlement. (Hezbollah 2015c)

Similarly, Hezbollah claimed in 2016 that, after what the party considered various missed opportunities for dialogue, Saudi Arabia had ruined and undermined any attempts at finding a political solution to the conflicts in Bahrain, Syria, Iraq and Yemen (Hezbollah 2016c, 2016e) – which disqualified them from becoming a dialogue partner. In this sense, dialogue is the counterpart to legitimate violence as discussed in the previous section. Where the former leads nowhere or is intentionally undermined to prevent a conflict being settled by peaceful means, the use of violent means becomes necessary as a last resort in circumstances of war or oppression.

Besides normative standards for dialogue, Hezbollah also defines the virtues and qualities a political actor must have: truthfulness and rationality. Opinions should always be based on facts and information (Hezbollah 2011h). These facts should always be verified and not simply taken for granted, in particular in the context of false media reports and the spread of misinformation in a digital age (Hezbollah 2011h, 2013b). Claims should always follow the methodology and rules of logic and objectivity (Hezbollah 2011h, 2012d). As the truth is often hidden, it needs to be exposed through careful argumentation and the search for the bigger picture (Hezbollah 2013d, 2015g). If new facts emerge, there is no shame in reconsidering an earlier stance (Hezbollah 2014e). However, it is equally important to keep one's word and honour one's commitments (Hezbollah 2016m). Besides being a religious duty, telling the truth is important for credible deterrence of the enemy (Hezbollah 2013b, 2016h). For 'those who make false claims and exaggerate are normally exposed by the enemy. So once the enemy finds out that any medium is lying, what kind of psychological war does that become? It turns into nonsense!' (Hezbollah 2013b).

Rationality and cool-headedness are also an 'ethical stance' (Hezbollah 2013c) but play an important role in preventing conflict, too: 'How does strife usually begin? People face their guns at others when they decide to stop thinking logically and allow their temper or anger to control them. That's when they turn crazy and start killing each other' (Hezbollah 2013d). Provocations and accusations should be avoided; actions and reactions should be considerate and only carried out after contemplation and careful evaluation of the situation (Hezbollah 2013e, 2014e, 2015h). The composition of Lebanon is like a powder keg which can easily be detonated by sectarian rhetoric and incitement (Hezbollah 2011e, 2011i, 2012a, 2013d, 2014e) – which 'the other camp' or the March 14 bloc all too often employs for personal and political gains (Hezbollah 2011e, 2012c, 2013d, 2013e). Those who want to rule strive to divide people, alienating Sunnis from Shi'a and Arabs from Persians (Hezbollah 2011h). Among the more cunning and dangerous lies that Hezbollah regularly takes a stand against in its discourse is the claim that it was a puppet of the Iranian government, which tried to exercise hegemony over Lebanon, interfere with elections and install a regime under its patronage (Hezbollah 2014c, 2015i, 2016f, 2016m). This goes hand in hand with the typical allegation made against Islamists, as seen in the Ennahda case, according to which Hezbollah was intent on seizing power and unilateral control over the state – and would not hesitate to use its arms for the achievement of its goals (Hezbollah 2011b, 2011l, 2013c, 2016d).

To counter these vicious tactics employed by political opponents, Nasrallah presents an image of righteousness and wisdom. He is widely perceived as a man who has good arguments, follows a line of reasoning and keeps his word (Interview 6). Nasrallah is not shy of publicly showcasing what he considers his own and the party's ethical qualities, which, besides truthfulness and rationality, include empathy and a willingness to try to understand the positions and, even more importantly, fears of others (Hezbollah 2012b, 2013c). From such a stance, it follows that Hezbollah embraces a cooperative attitude, refrains from pushing its own interests and offers concessions (Hezbollah 2012a, 2013c). While some try to frame this as a weakness, Nasrallah considers Hezbollah's principles a strength: '[O]ur allies realize our ethics. Personally, I'm absolutely ready to offer anything I can. So is this shameful?!' (Hezbollah 2013c). If all Lebanese political parties were to follow the example set by Hezbollah and refrain from '[e]xchanging accusations[, which] is something very largely widespread in Lebanon' (Hezbollah 2014b), the country would be better equipped to face regional and domestic challenges, and also to ward off attempts by external forces to mislead public opinion through psychological warfare and meddle in Lebanese politics (Hezbollah 2011f, 2011i, 2013a, 2013e).

Discussion

As Chapter 6 will show, Hezbollah sees itself, and indeed Lebanon as whole, as caught in the middle of a global fight between good and evil – and this general understanding of its position in the world order determines Hezbollah's ideas on legitimacy. In the background of what can only be called a very belligerent worldview hovers the positive idea of community-based legitimacy. A political order should be adapted to the people for which it is designed and respond to society-specific characteristics and problems. As a consequence, Hezbollah considers an Islamic state according to the Iranian model to be unsuited to Lebanon, despite recognising its virtues. It is noteworthy that, in its discourse, Hezbollah praises the democratic qualities of this system more than its Islamic principles. This already points to a certain discursive inescapability of global standards of legitimacy. Today, it seems, no one can argue against democracy – however far removed it may be from actual political practice. Similarly, Hezbollah's take on international institutions and law affirms their norms and procedures in principle but criticises the hypocrisy practised regarding human rights and other (democratic) norms (Hezbollah 2011b, 2011e, 2016i, 2016n), the partiality of certain bodies like the UN (Hezbollah 2015l) and the politicisation of institutions like the STL (Hezbollah 2011c, 2011i, 2011j). This confirms earlier findings that in its discourse, Hezbollah embraces and, to a certain degree and for some time, has empirically complied with international norms (Dionigi 2014) – at least until its involvement in the Syrian Civil War. Similarly, Hezbollah's normative standards of dialogue resonate well with discourse ethics and deliberative legitimacy (Habermas 1996), even if they are not integrated in a refined and sophisticated broader model of democratic politics. At least with regard to certain normative principles, Hezbollah is not as resistant as the term *al-Muqawama al-Islamiyya* suggests – or as it would like to see itself and be seen (Dudouet 2021, 243). There is a high degree of convergence between Hezbollah's and Western discourse when it comes to the legitimacy claims Hezbollah formulates for the Lebanese context.

What is undeniably resistant, however, is the party's self-positioning in regional conflicts and how it resorts to violent means according to its own assessment of which actions are necessary in these violent conditions. But even here, its resistant stance is limited. To put it simply, in the view of the West, Hezbollah positions itself on the 'wrong' side of the conflict yet it undermines very few principles of the Western world order, other than the use of force and intervention in conflicts as a non-state actor. In a sense, then, Hezbollah is resistant primarily because it is not a state – and because Western world order concepts are geared towards the nation-state based on the Westphalian ideal (Pfeifer forthcoming). Indeed, international law still normatively privileges states (Chiu 2019, 193–233) and international relations are often still imagined and studied as a practice of states, thereby ignoring the empirical reality that (armed) non-state actors are an important part of international politics and conflicts (Clément, Geis and Pfeifer 2021, Darwich 2021b, see also Chapter 6). Thus, Hezbollah's practice and discourse are provocative – or resistant – to the Western world order, because they extend its norms to a militant non-state actor – and because the party sides with countries that have been labelled 'rogue states' and enemies of the West, while engaging in violent conflict with Israel, not only one of the most important allies of the West in the region but the relationship with which is of high moral value for many states (Gardner Feldman 1999, Marsden 2009). In this sense, Hezbollah's ideas on legitimate violence challenge sovereignty more than legitimacy norms (see Chapter 4).

Turning to the articulation of the normative principles that should guide behaviour in situations of conflict and restrict violence, Hezbollah's discourse is based on the assumption of a permanent state of conflict in which Lebanon and the region are caught up. The only way of countering oppression, unjust rule and illegitimate war is self-defence or, in Hezbollah's words, resistance. Nasrallah's moral assessment of conflict behaviours is reminiscent of just-war theory (Walzer 1977) with the addition of the Muslim, or rather Shi'i, duty to oppose certain forms of violence (Kızılkaya 2017). There is an obvious tension between the standards articulated by the party, on the one hand, and, on the other, the brutality of the Hezbollah-supported Assad regime, whose methods include targeting civilians, long-term sieges and food deprivation as well as the use of chemical weapons banned by international law, to name just a few. These crimes and excessive use of violence by Assad and his allies constitute a glaring void in Hezbollah's discourse. It was thus all the more important for Hezbollah to construct a mighty 'Takfirist' threat and enemy image that could still legitimise its choice of sides in the Syrian war. The analysis also shows that Hezbollah struggles to demonstrate by means of its discourse that it does commit to normative standards – even more so than the hypocritical West. The latter uses a rhetoric of liberal norms and institutions and 'gives lectures . . . on civilization, democracy and the will of the majority' (Hezbollah 2011b), while devising self-interested plans and intervening when a regime that does not serve its interests is in power. By emphasising its ethics in the use of violence and its confirmation of norms (Dionigi 2014), Hezbollah also hopes to gain recognition as being different from actors like ISIS and al-Qa'ida.

Finally, Hezbollah draws a sharp line between the domestic and the international logic of legitimacy. The former requires dialogue and cooperation across sects, Hezbollah claims, presenting itself as a national Lebanese actor and de-emphasising its Shi'i and resistance identity (Matar 2014, 173). Calls to abstain from sectarian instigation were loudest between early 2012 and early 2014, when terrorist attacks hit Lebanon, as a way of easing sectarian tensions. And still, Nasrallah's rhetoric remains ambiguous in this regard, with his messages often at once rejecting and reproducing sectarian categories (Khatib and Matar 2014, 187). The results presented above confirm earlier findings on Nasrallah's ability to design and convey audience-specific messages with a corresponding rhetoric and style, 'adapting different linguistic, cultural and religious registers' (Matar 2014, 172). For instance, when Hezbollah's secretary general addresses his partisans, he frames jihad in terms of a religious duty and the Israelis as infidels. When he talks to a broader Lebanese audience, he puts an emphasis on the non-sectarian character of resistance which brought freedom to the Lebanese homeland and nation (Harik 2007, 66, 71). His speeches are said to address five audiences: his partisans, the larger Shi'i community, the Lebanese people, the Arab-Islamic world and Israel (Interview 6). A sixth overhearing global audience is clearly taken into account in the design of Nasrallah's speeches and sometimes even explicitly addressed. For the message he wants to convey to the hostile international environment is: Hezbollah can see right through the schemes devised for the region. As Chapter 6 will show, the party believes that hegemonic plans that would result in the submission, domination and oppression of Arabs and Muslims are underway. And to counter such plans, resistance and self-defence are not merely legitimate – they are a duty.

Notes

1. 'There is no longer a justification for political Islam in Tunisia. We are leaving political Islam to enter Muslim democracy. We are democratic Muslims who no longer rely on political Islam.'
2. Indeed, two legitimacy categories were of significant quantitative importance in the empirical material but will only be briefly touched upon at the end of this chapter: the illegitimacy of the old regime and output legitimacy. The former gives an idea of legitimacy *ex negativo*, through the distancing from practices and institutions of the old regime, but does not necessarily provide clues about Ennahda's specific conception of legitimacy. Output legitimacy, on the other hand, concerns the socio-economic conditions of democratic legitimacy and central questions of economic development and social justice. However, given the focus placed on input legitimacy in Chapter 2 and because output legitimacy can be achieved via non-democratic means, it will be de-emphasised here as well.
3. The other core demand, for (economic) dignity, is something that needs to be restored through the socio-economic transformation of Tunisian society and will briefly be touched upon in the discussion of output legitimacy.
4. 'Our identity is not a cause of debate among Tunisians. We are an Arab-Muslim country: this is a fact accepted by everyone.'

5. According to Saïd Amir Arjomand (2009, 571), the term *umma* originally designated 'the unified political community of Medina' and only later came to mean 'community of believers', which allowed a distinction to be drawn between 'the *ummas* of Moses and Jesus . . . [which] were now excluded from the *umma* of Muhammad'.

6. 'Evoking the "khalifa arrachida" only aimed at taking inspiration from our values and our political patrimony and the civilisational heritage of Tunisian society to which we so proudly belong.'

7. http://edition.cnn.com/videos/tv/2016/05/23/intv-amanpour-rached-ghanno uchi-tunisia-ennahda-islam.cnn (accessed 12 October 2023).

8. 'A constitution cannot be built on a majority of 51 per cent, but [must be built] on consensus. It should contain clear ideas on which everyone can agree.'

9. He does not formally belong to a party, but is considered as being close to Nidaa Tounes.

10. https://data.worldbank.org/country/tunisia (accessed 13 October 2023).

11. 'The people want a party that talks about their everyday problems, about the lives of families and individuals, and not a party that tells them about the Last Judgment, paradise etc.'

12. '*Die Christdemokraten in Deutschland sind ein gutes Vorbild für uns, wie religiöse Werte zwar Grundlage politischen Handelns sein können, aber nie zum Selbstzweck werden.*'

13. Hezbollah's interpretation of jihadism differs from the one introduced in Chapter 1. When Nasrallah calls Hezbollah a jihadist group he refers to jihad as a noble cause. The Salafi jihadism used in this book refers to groups such as ISIS or al-Qaʿida, which Nasrallah refers to as 'Takfiris'. Finally, by 'Islamists' Nasrallah exclusively means Sunni groups. To avoid terminological confusion, Hezbollah's use of the terms will be flagged through the use of inverted commas.

14. Zeynab is not only the Prophet's granddaughter and Imam Ali's daughter, but also the sister of Husayn and Hassan and an important figure in the Shiʿi tradition. Nasrallah refers to her in several speeches as a role model of courage and steadfastness.

15. *Nakba* (catastrophe) is the term used in the Arab and Muslim world to refer to the foundation of the state of Israel. In particular, it refers to the forced displacement of an estimated 700,000 Palestinians from their land (Allan 2005, 47).

16. This is a reasonable attribution. Even if one were to support it, however, Hezbollah, like Iran, adheres to Twelver Shi'ism, which ʿAlawites do not. The theological similarity is therefore highly contestable (Balanche 2018, 3).

6

TELOI

Ennahda

At the time of writing, the euphoria of the early 2010s about what seemed to be a fundamental transformation of politics in North Africa and the 'Middle East' seems very remote. What Souad Abdelrahim, an Ennahda member and since 2018 Tunis's first female mayor, formulated in an opinion piece in 2011 mirrors the Tunisian zeitgeist and is reminiscent of the widespread spirit of optimism at the time:

> Tunisia has already led the way in the region in showing how brutal dictatorship can be brought to an end through peaceful means. We hope we can now lead the way in building a genuine democratic, pluralistic and fair society that can provide a model for the entire region. (Ennahda 2011j)

For a long time, Tunisia was seen as the first and then the last remaining country to have turned the legacies of the Arab uprisings into a (more) democratic future. Since a series of terrorist attacks committed in 2015, however, a state of emergency has been in place. In July 2021, the president of Tunisia, Kais Saied, issued yet another extension of the state of emergency and announced the enforcement of Article 80 of the Tunisian Constitution according to his own interpretation (Ben Hamadi 2021). Since then, all democratic institutions have slowly but surely been dismantled (Weipert-Fenner 2022). Indeed,

Ennahda had anticipated these very developments in what was one of various dystopic trajectories the party had dreaded between 2011 and 2016. The danger of authoritarian relapse hanging over Tunisia since the ousting of Zine el Abidine Ben Ali became more concrete with the military coup in Egypt in 2013. It was briefly eclipsed by the successful conclusion of the constitutional process and the adoption of a democratic Tunisian constitution in 2014, but started to reappear when President Beji Caid Essebsi, in response to the wave of terrorist attacks and with the reluctant support of Ennahda, declared a state of emergency in 2015.

Ennahda was very aware of the precarious nature of the nascent Tunisian democracy, and the various domestic, regional and global threats it faced. Still, as present as dystopian elements of its discourse were, the party consistently and enthusiastically presented what it saw as a utopia for Tunisia and the region: the Tunisian people taking another step towards Arab and Islamic liberation. As the people had now 'tasted freedom', they would 'not go backward' and, eventually, there would be 'no escape from democratisation' (Ennahda 2015d). Ennahda sees Tunisia as a shining example of a region that was bound to democratise and liberate itself at some point. And, as a result of its own transformation, it now considers itself not only as a facilitator and a mirror of Tunisia's development, but also as a role model for other Islamist movements in the region who want to play a conducive role in processes of democratic transition. Figure 6.1 displays Ennahda's utopia on three levels: regional history, Tunisian politics and the evolution of the Islamic movement in Tunisia. This teleology leads to a region in the 'Middle East' and North Africa in which democracies peacefully coexist and are at eye level with other states in a multipolar world. The other side of the story, however, are the manifold threats and obstacles that stand in the way of the utopia becoming reality. Besides authoritarian persistence and resurgence, these threats comprise polarisation and civil war, anarchy and state failure, terrorism but also the demonisation of Islamists and, finally, external intervention. Ennahda's utopia must be protected from these threats – an ambition that, as we now know, Ennahda was unable to fulfil.

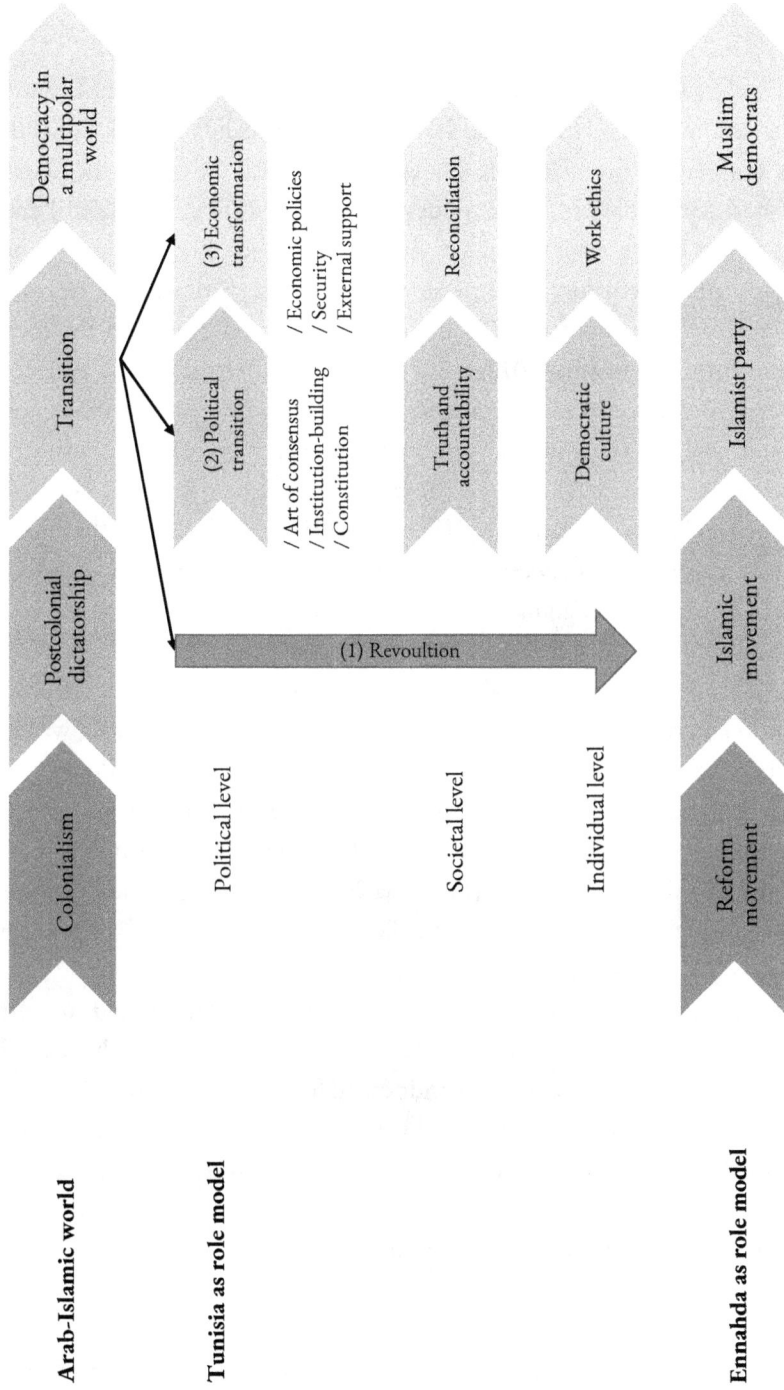

Arab-Islamic world

Colonialism — Postcolonial dictatorship — Transition — Democracy in a multipolar world

Tunisia as role model

Political level: (2) Political transition — (3) Economic transformation

/ Art of consensus
/ Institution-building
/ Constitution

/ Economic policies
/ Security
/ External support

(1) Revoultion

Societal level: Truth and accountability — Reconciliation

Individual level: Democratic culture — Work ethics

Ennahda as role model

Reform movement — Islamic movement — Islamist party — Muslim democrats

Figure 6.1 Ennahda's utopia

Utopia: A Story of Regional Liberation Following the Tunisian Model

In full awareness of the 'civilisational and strategic depth to which our country belongs at the Maghreb, Arab and Islamic levels' (Ennahda 2011a), Ennahda views Tunisia's future as inextricably intertwined with the fate of the neighbourhood with which it shares 'values and history' (Ennahda 2012ah) and with Islam as both a religion and a civilisation (Ennahda 2012ag). The region also has a common history of oppression. Colonial rule had prevented it from developing its own model of (Islamic) democracy and destroyed the local political culture (Ennahda 2012af, 2013c, 2013f). After the people achieved liberation, postcolonial authoritarian rule was established across the region (Ennahda 2011r). These dictators pursued a 'forced westernisation hostile to Arab-Muslim identity' (Ennahda 2014ac) and fuelled 'economic, political, and social exclusion and inequality' (Ennahda 2016h). In the 2010s, the region stood 'at a crossroads: between going forward towards democracy, development and progress, and going towards chaos and terrorism, civil war and sectarianism' (Ennahda 2014ae).

In 2011 and 2012, Ennahda's discourse seemed optimistic about the postrevolutionary future of the region. 'Arab regimes face implosion from within and change from without. This . . . [is] a natural outgrowth of decades of oppression and misrule. There is a similar set of socio-economic and political conditions in all the Arab countries and the dynamic of change appears unstoppable,' the party declared (Ennahda 2011e). The geographical proximity, shared language and culture and intellectual traditions of Arab reformism (Ennahda 2013l) allowed for the spread of the revolution and would ultimately put 'an end to the old doctrine of "Arab exceptionalism" and support for authoritarian regimes' (Ennahda 2013l). After the 2013 coup in Egypt and with the war in Syria escalating, Ennahda called for the people to remain steadfast. For what looked like victories of old or new dictators was only 'temporary and superficial – the Arab Spring is irreversible' (Ennahda 2014ad). Change does not happen overnight, and, as in other regions, including Europe, processes of democratisation would take time.

> The whole world is heading to democracy at different speeds, and the Arab world is part of the world. Democracy was delayed in this region for many

reasons . . . The other Arab countries are also headed toward democracy but at a different pace. (Ennahda 2012d)

But with violence escalating in Libya, Syria and Yemen, and the new Egyptian dictatorship consolidating, Ennahda explicitly referred to a utopia of regional liberation less and less often. Instead, it opted for leading by example. Tunisia's revolution had not only 'amazed the world' (Ennahda 2011i) and 'initiated a major Arab will for emancipation and liberation' (Ennahda 2011b), thereby sparking 'the flame of the Arab Spring' and opening a 'horizon of hope' (Ennahda 2014f). It also demonstrated how a revolution can be achieved with peaceful means (Ennahda 2011j) and set an 'an inspiring example of Islamic–secular co-operation for the greater national interest' (Ennahda 2011i, 2011j, 2013l) for the difficult task of transitioning to democracy, establishing its own 'brand of radical political moderation' (Ennahda 2016j). Tunisia thus became the '[f]irst Arab democracy' (Ennahda 2013e) and with it a 'light house or an example to the rest of the Muslim world' (Ennahda 2012g). As circumstances were similar in other Arab countries (Ennahda 2015d), Tunisia would be able to export its model of transition (Ennahda 2013i) and its experience of liberation.

Tunisia's liberation is built on the back of 'generations of women and men of diverse political and intellectual persuasions against despotism and for freedom, equality and dignity' (Ennahda 2011i) and can be told as a story of three generations of martyrs. First, after a long history of struggles and sacrifices, the brave Tunisian people had freed themselves from French colonial rule in their 'glorious revolution' (Ennahda 2013n) in 1956.[1] The next generation of Tunisians achieved the second step of liberation in 2010, after 'martyr Mohamed Bouazizi [had sparked] the beginning of the revolution of freedom and dignity' (Ennahda 2013ab) or the 'blessed revolution' (Ennahda 2011b). The final step that Ennahda projects to the future and integrates seamlessly into the teleology is Tunisia's liberation from terrorism. At the end of the process, Tunisia will emerge as a full, secure democracy in a multipolar world (see Chapter 5): 'Our vision . . . remembers with pride all the country's martyrs: those who struggled against occupation, those who struggled against dictatorship and injustice and those who lost their lives fighting terrorism' (Ennahda 2014z). '[T]hey are the third generation of martyrs, after the martyrs for independence and the martyrs of the struggle against dictatorship, these fell as martyrs for the defense of the revolutions of freedom, dignity and democracy' (Ennahda 2013ad). Ennahda came to perceive terrorism as the greatest threat to Tunisian democracy (see also next section), believing it would only be defeated by the conclusion of Tunisia's transition model.

Looking at this model more closely, a sequence of three phases can be determined: (1) revolution, (2) political transition and (3) economic transformation (see Figure 6.1).[2] All three need to occur on the levels of politics, society and the individual. The first phase put an end to dictatorship and culminated in the first democratic elections in 2011 (Ennahda 2014q). The second and third phases achieve two of the revolution's goals: (political) freedom and (economic) dignity (Ennahda 2014w). The political transition or second phase comprises restoring political freedom by building a democratic system of governance (Ennahda 2012a). This phase ended with the adoption of the constitution in 2014 and the second free elections, which 'crown[ed] . . . the transition phase' (Ennahda 2014y). The 'peaceful alternation of power' (Ennahda 2015l) marked the end of the transition phase in the narrow sense and took the 'country . . . into the phase of stability within a democratic pluralistic state' (Ennahda 2012u, 2014y). In this third phase of consolidation (Ennahda 2014y, 2016a), the priority shifts to economic transformation. 'Tunisia is today on the verge of a new phase in fulfilling its dreams of economic and social development and consolidating its pioneering position: prosperity and dignity for all its citizens,' Ennahda declared in 2014 (2014z). It would bring with it 'major economic and social reforms' (Ennahda 2015y) – and, thus, a difficult task requiring broad support and consensus among political and social partners (Ennahda 2016i). The *Pacte de Carthage* of 2016 could be considered a key document of this third phase. Several parties, civil society organisations – except for the UGTT – and 'national figures' had participated in setting up its agenda (Ennahda 2016o), which included, among other things, combatting terrorism, fighting unemployment and fostering development.

The political transition and economic transformation go hand in hand with changes on the societal and individual levels. Ennahda wanted to combine 'the principles of accountability and transitional justice with a spirit of reconciliation' (Ennahda 2011b). The first step, and Ennahda's priority, was accountability and the prosecution of perpetrators (Ennahda 2011l, 2012k, 2012ah). This was reflected in the establishment of the Ministry for Transitional Justice and Human Rights under the Troika government (Ennahda 2012ah), which was later replaced by the Truth and Dignity Commission (Ennahda 2014z). But Ennahda's efforts in 2011 and 2012 were perceived as a politicisation of the transitional justice process, as it pushed for the exclusion of old regime figures from the political system. At the same time, however, it secretly negotiated with RCD cadres and Rached al-Ghannouchi eventually even withdrew a bill called the Law for the Protection of the Revolution. This sparked a lot of criticism among Nahdawis, especially among those who had been political prisoners (Marks 2014). What is more, Ennahda relied on the business and security networks the old regime had left behind, which confirmed the impression that the party was only reluctantly starting to work through the past. It was very slow to initiate actual trials and truth-seeking processes and these only targeted low-ranking RCD members. And finally, as a way of making its constituency happy, Ennahda also prioritised securing compensation for victims among its own ranks (Boubekeur 2016).

Ennahda itself admitted that the Troika government had 'indeed fallen short on some of the revolution's goals, beginning with corruption, the dismantling of the tyrannical system, rehabilitating the victims of dictatorship, and transitional justice' (Ennahda 2013f, 2013ad), which can be interpreted as a concession to its base. But from 2013 onwards, the party officially started changing its policy, adopting a more accommodating stance towards old regime cadres, thus entering the phase of reconciliation. Tunisia now needed an 'approach [that would] enable our country to address the wounds of the past in a manner that allows us to move forward without planting seeds of animosity among our younger generations' (Ennahda 2014c). In 2015, Ennahda eventually even supported and garnered support for President Essebsi's contentious Reconciliation Law (Ennahda 2015u), which aimed to 'protect public servants and businessmen from prosecutions, even if they were involved in corruption and embezzlement of public funds' (Andrieu 2016, 290). Ennahda did propose some amendments to the first draft, but generally affirmed that it was also in favour of 'economic reconciliation' (Salehi and Weipert-Fenner 2017) – which is another manifestation of the priorities it set for the third phase of transition.

Finally, on an individual level, Ennahda pursued a twofold citizen education project. Tunisians would have to learn, first, to engage in democratic politics and, second, to develop a work ethic. Democracy must be institutionalised but also lived and experienced, in order to establish it as a new 'political culture' (Ennahda 2012y). Ennahda sought 'to promote and strengthen the values of moderation, balance, tolerance and openness' (Ennahda 2014z) among Tunisians. This would pave the way for the second step, learning 'to value the culture of work, action, initiative' (Ennahda 2014m). Such a work ethic had been crippled under the old regime, where '[s]uccess [was] usually achieved through illegal means or nepotism, not through hard work' (Ennahda 2014m). The call for individual virtues was simultaneously an attack on the UGTT, which had contributed to establishing a 'culture of strikes' after the revolution at the expense of a much-needed 'culture of work . . . – meaning appreciating the value and importance of work' (Ennahda 2015b). Again, this demonstrates Ennahda's apprehension vis-à-vis an economic situation that would simply not improve.

Dystopic Fragments: Multiple Threats to Tunisian Exceptionalism

While Ennahda may have hoped and believed that Tunisia would eventually be located in a free, peaceful and democratic neighbourhood, there was also a clear awareness of the dangers the surrounding countries faced and posed to Tunisia. Accordingly, the party regularly promoted and showcased Tunisian exceptionalism in metaphoric and emphatic language, almost as if it were trying to place a protective spell around its country and people so as to avert any harm from outside. While Ennahda emphasised Tunisia's particularism immediately after the revolution as a way of reassuring neighbours such as Algeria that no one intended to try to impose their revolution on them (Ennahda 2011r, 2013h, 2014d), the dire fate of the Arab Spring societies made the Tunisian path an incantation. Just a few years after the Arab uprisings of 2010 and 2011, Tunisia had become 'the last remaining candle of the Arab Spring over coups, terrorism, and internal and external conspiracies' (Ennahda 2013e, 2014b, 2014ae), 'despite all the winds that are blowing at it' (Ennahda 2013i); the 'sole peaceful island in a turbulent region' (Ennahda 2014g) and the 'sole success of the Arab Spring' (Ennahda 2015g); it remained the 'shining light of the region' (Ennahda 2016j) and the only 'alternative to the terrifying images of terror and tyranny here and there' (Ennahda 2014z).

And while Ennahda always also had an eye on the region as a whole, it sensed that the actual dangers to Tunisian democracy came from inside. Besides the lack of economic success, which was a necessary condition for democratic consolidation, Ennahda identified several specific dangers to the young Tunisian democracy. These threat scenarios in or dystopian elements of Ennahda's discourse emerge and begin to dominate in line with actual events. Immediately after the revolution, Ennahda was worried about external interference in Tunisian affairs and about becoming demonised as Islamists – or, put differently, that the results of the 2011 elections would not be accepted at home and abroad should Ennahda emerge as the winning party. The fear of an authoritarian backlash became particularly pronounced after the coup in Egypt in 2013 but lost importance after the adoption of the constitution in 2014. In 2015 and 2016, the party dedicated a large share of its discursive resources to the topic of terrorism.

Ennahda's fear of being stigmatised as dangerous Islamists was a legacy of the party's persecution under Ben Ali. The regime '*[avait] utilisé les islamistes comme un épouvantail, pour faire peur aux progressistes, aux femmes et à l'Occident, et pour faire taire tous ceux qui s'élevaient contre lui*' (Ennahda 2011d).[3] After the revolution, some of Ennahda's opponents continued the old regime's discourse and practices, urging citizens 'not to vote for Ennahda, as well as defaming the latter and spreading falsehoods against it' (Ennahda 2011p). They used clichés about Ennahda's supposed Islamist agenda and claimed it wanted to reintroduce polygamy, force the veil upon Tunisian women and take over state power for good (Ennahda 2011h, 2011i, 2011j, 2011p). When it was founded in 2012, Nidaa Tounes, the party that would become Ennahda's fiercest competitor and that provided a home for former RCD politicians, 'specialised in hostility' towards Ennahda. Some of its party leaders called 'for eliminating Al-Nahda from the scene . . . in a neo-Nazi exclusionist language' (Ennahda 2013e). It was only after the success of the Quartet roadmap and the reconciliation with Nidaa Tounes that Ennahda's fear of demonisation subsided.

Ennahda also condemned Western media reports in this phase, for instance when they suggested that the party planned to establish an Islamic state that would suppress women and that it received funding from Qatar. Ennahda regularly wrote open letters to Western media outlets that had distorted its image, correcting what the party perceived as false information and even filing a law suit against one international newspaper (Ennahda 2012f, 2012h, 2012aa, 2014u, 2014x). 'Some are presenting me as a Khomeini who will return to Tunisia – I am no Khomeini,' Ghannouchi indignantly clarified (Ennahda 2016e). Worried about a refusal by the international community to accept the results of the first free and fair Tunisian elections – which had not been without precedent in the region – Ennahda reminded Western politicians that they were obliged to respect the results of the elections even if they were nervous 'about the victory of democratic Islamic parties like Ennahda, mistakenly grouping them with radical extremists' (Ennahda 2014i). Ennahda responded to these allegations of closeness to the Salafist scene by pursuing two strategies. First, it claimed that any engagement with Salafists was aimed at persuading them 'to commit to legal and civic activism and peaceful coexistence' (Ennahda 2012x). Second, Ennahda insisted that the distinction between violent fundamentalists and political strands be maintained. 'Salafists are part of the Tunisian people, enjoying the same rights and bound by [the] same duties. We defend their right to freely express their views and all their rights, but they should abide by the law,' the party declared (Ennahda 2012f). Finally, as a former victim of demonisation, Ennahda knew that such stigmatisation would not prevent Salafists from playing a political role in the future: '*Si nous voulons diaboliser les salafistes, dans dix ou quinze ans, ce seront eux qui seront au pouvoir*' (Ennahda 2012e).[4]

Toning down aggressive discourse towards Salafists was also important with regard to a second scenario Ennahda dreaded: the escalation of polarisation into a civil war-like state of affairs. Ennahda had tried to avoid any societal tensions along the secular–Islamist line by forming a coalition government with the two secular parties Ettakatol and the CPR so as to make sure 'that the debate is not between Islamist and non-Islamist or Islamist and secular' (Ennahda 2011r). Ennahda described this phase between 2012 and 2013 as one of 'extreme polarisation' (Ennahda 2015h) and as '*une période de crise où la société a été divisée en deux parties*' (Ennahda 2015w)[5] in which '[t]wo trains were heading into an inevitable crash' (Ennahda 2015h). The political assassination of two leftist politicians, Chokri Belaïd and Mohamed Brahmi, constituted the sad culmination of this conflict which pitted government and opposition, Islamists and secularists, Ennahda and UGTT against one another and led to 'a loss of trust between many parties of the political class' (Ennahda 2013a). Ennahda suspected that polarisation was not a result of societal and political dynamics, though, and reminded Tunisians: '[I]deological polarisation and remaining in the cycle of traditional conflicts between the two sides [is what] the dictatorships benefitted from, and [what] the counter-revolution forces tried to revive and feed' (Ennahda 2013f). Ennahda sought to counter a simplistic polarisation between Islamists and secularists in its discourse and also wanted the resignation of Hamadi Jebali after Belaïd's murder to be interpreted as contributing to this: 'We sacrificed our government to avoid civil war' (Ennahda 2014ah).

Other societies had been less successful in taming violence and managing difference. Ennahda was worried about polarisation before the coup in Egypt (Ennahda 2013s). After Mohamed Morsi, Muslim Brother and Egyptian president (2012–13), was removed from power, Ennahda warned against 'zero-sum conflicts that rule out the possibility of dialogue and reconciliation between political rivals' (Ennahda 2015o) and violent escalation between conflicting factions (Ennahda 2013h). As for Syria, Ennahda considered sectarian division among those who confronted the regime to be the core problem (Ennahda 2014j, 2015t). Similarly, Yemen had 'sunk into a cycle of tribal and sectarian conflicts . . . and a rise in the dangers of division between north and south' (Ennahda 2014j), and Iraq had 'tapped into Sunni resentment over Shiite sectarian repression' (Ennahda 2016h). On an interstate level, Ennahda was also worried about increasing tensions between Saudi Arabia and Iran, and the dangers an escalation would hold for the whole region (Ennahda 2016l). On a global level, Ennahda warned against the threat of a 'clash of civilizations' (Ennahda 2012q, 2014ae) rhetoric, which was prone to reifying and worsening the 'Islamists vs. secularists division' (Ennahda 2014i). In particular, the medial presence of and global focus on the ISIS organisation and the fight against it increased the risk of 'conflating Islam and terrorism[, which] can only benefit terrorists themselves who misuse religion and oppose democracy as unislamic' (Ennahda 2014ae).

Indeed, the terrorist threat became the most important dystopian element of Ennahda's discourse. In 2011, the party had still assumed that the jihadi trend involved a negligible minority among Salafists and claimed that it enjoyed no popularity among Tunisians (Ennahda 2011e, 2011r). Ennahda also did not mention 'terrorists' at the time, referring instead to perpetrators of specific instances of violence as 'jihadi Salafists' (Ennahda 2011e), 'groups of delinquents' (Ennahda 2012p), '(violent) extremists' (Ennahda 2012c, 2012ad) or 'conspiring parties' (Ennahda 2013ac). However, this changed in 2013. There were violent clashes between the police and the Salafi-jihadist group Ansar al-Sharia in Kairouan in May; the number of attacks by violent groups in Jebel ech Chambi, a mountain close to the city of Kasserine near the Algerian border, increased over the summer; and Mohamed Brahmi was assassinated in July – an event which Ennahda initially called a crime (Ennahda 2013u, 2013ak), but later condemned as a terrorist act (Ennahda 2013k). In response, the party took a tougher line towards violent groups. It asserted that there was no place for extremism and terrorism in Tunisia (Ennahda 2013p). Ennahda would not seek dialogue with terrorists, nor grant them immunity (Ennahda 2013f, 2013ag), thereby confirming a taboo typical of Western discourse (Toros 2008, Pfeifer, Geis and Clément 2022). According to Ennahda's retrospective view, the government's 'war against terrorism' (Ennahda 2014ae) had begun immediately after Brahmi's assassination and also taken a toll on the party itself. For 'terrorists [had been] the principal cause of toppling the two Ennahdha-led Troika governments in Tunisia' (Ennahda 2014ae) in 2013 and 2014. The issue of terrorism and how to combat it became prevalent in Ennahda's discourse and the 2014 election programme alone contained ten references to countering terrorism (Ennahda 2014z).

From the second half of 2013 until the beginning of 2015, Tunisia witnessed a series of terrorist attacks, most of which were not covered in detail by the international press. This included, for example, attacks in Sidi Ali Ben Aoun and Menzel Bourguiba (Ennahda 2013y) and attempted attacks in Sousse in October 2013 (Ennahda 2013z), attacks in Jendouba in February 2014 (Ennahda 2014l), an assault on the military in Jebel ech Chambi in July 2014, and attacks in Kasserine in February 2015 (Ennahda 2015m). But terrorism reached a new level with the attacks on the Bardo Museum in Tunis in March 2015 which claimed twenty-four casualties. As the Bardo neighbourhood is home not only to the important national museum but also to the Tunisian Assembly of the Representatives of the People, this was interpreted as an 'attempt to destroy our young and successful democracy' (Ennahda 2015a, 2015f, 2015g, 2015n). In June 2015, a young man shot and killed thirty-eight people on a beach and in a hotel in Port El Kantaoui. Again, Ennahda framed this incident as a deliberate targeting of 'the revolution, Tunisians' freedom and the economy – whose pillar is tourism' (Ennahda 2015aa). President Essebsi declared a state of emergency and despite reservations (Ennahda 2015c), Ennahda supported his decision (Ennahda 2015r, 2015s). In November 2015, twelve members of the Presidential Guard died in a bus explosion in the heart of Tunis (Ennahda 2015v). Another state of emergency was declared and has remained in place ever since. In March 2016, the Tunisian military defeated an ISIS-led attack on the city of Ben Gardane, close to the Libyan border. The militants had tried to seize the city and more than eighty people, among them fighters, soldiers and civilians, lost their lives (Ennahda 2016f).

Ennahda pointed out that a wave of violence committed by the 'enemies of democracy' (Ennahda 2016h) always seemed to hit Tunisia whenever important political events were imminent (Ennahda 2014m, 2014q, 2014v). It explained that the roots of terrorism can be found in the era of dictatorship (Ennahda 2012d). At the time, moderate Islamic movements had been suppressed, which created a religious vacuum to be filled by extremists (Ennahda 2011r, 2012d, 2012v). People learnt that, in the absence of legitimate channels, change could only occur through violence (Ennahda 2011r). Terrorism is fed by economic hardship and social injustice, which, after the revolution, remained unaddressed for too many for too long (Ennahda 2012d, 2012e, 2014aa, 2014ah):

> Violent extremism is a multi-dimensional problem that has been decades in the making. We need to take urgent action to address the needs of young people who find themselves on the margins, who grew up in the shadow of repression and now are trying to cope with the painful transition period. We must offer them the promise of hope to ensure they have something to work for, not something to work against. (Ennahda 2015g)

Ennahda insisted that terrorism could be combatted more effectively with more, not less, freedom (Ennahda 2014g). Moreover, countering terrorism must not be reduced to the security dimension. Rather, the dialogue option must be kept open (Ennahda 2013f, 2015f) and alternative interpretations of Islam by eminent Muslim scholars who 'champion Islamic moderation and refute extremism in the name of Islam' (Ennahda 2015i, 2016i, 2016p) must be offered (see also Chapter 5). Not untypically for government representatives dealing with groups adhering to Salafi jihadism (Toros and Sabogal 2021), Ennahda claimed that this ideology was alien to Tunisian society and an import 'from the Gulf . . . due to the absence of a moderate school [t]here' (Ennahda 2012d).

The reason terrorist groups like the ISIS organisation were so successful, Ennahda claimed, was because 'the region offer[ed] few other models that succeed in providing economic security, social and political inclusion, and respect for human dignity' (Ennahda 2016h). Especially young Arabs therefore sometimes gained the impression that their only choice was between joining an armed group or living under authoritarianism (Ennahda 2016i). Ironically, we now know that combatting terrorism contributed significantly to the trajectory of authoritarian backsliding by legitimising exceptional measures. 'The virus of terrorism spreads in weak states and ill societies, but Tunisia is healthy and will defeat this virus,' Ghannouchi stated in 2015 (Ennahda 2015x). This was the year in which the state of emergency was introduced as an antidote to terrorism, a move which would turn out to be fatal for Tunisian democracy. Renewed year after year, its extension under Saied in 2021 and 2022 eventually justified and became a basis for the incremental abolition of Tunisia's democratic institutions.

Ennahda had always feared such a relapse into authoritarianism. Between the inception of Nidaa Tounes in 2012 and the conciliatory meeting between Ghannouchi and Essebsi in Paris in 2013, Ennahda had watched with concern as old RCD members came back together under new auspices but constituting no more than a 'recycling of the RCD against which the revolution [had taken] place' (Ennahda 2012ad). Having witnessed the Egyptian coup in 2013, Ennahda also called upon military institutions to keep the 'civil nature of the state' (Ennahda 2013e, 2013x, 2013ah), warning 'that some people want[ed] to import one of the most brutal and violent military coups in history to Tunisia' (Ennahda 2013b). The 'terrifying nightmare' (Ennahda 2013e) Egypt went through after the ousting of Morsi was accompanied by massive state violence committed by the newly installed military regime under President Abdel Fattah el-Sisi (Ennahda 2013h, 2014n, 2015j). The coup reintroduced the narrative 'that that the best option for the region is dictatorship in order to preserve peace. Just as [the Tunisian] people are told that they can only enjoy security, prosperity and progress under despotic regimes' (Ennahda 2014ae). Ennahda rejected an imposed 'choice between security and freedom' (Ennahda 2016i). Tunisia, the party claimed, had chosen the right way of sharing power and seeking consensus (Ennahda 2013h). In 2016, Ghannouchi still believed that

> Tunisia's ship was the exception. It was able to overcome the storms of the counter-revolution, chaos and destruction, thanks to Tunisians adopting the principle of dialogue, acceptance of the other, and avoidance of exclusion and revenge. We were able, by God's grace, to bring Tunisia to the shores of safety. (Ennahda 2016p)

Discussion

Ennahda had always appealed to European states and the EU to provide economic support to the young Tunisian democracy, showcasing the Tunisian model's 'immense potential as a democratic beacon in the Arab region, and as a gateway between Europe, Africa and the Middle East' (Ennahda 2013aj, 2014ae, 2014ah, 2015i). Tunisia could become Africa's bridge 'to EU countries and the rest of the world' (Ennahda 2014z). These appeals and ideas express Ennahda's awareness that, if Tunisian democracy was to survive, an economic transformation would have to occur and bring tangible changes to the everyday life of the Tunisian people. Over time, the pride in having 'exported revolution' to the region and the hope of eventually 'export[ing] . . . a working democratic model' (Ennahda 2013i) to the rest of the Arab world, showing that there was an alternative to both dictatorship and terrorism, gave way to sober realism. Ennahda saw that the existential and material threats posed by terrorism and socio-economic precarity would deprive the post-revolutionary Tunisian system of its foundation. And it was painfully aware that Tunisia's fate was closely connected to a region that was disintegrating before its eyes.

Ennahda's discourse oscillates between, on the one hand, the utopia of an Arab and Muslim world, liberated from colonialism, postcolonial dictatorship and terrorism, having established thriving societies and states as equals in a cooperative world order – and a whole variety of threat scenarios, on the other. The latter constitute dystopic fragments in its discourse rather than a coherent narrative or negative teleology. They are intrusions of realism into what was initially a regional and then became an increasingly distinctive Tunisian success story that Ennahda clung onto at least until late 2016, the end of the period under investigation in this book. Six years later, the Tunisian state appears to have slid back into authoritarianism and, at the time of writing in October 2023, it seems increasingly improbable that 'Tunisia will return to a democratic path' (Yerkes 2022) in the near future.

Ennahda's *teloi* and interpretations of the past and future fall entirely within the range of Western world order discourse. The party's utopia contains ideas of liberal convergence and a teleological view of political and economic transition. Its specific transition model is reminiscent of established ideas in the Western-dominated global order and even closely resembles ideal-typical models of transition (critically Carothers 2002). Nevertheless, as with its conception of legitimacy (see Chapter 5), Ennahda's projection of Tunisia's future and its international environment is built on the conviction that MENA cultural specificities and identity traits must be enshrined in the regional or global order. Because there is no universal model of domestic order, the world order must recognise diversity and be organised in a way that can accommodate plural forms of order – while assuring exchange and negotiation on equal footing. As for the dystopic elements, these sometimes echo the Western 'war on terror' discourse but also the tensions between security and freedom that have been debated within this framework. Importantly, there is also clear criticism of Western hegemony. In Ennahda's discourse, it serves as an amplifier of many threat scenarios but also as a mini-dystopia in its own right.

The past has proven that Western interference in the region is extremely harmful. Colonial rule prevented the region from developing its own model of (Islamic) democracy and destroyed the local political culture (Ennahda 2012af, 2013c, 2013f), suggesting that the Arabs were not capable of establishing order without tutelage and imposition (Ennahda 2011f). In the postcolonial authoritarian phase, the West repeatedly took the side of the ruling dictators against the people, intervening on their behalf and preventing democratic change (Ennahda 2011e, 2011g, 2012i, 2014g, 2014j, 2014ae, 2015b, 2016i). They refused to recognise the results of elections if these did not correspond to their interests (Ennahda 2015j) and looked for pretexts not to support democratic change (Ennahda 2012j). Beyond the direct harm this caused, Western hypocrisy also made Arabs lose faith in democracy (Ennahda 2015k) and perpetuated an image of the Arab region as having no hope of democratisation and peace (Ennahda 2014ae, 2014af). Western states created the illusion that, when it came to the Arab world, there was only a choice between stability and freedom (Ennahda 2014i, 2015e, 2015g) – and formulated their foreign policies accordingly. But these choices backfired through transnational terrorism. Western states' cooperation with Arab dictators proved unable to prevent and indeed actually exacerbated the problem of terrorism in the long run (Ennahda 2011r, 2014ag, 2016e). Consequently, Soumaya al-Ghannouchi, the party head's daughter, offered a 'small word of advice to western politicians and army of commentators and "experts": trust me, when it comes to democracy in the region, silence is best' (Ennahda 2015k). And yet, Ennahda realises that Tunisia will not be able to implement a functioning and successful democracy without Western support.

This tension between an anti-(post)colonial impetus and simultaneous dependence on foreign aid is a well-known conundrum for Arab states (Abou-El-Fadl 2014). Ennahda repeatedly called upon Western states to provide support for the Tunisian model 'in words and action' (Ennahda 2014i, 2014af, 2015d) – while simultaneously rejecting any form of interventionism. '[L]ocal governments . . . must take the lead role in designing solutions, with strong support from the international community,' Ennahda insisted (2016h). The parallel Ennahda drew between Tunisia's liberation and its own evolution is mirrored in a double quest for recognition: Tunisia must be recognised as a state with equal rights (see Chapter 4) and Ennahda as a Muslim democratic party. Indeed, the party feared that interventionism in Tunisia would go hand in hand with its own demonisation and a reinforcement of the global clash-of-civilisations frame between Islam and the West, and Islamism and secularism. Confronted with those who did not recognise 'democratic Islamic parties like Ennahda, mistakenly grouping them with radical extremists' (Ennahda 2014h), or the 'lumpers' as it were (Lynch 2017), Rached al-Ghannouchi warned that

> putting all Islamists in the same bucket, or linking Islam itself to violence, only serves the aims of terrorists who consider democracy to be un-Islamic.

In the past, such an Islamists vs. secularists division was propagated by authoritarian regimes to distract from their own suppression of pluralism and all forms of opposition. (Ennahda 2014h)

Ennahda promoted itself as North Africa's equivalent of the German Christian Democrats (Ennahda 2016k) and as a role model for other Islamists, and Tunisia as a model democracy in the region. Its strategy could be described as gaining recognition by embracing a role conception ('Muslim democrats') deemed familiar and acceptable to a Western audience, and recognising the principles underlying the global order under Western hegemony. At the same time, it denounced the West's hypocrisy and failure to meet its own normative standards. Ennahda offers good reasons for, and wants to lead by example in the hope of, transforming the patterns of perception in the West. In this sense, and contrary to the obvious conclusion that might be drawn, Ennahda actually challenges the principles of ordering and constructions of identity and difference as can be observed in the Western hegemonic practice since the GWOT (see Chapter 1). In this sense, Ennahda therefore offers a trajectory into a possible alternative future.

Hezbollah

In contrast to Ennahda's 'recognition through recognition' strategy, Hezbollah's approach could be described as the performance of resistance on the stage of an eternally recurring play: the struggle between the oppressors and the oppressed, portrayed by different actors over the course of history. While Ennahda generally has a utopian view of Tunisia as a model for Arab-Islamic liberation which needs to be protected from specific threat scenarios and obstacles, the opposite is true for Hezbollah. On a general level, it holds a dystopian worldview according to which an eternal struggle between the oppressors and the oppressed prevails. Only very specific utopian elements can be found in its discourse, and they do not seem to stand a chance of changing the fundamental conflict structure of the world. They are intrusions of hope and optimism into an otherwise gloomy but realistic narrative of inescapable struggles in the here and now. Indeed, Hezbollah's Shi'i legacy is the most tangible in its teleology. Counterintuitively, its discursive resistance to the Western world order actually reproduces and reifies the categories of identity

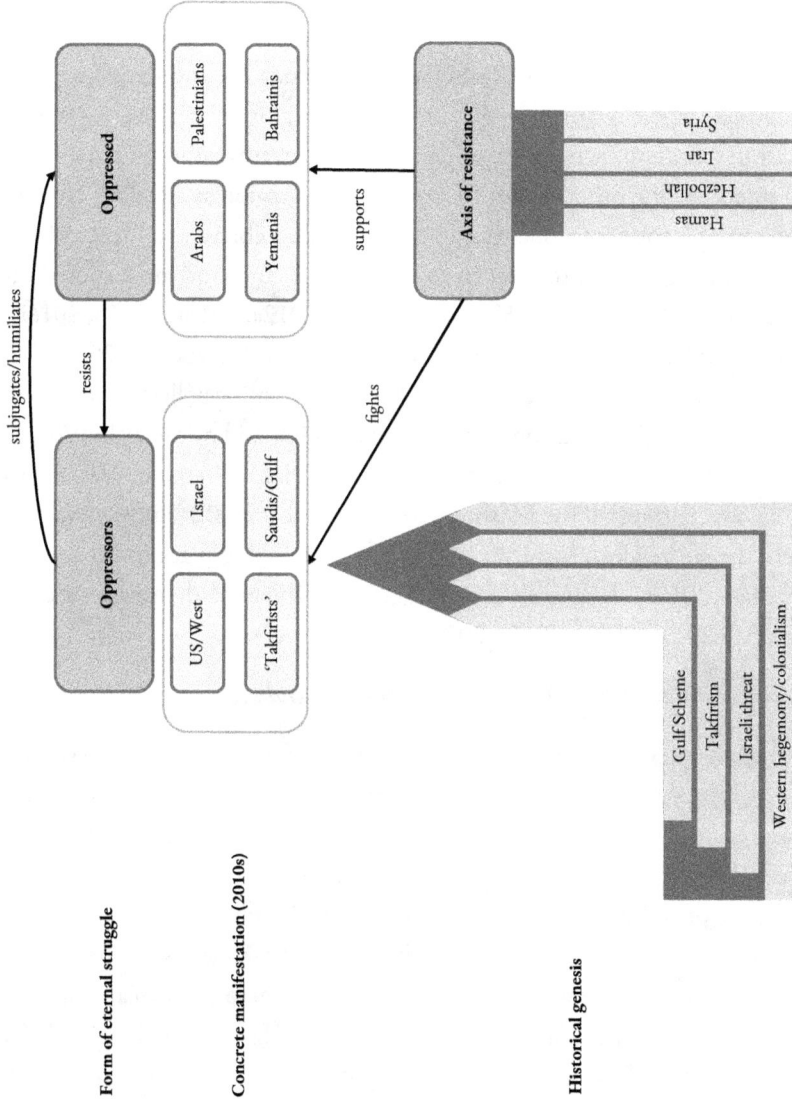

Form of eternal struggle

Concrete manifestation (2010s)

Historical genesis

Figure 6.2 Hezbollah's dystopia

and difference, as well as patterns of conflict, that have come to prevail in the Western-dominated world order over the last two decades. When it comes to *teloi*, Hezbollah's discourse can thus be considered resistant on the surface. But on a practical level, it actually affirms rather than challenges Western ordering.

Similar to Ennahda and as a corollary of its community-based conceptions of legitimacy (see Chapter 5), Hezbollah understands Lebanon's and its own destiny as inextricably linked to the future of the region. In Nasrallah's words, 'the fate of Lebanon, Syria, Iraq, Jordan, Egypt, Libya, Saudi Arabia, Bahrain, and Yemen, among other countries, is made in the region as a region. No fate is made in one country alone' (Hezbollah 2015c). Lebanon is 'most vulnerable' (Hezbollah 2015c) to the events that take place in and are imposed on the 'Arab and Islamic world' (Hezbollah 2011e, 2012a, 2013f, 2015h, 2016i), 'nation' (Hezbollah 2011c, 2011l, 2012c), 'peoples' (Hezbollah 2011b) or 'states' (Hezbollah 2015g). Besides Arab Muslims, framing collective identities in this way serves the inclusion of non-Arab Muslims and non-Muslim Arabs, too. While North Africa also plays a role in Hezbollah's discourse, Nasrallah's analyses concentrate on the Mashreq, the Gulf and Iran. But in his view, 'the globe – the entire globe – is influenced by what is taking place in the region' (Hezbollah 2015c). It is subjected to a cunning 'New Middle East scheme' (Hezbollah 2011f, 2011l, 2012a, 2012d, 2013a, 2016j).

Dystopia: Eternal Struggle between the Oppressors and the Oppressed

Hezbollah has developed a Shi'i version of a Manichaean worldview according to which history unfolds as an eternal struggle between the oppressed and the oppressors, 'righteousness and falsehood, between faithfulness and treachery and between justice and oppression' (Hezbollah 2011b). The key reference narrative is the story of the martyrdom of Husayn and the subsequent treatment of his family and followers by the tyrant Yazid (see Chapter 5). Hezbollah repeatedly reaffirms its 'pledge of allegiance' to Husayn and his heritage: 'the values of Karbala, the significance of Karbala, the morals of Karbala, the spirituality of Karbala, and the loyalty of Karbala' (Hezbollah 2014g). According to Karbala's promise, resistance is the 'path to dignity, honor, liberation and victory' (Hezbollah 2012f) and those who follow it will be under divine protection (Hezbollah 2015d, 2015i, 2016i, 2016l). The resistance does not fear death, for there is no higher honour than dying as a martyr in a noble struggle and it will be rewarded in the afterlife (Hezbollah 2011k). Martyrdom is a virtuous and heroic act that is celebrated on various regularly recurring occasions: 'Ashura' Day, Arbaeen Day, which commemorates the fortieth day after Husayn's martyrdom, the Day of the Wounded Fighters of the Islamic Resistance, and the Leader Martyrs' Day. The historical role model for martyrs is 'Ali ibn Husayn Zayn al-'Abidin, Husayn's son and the fourth imam. He had not been able to fight in the Battle of Karbala because of his poor health. As he stood in front of 'Ubayd Allah ibn Ziyad, the general who had killed his father, he said: 'O son of the freed! Are you threatening us with death? Killing is a habit to us and our dignity from Allah is martyrdom' (Hezbollah 2011g, 2015a). Moreover, the story of al-'Abbas ibn 'Ali, Husayn's half-brother, is told as a reference for the virtue of steadfastness:

> [H]is right arm was amputated, but he still went on. His left arm was amputated, too, but he went on, disregarding these harsh amputations . . . After that, an arrow hit him in the eye, but he still carried on until he was martyred and his soul ascended to the Heaven of Allah the Almighty. (Hezbollah 2013g)

Finally, there is also a central female figure whose heroism is regularly commemorated: Husayn's sister Zeynab, who is celebrated for her 'bravery and courage' (Hezbollah 2015a). When she was dragged before 'Ubayd Allah ibn Ziyad, who mocked the death of her brother and, in an attempt to humiliate her even further, asked her how she felt about what she had seen, she responded: 'I did not find but beauty. I did not see but beauty. These men were fated to be killed. They only had to show up for their death . . . May your mother mourn you, Ibn Marjana' (Hezbollah 2015a).[6]

Martyrdom, steadfastness and courage are the core virtues that are instilled in Hezbollah members, adherents, fighters and their families through the life stories of these Shi'i icons. These narratives are also invoked when martyrs are commemorated. Their life stories are told, their convictions and virtues are praised, and their deeds serve as a parable that teaches moral lessons about honourable behaviour among the oppressed (Hezbollah 2013g, 2014h, 2015a, 2015f, 2015j, 2016e, 2016g, 2016k). These ceremonies serve as opportunities for the self-reassurance and toughening of the resistance, the Shi'i community and especially the martyrs' families, who are thanked for their perseverance and sacrifice (Hezbollah 2015a). The readiness to become a martyr or bear the martyrdom of a loved one is presented as both commendable and self-evident. While martyrs' 'rewards, status, and dignity are continuously being upgraded by Allah Almighty' (Hezbollah 2016b), jihad is also a religious duty (Hezbollah 2015f, 2016a, 2016m). 'Whoever sits at home dies on his deathbed . . . In the Hereafter, Allah will call us all to account,' Nasrallah reminded his followers (Hezbollah 2016h).

Promoting the readiness to make sacrifices and die in battle as both virtuous and honourable became a particularly important part of Hezbollah's discursive strategy when it started its military engagement in Syria. This war could not easily be showcased as a resistance project. Hezbollah's discursive strategy to legitimise its engagement and continuously mobilise fighters involved making the case that the Arab-Islamic world found itself faced with a Husayn-like choice: 'war or disgrace' (Hezbollah 2014f). Nasrallah eventually claimed that this choice was imposed by 'the Americans, the "Israelis", the Takfiris, and tyrant[s]' in the Gulf (Hezbollah 2016a, 2016n). This was made possible by applying the Husayn legend, in both senses of the term, to the present. It was used as a prism through which to view schemes of oppression (legend as reading aid) and also moral lessons were drawn from it (legend as religious-historical narrative). On the one side of the conflict are the oppressed and those who defend them: the axis of resistance, consisting of Iran, Syria, Hamas and Hezbollah. And on the other side are a group of states and their proxies, which constitute the oppressors attempting to break the resistance. The latter grew out of the Western colonial project, transformed into a US–Israeli-led hegemonic project which was at first supported but now increasingly jointly run by submissive Arab regimes. What were four separate dystopian threads in the beginning of the post-Arab-uprisings era became interwoven until a cunning master plan came to light.

The first thread was the project of Western hegemony, which was already well known. Today, it is led by the US as the 'greatest devil' (Hezbollah 2015h), the 'head of occupation, tyranny and hegemony in the world' (Hezbollah 2011l), but it dates back to before the foundation of the Israeli state. While its concrete manifestations have changed over time, its core interests have remained the same: exerting power and establishing hegemony in the Middle East 'for hundreds of years to come' (Hezbollah 2016j). The project of Western hegemony began with colonialism, followed by the mandate period and the reorganisation of the region by and among the British and French. The Sykes–Picot Agreement divided the region with the intent to make Arabs 'remain [p]reoccupied with [their] wars ... until [they] get exhausted' (Hezbollah 2014b). Next was the moment of the Balfour Declaration 'when he who [did] not possess land [the British] gave [to him] who does not own land [the Jewish community]' (Hezbollah 2016f). According to Hezbollah, the mandate power allowed the Zionist movement to come to Palestine and establish

> an advanced, military, security barrack in the heart of our region in order to distort our region, to destroy it, and to waste all chances for human and economic development as well as all choices of unity and of developing the Arab and Islamic region. (Hezbollah 2014b)[7]

The US started to replace the old powers and the shift towards American hegemony coincided with the end of the Soviet empire, when the US 'became the only great power above all powers' (Hezbollah 2011d). Finally, the War in Afghanistan launched in 2001 foreshadowed an 'era of hegemony and control' (Hezbollah 2011d) at the peak of American power (Hezbollah 2014e). The invasion of Iraq in 2003, the July War in Lebanon in 2006 and the Gaza war of 2008–9 were soon to follow – the latter two being waged by the US proxy Israel. These instances served the plan to realise a 'Neo Middle East' (Hezbollah 2011d) as devised by George W. Bush and Condoleezza Rice. Its goals included breaking the axis of resistance and 'adjoin[ing] Lebanon and the whole region to the US–"Israeli"-yielding Arabs axis project' (Hezbollah 2012b, 2016j). While Hezbollah averted this danger for Lebanon, thereby thwarting the plan, the victory was only temporary – the scheme remained the same and was merely adapted (Hezbollah 2014b).

The US continued to pursue its interests: oil (Hezbollah 2011j, 2014e), protecting Israel's security (Hezbollah 2012d), 'liquidating the Palestinian cause' (Hezbollah 2014e), and turning Arabs into 'singers and dancers' (Hezbollah 2011g) rather than a respected and independent people. But the means had to be adapted after the US lost its puppet regimes following the Arab uprisings. They now aimed at 'spreading chaos, demolishing the region [and] igniting sectarian, factional, national, racial, and tribal conflicts' (Hezbollah 2012a, 2014b) so as to be able to reinstall compliant regimes in the region (Hezbollah

2011b, 2011d, 2011e, 2011k, 2011l). As Nasrallah explains, self-determination jeopardises US interests:

> When the peoples of our region revolt and call for unity, cooperation, coalition and putting all conflicts and struggles aside, that means that these peoples have set on the path of resorting their decision making, sovereignty, independence, oil, markets and future and this is not allowed by the tyrants and the gigantic companies that have control on decision making in the world. (Hezbollah 2011h)

The US also actively tried to overthrow the Assad regime and, thus, a core element of the axis of resistance. If one were to 'search for the "Israeli" and the American hand' (Hezbollah 2012d) in the Syrian war, one would find that it was just a new 'battlefield' (Hezbollah 2014b) for the US project. To achieve their goal, the US employed new means that went beyond the familiar trick of 'toppling regimes and establishing alternative authorities' (Hezbollah 2014e). Rather, they now tried to 'destroy, crush, and ruin everything' (Hezbollah 2014e) using proxies on the ground to reintroduce themselves as heroes and liberators who can restore order (Hezbollah 2015d, 2016j). This would be the moment to draw a new map of the region (Hezbollah 2014e).

The second thread concerns the enmity with Israel. While Israel is also a part of the Western hegemony project, it also constitutes a more concrete, aggressive danger. Nasrallah's descriptions of Israel, which is always put in inverted commas, are framed in a hostile language. He often refers to the country simply as 'the enemy', the 'Zionist' or the 'usurping entity' (Hezbollah 2012c, 2013f, 2014b), the 'Zionist hegemonic project' (Hezbollah 2016o) that 'longs to engulf [Arab] territories and wealth' (Hezbollah 2016l). More dramatically, Nasrallah also frames Israel as a 'cancerous gland, a terrorist state, an aggressive entity, a corruptive germ, and a title for tyranny and arrogance' (Hezbollah 2015a). The country has 'one of the strongest armies of the world' (Hezbollah 2015i) at its disposal. It is a 'waylaying' (Hezbollah 2011c) threat to its neighbours and attacks can happen at any time and without pretext (Hezbollah 2013c, 2013d, 2014c, 2016i). It is also an unjust enemy that conducts wars of destruction, attacks civilians, aims at annihilating populations (Hezbollah 2012b, 2014a, 2014c) and is 'aggressive in nature' (Hezbollah 2012c). No change in government would transform its character as an eternal enemy (Hezbollah 2011k, 2012a): 'Whether the parties are made of right-ists, extreme rightists, leftists, extreme leftists, moderates, or whoever, they all threaten the regional governments and peoples' (Hezbollah 2013f). Its greed transcends the Palestinian territories and goes beyond the Sinai, Golan and Lebanon: it is a danger to 'all the states . . . and the Arab and Islamic peoples in the region' (Hezbollah 2014c). Like the US, the Israelis have an interest in regional chaos. Arab distraction allows them to enforce a settlement on their terms on Palestinians (Hezbollah 2011f, 2013b, 2014c) and expedite their 'Judaisation' project (Hezbollah 2011e, 2011g, 2012d, 2012f, 2014f). Nasrallah holds that 'any ordeal must be judged against [the] background of [the] Zionist project; we must search for the "Israeli" hands behind the chaos spread in our region' (Hezbollah 2012a). This image of an unchange-able, omnipresent and omnipotent enemy clearly resonates with antisemitic stereotypes, even though Hezbollah distinguishes between Jews and Zionists in its discourse (Alagha 2011, 19).

The third thread evolved during the period between 2011 and 2016 and changed significantly in this time: the Saudi–Gulf scheme. Hezbollah was critical of the Gulf monarchies even before the Arab uprisings. But in the first years after the mass protests, its rhetoric was still indirect and constrained. Nasrallah talked about 'moderation countries' (Hezbollah 2011h), 'yielding Arabs' (Hezbollah 2012b) or 'oil-producing Arab states' (Hezbollah 2013a). An exception was the Khalifa dynasty in Bahrain, which Nasrallah openly shamed for its massive crackdown on the protestors in 2011 (Hezbollah 2011e, 2012a, 2013b). After the so-called Arab Coalition started its war on Yemen, Nasrallah's framing of the Saudis became more hostile. Nasrallah refers to Saudi Arabia sarcastically as the 'Kingdom of "Benevolence"' (Hezbollah 2015l) where '[w]hoever talks is beheaded, and whoever objects is beheaded' (Hezbollah 2016i), or the 'killing machine that is . . . allied with other worldly devils' (Hezbollah 2016a). Eventually, he even perceives the Saudis as 'more "Israeli" than the "Israelis"' (Hezbollah 2015e, 2015h, 2016h).

According to Hezbollah, the Saudi–Gulf scheme's goal is twofold. First, it aims at establishing US–Saudi hegemony in the region by eliminating any challenge to the Gulf monarchies' power. Second, the Saudis try to dissemi-nate the 'Takfirist' mindset and teachings, which, in the end, are indistinguish-able from Wahhabi ideology. Hezbollah alleged early on that Saudi Arabia had financed and planned the 'Takfirist' scheme in Syria and Iraq, as well as supporting al-Qaʻida and ISIS in Yemen (Hezbollah 2015i, 2015l, 2016e). Nasrallah mysteriously uttered his suspicions:

> [W]e always took pains not to talk overtly despite the information we had on what is taking place in Syria during the past four [years] . . . We knew everything that used to take place in Iraq since 2003, but we did not talk overtly. (Hezbollah 2015l)

This caution should be seen as a tribute to the close relations that exist between Lebanon and Saudi Arabia through the Hariri family, on the one hand, and the Lebanese living and working in Saudi exile, on the other.

But Hezbollah abandoned its caution once the Yemen war started in 2015 – and Nasrallah then no longer minced his words. He claimed that Saudi activities dated back decades before the regional crises that began in 2011. According to Nasrallah, the kingdom had supported Saddam Hussein's Iraq in attacking Iran, the US in ruining Iraq and different Lebanese Civil War parties in fighting each other (Hezbollah 2015i, 2015l). With their behaviour after the Arab uprisings, however, the Saudis reached an unprecedented 'degree of inferiority and moral deterioration' (Hezbollah 2016i). This manifested itself in not only the ruthless war waged in Yemen but also the other wars of the region in which 'they acted by proxy', such as in Syria and Iraq, where 'the financing is Saudi, the instigation is Saudi, the management is Saudi' (Hezbollah 2015l). Those who deemed Saudi Arabia a reliable ally eventually woke up and grasped the role the kingdom was playing in the spread of 'Takfirism': 'The entire world is now . . . well aware that all the terrorism in this world and in any corner in the world is due to the intellect and money of the [Saudis]' (Hezbollah 2016n).

The fourth thread, thus, initially seems rather similar to the third one: the threat posed by Salafi jihadism in the ISIS or al-Qaʻida version. In Nasrallah's language, they are dubbed terrorists and 'Takfirists' rather than jihadists – a term which has positive connotations in Hezbollah's discursive universe. Nasrallah rejects any attempt to differentiate between strands of 'Takfirism' or 'the good "Daesh" and the bad "Daesh", because they are both "Daesh"' (Hezbollah 2015c) at the end of the day. There is only one 'Takfirist' mindset because 'they learn from the same religious educational books' (Hezbollah 2016i), irrespective of whether the individual groups call themselves al-Qaʻida,

ISIS, JN or Boko Haram. According to Hezbollah, 'Takfirism' grew to become an existential menace to the whole region, its peoples and 'their civilization, their history, their diversity, their right to live a dignified peaceful life, their right to partnership, and their right of free expression' (Hezbollah 2013g, 2014c, 2014e, 2015c, 2015d, 2015f). 'Takfirists' also threaten Islam itself as they commit atrocities in its name, which is the 'worst deformation in human history for a divine religion' (Hezbollah 2015c). No one should see themselves as exempt from the danger posed by ISIS, not even those who support it today as they will be its victims tomorrow. If left unchallenged, this 'Nakba' (Hezbollah 2015h) will make 'the entire region . . . see [its] worst days ever' (Hezbollah 2013a).

In the course of the events that unfolded between 2011 and 2016, Nasrallah slowly but surely connected these four threads of oppression to eventually create one overarching dystopia which he described as the 'US, "Israeli", Takfiri, Saudi scheme that wants to practice hegemony and control' (Hezbollah 2016h). As early as 2012, Nasrallah hinted at a 'deep penetration into . . . Takfiri fighting groups by US and "Israeli" intelligence' (Hezbollah 2012a). In 2013, Nasrallah considered the possibility that the US had brought 'Takfirist' groups to Syria and provided them with money and other assistance in order to overthrow the Assad regime (Hezbollah 2013a). But he still articulated a degree of uncertainty, admitting that the only trustworthy information he had was 'that the Americans kept a blind eye on that, offered facilitations, and opened the gates to exploit this phenomenon [of "Takfirism"]' (Hezbollah 2014e) – ISIS and similar groups offered themselves as a 'natural ally' (Hezbollah 2015a) to the US and Israel. The Saudi funding of 'Takfirist' projects made their project even easier, Nasrallah claimed: ISIS, as the 'new savage black army with its arms, ensures [the achievement of] all the US–"Israeli" goals in the region while the Americans and the "Israelis" watch without paying any penny' (Hezbollah 2016h, 2016j).

Nasrallah's final assessment of the situation seems to be that the US deliberately counted on chaos to spread and conflicts to deteriorate without the need for direct engagement. His argument is that the US is responsible at least in so far as it cannot have failed to notice the growth of 'Takfirism', how the 'Takfirists' were financed and armed, and that its regional allies were behind these groups ideologically, financially and logistically (Hezbollah 2016j). The

Western and Israeli goal in the Middle East was to make Arabs fight Arabs and Muslims fight Muslims so as to impede the creation of a unified popular will and so that they would develop and pursue their own independent interests. In particular, this was implemented by inflaming a global fight against the axis of resistance in which more and more regional actors became involved. Aspects of this fight included a demonisation of Iran, which served as a pretext for the Saudi-led war on Yemen (Hezbollah 2015i), attempts by Turkey and the Gulf states to establish a more 'friendly' government in Syria (Hezbollah 2015i), and the designation of Hezbollah as a terrorist actor by the GCC and the Arab League (Hezbollah 2016c, 2016k). Eventually, 'the truth which [was] being revealed day after day' (Hezbollah 2016o) was that all conflicts in the region were working towards the same goal: putting an end to the resistance. As the Arab uprisings had yielded a 'peak of the resistance project' (Hezbollah 2016l), at least according to Hezbollah, the US, Western, Israeli and Arab allies did everything to quash it. 'The true supporters of the resistance are being fought and killed around the world, whether in Syria, Iraq, Bahrain, Yemen, Nigeria, and other countries in the world where people demonstrate in the hundreds of thousands for Palestine and for Al Quds' (Hezbollah 2016o). The cunning twist in the scheme, according to Nasrallah, is that the escalation of violence would eventually serve as a pretext for the US to legitimise the renewed presence of military bases and troops in the region: 'they will present themselves to the peoples of the region as fake protectors and defenders' (Hezbollah 2016h, 2016n).

Utopian Fragment(s): Victory of the Resistance (and Peaceful Coexistence in Difference)

The comprehensiveness and complexity of Hezbollah's dystopia is contrasted with a flat and tentative utopian outlook: the victory of the oppressed and the resistance. The axis 'made great accomplishments and victories' (Hezbollah 2013c) in the face of a variety of oppressive schemes and managed to remain 'intact' (Hezbollah 2014b) in spite of all efforts to destroy it. Its new challenges and battles made the resistance 'emerge firmer and stronger' (Hezbollah 2016l, 2016o). But this glimpse of utopia is relativised by the predictable recurrence of Husayn's choice, the inescapability of the conflict between the oppressors and the oppressed.

Serving as a mobilising narrative, the prospect of victory builds on the past track record of the resistance and Shi'i accomplishments. For Hezbollah, the era of victory began with the Islamic Revolution in Iran in 1979. With the ousting of the Shah, the US lost an important ally, which reconfigured the regional political game (Hezbollah 2016l). The second event was the development of the resistance in southern Lebanon and the invention of new tactics to counter the Israeli invasion (Hezbollah 2011k, 2012c). Over the years of the Israeli occupation of Lebanon, Hezbollah successfully resisted attempts to reduce its room for manoeuvre and stop its military activities against the IDF and Israeli territory (Hezbollah 2011i, 2016h). Then came the liberation of Lebanon in May 2000, which Hezbollah celebrates as 'the fruit of the accumulation of all sacrifices since 1948 until today offered by all factions, groups and parties which remained steadfast' (Hezbollah 2011l) in their resistance. The Israeli withdrawal in 'humiliation and defeat' (Hezbollah 2011i) constituted yet another shift in the regional balance because it 'hammered the last pin in the coffin of Greater "Israel"' (Hezbollah 2012c). While this triumph had to be credited to the resistance, it had to be celebrated as a 'Lebanese-Arab-national-Islamic achievement" (Hezbollah 2014b) and a day of liberation for all Lebanese (Hezbollah 2011i).

The next step in what would become a history of the resistance's victory was the Israeli withdrawal from Gaza in 2005 (Hezbollah 2011g, 2012f, 2013a). With the July War in southern Lebanon just one year later, Israel had to accept what Hezbollah considers a critical defeat. The fact that 'they flopped and were defeated and broken' (Hezbollah 2015k) caused a severe crisis of confidence and left psychological wounds in Israeli society (Hezbollah 2011f). Israelis no longer trusted the military abilities and capabilities or the strategic abilities of their military and political leaders (Hezbollah 2012d, 2015a, 2016j). At the same time, the victory boosted Arab confidence because the July War had proved that '"Israel" is no more unbeatable in the eyes of Arabs' (Hezbollah 2011l, 2016i). Never before had an Arab army achieved victory against Israel. Hezbollah had thus achieved a long-term victory on the psychological level (Hezbollah 2011f). The next decisive blow to the 'New Middle East' scheme, according to Hezbollah, was the forced US withdrawal from Iraq in 2011, for which it credits the resistance of the Iraqi people and the support provided by Iran and Syria (Hezbollah 2011g, 2011k, 2012f).

Since the 2006 victory, Lebanon was successful in deterring Israel through its army–people–resistance formula (Hezbollah 2011j, 2014f, 2015a, 2016a). Resistance 'is a culture' (Hezbollah 2014a) in Lebanon now and this is what grants its victory (see also the 'society of resistance' as discussed in Saade 2016, 29, 138).

The new battles in Syria, Iraq, Yemen and Bahrain as well as the continued struggle in Palestine demand sacrifices (Hezbollah 2014c). For these conflicts, Hezbollah formulates micro-utopias. In Palestine, the day will come 'when an independent Palestinian state is established on the entire land of Palestine from the Sea to the River' (Hezbollah 2011j). The Yemeni people will never give up defending 'their dignity, existence, land, and honor' (Hezbollah 2015i), which, according to the laws of history and 'Divine Justice' (Hezbollah 2016k), will allow them to emerge victorious. Even the 'Takfirist' scheme can be averted by those who were able to defeat the Zionist projects (Hezbollah 2014c, 2014e, 2016h). The fact that the 'Takfirists' did not manage to take control of the Syrian government should be considered a 'great victory' (Hezbollah 2014f) – brought about by the joint efforts of the Syrian government troops and Hezbollah, as Nasrallah emphasises (Hezbollah 2015h, 2016d).

Beyond martial discourse and the belief that resistance and steadfastness will be rewarded, Hezbollah has little to offer in terms of utopia. One dim vision that shines through its discourse here and there is the idea of Islamic unity and intercivilisational peace. Arab liberation can only manifest itself once religious communities become aware of their commonalities rather than their differences. For instance, as Nasrallah elaborates:

> Muslims might differ on the issue of Imamate, caliphate and the rule after the Prophet of Allah, but they do not differ over their love to those near of kin to the Prophet of Allah and their love to the Household of the Prophet of Allah. (Hezbollah 2011h)

In line with its community-based conception of legitimacy (see Chapter 5), Hezbollah advocates the idea that a Muslim self-understanding as one nation should prevail, common causes and interests be identified, and reconciliation processes be initiated where sects have grown apart (Hezbollah 2011h, 2011l, 2016o). Muslim unity is not, however, a synonym for 'melting the various sects in one sect' (Hezbollah 2011h). In contrast to ISIS's programme of eliminating difference, Hezbollah foregrounds intra-Islamic pluralism as a value that constitutes Islamic unity (Hezbollah 2015e, 2016d, 2016i, 2016o) – or as one interviewee put it, rephrasing what, according to a hadith, the Prophet said: '*Ikhtilāf ummati raḥma* –differences in my nation are a blessing' (Interview 7). Such appreciation of difference should be extended to Christians, too (Hezbollah 2015c). As Nasrallah formulates it, '[p]eople are one of two groups: either a brother of yours in religion or a fellow of yours in creation' (Hezbollah 2011h). As a faint hope on the horizon, he describes 'a state of harmony between the governments and the peoples' (Hezbollah 2011l) in the Arab and Islamic world. For while 'the slaves of wealth, authority, and this mundane world will court the tyrant', he assures, 'this nation is full of scholars, politicians, leaders, elites, educated men, journalists, peoples, and free men and women' (Hezbollah 2016i).

Discussion

It is in Hezbollah's bleak outlook on a world caught up in eternal conflict that its identity as resistance is most clearly articulated. As new oppressive schemes potentially hide behind every turn of history, Hezbollah and all those who are neither naive nor arrogant have to remain alert (Hezbollah 2014c, 2014e). The party claims that it is a defender not only of Shi'a in Lebanon or of the Lebanese nation against outside threats but of the poor, marginalised, oppressed and subjugated in a more global sense (Interview 5). While this mission of defence refers to oppressive schemes of any sort and is thus generalised, it stems from a very particular Shi'i narrative of Husayn's and his followers' resistance in the face of humiliation by an unjust ruler. The potential to mobilise fighters and promote steadfastness among their families is an important function of the celebration of historical and contemporary heroes, the ritualised memory of the fallen in the times of the Prophet and Husayn and of those who gave their lives in the resistance projects designed to fend off plans for a 'New Middle East'. The reference to religious tradition and values is, hence, most affective and pronounced in Hezbollah's dystopian view, which it derives from an understanding of history as a series of struggles.

But the idea of resistance became increasingly hard to sell. The reason why Hezbollah had to engage in the Syrian war was not immediately evident from its previous legitimation of the use of force, nor was it easily reconcilable with the resistance project. Its deployment of fighters to Syria imposed costs on the Shi'i community in Lebanon, both directly through the loss of fighters in the war and more indirectly through attacks in Shi'a neighbourhoods in Lebanon (Lob 2014, Farida 2020, 122). The amalgamation of the four threat scenarios into one big dystopia has to be seen in this light. It allows the continual production and reproduction of identity and the legitimation of the practice of resistance as resistance. Only if Syria is threatened by a hegemonic scheme can helping the Assad regime be framed as a case in which Husayn's imperative applies. Its intervention was necessary, Hezbollah claimed, because outside powers attempted to break the axis of resistance by hijacking the Arab uprisings and pursuing an agenda of, first, regime change and, when that failed, chaos. Consequently, Hezbollah became a regional intervention force, active first and foremost in Syria, but also in Yemen and Iraq in the name of resisting the 'US, "Israeli", Takfiri, Saudi scheme' (Hezbollah 2016h).

This perpetuation of the resistance narrative in Hezbollah's discourse was aimed at distracting from the very pragmatic reasons Hezbollah had for engaging in Syria, as long-time observers of the party have pointed out (Khatib 2015). Among them are its interest in securing a constant supply of weapons and the direct order from Iran to help keep the Assad regime in power. The former is important for Hezbollah to keep its position of power in Lebanese domestic politics, where its weapons serve as a latent and sometimes manifest and credible threat. The latter is an immediate consequence of the allegiance to *wilāyat al-faqīh*, according to which the involvement in war is to be decided by the supreme jurist (Khatib 2015, 110–11, Qassem 2010). Neither, however, are reasons that Hezbollah gives in its discourse – they are not consistent with its ethics of the legitimate use of force, nor its insistence on being a Lebanese and independent actor (see Chapter 5). These reasons, therefore, constitute important instances of the unsaid. Beyond the legitimation of Hezbollah's involvement in Syria, the direct and indirect consequences of this involvement also had to be processed discursively and, in turn, yielded new legitimation problems (Farida 2020, 120–39). In addition to the human losses that Hezbollah's participation in the Syrian war caused, its support of the Assad regime was costly in other respects as well. Even though Hezbollah went to great lengths to claim the opposite in its discourse, its support of the Assad family, the Houthis in Yemen and Bahraini protestors was read as being motivated by sectarianism – and it contributed to sectarian tensions and violence in Lebanon (Khatib 2015, see also Chapter 3). Conjuring up Arab and Muslim unity and identifying Western hegemony, the Israeli threat, 'Takfirism' and Saudi aggressions as a danger to all Arabs and Muslims in their diversity was one alternative framing of conflict dynamics that Hezbollah tried to discursively construct as reality (see Chapter 2). The creation of new enemy images served both to keep 'resistance' plausible and to mitigate the sectarianising effects of Hezbollah's actions. Yet none of this prevented Hezbollah from casually using sectarian rhetoric and reproducing sectarian categories, while simultaneously claiming to reject them. This ambiguity allows for the mobilisation of the Shi'i community, in particular, and the appeasement of the Lebanese public, in general, at the same time. But as we know today, this 'playful' sectarianism – which is by no means unique to Hezbollah – was a game that, at some point, the Lebanese were all too familiar with, and they were thus well aware of its ability to gloss over the failure to actually address political, social and economic problems. In 2019, they decided to no longer play along and mass protests erupted in Lebanon, markedly turning against the sectarian system and politics (see the Conclusion of this book).

While Hezbollah insists on being resistant, the extent to which its discourse reflects both the clash of civilisations and the dystopias of the Western hegemony is striking. While the addition of the 'Takfirists' and the Gulf states to the list of oppressors seems to relativise a marked 'West' versus 'Islam' dichotomy, Hezbollah ultimately considers both tools in the hands of the US and its allies in their endeavour to continue the subjugation of the region. The Others created in Hezbollah's discourse are not equally distal and different (Hansen 2006), and whereas 'the West' and Israel appear unchangeable, the 'Takfirists' and the Gulf states seem to be more of a temporary (albeit no less urgent) problem. In this sense, Hezbollah reifies rather than resists the epistemology offered by Western hegemonic discourse, especially the antagonistic relations between the Western Others and Arab-Muslim Selves. However, the derivation of these categories and, more broadly, the lens through which global conflict dynamics are interpreted stem from Shi'i religious discourse – and, therefore, can be considered a transformation of the dystopias present in Western discourse or a form of resistance against the Western world order. They are used to expose Western hypocrisy and denounce its stance towards the 'Middle East' and North Africa as one claiming to be underpinned by morals but in fact driven by interests. '[T]he ruler of the American, western and other world administrations is not united norms. Right[s] and values are not the adopted norms,' Nasrallah explains. 'Norms are rather political considerations and interests' (Hezbollah 2011b).

Analysing the lens through which an armed non-state actor perceives reality is important, and not only from the perspective of Islamist and area studies. Rather, Hezbollah illustrates the high relevance of non-state actors for trans- and international conflict dynamics. Rebel groups and other ANSAs tend to be analysed in their 'domestic' context, for example the civil war or local conflict dynamics of which they are part (Pfeifer and Schwab 2023a), even though the transnational character and properties of these conflicts are well known (Salehyan 2009). The transnational aspect has often been seen as a function of 'strategic calculations at domestic and regional levels' (Darwich 2021b, 5), although the above would suggest the opposite. It is because of a certain worldview and ideas of what its basic operating principles and conflict structures are that Hezbollah acts in a certain way domestically, regionally and globally. As May Darwich (2021b, 5) rightfully demands, approaches of foreign policy analysis should be applied to actors such as Hezbollah, so as to study them as a more disaggregated phenomenon and come to more fine-grained conclusions. Following her impetus, the above could be read as an analysis of Hassan Nasrallah's operational code (Holsti 1977, S. G. Walker 1983), for it reveals his beliefs about the conflictual nature of global politics and links them to actions taken by Hezbollah to influence its international environment. 'Today, the globe – the entire globe – is influenced by what is taking place in the region,' as Nasrallah has put it (Hezbollah 2015c). For Hezbollah, this means that it must take action to influence global politics by confronting the regional manifestation of hegemonic schemes.

Notes

1. France is never explicitly named as the former colonial power, even though colonial rule and its injustice are frequently referenced. This can only be interpreted as a strategy to avoid confrontation with an important cooperation partner. Similarly, while the old regime is often explicitly associated with Ben Ali, Habib Bourguiba is never named as a culprit. On the contrary, he is sometimes lauded as an impor-

tant leader in the liberation movement. For the ambivalent relationship between *Nahdawis* and Bourguiba, see also Ounissi (2016).

2. It is astonishing how close some of Ennahda's considerations are to what is referred to as a 'transition paradigm' in the democratisation literature; see, for example, Carothers (2002).

3. The regime 'used Islamists as a scarecrow in order to frighten progressives, women and the West, and to silence all those who spoke out against it'.

4. 'If we want to demonise the Salafists, it will be them who will be in power ten to fifteen years from now'.

5. 'A period of crisis when society was divided into two parts'.

6. Marjana was 'Ubayd Allah's mother. 'Ibn Marjana' translates as 'son of Marjana'.

7. This narrative is misleading because the first two *aliyot* or waves of Jewish migration had already occurred in the nineteenth century to Ottoman Palestine. See, for example, Gelvin (2021).

CONCLUSION: ISLAMISTS AS (WORLD) POLITICAL ACTORS AND CO-PRODUCERS OF GLOBAL ORDER

The Global Order in Ennahda's and Hezbollah's Discourse: More Recognition than Resistance

This study set out to explore Islamists' position on the Western-dominated global order. It aimed to move beyond the position of rejectionism that is sometimes ascribed to all Islamists by universalising a stance that is particular to Salafi jihadism. In the course of the 'global war on terror' (GWOT), groups belonging to this latter strand have hegemonised the public imaginary of 'Islamists' as 'terrorists'. This shortcut glosses over two important distinctions: the one between Islamists and terrorists, and the one between Islamists and Salafi jihadists. The findings of this book confirm that sustaining these conceptual differences is important. It has found that Ennahda and Hezbollah, two – albeit unique – representatives of statist Islamism, do not engage in the type of politics of rejectionism that al-Qaʻida or the ISIS organisation do. They do not even strongly resist, that is, object to or aim to transform, elements of order that mark the boundaries with Western world order discourse. Rather, their Islamism manifests in the nuances given to conceptions of sovereignty and legitimacy and, more prominently, in their understanding of the unfolding and *telos* of history. But what is just as important for their take on the Western-dominated world order as their Islamism is their anti-colonial identity and positionality in a postcolonial political context. It is from this point of view that they criticise, denounce and reject practices of ordering, especially when these deviate from or even clash with the principles and norms upheld in the discourse of powerful actors in the global order. This is the (modest) resistance part of the story.

But recognition is much more prominent in both Islamist discourses. Ennahda and Hezbollah argue (from) within the epistemological and normative universe spanned by Western world order discourse. In their own respective versions, they recognise the principles of global order as posited by at least one, and more often a combination of several, of the strands of Western discourse. They also both seek recognition within the global order. In Ennahda's case, this translates into a discursive strategy of foregrounding categories of identity (similarity, comparability, translatability, consensus). It thereby hopes to prove worthy of being considered as equal. The method Ennahda employs for gaining recognition as part of the global order is to visibly and explicitly signal recognition of the order's principles. For Hezbollah, however, the recognition project seems a bit more complicated. Its self-proclaimed 'resistance' is not directed against the foundations of Western world order discourse. Although its behaviour may appear deviant to others, Hezbollah tries to show that, upon closer inspection, its actions do not even infringe upon a given normative principle of global order, or it attempts to make a convincing case for why an exception is appropriate. This discursive practice, then, confirms the respective norm or order principle at hand.[1] Its resistance targets specific actors and their practices (which are illegitimate according to Hezbollah's own standards) and some strands of Western discourse. Hezbollah's position on global order is far from one of rejectionism and is resistant in limited respects. What is more, while Hezbollah demonstratively performs 'resistance' (self-defence, protection, alertness, steadfastness), it actually seems to seek recognition of its legitimacy according to the standards of a Western-dominated global order, or even for being a morally superior actor who defends the powerless and disenfranchised. Its strategy is thus geared towards being recognised as different but not radically different, as being an equal in a struggle that is inescapable. It thereby reproduces the antagonisms to which two decades of GWOT rhetoric have given rise: the West versus the Muslim world. In contrast, Ennahda is able to offer a transforming and, therefore, resistant impetus to this structuring of global conflict and mutual Othering. For both Tunisia and itself, it claims a bridge-building role: between Islamism and secularism, between Europe and Africa, between Western and Arab-Muslim models of political (or rather, democratic) order, for a future that can unite in diversity.

Ennahda: The Muslim Democratic Role Model for Living in Harmony

As the previous chapters demonstrated, Ennahda's discourse on global order is best described as the consensus-oriented navigation of an unstable yet promising domestic situation in Tunisia. The country was, on the one hand, in the very process of transitioning from authoritarianism to democracy. For Ennahda, this created a window of opportunity to leave behind its shadowy existence as suppressed opposition and emerge as a regular part of Tunisian political life. But both Tunisia's transition and Ennahda's transformation were precarious and preliminary, threatened by the danger of authoritarian backsliding and societal polarisation. On the other hand, Ennahda was aware of the external conditions required for this change to succeed and the risks that might undermine it. Among these risks were the contagion of coups and civil wars, transnational terrorism and the misrecognition of Tunisia as an inferior country rather than a free and equal state, and of Ennahda as 'radical extremists' (Ennahda 2014i) rather than a legitimate political party (for a discussion of misrecognition of non-state actors, see Clément, Geis and Pfeifer 2021). Ennahda's world order discourse between 2011 and 2016 is, therefore, a dual survival strategy. The international audience is approached as the producer of a global order the structure of which will determine the persistence of Tunisian democracy and Ennahda's (thin) recognition as part of the domestic and regional political game.

Ennahda's conception of sovereignty is marked by an insistence on both popular and absolute sovereignty and a negotiation of the tensions between them. But, in the end, for Ennahda, there is 'not much to say' about sovereignty, because it has firmly internalised the idea that the world order consists of equal states inhabited by self-determined peoples. Its rejection of external intervention by third parties is a confirmation of these two sovereignty principles and equates to a stance taken against conditional sovereignty. While Ennahda tentatively formulates ideas on supranational and, more importantly, subnational versions of shared sovereignty, the conception does not play a prominent role in its discourse. If Ennahda's sovereignty discourse is connected to the hope of Tunisia being recognised as an equal member of the world order, its legitimacy conception mirrors its struggle for recognition as a normal political party whose right to participation in Tunisian democracy is irrevocable. The addressees of this quest are Tunisian and international secularists who are suspicious of Islamists and convinced that Islamic democracy is a contradiction in terms.

Ennahda's methodology of consensus is the party's way of demonstrating that it is radically unradical. Its model of Islamic democracy is presented as a version of realising community-based legitimacy which is easily reconcilable with individualist, liberal values and deliberative democracy. When this was found to be insufficient to prove the harmlessness of its Islamist project, Ennahda discursively sacrificed its self-identification with political Islam. From then on, it promoted itself as a party of Muslim democrats, the North African version of a 'normal' (read: familiar to Europeans) conservative party. Both its sovereignty and its legitimacy discourse were meant to smooth the bumpy road to a utopia in which a democratic Tunisia, inhabited by a prosperous and free people and enriched by a thriving civil society, would enter international relations in the spirit of cooperation and recognition as equal in difference. As its discourse on *teloi* showed, however, the party was acutely aware of the dangers that could stand in the way of it fulfilling this normative vision. Ennahda's discourse on world order is couched in a language fully intelligible and accessible to Western audiences. Where there are frictions, Ennahda offers to solve the underlying contradictions or to adapt its conceptions and even its identity. It is open to such change because history has demonstrated that the Islamic movement needs to work through reality as it asserts itself, which includes large-scale transformations from colonisation to dictatorship to revolution to terrorism. Ennahda wants Tunisia to become a model for the region, and it wants to be a shining example itself. It believes that this can inspire change in others, too.

Hezbollah: Husayn's Choice and the Duty to Resistance on Behalf of the Oppressed

While Hezbollah's discourse pushes the boundaries of Western conceptions of global order more tangibly than Ennahda's, it does so in ways that cannot simply be ascribed to its 'Islamism'. Religion plays a role but in ways that are much more subtle. Hezbollah's discourse between 2011 and 2016 is also far from inaccessibly irrational, as vulgar versions of securitised secularist discourse would have it. The ideological framework within which Hezbollah has to act and present its arguments is determined by the party's adherence to *wilāyat al-faqīh*. As Naim Qassem explains, Hezbollah sees 'Sharia's verdicts and judgments' as revealed by the jurist-theologian as 'the spiritual authority of last resort' (Qassem 2010, 113) and complies with the 'general political commandments' (Qassem 2010, 119) defined by him. These include the rejection of hegemony, the common pursuit of unity, the fight against Israel and caring for the needy. This commitment does not, however, 'limit the scope of internal work at the level of forging relations with the various powers and constituents of Lebanon' (Qassem 2010, 121). Qassem goes on to claim that Hezbollah is also free 'in the sphere of regional and international cooperation with groups with whom the Party's strategic direction or concerns meet' (Qassem 2010, 121). But this already hints at a distinction between two logics of operation that are more manifest in Hezbollah's political discourse, those being internal and external affairs. The former realm mainly refers to Lebanon but is sometimes extended to the Arab-Islamic world. In it, Hezbollah strives for unity. The latter works through difference or, rather, antagonism. Here, Hezbollah is concerned with 'resistance' understood as (collective) self-defence.

Hezbollah is a strong advocate of both popular and absolute sovereignty. But it adds a notion of shared sovereignty to the conceptual mix which creates tensions in its overall sovereignty discourse. The party tries to solve this problem by applying its 'two worlds' logic. It distinguishes between a domestic and an international realm as 'scope conditions' for the applicability of sovereignty principles. For Hezbollah, absolute and popular sovereignty are permanently put in jeopardy by scheming third parties and external forces. As both principles need to be upheld, the 'army–people–resistance formula' comes in as a type of auxiliary conception of sovereignty. Only by supplementing the weak state and military capacities can the Lebanese borders be secured and the people remain free. Because absolute and popular sovereignty are threatened and weakened from the outside, they need to be defended with additional means from the inside (support from the armed resistance) – which actually further undermines the two principles. This is an element of resistance in Hezbollah's discourse on global order. For while it reproduces notions of absolute and popular sovereignty, it innovates upon and pushes the boundaries of the conceptions of shared sovereignty articulated in Western discourse. The transformative impulse with regard to sovereignty is the claim that non-state actors have sovereignty, too.

This is mirrored in Hezbollah's conception of legitimacy, which follows the 'two worlds' logic, too. For Lebanese society, a dialogue-, compromise- and cooperation-oriented political process (the 'budget version' of deliberative legitimacy) and a community-based political system (doing justice to the sectarian composition of Lebanese society) are adequate. They are intended to bring about a fairly peaceful coexistence and enough cohesion for the Lebanese to stand as one 'society of resistance'.[2] Only then will Lebanon be equipped to confront a hostile outside world and a global order in and through which great powers seek to impose hegemony and heteronomy on the Arab-Islamic world. For Hezbollah, any consideration of legitimacy is inextricably linked to the question of violence. It is completely preoccupied with legitimating and delegitimating acts, forms, perpetrators, victims and structures of violence in its discourse. It tries to argue that non-state actors can resort to violence in legitimate ways that are similar to state practices. This is another instance of resistance to Western discourse.

However, it also seeks to be recognised as acting in accordance with the standards and norms regarding the legitimate use of force as established in international norms (and Western discourse) and as being different from other, illegitimate, ANSAs: 'Takfirists' or 'terrorists'. It understands its resort to violence as a necessity to counter schemes of domination and hegemony devised by Western powers, Israel and their allies for the region. The legitimacy of Hezbollah's violence derives from the blatant injustice and illegitimacy of the violence committed by the oppressors. Hezbollah claims that it is one of the few groups that resist and defend the oppressed. It thereby fulfils its religious duty and follows Imam Husayn and his companions, the antetypes of steadfastness in the face of humiliation. The underlying structure of the conflict between the oppressors and the oppressed is unchangeable but its concrete manifestation varies throughout history. The task for Hezbollah and the Arab-Islamic world, then, is to reveal and uncover the disguise of new plans and schemes. This essentialised image of an inescapable conflict is simultaneously the motor of history. It is as evocative of the clash-of-civilisations imaginary as it is reminiscent of the dystopia of Western hegemony. In this sense, Hezbollah's discourse echoes Western dystopias of the global order and thereby also reproduces enemy images. Rather than resisting hegemonic discourse, Hezbollah reifies, reproduces and, counterintuitively, recognises the basic parameters which Western discourse sets for the interpretation of conflicts in MENA and their future evolution. But within this structure of conflict, the party ends up on the opposite side from the West. The resistant part, then, is the religious legitimation, the evocation of Shi'i tradition and the application of Husayn's story as a script for contemporary conflict, which all justify Hezbollah's choice of sides and militant action. The group believes that necessary change or rather the prevention of evil plans can only be achieved through (violent) intervention in regional and global politics.

Widening the Space–Time of Islamist World Order Discourse: Other Cases and Contexts

This book has presented an in-depth study of two statist Islamist actors after the Arab uprisings. It has shown that there are large overlaps between what has been presented as Western conceptions of sovereignty and legitimacy, and utopias and dystopias, on the one hand, and both Ennahda's and Hezbollah's discourse on global order, on the other. But the scope conditions of these findings are a particular place and world time: the first hopeful years of the 2010s. Over time, euphoria gave way to disappointment about what, for proponents of the liberal world order, should have been the fulfilment of the liberal promise for the last democracy-free zone. What finally prevailed was despondency about the crisis of the world order the West itself had caused (see Chapter 2). At the latest since the 2016 election of Donald Trump as president of the United States of America, the main debates in IR have revolved around the transformation and contestation of the liberal international order from within and without (Acharya 2017, Duncombe and Dunne 2018, Adler-Nissen and Zarakol 2020, Zürn and Gerschewski 2021), the 'end of American world order' (Acharya 2018b), the decline of the West and 'rise of the rest' (Zarakol 2019) and a 'post-Western world' (Wæver 2018, 75).

The age of a global order under Western hegemony, and therefore the context in which Ennahda and Hezbollah articulated their world order conceptions, may be time-bound. This means that the two Islamist discourses were studied under particular world-political and domestic conditions. This section will, therefore, first provide an outlook on the unfolding of events in and beyond MENA after 2016. This allows an appraisal of Ennahda's and Hezbollah's (discursive) practices of the early 2010s in a larger temporal context and a rough assessment of the consequences they had for Tunisia's and Lebanon's future. Second, it relates the findings on Ennahda and Hezbollah to the broader phenomenon of Islamism, asking what we can learn for other cases and what the limits to this are.

Beyond the Aftermath of the Arab Uprisings: Ennahda and Hezbollah in Tunisia and Lebanon at the Turn of the Decade

While a strategic shift had already occurred under President Barack Obama with the US's 'pivot to Asia' in 2011 (Campbell and Andrews 2013), the early 2010s still drew Western attention and resources to MENA. Only three years since withdrawing from Iraq, the US returned with the GCAD in September 2014. Following his 'America first' ideology, Donald Trump made the end of the US presence in the region a priority and radicalised both the support of allies such as Israel and Saudi Arabia and the pressure on American 'enemies' such as Iran. In early 2019, Trump declared ISIS '100 per cent' defeated and announced a full US withdrawal from Syria (Lister 2019). By January 2021, shortly before Joe Biden took office as president, the US had also reduced its presence in Iraq to 2,500 troops. The US military announced the end of its combat mission later that year, after the disastrous withdrawal from Afghanistan had captured attention and shocked the global public (Arraf 2021). While the failure of this twenty-year military mission briefly sparked intense debates, the world was preoccupied with the COVID-19 pandemic from early 2020. The global health crisis entailed myriad additional problems for MENA (Lynch 2022). Finally, the Russian invasion of Ukraine in 2022 resulted in existential economic and food crises for many people living in those countries (Süß and Weipert-Fenner 2022). But it also further distracted attention away from MENA even though none of the crises and conflicts had ended, some having been exacerbated by these global (political) developments, others having entered a phase of de-escalation, at least temporarily.

At the time of writing, in autumn 2023 and more than ten years after the beginning of the Arab uprisings, Lebanese and Tunisian society are facing dire political and economic circumstances. Not only have these two countries, like so many others in the world, struggled with the effects of the COVID-19 pandemic and the Russian war. They have both also witnessed other severe, country-specific crises since 2017. For a long time, Tunisia was seen as the exceptional case in terms of the outcomes of the Arab uprisings that began in 2010 and 2011, having achieved 'a tenuous transition towards democracy' (Weipert-Fenner 2021, 566), while all other states either experienced an authoritarian backlash or descended into armed conflict. Lebanon was the only Arab country that had been classified as a democracy prior to the Arab uprisings, more precisely since the Syrian occupation ended after almost thirty years in 2005.[3] This does not mean that the political systems in the two countries were without flaws. Lebanon has been notorious for foreign involvement in its domestic politics, the paralysing effects of sectarian politics and the corruption of the political elite as a whole, resulting in neglect in the provision of public goods and services. As for Tunisia, even though the transition and constitutional process exceeded the expectations of many observers of political transformations, the country suffered from terrorist attacks and a severe economic crisis. The process of transitional justice that accompanied the political transition and was lauded for its inclusivity and comprehensiveness grew increasingly contentious (Salehi 2022). The year 2019 can be seen as the turning point for the worse in both countries.

Lebanon was among the countries of the so-called second wave of Arab uprisings. Mass protests erupted in Algeria, Sudan, Iraq and Lebanon, leading to the ousting of a dictator in the first of these two cases and forcing the governments out of office in the second two. Protests in Lebanon were motivated by socio-economic grievances and directed against the corrupt political class as a whole, as 'condensed in the overarching slogan "*Killun ya'ni killun*" (All of them means all of them)' (Della Porta and Tufaro 2022, 7). What was special about these protests was the cross-sectarian mobilisation. Among other things, it led to the demand to abolish the ethno-religious quotas from the political system and electoral law, thereby breaking with what used to be known as the most divisive conflict line in Lebanon (Bou Khater and Majed 2020, Pfeifer and Weipert-Fenner 2022). Such protests were not without precedent. In 2015, for instance, the garbage crisis and political stalemate had triggered protests led by the 'You Stink' and '*Isqāṭ al-Niẓām al-Ṭāʾifī*' ('Downfall of the Sectarian System') movements, denouncing the corruption of the political system and the collusion of private companies and demanding an end to the sectarian system (AbiYaghi, Catusse and Younes 2017). But in 2019, the scale and effects of the protests reached a level that was indeed unprecedented – and so, too, did the economic crisis. It deteriorated from a recession that began in 2017 into what the World Bank calls 'one of the world's worst economic and financial crises in the last 150 years' (World Bank 2021). It is also considered a 'deliberate depression', having been 'orchestrated by the country's elite that has long captured the state and lived off its economic rents' (World Bank 2022). The inflation rate skyrocketed from 3 per cent in 2019 to roughly 155 per cent in 2021.[4] The Lebanese middle class virtually vanished, with an estimated '75% of the population . . . struggling to put food on the table' (Gallagher 2022).

The resignation of Saad al-Hariri's government in October 2019, which had been in a coalition with several parties, came as a shock to Hezbollah. As one of the ruling parties, it had advocated not giving in to the protestors' demands (Reuters 2019). In January 2020, what was seen as a technocratic government took office. It was suspected of being 'exclusively beholden to a parliamentary coalition led by . . . Hezbollah . . . and in fact affiliated with the political establishment that drove the country into its current critical condition' (Maksad 2020). In August 2020, a massive explosion in the Port of Beirut killed over 200 people, wounded more than 7,000, destroyed large parts of the city and forcibly displaced over 300,000 people.[5] Investigations conducted by, among others, the investigative art collective Forensic Architecture found that the explosion had been caused by improper storage of chemicals, explosives and contaminants in a warehouse (Hilburg 2020). Leaked documents showed that the authorities had been warned on multiple occasions about the dangers of the situation but chose to ignore it.

The Beirut port blast was followed by the resignation of the technocratic government under Hassan Diab, which had acted as a caretaker government until September 2021. Moreover, a domestic investigation into the government was launched. As several Lebanese and international NGOs documented, it had a 'range of procedural and systemic flaws . . . including flagrant political interference, immunity for high-level political officials, lack of respect for fair trial standards, and due process violations' from the beginning.[6] When some of their MPs became subjects of the investigation, Hezbollah tried to undermine the process, including by threatening judges. Supporters of Hezbollah and Amal, the other main Shi'i party, took to the streets in 2021 to protest against the investigation, triggering massive street violence in Beirut (Chulov 2021). It was not until May 2022 that new elections took place, with the aim of putting an end to yet another interim government under Najib Mikati (El Dahan and Bassam 2021). The formation of a new cabinet is still stalled at the time of writing in autumn 2023. But it is clear that Hezbollah and its allies have lost their parliamentary majority. According to the annual report published by the V-Dem Institute in 2022, Lebanon is now considered an electoral autocracy (V-Dem Institute 2022).

Beyond these domestic developments, Lebanon struck a historical deal with Israel in October 2022 when, with the help of US diplomacy, a new line was drawn to redefine the two exclusive economic zones in the Mediterranean. This solved the question of who was permitted to exploit the gas fields – and is considered by some observers as a step towards the normalisation of Lebanese–Israeli relations (Byman 2022). Hezbollah had still sent drones to Israel when the country was about to start gas production a couple of months earlier. But it did not stop the two governments from negotiating the deal and 'eventually even praised it' (Byman 2022). While Hezbollah is still caught up in engagements abroad, believed by many to be on direct Iranian orders, it has all but ended its military mission in Syria, even though the conflict there is far from over (Ghaddar et al. 2022).

Hezbollah's strategy of keeping everything calm on the Lebanese domestic level to provide room for manoeuvre for its resistance projects must at this point be considered as having failed, at least for the time being. Hezbollah has for a long time prioritised transnational projects and, along with virtually all other parties, neglected social and economic grievances in Lebanon. The mass protests show that this strategy no longer works. Hezbollah has also lost reputation in recent years, as part of the political elite but also because it resorted to violence against protestors. Being caught up in Lebanese politics may threaten its domestic position, which has thus far been stable, and, as a consequence, place restrictions on its external agency. While it developed into an important regional and even global player in the 2010s,[7] Hezbollah may now have to redirect its resources to the Lebanese domestic context, at least for a certain amount of time. Should this be the case, the 'two worlds' strategy Hezbollah pursued in the past may have contributed to its own downfall. By focusing on trans- and international conflicts, Hezbollah may have hindered the reproduction of necessary resources for the resistance project at the domestic level.

It is too early to tell whether Hezbollah's role in regional politics will be diminished. Its accommodation of the gas deal is astonishing and will be hard to reconcile with the resistance image. However, only a couple of days before writing these words in October 2023, the Israeli–Palestinian conflict escalated to a degree that is considered unprecedented by many observers. Hamas, the Islamist Palestinian faction ruling in Gaza and part of the 'axis of resistance', together with other militant groups in Gaza assaulted Israel, killing around 1,100 Israelis and foreigners, more than 750 of them civilians, injuring several thousand and abducting more than 200 persons in a series of guerrilla and terrorist attacks on 7 October. Israel responded with a massive military operation, including not only air strikes but also ground forces. A couple of weeks into the war, the death toll among Gazans is already estimated to have reached 8,000, about 40 per cent of them children.[8] There were also clashes at the Israeli–Lebanese border between Hezbollah and the IDF, which caused the death of dozens of fighters on both sides. But it also seems that both sides are currently still trying to contain the violence and avoid full escalation (Bassam and Perry 2023). At the moment, it is hard to predict whether the war will expand regionally or whether this can be avoided. What is clear, however, is that regional politics and in particular alliance politics are crucial for understanding the dynamics of escalation – and will be severely affected by this war. This includes the 'axis of resistance'.

Hezbollah's relationship with the Iranian regime has been close since its inception. But the degree and quality of Iranian influence on Hezbollah has been a subject of debate. Some claim the party is a mere extension of the Islamic Republic's regime in Lebanon and that Hezbollah acts as an Iranian proxy. Others, however, have suggested that Hezbollah has significant freedoms or has sometimes even reversed the power relations with Iran. There have, for instance, been reports of commanders of the Islamic Revolutionary Guard Corps taking 'many of their operational decisions . . . after consulting Hizbullah' (Leenders and Giustozzi 2022, 629). The popularity and success of its 'golden formula' or the '"resistance" template' in other contexts like Iraq and Yemen may have 'allowed Hizbullah to enjoy some autonomy towards

Iran' (Leenders and Giustozzi 2022, 629). Nevertheless, it is clear that any drastic political change in the domestic politics of Iran (like a revolution, or far-reaching reforms in response to the massive protests the regime has kept facing since 2021) or in its organisation of alliances would also have a profound impact on Hezbollah financially in terms of weapons supply and transnational support from other non-state actors and Shiʿi communities. Such developments would certainly limit its room to manoeuvre. They would also further alter the regional political game. While it is impossible to predict how Hezbollah would react to such changes in terms of its strategies and tactics, its world order discourse might be affected less strongly and more indirectly than we would expect. It is conceivable that its interpretations of regional politics would change slightly according to its own perceived agency. But Iran and *wilāyat al-faqīh* do not feature prominently in Hezbollah's discourse. What is more, Hezbollah has created its own trademark of Islamic resistance and an original Shiʿi outlook on the unfolding of history and what the future holds. Even if major changes were to occur in the Iranian political system, I would, therefore, expect a high degree of continuity in Hezbollah's world order discourse. What would change rather dramatically, however, is the power of its speaker position and its material capabilities, which, in turn, might significantly alter its take on world order in the long run.

As for Tunisia, drastic change in the form of authoritarian backsliding has already occurred: at the time of writing in autumn 2023, President Kais Saied was slowly but surely consolidating his rule, systematically shutting down democratic institutions and repressing those who had become the opposition, from leftists to Islamists (Agence France-Presse 2023, Yee 2023). The 2019 legislative elections had seen Ennahda emerge as still the strongest party in parliament but had left the legislature fractured, with 'no political force gaining more than 20% of the votes' (Sebei and Fulco 2022, 12). There were several failed attempts to form a government, which led to a short period of rule by Prime Minister Elya Fakhfakh (February–September 2020) and his deposition through a vote of no confidence initiated by Ennahda. Fakhfakh had not responded positively to several of Ennahda's requests. Among other things, he had not included a secular and a Salafist party in the cabinet. The latter had not 'backed President Saied in the second round of the 2019 presidential elections' (Sebei and Fulco 2022, 13). Its exclusion from government enraged Rached al-Ghannouchi, who also served as the parliament's speaker at the time. In this tense situation, Hichem Mechichi succeeded Fakhfakh as the new head of government. He was simply appointed by President Saied against the will of the political parties represented in parliament.

In the coming months, none of the bills issued by the 'president's government' were passed by the parliament. The country had now not only been hit heavily by COVID-19. It also faced further economic decline, with the GDP growth rate having dropped to minus 8.7 per cent in 2020 and public debt hitting 87.6 per cent (Meddeb 2022). Tunisia also faced a fiscal crisis, given that the deadlock between government, parliament and president prevented the necessary reforms to secure a new loan. Mechichi tried to solve the impasse by reshuffling his cabinet and appointing new ministers that would be backed by the Assembly of the Representatives of the People. While he managed to gain the parliament's support, including Ennahda's, President Saied blocked the process in January 2021. Saied also started introducing reforms without involving the government or parliament. As no agreement had ever been reached on how to staff the Constitutional Court, it had never started work. This meant that questions of authority could not be solved. Meanwhile, anti-Ennahda sentiment continued to grow in parliament and among the public. When the chairman of Ennahda's Shura Council 'publicly demanded financial reparations for the victims of Ben Ali's dictatorship while the country was experiencing the deadliest phase of the epidemic' in summer 2021, mass protests erupted against the government, corruption and 'the looting of public money' (Sebei and Fulco 2022, 15). Many of the protestors directly attacked Ennahda buildings, as the stalemate was mainly blamed on the party. Ennahda was also accused of political manoeuvring in an escalating health and economic crisis.

In July 2021, President Saied announced the enforcement of Article 80 of the Tunisian Constitution – or rather, his interpretation of the law (Ben Hamadi 2021). He suspended the parliament, fired the prime minister and deprived the members of parliament of their immunity from criminal prosecution. While protestors initially welcomed his move, it soon became clear that Saied was leading the country back into authoritarianism. Saied rapidly tightened his grip on power. He restructured the ISIE in April 2022, having dissolved the suspended the parliament a month earlier (Middle East Eye 2022). In June 2022, he sacked several dozen judges (Reuters 2022). In winter

2022, the country saw its first elections since the de facto coup d'état of Kais Saied. They were boycotted by almost all opposition parties as they took place under a new constitution that the president had himself designed and put to a referendum in July 2022. His draft constitution had been passed with 97 per cent of the vote, but only 30 per cent of Tunisians participated in the referendum (Amara 2022). And still, the opposition did not manage to unite against Saied, even when the parties and civil society had long realised what was going on. Ennahda and a few other groups had immediately called the July events a coup, though others were more reluctant to do so. What most parties agreed on, however, was that Ennahda was to blame for the stalemate that had preceded the president's dismantling of democratic institutions and the constitution. Moreover, when Ghannouchi reached out to Saied to try to prevent him from abandoning the 2014 constitution, internal rifts within the party deepened. When the president declined the offer to negotiate, Ennahda returned to its firm stance against his actions. And yet, the party remained isolated. It was not until shortly before the constitutional referendum that it was 'allowed' to join the National Salvation Front, which mobilised against the vote (Sebei and Fulco 2022).

Despite the 'methodology of consensus' it had practised for almost a decade in post-revolutionary Tunisia, Ennahda found itself in a marginalised political position at the beginning of the 2020s and, at the time of writing, the Court of Appeal in Tunis has just extended Ghannouchi's prison sentence from twelve to fifteen months, confirming that he is guilty of terrorism and incitement charges (Associated Press 2023, Middle East Eye 2023a). It seems that not only has Ennahda's fear of authoritarian backsliding become reality but the other political and civil society actors sided against Ennahda once the dialogue- and consensus-oriented formats failed. In a situation where they could agree on barely anything else, what united them was 'their will to sideline Ennahda' (Sebei and Fulco 2022, 26). This shows that antagonism did not transform into agonism and Ennahda did not manage to establish itself as a normal political actor recognised by others even in times of disagreement. In its own perception, then, Ennahda is still demonised as an Islamist danger and it seems that the increasingly authoritarian regime under Saied is indeed reviving the terrorism narrative. This may exacerbate the party's fears for survival. In this sense, the moment in which Ennahda reached out to Saied can be interpreted as an attempt to avert renewed repression or a ban. But this move was immediately punished within the party. The party is still struggling with the legacy of the Ben Ali regime's strategy of managing the opposition by dividing it. In case of doubt, the rest of the opposition still unites against the Islamist party, the UGTT being its most outspoken critic and opponent. Meanwhile, Ennahda's attempts to negotiate with the regime were not only fruitless, they were also unacceptable to many Nahdawis who vividly remember the repression the party experienced under the old authoritarian regime.

The consensus methodology was Ennahda's attempt to mitigate these tensions. However, 2021 made the limits of this strategy painfully clear. Moreover, by lulling the party into a false sense of security, striving for consensus may even have contributed to Ennahda finding itself in a precarious position again. Following the line of argument of radical democratic theorists (Mouffe 2000), Ennahda's attempt to replace antagonism by consensus is dangerous in two respects. First, it can make difference disappear by formulating a consensus that strives to be as encompassing as possible. This may lead to actually existing difference articulating itself through other channels than the legitimate political game. The emergence of violent forms of Salafism and terrorism could then be interpreted not only as a reaction to exclusion but also as an expression of consensus being too pervasive in the political realm. Second, there is a danger of the political struggle remaining antagonistic, where hegemony can become deadly for the opponent that is still perceived as the enemy. In the democratic game, the inevitable moment of closure constituted by the political decision is meant to be temporary. Thus, striving for consensus may be an understandable strategy of survival, given Ennahda's historical experience, but it may prove dangerous, assuming antagonism is not transformed into agonism. Ennahda's instinct to seek recognition can, then, be interpreted as one way to pursue such a transformation.

As the events between 2019 and 2022 show, however, Ennahda has failed to achieve this in Tunisia – or internationally. While European countries and the EU were not happy about Saied's power grab, they also found reasons for not taking a stance against it. They wanted to avoid allegations of neocolonialism and the EU being replaced as one of the main international partners by other powers like China. But their laissez-faire attitude also reflected wishful thinking that 'Saied's popularity and determination would lead to more effective governance and facilitate overdue economic and administrative reforms' (Werenfels 2022, 4). As in the past, the West seems to favour (the illusion of) stability over a serious commitment to democracy. There were expressions of support from the far right in the European Parliament, celebrating Saied as an ally in fighting Islamists (Middle East Monitor 2022). Similar calls to finally ban Ennahda came from the UAE in support of those Tunisian politicians who portray the party as a dangerous Muslim Brotherhood disciple (Werenfels 2022). Beyond Qatar, Ennahda cannot really count on external support. As the party comes under increasing domestic pressure due to Saied's repressive measures against his opponents, the international community has remained audibly silent. The failure of its recognition project on both the domestic and the international levels will strengthen those within and outside the party who were critical of Ennahda's path of compromise and consensus-seeking to begin with.

Beyond Ennahda and Hezbollah, Recognition and Resistance: What Lessons Can Be Learned for Other Islamists and for Rejectionists in the Global Order?

As the recontextualisation of the results of this book in another phase demonstrates, Islamist discourses are fundamentally context-bound. This holds for not only temporal but also spatial contexts. The analysis in this book has shown that, like other political actors, Islamists need to react to the political structures and constraints of which they are part, both domestically and globally. They face enemies and opponents, crises and problems, the opening and closing of windows of opportunity in the here and now. This is reflected in their utterances. Islamists have unique ways of processing their reality through language. Consequently, if we were to analyse another Islamist discourse, or Ennahda's and Hezbollah's discourse at another point in time, we would get different results. This does not mean, however, that more general conclusions cannot be drawn. There are some commonalities between Ennahda's and Hezbollah's discourse which may be representative of larger evolutions in Islamist politics and prove valid in other contexts. But generalisable conclusions are limited.

First, this is linked with the similarity of the two parties. They consider themselves part of the Arab-Islamic world. The relations of closeness and remoteness, of identity and difference found in their discourses have important overlaps. But ultimately, Hezbollah is an actor in the Mashreq oriented towards the East and the Gulf, whereas Ennahda is rooted in the Maghreb and conceives itself as a bridge between Africa and Europe. These geographical orientations and the parties' self-positioning within them are distinct, even though they share a (problem) horizon and both revolve around the notion of an Arab-Islamic world. Ennahda and Hezbollah also share the rejection of Western intervention, interference and hegemony in this space. Where Ennahda tentatively develops a concrete positive vision of what a global order without hegemony could look like, Hezbollah calls for action and self-defence against the unchangeable invasiveness of the West. This anti-colonial impetus will certainly be found not only in other Islamist discourses but also more broadly in world order discourse in formerly colonised areas.

Second and relatedly, Ennahda and Hezbollah both have deeply internalised conceptions of absolute and popular sovereignty. Divine sovereignty plays no practical role in their political discourse. Similarly, with regard to legitimate forms of authority, neither of them still seeks to establish an Islamic state. This is evident in their official platforms as well as their discursive interactions as observed in this book. Both, then, are truly post-Islamist (Bayat 2013, Boubekeur and Roy 2012b) in the sense that they no longer strive for a top-down Islamisation of society through the state or make strong truth claims about (political) Islam. Rather, they emphasise intra-religious pluralism and that different interpretations of Islam are possible and desirable. And still, both have their own way of bringing Islam into their (world) order political discourse. For Ennahda, the constant reinterpretation of religion and politics, as well as renegotiation and adjustment of the line between them, is at the core of its conception of Islamic democracy and community-based legitimacy. In Hezbollah's discourse, Islam features as a practised cultural form of conflict interpretation and moral guidance from which it draws its repertoire and legitimation of action. The ways in which Islam feeds into Ennahda's and Hezbollah's discourses is both specific and complex. It exceeds mere 'cultural' traces or 'value' orientation. Islam is still constitutive of Islamist politics and discourse – but no more than other identities, political circumstances and the position Islamists occupy in a world-political and domestic context. Islamists' Islam moves with time.

Third, this separates the two parties from Salafi jihadism. This book clearly demonstrates that such a distinction makes sense, in terms not only of ideology but also of ordering practice. Ennahda and Hezbollah have entered a global discourse on world order, or rather, they are part of it and articulate their positions in ways that are accessible and contestable for other speakers rather than opaque or otherworldly. Neither group positions itself outside the (hegemonic discourse on) world order but rather both are deeply entangled in it, sometimes stretching and pushing its boundaries, but mostly accepting it as so 'normal' that they do not even feel the need to reaffirm certain standards. In this regard, they also position themselves on the side of a global order which depicts Salafi jihadism as its Other. Ennahda had to walk the line between engaging the Salafist spectrum and credibly distancing itself from these 'radicals'. At the same time, as part of the government, it also needed to deal with and respond to the terrorist attacks in Tunisia. This has made emphasising difference from Salafi jihadism even more pressing. As for Hezbollah, the enemy image of 'Takfirism' is a core part of the legitimation of its intervention in Syria. Both Ennahda and Hezbollah, therefore, reject Salafi-jihadist rejectionism. They characterise the 'Jihadi' (Ennahda) or 'Takfiri' (Hezbollah) project as distorting the meaning of Islam, misusing religion for the legitimation of excessive and appalling violence and eliminating difference within and beyond Islam. They explicitly make use of the Salafi-jihadist Other to articulate their identity by setting themselves apart from these 'terrorists'. While actors such as the ISIS organisation or al-Qaʿida may be considered an 'easy' target to agree on, the rejection of these groups still marks common ground between 'Islamists' and 'the West'. At the same time, Ennahda and Hezbollah are also careful to maintain a clear-cut enemy image. They warn against equating Salafi jihadism with non-violent Salafism (Ennahda) or stylising it as a Sunni form of extremism, thereby exacerbating sectarian tensions (Hezbollah). As the analysis in this book has shown, this degree of differentiation is important for both Islamist parties in their respective contexts because a wrong discursive move could escalate conflicts.

Fourth, Ennahda and Hezbollah also share their scepticism towards Saudi Arabia's role in MENA. While Ennahda formulates its concerns more indirectly (referring to 'views from the Gulf', Ennahda 2012d), Hezbollah openly shames the kingdom: 'The entire world is now . . . well aware that all the terrorism in this world and in any corner in the world is due to the intellect and money of the [Saudis]' (Hezbollah 2016n).[9] These positions certainly involve both a real concern with Wahhabi ideology and a regional rivalry perspective. But one important dimension of the relationship with Saudi Arabia is the kingdom's long-lasting and proactively pursued ambition to provide the only model of an Islamic polity (Darwich 2016, Hegghammer 2010). With its Muslim Brotherhood legacy and closeness to Qatar and the Turkish AKP, Ennahda sides with actors that propose a competing model of Sunni Islamic political order. Hezbollah's *wilāyat al-faqīh* commitment, closeness to Iran and key role in maintaining (and extending) the axis of resistance make it a thorn in the kingdom's flesh. The antagonism increased when Saudi Arabia had reason to fear that Iran's isolation would come to an end with the JCPOA nuclear deal under the Obama administration (Stein 2021, 183–208). Ennahda and Hezbollah offer ideas on how to calibrate the relationship between Islam and politics in the twenty-first century that strongly diverge from the Saudi-Wahhabi system. In contrast to Islamists, however, Saudi Arabia does not have to struggle with Western securitisation and demonisation, it enjoys the privileges of being a state actor, and its regime does not have to engage in 'risky' democratic politics. The kingdom is simply not met with the same amount of scepticism and enjoys recognition as a strategic partner of the West in the region – in spite of despicable violations of humanitarian law in its war on Yemen.

This points to a final finding that applies to both Ennahda and Hezbollah: enmity towards them is based on interests rather than their alleged radicalism, fanaticism or religious irrationalism. Their discourse is largely conducted within a discursive space spanned by Western conceptions of world order, albeit sometimes pushing the boundaries of the latter. But, based on their utterances, they are also clearly identifiable as (post-)Islamists, as both have specific ways of bringing Islam into politics. And yet, nowhere did the reference to religion render their normative and epistemic universes irreconcilable with the Western equivalent. The results of this book, therefore, refute the unintelligibility or inaccessibility of religious reasons that is sometimes formulated as a central argument in favour of political secularism and against talking to Islamists. No good reasons to refuse cooperation with Islamists can be found in their 'Islamism'. Rather, it seems that Western Othering practices are grounded in a habitualised and generalised suspicion of 'Islamists' in the case of Ennahda. The West may also hope to benefit from cooperation with known 'secularists' for the sake of 'stability'. When it comes to Hezbollah, the West pursues divergent, sometimes diametrically opposite interests. Not only does the West not accept the self-authorisation of a non-state actor to conduct military interventions and other sovereign practices reserved for states. Hezbollah's calls for Israel to be eradicated make even thin recognition inconceivable to Western states committed to the non-negotiability of Israel's right to exist. And finally, Hezbollah is simply on the 'wrong side' of regional conflict dynamics from a Western perspective in which the 'axis of resistance' is seen as an 'axis of evil'.

What Islamists Tell Us about Global Order (Discourse) – and Vice Versa

This book demonstrates that the clichéd view on the position of Islamists towards the world order is too simple. Divine sovereignty does not play any practical role in Ennahda's and Hezbollah's discourse. Neither of the two Islamist parties question the state-based system or seek to establish an Islamic state. The afterlife does not extend into their very realistic and this-worldly assessments of political developments and their room for manoeuvre. They do not hold up irrevocable truth claims that make certain positions non-negotiable. Hezbollah does use an epistemic and ethical apparatus derived from religious tradition to interpret conflict and determine acceptable behaviour. But what results from this are tactical decisions and tangible actions to best pursue its interests in the here and now. Ennahda does try to transform democracy to make it more fitting for a society of Muslims and Islamic tradition. But it privileges and is ready to make concessions for the sake of consensus. Ennahda is deeply recognisant of the global order and strives to be recognised within it and by powerful speakers in the world order discourse. Its position is one of restraint and leading by example. Hezbollah is moderately resistant to the global order and more recognisant than it might wish to appear. Its position is one of imposition and intervening to actively bring about or prevent change.[10]

This book also provides strong evidence that Islamists must be taken seriously as (world-)political actors – rather than be conceptualised as primarily religious-ideological or rational-opportunistic. They are not, as some have suggested, in principle and *a priori* actors who show a moderate, compromising face until they are in power, only to reveal their true, radical selves. Nor are they in principle more irrational or prone to violence than other actors. By qualifying them as political, I mean, first, that Islamists have ideas about how the global order should be designed and how we should live together in this rather than the next world. Second, Islamists, like other actors, are context-bound. This implies that their goals and means are subject to change and adaptation. They are actors who respond to different interests addressed to them by various Others. They must negotiate and strike compromises, they sometimes act pragmatically, and must reconcile competing ambitions and interests. In this sense, seeing Islamists as political actors also opens up spaces for negotiation and, potentially, cooperation. Finally, they are actors deeply embedded in and aware of the (world-)political context to which they must relate. Importantly, this means that they need to legitimise their action vis-à-vis different audiences and in relation to different normative structures and standards. This is why they formulate their conceptions and positions in a language that is accessible, give reasons that are comprehensible and provide justifications that are acceptable to a global audience and within a normative structure born out of Western hegemony. This normative structure includes liberal elements that both actors accept and a secular settlement that both actors challenge – not least because it positions Islamists outside legitimate global politics and the Western-dominated world order. Both actors are aware of the normative power of secularism (Pfeifer 2019), and make concessions and adapt to it by downplaying their Islamism. But they also use the global normative structure to delegitimise Salafi-jihadist actors, to demand equal rights and to condemn Western practices that run counter to this structure: (military) interventions in other states, influencing the outcome of elections, favouring interests over norms that are claimed to be universal.

If Ennahda and Hezbollah do indeed reproduce many of the conceptions and norms of Western world order discourse, we can consider this finding as reaffirming the pervasiveness of Western power. A critical interpretation of this would claim that Western hegemony is inescapable and its structures significantly constrain agency for other world-ordering practices. A more practical take on this would be that utterances articulated in a global discourse on world order have to be intelligible for others who speak in it. These utterances have to be expressed in a normative and epistemic lingua franca and they are formulated in a context which has been shaped by centuries of Western dominance. But neither interpretation precludes actors' ability to push boundaries and transform structures. The fact that Islamists recognise but also resist is a sign that hegemony is not total (Deitelhoff and Daase 2021). In this sense, the study of Ennahda's and Hezbollah's world order discourse is one way of detecting the room for agency in and potential for the transformation of the global order under Western hegemony. The fact that non-state actors adopt a position on a global order underlines the importance of an emerging research agenda that aims at studying external – international, regional, global – relations of (armed) non-state actors (Huang 2016, Darwich 2021a, 2021b, Geis, Clément and Pfeifer 2021). And finally, for a long time it was assumed that 'non-Western states and peoples are ... without international politics or an interest in the world at large' (Zarakol 2022, 7), but this book shows that the global order shapes everyday politics in the MENA region and, conversely, actors from the region actively try to engage and transform the (discourse on) global order. The analysis of Ennahda's and Hezbollah's discourse, then, reveals that world ordering takes place beyond the state and beyond the West.

Notes

1. A similar argument has recently been made in norms research with regard to the question of how contestation affects the robustness of norms: as long as contestation concerns the application rather than the validity of a norm, it does not weaken and can even strengthen norm robustness (Deitelhoff and Zimmermann 2020).
2. For an interpretation of this term, coined by Naim Qassem, see Saade (2016, 138).
3. It had been classified as a democracy by the Polity data series since 2005, see http://www.systemicpeace.org/polity/Lebanon2010.pdf (accessed 16 October 2023). V-Dem provides the indices for different conceptions of democracy, but all indicators rose sharply in 2005 as well, see https://www.v-dem.net/data_analy sis/CountryGraph/ (accessed 16 October 2023).
4. https://data.worldbank.org/indicator/FP.CPI.TOTL.ZG?end=2021&location s=LB&start=2018 (accessed 16 October 2023).
5. https://english.legal-agenda.com/joint-letter-to-the-human-rights-council-calling-for-an-international-investigative-mission-into-the-beirut-blast/ (accessed 16 October 2023).

6. https://english.legal-agenda.com/joint-letter-to-the-human-rights-council-calling-for-an-international-investigative-mission-into-the-beirut-blast/ (accessed 17 October 2023).

7. https://www.washingtoninstitute.org/hezbollahinteractivemap/# (accessed 17 October 2023).

8. https://reliefweb.int/report/occupied-palestinian-territory/gaza-3195-children-killed-three-weeks-surpasses-annual-number-children-killed-conflict-zones-2019 (accessed 7 November 2023).

9. Square brackets in original.

10. For the distinction between restraint and imposition, see Sørensen (2006).

INTERVIEWS

Interview 1: Tunisian MP and former minister. 23 May 2017, Tunis.

Interview 2: Former Tunisian minister. 25 May 2017, Tunis.

Interview 3: Ennahda member. 25 May 2017, Tunis.

Interview 4: Member of Ennahda's Foreign Affairs Committee and of the Shura Council. 26 May 2017, Tunis.

Interview 5: Researcher at *Markaz ad-Dirasat* and university professor. 18 March 2015, Dahieh.

Interview 6: Journalist at *L'Orient le Jour*. 16 March 2015, Baabda.

Interview 7: Journalist at al-Manar TV. 31 March 2014, Beirut.

BIBLIOGRAPHY

References

Abdelkader, Deina, Nassef Manabilang Adiong and Raffaele Mauriello, eds. 2016. *Islam and International Relations. Contributions to Theory and Practice.* Basingstoke/New York: Palgrave Macmillan.

AbiYaghi, Marie-Noëlle, Myriam Catusse and Miriam Younes. 2017. 'From *Isqat an-Nizam at-Ta'ifi* to the Garbage Crisis Movement. Political Identities and Antisectarian Movements'. In *Lebanon Facing the Arab Uprisings. Constraints and Adaptation*, edited by Rosita Di Peri and Daniel Meier, 73–92. London: Palgrave Macmillan.

Abou-El-Fadl, Reem. 2014. 'Neutralism Made Positive. Egyptian Anti-colonialism on the Road to Bandung'. *British Journal of Middle Eastern Studies* 42 (2): 219–40. https://doi.org/10.1080/13530194.2013.878526

Acharya, Amitav. 2002. 'Regionalism and the Emerging World Order. Sovereignty, Autonomy, Identity'. In *New Regionalism in the Global Political Economy. Theories and Cases*, edited by Shaun Breslin, Christopher W. Hughes, Nicola Phillips and Ben Rosamond, 20–32. London/New York: Routledge.

Acharya, Amitav. 2014. *Rethinking Power, Institutions and Ideas in World Politics. Whose IR?* Abingdon/New York: Routledge.

Acharya, Amitav. 2017. 'After Liberal Hegemony. The Advent of a Multiplex World Order'. *Ethics and International Affairs* 31 (3): 271–85. https://doi.org/10.1017/S089267941700020X

Acharya, Amitav. 2018a. *Constructing Global Order. Agency and Change in World Politics*. Cambridge: Cambridge University Press.

Acharya, Amitav. 2018b. *The End of American World Order*. 2nd ed. Cambridge/Medford, MA: Polity Press.

Adiong, Nassef Manabilang, Raffaele Mauriello and Deina Abdelkader, eds. 2018. *Islam in International Relations. Politics and Paradigms*. Abingdon/New York: Routledge.

Adler-Nissen, Rebecca, and Ayşe Zarakol. 2020. 'Struggles for Recognition. The Liberal International Order and the Merger of Its Discontents'. *International Organization* 75 (2): 611–34. https://doi.org/10.1017/s0020818320000454

Adraoui, Mohamed-Ali, ed. 2018. *The Foreign Policy of Islamist Political Parties. Ideology in Practice*. Edinburgh: Edinburgh University Press.

Agence France-Presse. 2023. 'Tunisia Forces Arrest Senior Opposition Figure as Crackdown Escalates'. *The Guardian*. 24 February. https://www.theguardian.com/world/2023/feb/24/tunisia-forces-arrest-senior-opposition-figure-as-crackdown-escalates (accessed 7 November 2023).

Agnew, John. 2005. 'Sovereignty Regimes. Territoriality and State Authority in Contemporary World Politics'. *Annals of the Association of American Geographers* 95 (2): 437–61. https://doi.org/10.1111/j.1467-8306.2005.00468.x

Ahram, Ariel I. 2020. *War and Conflict in the Middle East and North Africa*. Cambridge: Polity Press.

Al-Azmeh, Aziz. 2020. *Secularism in the Arab World. Contexts, Ideas and Consequences*. Edinburgh: Edinburgh University Press.

Al Jazeera. 2016a. 'New Government Announced under PM Saad al-Hariri'. 18 December. http://www.aljazeera.com/news/ 2016/12/lebanon-announces-government-saad-al-hariri-161218201145680.html (accessed 7 November 2023).

Al Jazeera. 2016b. 'Tunisian Parliament Votes to Dismiss PM Habib Essid'. 31 July. http://www.aljazeera.com/news/2016/07/tunisia-pm-habib-essid-loses-confidence-vote-160730174505286.html (accessed 7 November 2023).

Al Jazeera. 2016c. 'Tunisian President Names Youssef Chahed as New PM'. 3 August. http://www.aljazeera.com/news/2016/08/tunisian-president-nominates-prime-minister-160803134622999.html (accessed 7 November 2023).

Alagha, Joseph. 2011. *Hizbullah's Documents. From the 1985 Open Letter to the 2009 Manifesto*. Amsterdam: Pallas.

Allan, Diana. 2005. 'Mythologising Al-Nakba. Narratives, Collective Identity and Cultural Practice among Palestinian Refugees in Lebanon'. *Oral History* 33 (1): 47–56. https://www.jstor.org/stable/40179820

Amara, Tarek. 2022. 'Tunisian Officials Say New Constitution Passed in Vote with Low Turnout'. Reuters. 27 July. https://www.reuters.com/world/africa/tunis ian-electoral-commission-says-yes-won-constitutional-referendum-2022-07-26/ (accessed 7 November 2023).

Amara, Tarek, and Patrick Markey. 2016. 'Border Attack Feeds Tunisia Fears of Libya Jihadist Spillover'. Reuters. 13 March. http://www.reuters.com/article/us-tunisia-security-idUSKCN0WF072 (accessed 7 November 2023).

Ammar, Muhammad. 2022. 'From Dignity Violation to Self-Immolation'. *Peace Review* 33 (4): 444–52. https://doi.org/10.1080/10402659.2021.2042996

Anderson, John. 2009. 'Does God Matter, and If So Whose God? Religion and Democratization'. In *The Routledge Handbook of Religion and Politics*, edited by Jeffrey Haynes, 192–210. Abingdon/New York: Routledge.

Andrieu, Kora. 2016. 'Confronting the Dictatorial Past in Tunisia. Human Rights and the Politics of Victimhood in Transitional Justice Discourses since 2011'. *Human Rights Quarterly* 38 (2): 261–93. https://doi.org/10.1353/hrq.2016.0028

Appleby, R. Scott. 2000. *The Ambivalence of the Sacred. Religion, Violence, and Reconciliation*. Lanham, MD: Rowman and Littlefield.

Appleby, R. Scott. 2011. 'Rethinking Fundamentalism in a Secular Age'. In *Rethinking Secularism*, edited by Craig Calhoun, Mark Juergensmeyer and Jonathan VanAntwerpen, 225–47. New York: Oxford University Press.

Archibugi, Daniele. 2004. 'Cosmopolitan Democracy and Its Critics. A Review'. *European Journal of International Relations* 10 (3): 437–73. https://doi.org/10 .1177/1354066104045543

Arjomand, Saïd Amir. 2009. 'The Constitution of Medina. A Sociolegal Interpretation of Muhammad's Acts of Foundation of the *Umma*'. *International Journal of Middle East Studies* 41 (4): 555–75. https://doi.org/10.1017/s002074380999 0067

Arraf, Jane. 2021. 'U.S. Announces End to Combat Mission in Iraq, but Troops Will Not Leave'. *New York Times*. 9 December. https://www.nytimes.com/2021 /12/09/world/middleeast/us-iraq-combat-mission.html (accessed 7 November 2023).

Asad, Talal. 1983. 'Anthropological Conceptions of Religion. Reflections on Geertz'. *Man* 18 (2): 237–59. https://doi.org/10.2307/2801433

Asad, Talal. 1993. *Genealogies of Religion. Discipline and Reasons of Power in Christianity and Islam*. Baltimore, MD: Johns Hopkins University Press.

Asad, Talal. 2003. *Formations of the Secular. Christianity, Islam, Modernity*. Stanford, CA: Stanford University Press.

Asad, Talal. 2006. 'Trying to Understand French Secularism'. In *Political Theologies. Public Religions in a Post-Secular World*, edited by Hent de Vries and Lawrence E. Sullivan, 494–527. New York: Fordham University Press.

Asad, Talal. 2009. 'Free Speech, Blasphemy, and Secular Criticism'. In *Is Critique Secular? Blasphemy, Injury, and Free Speech*, edited by Talal Asad, Wendy Brown, Judith Butler and Saba Mahmood, 20–63. Berkeley: Townsend Center for the Humanities, University of California.

Asseburg, Muriel, Wolfram Lacher and Mareike Transfeld. 2018. 'Mission Impossible? UN Mediation in Libya, Syria and Yemen'. *SWP Research Papers* 8: 1–62.

Associated Press. 2012. 'Syrian Kidnapping of Lebanese Pilgrims Raises Fears Conflict Will Cross Border'. *The Guardian*. 22 May. https://www.theguardian.com/world/2012/may/22/syrian-kidnap-lebanese-pilgrims-shia (accessed 7 November 2023).

Associated Press. 2023. 'Tunisian Party Leader Sentenced to 15 Months in Prison for Terrorism Support, Incitement'. Fox News. 31 October. https://www.foxnews.com/world/tunisian-party-leader-sentenced-15-months-prison-terrorism-support-incitement (accessed 7 November 2023).

Ayoob, Mohammed. 2008. *The Many Faces of Political Islam. Religion and Politics in the Muslim World*. Ann Arbor: University of Michigan Press.

Azani, Eitan. 2009. *Hezbollah. The Story of the Party of God. From Revolution to Institutionalization*. New York: Palgrave Macmillan.

Azani, Eitan. 2013. 'The Hybrid Terrorist Organization. Hezbollah as a Case Study'. *Studies in Conflict and Terrorism* 36 (11): 899–916. https://doi.org/10.1080/1057610X.2013.832113

Bachman, Jeffrey Scott. 2015. 'The Lawfulness of US Targeted Killing Operations outside Afghanistan'. *Studies in Conflict and Terrorism* 38 (11): 899–918. https://doi.org/10.1080/1057610X.2015.1072390

Bächtiger, André, John S. Dryzek, Jane Mansbridge and Mark Warren. 2018. 'Deliberative Democracy. An Introduction'. In *The Oxford Handbook of Deliberative Democracy*, edited by André Bächtiger, John S. Dryzek, Jane Mansbridge and Mark Warren, 1–32. Oxford: Oxford University Press.

Bakali, Naved, and Farid Hafez, eds. 2022. *The Rise of Global Islamophobia in the War on Terror. Coloniality, Race, and Islam*. Manchester: Manchester University Press.

Balanche, Fabrice. 2018. 'From the Iranian Corridor to the Shia Crescent'. Stanford, CA: Hoover Institution.

Bamber, Matthew, and Isak Svensson. 2023. 'Resisting Radical Rebels. Variations in Islamist Rebel Governance and the Occurrence of Civil Resistance'. *Terrorism and Political Violence* 35 (5): 1126–46. https://doi.org/10.1080/09546553.20 21.2019023

Bamber-Zryd, Matthew. 2022. 'Cyclical Jihadist Governance. The Islamic State Governance Cycle in Iraq and Syria'. *Small Wars and Insurgencies* 33 (8): 1314–44. https://doi.org/10.1080/09592318.2022.2116182

Bank, André, and Jan Busse. 2021. 'MENA Political Science Research a Decade after the Arab Uprisings. Facing the Facts on Tremulous Grounds'. *Mediterranean Politics* 26 (5): 539–62. https://doi.org/10.1080/13629395.20 21.1889285

Bapat, Navin A. 2019. *Monsters to Destroy. Understanding the War on Terror*. New York: Oxford University Press.

Barnard, Anne. 2014. 'A Lebanese Battle with Syrian Overtones'. *New York Times*. 26 October. https://www.nytimes.com/2014/10/27/world/middleeast/a-lebanese-battle-with-syrian-overtones.html (accessed 7 November 2023).

Barnard, Frederick M. 2001. *Democratic Legitimacy. Plural Values and Political Power*. Montreal: McGill-Queen's University Press.

Barnett, Michael. 2011. 'Another Great Awakening? International Relations Theory and Religion'. In *Religion and International Relations Theory*, edited by Jack Snyder, 91–114. New York: Columbia University Press.

Bassam, Laila and Tom Perry. 2023. 'Lebanon's Hezbollah Works to Curb Hefty Losses in Israel Clashes, Sources Say'. Reuters. 31 October. https://www.reuters .com/world/middle-east/lebanons-hezbollah-works-curb-hefty-losses-israel-clashes-sources-say-2023-10-30/ (accessed 7 November 2023).

Baumgart-Ochse, Claudia. 2010. 'Religiöse Akteure und die Opportunitätsstruktur der internationalen Beziehungen. Eine Replik auf Karsten Lehmann'. *Zeitschrift für Internationale Beziehungen* 17 (1): 101–17. https://doi.org/10.5771/0946 -7165-2010-1-101

Baumgart-Ochse, Claudia. 2016. 'Substanziell, funktional oder gar nicht? Der Religionsbegriff in der Friedens- und Konfliktforschung'. In *Religion in der Friedens- und Konfliktforschung. Interdisziplinäre Zugänge zu einem multidimensionalen Begriff*, edited by Ines-Jacqueline Werkner, *Zeitschrift für Friedens- und Konfliktforschung* Sonderband 1, 29–59. Baden-Baden: Nomos.

Bayat, Asef. 2013. *Post-Islamism. The Changing Faces of Political Islam*. New York: Oxford University Press.

Bayulgen, Oksan, Ekim Arbatli and Sercan Canbolat. 2018. 'Elite Survival Strategies and Authoritarian Reversal in Turkey'. *Polity* 50 (3): 333–65. https://doi.org/10.1086/698203

BBC News. 2011. 'Israel–Lebanon Sea Border Dispute Looms over Gas Fields'. 11 July. https://www.bbc.com/news/world-middle-east-14104695 (accessed 7 November 2023).

BBC News. 2012. '"Nine Killed" in Syria-Linked Unrest in Lebanon's Tripoli'. 3 June. http://www.bbc.com/news/world-middle-east-18309534 (accessed 7 November 2023).

BBC News. 2014. 'Lebanon Army Steps Up Tripoli Battle against Militants'. 26 October. http://www.bbc.com/news/world-middle-east-29778462 (accessed 7 November 2023).

BBC News. 2015. 'Three Killed as Israel and Hezbollah Clash on Lebanese Border'. 28 January. http://www.bbc.com/news/world-middle-east-31015862 (accessed 7 November 2023).

Bech, Emily Cochran, and Jack Snyder. 2011. 'Conclusion. Religion's Contribution to International Relations Theory'. In *Religion and International Relations Theory*, edited by Jack Snyder, 200–10. New York: Columbia University Press.

Bell, Daniel. 2023. 'Communitarianism'. In *The Stanford Encyclopedia of Philosophy (Fall 2023 Edition)*, edited by Edward N. Zalta. https://plato.stanford.edu/archives/fall2023/entries/communitarianism/.

Bellamy, Richard, and Dario Castiglione. 1998. 'Between Cosmopolis and Community. Three Models of Rights and Democracy within the European Union'. In *Re-imagining Political Community. Studies in Cosmopolitan Democracy*, edited by Daniele Archibugi, David Held and Martin Köhler, 152–78. Cambridge: Polity Press.

Ben Hamadi, Monia. 2021. 'How Did Kaïs Saied Apply Article 80? Comparing the Legal Text to His Speech'. *Inkyfada*. 29 July. https://inkyfada.com/en/2021/07/29/kais-saied-article-80-constitution-legal-text-speech-tunisia/ (accessed 18 October 2023).

Benhabib, Seyla. 1996. 'Toward a Deliberative Model of Democratic Legitimacy'. In *Democracy and Difference. Contesting the Boundaries of the Political*, edited by Seyla Benhabib, 67–94. Princeton, NJ: Princeton University Press.

Berger, Mark T. 2008. 'The Real Cold War Was Hot. The Global Struggle for the Third World'. *Intelligence and National Security* 23 (1): 112–26. https://doi.org/10.1080/02684520701798171

Berger, Peter L. (1967) 1990. *The Sacred Canopy. Elements of a Sociological Theory of Religion*. New York: Anchor.

Berger, Peter L. 1999. 'The Desecularization of the World. A Global Overview'. In *The Desecularization of the World. Resurgent Religion and World Politics*, edited by Peter L. Berger, 1–18. Washington, DC: Ethics and Public Policy Center/ Grand Rapids, MI: W. B. Eerdmans.

Bergström, Anders, Göran Ekström and Kristina Boréus. 2017. 'Discourse Analysis'. In *Analyzing Text and Discourse. Eight Approaches for the Social Sciences*, edited by Kristina Boréus and Göran Bergström, 208–41. Thousand Oaks, CA: Sage.

Bettiza, Gregorio. 2014. 'Civilizational Analysis in International Relations. Mapping the Field and Advancing a "Civilizational Politics" Line of Research'. *International Studies Review* 16 (1): 1–28. https://doi.org/10.1111/misr.12100

Biersteker, Thomas J., and Cynthia Weber. 1996. 'The Social Construction of State Sovereignty'. In *State Sovereignty as Social Construct*, edited by Thomas J. Biersteker and Cynthia Weber, 1–21. Cambridge: Cambridge University Press.

Blake, Jillian, and Aqsa Mahmud. 2013. 'A Legal "Red Line"? Syria and the Use of Chemical Weapons in Civil Conflict'. *UCLA Law Review Discourse* (61): 244–61.

Bohn, Miriam, and Erik Vollmann. 2021. 'Untangling Elite Networks and Decentralization in the Middle East and North Africa. Neopatrimonialism Revisited'. In *Decentralization in the Middle East and North Africa. Informal Politics, Subnational Governance, and the Periphery*, edited by Thomas Demmelhuber and Roland Sturm, 59–107. Baden-Baden: Nomos.

Böker, Marit. 2017. 'Justification, Critique and Deliberative Legitimacy. The Limits of Mini-Publics'. *Contemporary Political Theory* 16 (1): 19–40. https://doi.org /10.1057/cpt.2016.11

Börzel, Tanja A., and Michael Zürn. 2021. 'Contestations of the Liberal International Order. From Liberal Multilateralism to Postnational Liberalism'. *International Organization* 75 (2): 282–305. https://doi.org/10.1017/S0020818320000570.

Bou Khater, Lea, and Rima Majed. 2020. 'Lebanon's 2019 October Revolution. Who Mobilized and Why?' Beirut: Asfari Institute for Civil Society and Citizenship.

Boubekeur, Amel. 2016. 'Islamists, Secularists and Old Regime Elites in Tunisia. Bargained Competition'. *Mediterranean Politics* 21 (1): 107–27. https://doi.org /10.1080/13629395.2015.1081449

Boubekeur, Amel, and Olivier Roy. 2012a. 'Introduction. Whatever Happened to the Islamists . . . or Political Islam Itself?' In *Whatever Happened to the Islamists? Salafis, Heavy Metal Muslims and the Lure of Consumerist Islam*, edited by Amel Boubekeur and Olivier Roy, 1–16. London: Hurst.

Boubekeur, Amel, and Olivier Roy, eds. 2012b. *Whatever Happened to the Islamists? Salafis, Heavy Metal Muslims and the Lure of Consumerist Islam*. London: Hurst.

Boyle, Michael J. 2019. 'The Military Approach to Counter-terrorism'. In *Handbook of Terrorism and Counterterrorism*, edited by Andrew Silke, 384–94. Abingdon: Routledge.

Bruce, Steve. 2002. *God is Dead. Secularization in the West*. Oxford: Blackwell.

Buchanan, Allen. (2004) 2007. *Justice, Legitimacy, and Self-determination. Moral Foundations for International Law*. Oxford: Oxford University Press.

Bull, Hedley. 1995. *The Anarchical Society. A Study of Order in World Politics*. 2nd ed. Basingstoke: Macmillan.

Butler, Judith. 2004. *Precarious Life. The Powers of Mourning and Violence*. London/New York: Verso.

Buzan, Barry. 2009. 'The Middle East through English School Theory'. In *International Society and the Middle East. English School Theory at the Regional Level*, edited by Barry Buzan and Ana Gonzalez-Pelaez, 24–44. Basingstoke/New York: Palgrave Macmillan.

Byman, Daniel. 2017. 'How to Hunt a Lone Wolf. Countering Terrorists Who Act on Their Own'. *Foreign Affairs* 96 (2): 96–105. https://www.foreignaffairs.com/articles/2017-02-13/how-hunt-lone-wolf

Byman, Daniel L. 2022. 'Hezbollah's Dilemmas'. Policy Brief, Brookings. November. https://www.brookings.edu/research/hezbollahs-dilemmas/ (accessed 7 November 2023).

Cafiero, Giorgio, and Andreas Krieg. 2019. 'The Houthi–Hezbollah Surrogate Nexus'. *Lobe Log*. 26 August. https://lobelog.com/the-houthi-hezbollah-surrogate-nexus/

Cambanis, Thanassis. 2016. 'Michel Aoun Rises to Lebanese Presidency, Ending Power Vacuum'. *New York Times*. 31 October. https://www.nytimes.com/2016/11/01/world/middleeast/michel-aoun-lebanon-president.html (accessed 7 November 2023).

Camilleri, Joseph A. 2012. 'Postsecularist Discourse in an "Age of Transition"'. *Review of International Studies* 38 (5): 1019–39. https://doi.org/doi:10.1017/S0260210512000459

Campbell, Kurt, and Brian Andrews. 2013. 'Explaining the US "Pivot" to Asia'. Americas 2013/01. London: Chatham House.

Carothers, Thomas. 2002. 'The End of the Transition Paradigm'. *Journal of Democracy* 13 (1): 5–21. https://doi.org/10.1353/jod.2002.0003

Carter Center. 2015. *The Constitution-Making Process in Tunisia. Final Report, 2011–2014*. Atlanta, GA: Carter Center.

Casanova, José. 1994. *Public Religions in the Modern World*. Chicago: University of Chicago Press.

Casanova, José. 2006. 'Secularization Revisited. A Reply to Talal Asad'. In *Powers of the Secular Modern. Talal Asad and His Interlocutors*, edited by David Scott and Charles Hirschkind. Stanford, CA: Stanford University Press.

Casanova, José. 2007. 'Rethinking Secularization. A Global Comparative Perspective'. In *Religion, Globalization, and Culture*, edited by Peter Beyer and Lori Beaman, 101–20. Leiden: Brill.

Casanova, José. 2009. 'The Secular and Secularisms'. *Social Research* 76 (4): 1049–66. https://doi.org/10.1353/sor.2009.0064

Casanova, José. 2012. 'Rethinking Public Religions'. In *Rethinking Religion and World Affairs*, edited by Timothy Samuel Shah, Alfred Stepan and Monica Duffy Toft, 25–35. New York: Oxford University Press.

Cavanaugh, William T. 2009. *The Myth of Religious Violence. Secular Ideology and the Roots of Modern Conflict*. New York: Oxford University Press.

Cavatorta, Francesco, and Fabio Merone. 2013. 'Moderation through Exclusion? The Journey of the Tunisian Ennahda from Fundamentalist to Conservative Party'. *Democratization* 20 (5): 857–75. https://doi.org/10.1080/13510347.2013.80 1255

Cavatorta, Francesco, and Fabio Merone. 2015. 'Post-Islamism, Ideological Evolution and "*la tunisianité*" of the Tunisian Islamist Party al-Nahda'. *Journal of Political Ideologies* 20 (1): 27–42. https://doi.org/10.1080/13569317.2015.9 91508

Cesari, Jocelyne. 2014. *The Awakening of Muslim Democracy. Religion, Modernity, and the State*. New York: Cambridge University Press.

Chandler, David. 2012. 'Resilience and Human Security. The Post-interventionist Paradigm'. *Security Dialogue* 43 (3): 213–29. https://doi.org/10.1177/096701 0612444151

Chayes, Abram, and Antonia Handler Chayes. 1995. *The New Sovereignty. Compliance with International Regulatory Agreements*. Cambridge, MA: Harvard University Press.

Chayes, Sarah. 2014. 'How a Leftist Labor Union Helped Force Tunisia's Political Settlement'. Carnegie Endowment for International Peace. 27 March. https://carnegieendowment.org/2014/03/27/how-leftist-labor-union-helped-force-tunisia-s-political-settlement-pub-55143 (accessed 18 October 2023).

Chiu, Yvonne. 2019. *Conspiring with the Enemy. The Ethic of Cooperation in Warfare.* New York: Columbia University Press.

Chulov, Martin. 2012. 'France Funding Syrian Rebels in New Push to Oust Assad'. *The Guardian.* 7 December. https://www.theguardian.com/world/2012/dec/07/france-funding-syrian-rebels

Chulov, Martin. 2021. 'Six Dead as Beirut Gripped by Worst Street Violence in 13 Years'. *The Guardian.* 14 October. https://www.theguardian.com/world/2021/oct/14/gunfire-beirut-protest-judge-leading-port-blast-inquiry (accessed 7 November 2023).

Clément, Maéva, Anna Geis and Hanna Pfeifer. 2021. 'Recognising Armed Non-state Actors. Risks and Opportunities for Conflict Transformation'. In *Armed Non-state Actors and the Politics of Recognition*, edited by Anna Geis, Maéva Clément and Hanna Pfeifer, 3–29. Manchester: Manchester University Press.

Coggins, Bridget. 2015. 'Rebel Diplomacy. Theorizing Violent Non-State Actors' Strategic Use of Talk'. In *Rebel Governance in Civil War*, edited by Ana Arjona, Nelson Kasfir and Zachariah Mampilly, 98–118. New York: Cambridge University Press.

Cook, Joana, and Shiraz Maher, eds. 2023. *The Rule Is for None but Allah. Islamist Approaches to Governance.* London: Hurst.

Cox, Robert W. 1983. 'Gramsci, Hegemony and International Relations. An Essay in Method'. *Millennium. Journal of International Studies* 12 (2): 162–75. https://doi.org/10.1177/03058298830120020701

Crowcroft, Orlando. 2014. 'Hamas Official: We Were behind the Kidnapping of Three Israeli Teenagers'. *The Guardian.* 21 August. https://www.theguardian.com/world/2014/aug/21/hamas-kidnapping-three-israeli-teenagers-saleh-al-arouri-qassam-brigades (accessed 7 November 2023).

Daher, Joseph. 2016. *Hezbollah. The Political Economy of the Party of God.* London: Pluto Press.

Dalacoura, Katerina. 2015. 'Islamism, Democracy and Democratization and the 2011 Arab Uprisings'. *Mediterranean Politics* 20 (3): 420–6. https://doi.org/10.1080/13629395.2015.1042712

Dallmayr, Fred R. 2002. *Dialogue among Civilizations. Some Exemplary Voices.* New York: Palgrave Macmillan.

Dallmayr, Fred R. 2009. 'Justice and Cross-cultural Dialogue. From Theory to Practice'. In *Civilizational Dialogue and World Order. The Other Politics of Cultures, Religions, and Civilizations in International Relations*, edited by Michális S. Michael and Fabio Petito, 29–46. New York: Palgrave Macmillan.

Darwich, May. 2016. 'The Ontological (In)security of Similarity Wahhabism versus Islamism in Saudi Foreign Policy'. *Foreign Policy Analysis* 12 (3): 469–88. https://doi.org/10.1093/fpa/orw032

Darwich, May. 2018. 'The Saudi Intervention in Yemen. Struggling for Status'. *Insight Turkey* 20 (2): 125–41. https://doi.org/10.25253/99.2018202.08

Darwich, May. 2021a. 'Alliance Politics in the Post-2011 Middle East. Advancing Theoretical and Empirical Perspectives'. *Mediterranean Politics* 26 (5): 635–56. https://doi.org/10.1080/13629395.2021.1889300

Darwich, May. 2021b. 'Foreign Policy Analysis and Armed Non-state Actors in World Politics. Lessons from the Middle East'. *Foreign Policy Analysis* 17 (4): orab030. https://doi.org/10.1093/fpa/orab030

De Londras, Fiona. 2019. 'The Transnational Counter-terrorism Order. A Problématique'. *Current Legal Problems* 72 (1): 203–51. https://doi.org/10.1093/clp/cuz005

Deeb, Lara, and Mona Harb. 2013. *Leisurely Islam. Negotiating Geography and Morality in Shi'ite South Beirut*. Princeton, NJ: Princeton University Press.

Deitelhoff, Nicole, and Christopher Daase. 2021. 'Rule and Resistance in Global Governance'. *International Theory* 13 (1): 122–30. https://doi.org/10.1017/s1752971920000469

Deitelhoff, Nicole, and Lisbeth Zimmermann. 2020. 'Things We Lost in the Fire. How Different Types of Contestation Affect the Robustness of International Norms'. *International Studies Review* 22 (1): 51–76. https://doi.org/10.1093/isr/viy080

Della Porta, Donatella, and Rossana Tufaro. 2022. 'Mobilizing the Past in Revolutionary Times. Memory, Counter-memory, and Nostalgia during the Lebanese Uprising'. *Sociological Forum* 38 (S1): 1387–1413. https://doi.org/10.1111/socf.12843

Di Peri, Rosita, and Daniel Meier. 2017. 'Introduction'. In *Lebanon Facing the Arab Uprisings. Constraints and Adaptation*, edited by Rosita Di Peri and Daniel Meier, 1–12. London: Palgrave Macmillan.

Dionigi, Filippo. 2014. *Hezbollah, Islamist Politics, and International Society*. New York: Palgrave Macmillan.

Donker, Teije Hidde. 2013. 'Re-emerging Islamism in Tunisia. Repositioning Religion in Politics and Society'. *Mediterranean Politics* 18 (2): 207–24. https://doi.org/10.1080/13629395.2013.799339

Donker, Teije Hidde, and Kasper Ly Netterstrøm. 2017. 'The Tunisian Revolution and Governance of Religion'. *Middle East Critique* 26 (2): 137–57. https://doi.org/10.1080/19436149.2017.1285469

Donnelly, Jack. 2014. 'State Sovereignty and International Human Rights'. *Ethics and International Affairs* 28 (2): 225–38. https://doi.org/10.1017/S089267941400 0239

Donohue, John J., and John L. Esposito, eds. 2007. *Islam in Transition. Muslim Perspectives*. 2nd ed. New York: Oxford University Press.

Doyle, Michael W. 1983. 'Kant, Liberal Legacies, and Foreign Affairs'. *Philosophy and Public Affairs* 12 (3): 205–35. http://www.jstor.org/stable/2265298

Dryzek, John S. 2005. 'Deliberative Democracy in Divided Societies. Alternatives to Agonism and Analgesia'. *Political Theory* 33 (2): 218–42. https://doi.org/10. 1177/0090591704268372

Dryzek, John S. 2006. *Deliberative Global Politics. Discourse and Democracy in a Divided World*. Cambridge: Polity Press.

Dudouet, Véronique. 2021. 'From Rebels to Violent Extremists. Evolving Conflict Trends and Implications for the Recognition of Armed Non-state Actors'. In *Armed Non-state Actors and the Politics of Recognition*, edited by Anna Geis, Maéva Clément and Hanna Pfeifer, 237–56. Manchester: Manchester University Press.

Duncombe, Constance, and Tim Dunne. 2018. 'After Liberal World Order'. *International Affairs* 94 (1): 25–42. https://doi.org/10.1093/ia/iix234

Dunne, Tim, and Trine Flockhart, eds. 2013. *Liberal World Orders*. Oxford: Oxford University Press.

Durkheim, Émile. (1912) 1990. *Les Formes élémentaires de la vie religieuse*. Paris: Presses Universitaires de France.

Dworkin, Ronald. 2013. *Religion without God*. Cambridge, MA: Harvard University Press.

Eberl, Oliver. 2008. *Demokratie und Frieden. Kants Friedensschrift in den Kontroversen der Gegenwart*. Baden-Baden: Nomos.

Eickelman, Dale F., and James P. Piscatori. 1996. *Muslim Politics*. Princeton, NJ: Princeton University Press.

Eisenstadt, Shmuel N. 2000a. 'Multiple Modernities'. *Daedalus* 129 (1): 1–29. https://www.jstor.org/stable/20027613

Eisenstadt, Shmuel N. 2000b. 'The Reconstruction of Religious Arenas in the Framework of "Multiple Modernities"'. *Millennium. Journal of International Studies* 29 (3): 591–611. https://doi.org/10.1177/03058298000290031201

El Dahan, Maha, and Laila Bassam. 2021. 'Lebanon Agrees New Government to Tackle Economic Collapse'. Reuters. 11 September. https://www.reuters.com /world/middle-east/lebanons-pm-designate-mikati-visiting-president-about-cabinet-source-2021-09-10/ (accessed 7 November 2023).

Enayat, Hadi. 2017. *Islam and Secularism in Post-colonial Thought. A Cartography of Asadian Genealogies*. Cham, Switzerland: Palgrave Macmillan.

Erman, Eva. 2016. 'Global Political Legitimacy beyond Justice and Democracy?' *International Theory* 8 (1): 29–62. https://doi.org/10.1017/s175297191500 0196

Esposito, John L., Tamara Sonn and John O. Voll. 2016. *Islam and Democracy after the Arab Spring*. New York: Oxford University Press.

Etzioni, Amitai. 2011. 'On Communitarian and Global Sources of Legitimacy'. *Review of Politics* 73 (1): 105–22. https://doi.org/10.1017/s0034670510000884

Euben, Roxanne L. 1999. *Enemy in the Mirror. Islamic Fundamentalism and the Limits of Modern Rationalism*. Princeton, NJ: Princeton University Press.

Euben, Roxanne L. 2017. 'Spectacles of Sovereignty in Digital Time. ISIS Executions, Visual Rhetoric and Sovereign Power'. *Perspectives on Politics* 15 (4): 1007–33. https://doi.org/10.1017/s1537592717002134

Evans, Gareth. 2006. 'From Humanitarian Intervention to the Responsibility to Protect'. *Wisconsin International Law Journal* 24 (3): 703–22. https://wilj.law .wisc.edu/wp-content/uploads/sites/1270/2012/02/evans.pdf

Fakhoury, Tamirace. 2016. 'Lebanon's Consociational Politics in the Post-2011 Middle East. The Paradox of Resilience'. In *Lebanon and the Arab Uprisings. In the Eye of the Hurricane*, edited by Maximilian Felsch and Martin Wählisch, 21–30. Abingdon/New York: Routledge.

Farida, Mariam. 2020. *Religion and Hezbollah. Political Ideology and Legitimacy*. Abingdon/New York: Routledge.

Fermor, Ben. 2021. '"This Barbaric Terrorist Organization". Orientalism and Barack Obama's Language on ISIS'. *Critical Studies on Terrorism* 14 (3): 312–34. https://doi.org/10.1080/17539153.2021.1932750

Fierke, K. M. 2009. 'Terrorism and Trust in Northern Ireland'. *Critical Studies on Terrorism* 2 (3): 497–511. https://doi.org/10.1080/17539150903306212

Filiu, Jean-Pierre. 2015. 'The First Year of the Tunisian Revolution'. In *The Arab Revolution of 2011. A Comparative Perspective*, edited by Saïd Amir Arjomand, 167–86. Albany, NY: SUNY Press.

Fine, Robert, and Will Smith. 2003. 'Jürgen Habermas's Theory of Cosmopolitanism'. *Constellations* 10 (4): 469–87. https://doi.org/10.1046/j.1351-0487.2003.003 48.x

Finnemore, Martha, and Kathryn Sikkink. 2001. 'Taking Stock. The Constructivist Research Program in International Relations and Comparative Politics'. *Annual*

Review of Political Science 4: 391–416. https://doi.org/10.1146/annurev.polisci
.4.1.391

Flockhart, Trine. 2016. 'The Coming Multi-order World'. *Contemporary Security Policy* 37 (1): 3–30. https://doi.org/10.1080/13523260.2016.1150053

Flockhart, Trine. 2022. 'From "Westlessness" to Renewal of the Liberal International Order. Whose Vision for the "Good Life" Will Matter?' *Cambridge Review of International Affairs* 35 (2): 176–93. https://doi.org/10.1080/09557571.2021 .1999212

Flockhart, Trine, and Elena A. Korosteleva. 2022. 'War in Ukraine. Putin and the Multi-order World'. *Contemporary Security Policy* 43 (3): 466–81. https:// doi.org/10.1080/13523260.2022.2091591

Forst, Rainer. 1993. 'Kommunitarismus und Liberalismus. Stationen einer Debatte'. In *Kommunitarismus. Eine Debatte über die moralischen Grundlagen moderner Gesellschaften*, edited by Axel Honneth, 181–212. Frankfurt am Main: Campus.

Fox, Jonathan, and Nukhet A. Sandal. 2010. 'Toward Integrating Religion into International Relations Theory'. *Zeitschrift für Internationale Beziehungen* (1): 149–59.

Fox, Jonathan, and Shmuel Sandler. 2004. *Bringing Religion into International Relations*. New York: Palgrave Macmillan.

Friis, Simone Molin. 2015. '"Beyond Anything We Have Ever Seen". Beheading Videos and the Visibility of Violence in the War against ISIS'. *International Affairs* 91 (4): 725–46. https://doi.org/10.1111/1468-2346.12341

Friis, Simone Molin. 2018. '"Behead, Burn, Crucify, Crush". Theorizing the Islamic State's Public Displays of Violence'. *European Journal of International Relations* 24 (2): 243–67. https://doi.org/10.1177/1354066117714416

Fukuyama, Francis. 1989. 'The End of History?' *National Interest* 16 (3): 3–18.

Fukuyama, Francis. 1992. *The End of History and the Last Man*. New York: Free Press.

Gallagher, Adam. 2022. 'Amid Historic Crisis, Has a New Hope Emerged in Lebanon?' United States Institute of Peace. 23 June. https://www. usip.org/publications/2022/06/amid-historic-crisis-has-new-hope-emerged-lebanon (accessed 7 November 2023).

Ganor, Boaz. 2015. *Global Alert. The Rationality of Modern Islamist Terrorism and the Challenge to the Liberal Democratic World*. New York: Columbia University Press.

Gardner Feldman, Lily. 1999. 'The Principle and Practice of "Reconciliation" in

German Foreign Policy. Relations with France, Israel, Poland and the Czech Republic'. *International Affairs* 75 (2): 333–56. https://doi.org/10.1111/1468-2346.00075

Gartenstein-Ross, Daveed, Bridget Moreng and Kathleen Soucy. 2014. 'Raising the Stakes. Ansar al-Sharia in Tunisia's Shift to Jihad'. The Hague: International Centre for Counter-Terrorism.

Geis, Anna. 2013. 'The "Concert of Democracies". Why Some States Are More Equal than Others'. *International Politics* 50 (2): 257–77. https://doi.org/10.1057/ip.2013.2

Geis, Anna. 2018. 'The Ethics of Recognition in International Political Theory'. In *The Oxford Handbook of International Political Theory*, edited by Chris Brown and Robyn Eckersley, 612–25. Oxford: Oxford University Press.

Geis, Anna, Maéva Clément and Hanna Pfeifer, eds. 2021. *Armed Non-state Actors and the Politics of Recognition*. Manchester: Manchester University Press.

Geis, Anna, Harald Müller and Niklas Schörnig, eds. 2013. *The Militant Face of Democracy. Liberal Forces for Good*. Cambridge: Cambridge University Press.

Gelvin, James L. 2021. *The Israel–Palestine Conflict. A History*. 4th ed. Cambridge: Cambridge University Press.

Gerges, Fawaz A. 1999. *America and Political Islam. Clash of Cultures or Clash of Interests?* Cambridge: Cambridge University Press.

Gerges, Fawaz A. 2014. 'Introduction'. In *The New Middle East. Protest and Revolution in the Arab World*, edited by Fawaz A. Gerges, 1–38. New York: Cambridge University Press.

Gerges, Fawaz A. 2016. *ISIS. A History*. Princeton, NJ: Princeton University Press.

Ghaddar, Hanin, Matthew Levitt, Mona Fayad and Akeel Abbas. 2022. 'Hezbollah Turns 40. Implications of the Group's Internal, Regional, and Strategic Shifts'. *PolicyWatch* 3677, Washington Institute for Near East Policy. 2 December. https://www.washingtoninstitute.org/policy-analysis/hezbollah-turns-40-implications-groups-internal-regional-and-strategic-shifts (accessed 7 November 2023).

Ghannouchi, Rached. 1993a. 'The Participation of Islamists in a Non-Islamic Government'. In *Power-Sharing Islam?*, edited by Azzam Tamimi, 51–63. London: Liberty for Muslim World.

Ghannouchi, Rached. 1993b. *Al-Ḥurriyāt al-ʿĀmma fī al-Dawla al-Islāmiyya*. Beirut: Markaz Dirasāt al-Waḥda al-ʿArabiyya.

Ghannouchi, Rached. 2013. 'The State and Religion in the Fundamentals of Islam and Contemporary Interpretation'. *Contemporary Arab Affairs* 6 (2): 164–71. https://doi.org/10.1080/17550912.2013.783184

Ghannouchi, Rached. 2016. 'From Political Islam to Muslim Democracy. The Ennahda Party and the Future of Tunisia'. *Foreign Affairs* 95 (5): 58–75. https://www.foreignaffairs.com/tunisia/political-islam-muslim-democracy-ennahda

Glaser, Karin. 2013. *Über legitime Herrschaft. Grundlagen der Legitimitätstheorie.* Wiesbaden: Springer VS.

Gould, Carol C. 2012. 'Regional versus Global Democracy. Advantages and Limitations'. In *Global Democracy. Normative and Empirical Perspectives*, edited by Daniele Archibugi, Mathias Koenig-Archibugi and Raffaele Marchetti, 115–31. Cambridge: Cambridge University Press.

Gramsci, Antonio. 1971. 'The Intellectuals'. In *Selections from the Prison Notebooks of Antonio Gramsci*, edited by Quintin Hoare and Geoffrey Nowell Smith, 3–23. London: Lawrence and Wishart/New York: International.

Gunning, Jeroen, and Richard Jackson. 2011. 'What's So "Religious" about "Religious Terrorism"?' *Critical Studies on Terrorism* 4 (3): 369–88. https://doi.org/10.1080/17539153.2011.623405

Günther, Christoph. 2022. *Entrepreneurs of Identity. The Islamic State's Symbolic Repertoire.* New York: Berghahn.

Gutkowski, Stacey. 2014. *Secular War. Myths of Religion, Politics and Violence.* London: I. B. Tauris.

Gutkowski, Stacey. 2016. 'We Are the Very Model of a Moderate Muslim State. The Amman Messages and Jordan's Foreign Policy'. *International Relations* 30 (2): 206–26. https://doi.org/10.1177/0047117815598352.

Haas, Ernst B. 1961. 'International Integration. The European and the Universal Process'. *International Organization* 15 (3): 366–92. https://doi.org/10.1017/S0020818300002198

Habermas, Jürgen. 1996. *Between Facts and Norms. Contributions to a Discourse Theory of Law and Democracy.* Cambridge, MA: MIT Press.

Habermas, Jürgen. 2001a. *Glauben und Wissen.* Frankfurt am Main: Suhrkamp.

Habermas, Jürgen. 2001b. *The Postnational Constellation. Political Essays.* Cambridge, MA: MIT Press.

Habermas, Jürgen. 2004. *Der gespaltene Westen.* Frankfurt am Main: Suhrkamp.

Habermas, Jürgen. 2009. *Zwischen Naturalismus und Religion. Philosophische Aufsätze.* Frankfurt am Main: Suhrkamp.

Habermas, Jürgen, and Charles Taylor. 2009. 'Jürgen Habermas and Charles Taylor in Conversation. An Interview Led by Craig Calhoun'. *The Immanent Frame.* 20 November. http://tif.ssrc.org/tif/2009/11/20/rethinking-secularism-jurgen-habermas-and-charles-taylor-in-conversation/

Hadid, Diaa, and Anne Barnard. 2015. 'Commander of Hezbollah Freed by Israel Is Killed in Syria'. *New York Times.* 20 December. https://www.nytimes.com/2015/12/21/world/middleeast/samir-kuntar-hezbollah-syria-israel.html (accessed 7 November 2023).

Hafez, Mohammed, and Creighton Mullins. 2015. 'The Radicalization Puzzle. A Theoretical Synthesis of Empirical Approaches to Homegrown Extremism'. *Studies in Conflict and Terrorism* 38 (11): 958–75. https://doi.org/10.1080/1057610x.2015.1051375

Haid, Haid. 2016. 'Aleppo's Fall Won't End the Syrian Conflict – It Will Signal a More Terrifying Stage'. *The Guardian.* 8 December. https://www.theguardian.com/commentisfree/2016/dec/08/aleppo-fall-syria-conflict-assad (accessed 7 November 2023).

Hamdi, Mohamed Elhachmi. 1998. *The Politicisation of Islam. A Case Study of Tunisia.* Boulder, CO: Westview Press.

Hamid, Shadi. 2014. *Temptations of Power. Islamists and Illiberal Democracy in a New Middle East.* New York: Oxford University Press.

Hansen, Lene. 2006. *Security as Practice. Discourse Analysis and the Bosnian War.* Abingdon/New York: Routledge.

Hardt, Michael, and Antonio Negri. 2000. *Empire.* Cambridge, MA: Harvard University Press.

Harik, Judith Palmer. 2007. *Hezbollah. The Changing Face of Terrorism.* London: I. B. Tauris.

Harmon, Christopher C., and Randall G. Bowdish. 2018. *The Terrorist Argument. Modern Advocacy and Propaganda.* Washington, DC: Brookings Institution Press.

Hasenclever, Andreas, and Alexander De Juan. 2007. 'Grasping the Impact of Religious Traditions on Political Conflicts. Empirical Findings and Theoretical Perspectives'. *Die Friedens-Warte. Journal of International Peace and Organization* 82 (2–3): 19–47. https://www.jstor.org/stable/23773926

Hasenclever, Andreas, and Volker Rittberger. 2000. 'Does Religion Make a Difference? Theoretical Approaches to the Impact of Faith on Political Conflict'. *Millennium. Journal of International Studies* 29 (3): 641–74. https://doi.org/10.1177/03058298000290031401

Hashem, Ali. 2013. 'Why Hezbollah Is Fighting in Syria'. *Al-Monitor.* 21 April.

http://www.al-monitor.com/originals/2013/04/reasons-hezbollah-fighting-syria.html (accessed 7 November 2023).

Hashemi, Nader, and Danny Postel, eds. 2017. *Sectarianization. Mapping the New Politics of the Middle East*. New York: Oxford University Press.

Haynes, Jeff. 1998. *Religion in Global Politics*. London: Longman.

Haynes, Jeff. 2001. 'Transnational Religious Actors and International Politics'. *Third World Quarterly* 22 (2): 143–58. https://doi.org/10.1080/01436590120037009

Haynes, Jeffrey. 2008. 'Religion and Foreign Policy Making in the USA, India and Iran. Towards a Research Agenda'. *Third World Quarterly* 29 (1): 143–65. https://doi.org/10.1080/01436590701739668

Haynes, Jeffrey. 2014. *An Introduction to International Relations and Religion*. 2nd ed. Abingdon/New York: Routledge.

Heath-Kelly, Charlotte. 2018. 'Forgetting ISIS. Enmity, Drive and Repetition in Security Discourse'. *Critical Studies on Security* 6 (1): 85–99. https://doi.org/10.1080/21624887.2017.1407595

Hegghammer, Thomas. 2010. *Jihad in Saudi Arabia. Violence and Pan-Islamism since 1979*. Cambridge: Cambridge University Press.

Hegghammer, Thomas. 2014. 'Jihadism. Seven Assumptions Shaken by the Arab Spring'. In *Rethinking Islamist Politics*, edited by Marc Lynch. POMEPS Studies 6, 28–31. Washington, DC: George Washington University.

Held, David. 2006. *Models of Democracy*. Cambridge: Polity Press.

Hellmann, Gunther, and Benjamin Herborth, eds. 2017. *Uses of the West. Security and the Politics of Order*. Cambridge: Cambridge University Press.

Hellmuth, Dorle. 2021. '"The Same Procedure as Every Year". U.S. Counterterrorism Policy since 9/11'. *Humanitas* 34 (1–2): 29–54. https://doi.org/10.5840/humanitas2021341/23

Hemkemeyer, Leon. 2016. 'Tunesiens UGTT. Gegen "Islamismus", für "Säkularismus"?' Working Paper 14. Berlin: Center for Middle Eastern and North African Politics.

Henderson, Errol A., and Richard Tucker. 2001. 'Clear and Present Strangers. The Clash of Civilizations and International Conflict'. *International Studies Quarterly* 45 (2): 317–38. https://doi.org/10.1111/0020-8833.00193

Hensell, Stephan, and Klaus Schlichte. 2021. 'The Historical Mapping of Armed Groups' Recognition'. In *Armed Non-state Actors and the Politics of Recognition*, edited by Anna Geis, Maéva Clément and Hanna Pfeifer, 30–48. Manchester: Manchester University Press.

Heritage, John. 1985. 'Analyzing News Interviews. Aspects of the Production of Talk for an Overhearing Audience'. In *Handbook of Discourse Analysis, Volume 3. Discourse and Dialogue*, edited by Teun A. van Dijk, 95–117. London: Academic Press.

Heydemann, Steven. 2007. 'Upgrading Authoritarianism in the Arab World'. Analysis Paper 13. Washington, DC: Saban Center for Middle East Policy at the Brookings Institution.

Hilburg, Jonathan. 2020. 'Forensic Architecture Reconstructs the Port Blast That Crippled Beirut'. *Architect's Newspaper*. 24 November. https://www.arch paper.com/2020/11/forensic-architecture-reconstructs-beirut-blast/ (accessed 7 November 2023).

Hobbes, Thomas. 1965. *Leviathan, or the Matter, Forme, and Power of a Common-Wealth Ecclesiasticall and Civill*. Oxford: Clarendon Press.

Hobson, Christopher. 2009. 'Beyond the End of History. The Need for a "Radical Historicisation" of Democracy in International Relations'. *Millennium. Journal of International Studies* 37 (3): 631–57. https://doi.org/10.1177/03058298091 03237

Hobson, John M. 2012. *The Eurocentric Conception of World Politics. Western International Theory, 1760–2010*. Cambridge: Cambridge University Press.

Höffe, Otfried. 2007. *Democracy in an Age of Globalisation*. Dordrecht: Springer.

Holsti, Ole R. 1977. *The 'Operational Code' as an Approach to the Analysis of Belief Systems. Final Report to the National Science Foundation, Grant No. SOC 75–15368*. Durham, NC: Duke University.

Holzscheiter, Anna. 2014. 'Between Communicative Interaction and Structures of Signification. Discourse Theory and Analysis in International Relations'. *International Studies Perspectives* 15 (2): 142–62. https://doi.org/10.1111/insp .12005

Honig, Bonnie. 1993. *Political Theory and the Displacement of Politics*. Ithaca, NY: Cornell University Press.

Hosenball, Mark. 2012. 'Obama Authorizes Secret Support for Syrian Rebels'. Reuters. 2 August. http://www.reuters.com/article/us-usa-syria-obama-order -idUSBRE8701OK20120802 (accessed 7 November 2023).

Huang, Reyko. 2016. 'Rebel Diplomacy in Civil War'. *International Security* 40 (4): 89–126. https://doi.org/10.1162/ISEC_a_00237

HuffPost Tunisie. 2016. 'Le pacte de Carthage au bord de la crise. Des remises en question et des appels au consensus'. 6 December. http://web.archive.org/web/ 20161207153249/http://www.huffpostmaghreb.com/2016/12/06/pacte-de-carthage-crise-c_n_13458510.html (accessed 7 November 2023).

Huntington, Samuel P. 1993. 'The Clash of Civilizations? The Next Pattern of Conflict'. *Foreign Affairs* 72 (3): 22–49.

Hurd, Elizabeth Shakman. 2007. *The Politics of Secularism in International Relations.* Princeton, NJ: Princeton University Press.

Hurd, Elizabeth Shakman. 2012. 'The Politics of Secularism'. In *Rethinking Religion and World Affairs,* edited by Timothy Samuel Shah, Alfred Stepan and Monica Duffy Toft, 36–54. New York: Oxford University Press.

Hurd, Ian. 1999. 'Legitimacy and Authority in International Politics'. *International Organization* 53 (2): 379–408. https://doi.org/10.1162/002081899550913

Hurrell, Andrew. 2007. *On Global Order. Power, Values, and the Constitution of International Society.* Oxford: Oxford University Press.

Hussain, Ali J. 2005. 'The Mourning of History and the History of Mourning. The Evolution of Ritual Commemoration of the Battle of Karbala'. *Comparative Studies of South Asia, Africa and the Middle East* 25 (1): 78–88. https://doi.org /10.1215/1089201X-25-1-78

Hussain, Hana. 2018. 'Remembering Mohamed Bouazizi and the Start of the Arab Spring'. *Middle East Monitor.* 17 December. https://www.middleeastmonitor .com/20181217-remembering-mohamed-bouazizi-and-the-start-of-the-arab-- spring/

Ikenberry, G. John. 2009. 'Liberal Internationalism 3.0. America and the Dilemmas of Liberal World Order'. *Perspectives on Politics* 7 (1): 71–87. https://doi.org/ 10.1017/S1537592709090112

Ikenberry, G. John. 2011. *Liberal Leviathan. The Origins, Crisis, and Transformation of the American World Order.* Princeton, NJ: Princeton University Press.

Ikenberry, G. John. 2020. 'The Next Liberal Order. The Age of Contagion Demands More Internationalism, Not Less'. *Foreign Affairs* 99 (4): 133–42.

Ikenberry, G. John, Inderjeet Parmar and Doug Stokes. 2018. 'Introduction. Ordering the World? Liberal Internationalism in Theory and Practice'. *International Affairs* 94 (1): 1–5. https://doi.org/10.1093/ia/iix277

Isakhan, Benjamin, ed. 2015. *The Legacy of Iraq. From the 2003 War to the 'Islamic State'.* Edinburgh: Edinburgh University Press.

Ish-Shalom, Piki 2006. 'Theory as a Hermeneutical Mechanism. The Democratic-Peace Thesis and the Politics of Democratization'. *European Journal of International Relations* 12 (4): 565–98. https://doi.org/10.1177/1354066106069324

Jackson, Richard. 2007. 'Constructing Enemies. "Islamic Terrorism" in Political and Academic Discourse'. *Government and Opposition* 42 (3): 394–426. https:// doi.org/10.1111/j.1477-7053.2007.00229.x

Jafri, S. H. M. 2000. *The Origins and Early Development of Shiʻa Islam*. Karachi: Oxford University Press.

Jahn, Beate. 2005. 'Kant, Mill, and Illiberal Legacies in International Affairs'. *International Organization* 59 (1): 177–207. https://doi.org/10.1017/S00208 18305050046

Jahn, Beate. 2013. *Liberal Internationalism. Theory, History, Practice*. Basingstoke: Palgrave Macmillan.

Jones, Jennifer J. 2016. 'Talk "like a Man". The Linguistic Styles of Hillary Clinton, 1992–2013'. *Perspectives on Politics* 14 (3): 625–42. https://doi.org/10.1017/s1537592716001092

Josua, Maria. 2021. 'What Drives Diffusion? Anti-terrorism Legislation in the Arab Middle East and North Africa'. *Journal of Global Security Studies* 6 (3): ogaa049. https://doi.org/10.1093/jogss/ogaa049

Juergensmeyer, Mark. 2008. *Global Rebellion. Religious Challenge to the Secular State, from Christian Militias to al Qaeda*. Berkeley, CA/Los Angeles/London: University of California Press.

Jünemann, Annette. 2017. 'Zum Wandel arabischer Geschlechterdiskurse in Zeiten von Transformation, Restauration und Bürgerkrieg'. In *Arabellion. Vom Aufbruch zum Zerfall einer Region?* edited by Thomas Demmelhuber, Axel T. Paul and Maurus Reinkowski, *Leviathan* Sonderband 31, 303–24. Baden-Baden: Nomos.

Jung, Dietrich. 2011. *Orientalists, Islamists and the Global Public Sphere. A Genealogy of the Modern Essentialist Image of Islam*. Sheffield: Equinox.

Jung, Dietrich. 2012. 'Islamic Reform and the Global Public Sphere. Muhammad Abduh and Islamic Modernity'. In *The Middle East and Globalization. Encounters and Horizons*, edited by Stephan Stetter, 153–70. New York: Palgrave Macmillan.

Kadivar, Jamileh. 2020. 'Exploring Takfir, Its Origins and Contemporary Use. The Case of Takfiri Approach in Daesh's Media'. *Contemporary Review of the Middle East* 7 (3): 259–85. https://doi.org/10.1177/2347798920921706

Kagan, Robert. 2012. *The World America Made*. New York: Alfred A. Knopf.

Kandil, Hazem. 2015. *Inside the Brotherhood*. Malden, MA: Polity Press.

Kant, Immanuel. 1977. 'Zum ewigen Frieden. Ein philosophischer Entwurf'. In *Werkasugabe, Band XI. Schriften zur Anthropologie, Geschichtsphilosophie, Politik und Pädagogik, Band 1*, edited by Wilhelm Weischedel, 195–251. Frankfurt am Main: Suhrkamp.

Karakaya, Suveyda, and A. Kadir Yildirim. 2013. 'Islamist Moderation in Perspective. Comparative Analysis of the Moderation of Islamist and Western Communist

Parties'. *Democratization* 20 (7): 1322–49. https://doi.org/10.1080/13510347
.2012.696612

Katzenstein, Peter J. 2010. 'A World of Plural and Pluralist Civilizations. Multiple
Actors, Traditions, and Practices'. In *Civilizations in World Politics. Plural and
Pluralist Perspectives*, edited by Peter J. Katzenstein, 1–40. Abingdon/New York:
Routledge.

Kausch, Kristina. 2013. '"Foreign Funding" in Post-revolution Tunisia'. Arab Forum
for Alternatives/Fride and Hivos Working Paper.

Kazmi, Zaheer. 2022. 'Radical Islam in the Western Academy'. *Review of International
Studies* 48 (4): 725–47. https://doi.org/10.1017/s0260210521000553

Keohane, Robert O. 2002. 'The Globalization of Informal Violence, Theories of
World Politics, and the "Liberalism of Fear"'. *Dialogue IO* 1 (1): 29–43. https://
doi.org/10.1017/S7777777702000031

Kepel, Gilles. 1993. *The Revenge of God. The Resurgence of Islam, Christianity and
Judaism in the Modern World*. Cambridge: Polity Press.

Ketchley, Neil, and Michael Biggs. 2017. 'The Educational Contexts of Islamist
Activism. Elite Students and Religious Institutions in Egypt'. *Mobilization. An
International Quarterly* 22 (1): 57–76. https://doi.org/10.17813/1086-671x-22
-1-57

Khanani, Ahmed. 2021. *All Politics Are God's Politics. Moroccan Islamism and
the Sacralization of Democracy*. New Brunswick, NJ: Rutgers University
Press.

Khatib, Lina. 2015. 'Hezbollah's Ascent and Descent'. *Turkish Policy Quarterly*
14 (1): 105–11. http://transatlanticpolicy.com/article/744/hezbollahs-ascent-
and-descent-spring-2015 (acceessed 19 October 2023).

Khatib, Lina, and Dina Matar. 2014. 'Conclusion. Hizbullah at a Crossroads'. In *The
Hizbullah Phenomenon. Politics and Communication*, edited by Lina Khatib,
Dina Matar and Atef Alshaer, 181–90. New York: Oxford University Press.

Kirdiş, Esen. 2018. 'Wolves in Sheep Clothing [*sic*] or Victims of Times? Discussing
the Immoderation of Incumbent Islamic Parties in Turkey, Egypt, Morocco, and
Tunisia'. *Democratization* 25 (5): 901–18. https://doi.org/10.1080/13510347
.2018.1441826

Kızılkaya, Zafer. 2017. 'Hizbullah's Moral Justification of Its Military Intervention
in the Syrian Civil War'. *Middle East Journal* 71 (2): 211–28. https://doi.org/
10.3751/71.2.12

Knudsen, Are John. 2017. 'Syria's Refugees in Lebanon. Brothers, Burden, and
Bone of Contention'. In *Lebanon Facing the Arab Uprisings. Constraints and*

Adaptation, edited by Rosita Di Peri and Daniel Meier, 135–54. London: Palgrave Macmillan.

Kohler-Koch, Beate, and Berthold Rittberger, eds. 2007. *Debating the Democratic Legitimacy of the European Union*. Lanham, MD: Rowman & Littlefield.

Koss, Maren. 2018. *Resistance, Power and Conceptions of Political Order in Islamist Organizations. Comparing Hezbollah and Hamas*. Abingdon/New York: Routledge.

Kramer, Martin. 2003. 'Coming to Terms. Fundamentalists or Islamists?' *Middle East Quarterly* 10 (2): 65–77. https://www.meforum.org/541/coming-to-terms -fundamentalists-or-islamists (accessed 19 October 2023).

Krasner, Stephen D. 1999. *Sovereignty. Organized Hypocrisy*. Princeton, NJ: Princeton University Press.

Krause, Peter, Daniel Gustafson, Jordan Theriault and Liane Young. 2022. 'Knowing Is Half the Battle. How Education Decreases the Fear of Terrorism'. *Journal of Conflict Resolution* 66 (7–8): 1147–73. https://doi.org/10.1177/002200272210 79648

Kreuder-Sonnen, Christian, and Michael Zürn. 2020. 'After Fragmentation. Norm Collisions, Interface Conflicts, and Conflict Management'. *Global Constitutionalism* 9 (2): 241–67. https://doi.org/10.1017/s2045381719000315

Kubálková, Vendulka. 2009. 'A "Turn to Religion" in IR?' *Perspectives. Review of International Affairs* 17 (2): 13–42.

Kubicek, Paul. 2015. *Political Islam and Democracy in the Muslim World*. Boulder, CO: Lynne Rienner.

Kundnani, Arun, and Ben Hayes. 2018. *The Globalisation of Countering Violent Extremism Policies. Undermining Human Rights, Instrumentalising Civil Society*. Amsterdam: Transnational Institute.

Kuntz, Friederike, and Christian Volk. 2014. 'Souveränität und die transnationale Konstellation. Eine Einleitung'. In *Der Begriff der Souveränität in der transnationalen Konstellation*, edited by Christian Volk and Friederike Kuntz, 9–24. Baden-Baden: Nomos.

Kymlicka, Will. 2002. *Contemporary Political Philosophy. An Introduction*. 2nd ed. Oxford/New York: Oxford University Press.

Laborde, Cécile. 2017. *Liberalism's Religion*. Cambridge, MA: Harvard University Press.

Laclau, Ernesto. 2007. *Emancipation(s)*. New ed. London: Verso.

Laclau, Ernesto, and Chantal Mouffe. 1985. *Hegemony and Socialist Strategy. Towards a Radical Democratic Politics*. London: Verso.

Lafont, Cristina. 2015. 'Deliberation, Participation, and Democratic Legitimacy. Should Deliberative Mini-publics Shape Public Policy?' *Journal of Political Philosophy* 23 (1): 40–63. https://doi.org/10.1111/jopp.12031

Laustsen, Carsten Bagge, and Ole Wæver. 2000. 'In Defence of Religion. Sacred Referent Objects for Securitization'. *Millennium. Journal of International Studies* 29 (3): 705–39. https://doi.org/10.1177/03058298000290031601

Layne, Christopher. 1993. 'The Unipolar Illusion. Why New Great Powers Will Rise'. *International Security* 17 (4): 5–51. https://doi.org/10.2307/2539020

Lecocq, Sharon. 2020. 'Hamas and Hezbollah. Hybrid Actors between Resistance and Governance'. *International Affairs* 96 (4): 1069–79. https://doi.org/10.1093/ia/iiaa104

Leenders, Reinoud, and Antonio Giustozzi. 2022. 'Foreign Sponsorship of Pro-government Militias Fighting Syria's Insurgency. Whither Proxy Wars?' *Mediterranean Politics* 27 (5): 614–43. https://doi.org/10.1080/13629395.2020.1839235

Lepelletier, Pierre. 2020. 'Terrorisme: "Nous sommes en guerre" contre "l'idéologie islamiste", affirme Gérald Darmanin'. *Le Figaro*. 30 October. https://www.lefigaro.fr/politique/terrorisme-nous-sommes-en-guerre-contre-l-ideologie-islamiste-affirme-gerald-darmanin-20201030 (accessed 7 November 2023).

Lewis, Bernard. 1990. 'The Roots of Muslim Rage'. *The Atlantic*. September, 47–60. https://www.theatlantic.com/magazine/archive/1990/09/the-roots-of-muslim-rage/304643/ (accessed 19 October 2023).

Lindekilde, Lasse. 2015. 'Discourse and Frame Analysis. In-Depth Analysis of Qualitative Data in Social Movement Research'. In *Methodological Practices in Social Movement Research*, edited by Donatella della Porta, 195–227. Oxford: Oxford University Press.

Lipscy, Phillip Y. 2016. *Renegotiating the World Order. Institutional Change in International Relations*. Cambridge: Cambridge University Press.

Lister, Charles. 2019. 'Trump Says ISIS Is Defeated. Reality Says Otherwise'. *Politico*. 18 March. https://www.politico.com/magazine/story/2019/03/18/trump-isis-terrorists-defeated-foreign-policy-225816/ (accessed 7 November 2023).

Lob, Eric. 2014. 'Is Hezbollah Confronting a Crisis of Popular Legitimacy?' Middle East Brief 78. Waltham, MA: Crown Center for Middle East Studies.

Lord, Ceren. 2019. Review of *Islam and Secularism in Post-colonial Thought. A Cartography of Asadian Genealogies*, by Hadi Enayat. *British Journal of Middle Eastern Studies* 46 (4): 687–90. https://doi.org/10.1080/13530194.2019.1627047

Loyle, Cyanne E., Kathleen Gallagher Cunningham, Reyko Huang and Danielle F. Jung. 2023. 'New Directions in Rebel Governance Research'. *Perspectives on Politics* 21 (1): 264–76. https://doi.org/10.1017/s1537592721001985

Luckmann, Thomas. 1985. 'Über die Funktion der Religion'. In *Die religiöse Dimension der Gesellschaft. Religion und ihre Theorien*, edited by Peter Koslowski, 26–41. Tübingen: J. C. B. Mohr/Paul Siebeck.

Luckmann, Thomas. (1966) 1991. *Die unsichtbare Religion.* Frankfurt am Main: Suhrkamp.

Lynch, Marc. 2017. 'In the Same Basket, or Not?' *Diwan. Middle East Insights from Carnegie.* 28 April. https://carnegie-mec.org/diwan/68779 (accessed 19 October 2023).

Lynch, Marc, ed. 2022. *COVID-19 in the MENA. Two Years On.* POMEPS Studies 47. Washington, DC: George Washington University.

McCarthy, Rory. 2019. 'The Politics of Consensus. Al-Nahda and the Stability of the Tunisian Transition'. *Middle Eastern Studies* 55 (2): 261–75. https://doi.org/10.1080/00263206.2018.1538969

McInnis, Kathleen J. 2016. 'Coalition Contributions to Countering the Islamic State'. Congressional Research Service, Report R44135, 24 August. https://sgp.fas.org/crs/natsec/R44135.pdf (accessed 6 November 2023).

Mahdavi, Mojtaba. 2013. 'Ayatollah Khomeini'. In *The Oxford Handbook of Islam and Politics*, edited by John L. Esposito and Emad El-Din Shahin, 180–202. New York: Oxford University Press.

Maher, Shiraz. 2016. *Salafi-Jihadism. The History of an Idea.* London: Hurst.

Mahmood, Saba. 2015. *Religious Difference in a Secular Age. A Minority Report.* Princeton, NJ: Princeton University Press.

Maksad, Firas. 2020. 'Lebanon's Halloween Government'. *Foreign Policy.* 22 January. https://foreignpolicy.com/2020/01/22/lebanons-halloween-government/ (accessed 16 October 2023).

Malmvig, Helle. 2021. 'Allow Me This One Time to Speak as a Shi'i. The Sectarian Taboo, Music Videos and the Securitization of Sectarian Identity Politics in Hezbollah's Legitimation of its Military Involvement in Syria'. *Mediterranean Politics* 26 (1): 1–24. https://doi.org/10.1080/13629395.2019.1666230

Malthaner, Stefan, and Siniša Malešević. 2022. 'Violence, Legitimacy, and Control. The Dynamics of Rebel Rule'. *Partecipazione e Conflitto* 15 (1): 1–16.

Mandaville, Peter. 2007. *Global Political Islam.* Abingdon/New York: Routledge.

Mandaville, Peter. 2013. 'Islam and International Relations in the Middle East. From

Umma to Nation State'. In *International Relations of the Middle East*, edited by Louise Fawcett. 3rd ed., 167–84. Oxford: Oxford University Press.

Mandaville, Peter. 2021. 'Islam and Exceptionalism in the Western Policy Imagination'. In *Overcoming Orientalism. Essays in Honor of John L. Esposito*, edited by Tamara Sonn, online ed. New York: Oxford University Press.

Mansour, Renad. 2014. 'Rethinking Recognition. The Case of Iraqi Kurdistan'. *Cambridge Journal of International and Comparative Law* 3 (4): 1182–94.

March, Andrew F. 2015. 'Political Islam. Theory'. *Annual Review of Political Science* 18: 103–23. https://doi.org/10.1146/annurev-polisci-082112–141250

March, Andrew F. 2019. *The Caliphate of Man. Popular Sovereignty in Modern Islamic Thought*. Cambridge, MA: Belknap Press.

Marks, Monica. 2014. 'Convince, Coerce, or Compromise? Ennahda's Approach to Tunisia's Constitution'. Analysis Paper 10. Doha: Brookings Doha Center.

Marks, Monica. 2015. 'Tunisia's Ennahda. Rethinking Islamism in the Context of ISIS and the Egyptian Coup'. Washington, DC: Brookings Institution. https://www.brookings.edu/wp-content/uploads/2016/07/Tunisia_Marks-FINALE-5.pdf (accessed 19 October 2023).

Marks, Monica. 2016. 'A Response to Sayida Ounissi's "Ennahda from Within. Islamists or 'Muslim Democrats'?"' Washington, DC: Brookings Institution. https://www.brookings.edu/wp-content/uploads/2016/07/MonicaMarks_re2 SayidaOunissi3.pdf (accessed 19 October 2023).

Marks, Monica. 2017. 'Tunisia's Islamists and the "Turkish Model"'. *Journal of Democracy* 28 (1): 102–15. https://doi.org/10.1353/jod.2017.0009

Marsden, Lee. 2009. 'US–Israel Relations. A Special Friendship'. In *America's 'Special Relationships'. Foreign and Domestic Aspects of the Politics of Alliance*, edited by John Dumbrell and Axel R. Schäfer, 191–207. Abingdon/New York: Routledge.

Marty, Martin E., and R. Scott Appleby, eds. 1991–5. *The Fundamentalism Project*. 5 vols. Chicago: University of Chicago Press.

Matar, Dina. 2014. 'Hassan Nasrallah. The Central Actor in Hizbullah's Political Communication Strategies'. In *The Hizbullah Phenomenon. Politics and Communication*, edited by Lina Khatib, Dina Matar and Atef Alshaer, 153–80. New York: Oxford University Press.

Mattern, Janice Bially, and Ayşe Zarakol. 2016. 'Hierarchies in World Politics'. *International Organization* 70 (3): 623–54. https://doi.org/10.1017/s0020818 316000126

Matthews, Jamie. 2015. 'Framing Alleged Islamist Plots. A Case Study of British Press

Coverage since 9/11'. *Critical Studies on Terrorism* 8 (2): 266–83. https://doi.org /10.1080/17539153.2015.1042305

Mavelli, Luca. 2012. *Europe's Encounter with Islam. The Secular and the Postsecular.* Abingdon/New York: Routledge.

Mavelli, Luca. 2013. 'Between Normalisation and Exception. The Securitisation of Islam and the Construction of the Secular Subject'. *Millennium. Journal of International Studies* 41 (2): 159–81. https://doi.org/10.1177/0305829812463655

Mavelli, Luca. 2014. 'Secularism, Postsecularism, and States of Exception in the 2011 Egyptian Revolution and Its Aftermath'. In *Towards a Postsecular International Politics. New Forms of Community, Identity, and Power*, edited by Luca Mavelli and Fabio Petito, 171–96. New York: Palgrave Macmillan.

Mavelli, Luca, and Fabio Petito. 2012. 'The Postsecular in International Relations. An Overview'. *Review of International Studies* 38 (5): 931–42. https://doi.org/10. 1017/S026021051200040X

Mavelli, Luca, and Fabio Petito. 2014. 'Towards a Postsecular International Politics'. In *Towards a Postsecular International Politics. New Forms of Community, Identity, and Power*, edited by Luca Mavelli and Fabio Petito, 1–26. New York: Palgrave Macmillan.

Mearsheimer, John J. 2001. *The Tragedy of Great Power Politics.* New York: Norton.

Mearsheimer, John J. 2014a. 'Can China Rise Peacefully?' *National Interest.* 25 October. https://nationalinterest.org/print/commentary/can-china-rise-peacefully-10204 (accessed 19 October 2023).

Mearsheimer, John J. 2014b. 'Why the Ukraine Crisis Is the West's Fault. The Liberal Delusions That Provoked Putin'. *Foreign Affairs* 93 (5): 77–84.

Mearsheimer, John J. 2019. 'Bound to Fail. The Rise and Fall of the Liberal International Order'. *International Security* 43 (4): 7–50. https://doi.org/10. 1162/isec_a_00342

Meddeb, Hamza. 2022. 'Tunisia's Democratic Backsliding. The Revenge of the Economy'. In *Global Lessons for Tunisia's Stalled Transition*, by Sarah Yerkes, Jennifer Mccoy, Paul Stronski, Thomas De Waal, Saskia Brechenmacher, Marc Pierini, Yezid Sayigh and Hamza Meddeb. Carnegie Endowment for International Peace. 21 July. https://carnegieendowment.org/2022/07/21/global-lessons-for-tunisia-s-stalled-transition-pub-87541#economy (accessed 19 October 2023).

Meier, Daniel. 2016. 'The Blind Spot. Palestinian Refugees from Syria in Lebanon'. In *Lebanon and the Arab Uprisings. In the Eye of the Hurricane*, edited by Maximilian Felsch and Martin Wählisch, 104–18. Abingdon/New York: Routledge.

Meijer, Hugo, and Marco Wyss. 2019. 'Upside Down. Reframing European Defence Studies'. *Cooperation and Conflict* 54 (3): 378–406. https://doi.org/10.1177/0010836718790606

MEMRI. 2013. 'Assad and His Allies Threaten to Open a Front in Golan Heights'. *Special Dispatch* 5307, 21 May. https://www.memri.org/reports/assad-and-his-allies-threaten-open-front-golan-heights (accessed 7 November 2023).

Merone, Fabio. 2015. 'Enduring Class Struggle in Tunisia. The Fight for Identity beyond Political Islam'. *British Journal of Middle Eastern Studies* 42 (1): 74–87. https://doi.org/10.1080/13530194.2015.973188

Merone, Fabio. 2017. 'Between Social Contention and *Takfirism*. The Evolution of the Salafi-Jihadi Movement in Tunisia'. *Mediterranean Politics* 22 (1): 71–90. https://doi.org/10.1080/13629395.2016.1230949

Michael, Michális S., and Fabio Petito, eds. 2009. *Civilizational Dialogue and World Order. The Other Politics of Cultures, Religions, and Civilizations in International Relations*. New York: Palgrave Macmillan.

Middle East Eye. 2022. 'Tunisia Coup. Saied Seizes Control of Electoral Commission in Latest Power Grab'. 22 April. https://www.middleeasteye.net/news/tunisia-coup-saied-seizes-control-electoral-commission-latest-power-grab (accessed 7 November 2023).

Middle East Eye. 2023a. 'Tunisia. Authorities Extend Jail Term for Opposition Leader Rached Ghannouchi'. 31 October. https://www.middleeasteye.net/news/tunisia-jail-term-opposition-leader-rached-ghannouchi-extended (accessed 7 November 2023).

Middle East Eye. 2023b. 'Tunisia. Ennahda Leader Rached Ghannouchi Arrested in Home Raid'. 17 April. https://www.middleeasteye.net/news/tunisia-ennahda-leader-rached-ghannouchi-arrested-home-raid (accessed 7 November 2023).

Middle East Monitor. 2022. 'French MP Criticised for Calling on EU to Support Kais Saied against Islamists'. 22 October. https://www.middleeastmonitor.com/2021022-french-mp-criticised-for-calling-on-eu-to-support-kais-saied-against-islamists/ (accessed 7 November 2023).

Miller, Carl. 2011. 'Is It Possible and Preferable to Negotiate with Terrorists?' *Defence Studies* 11 (1): 145–85. https://doi.org/10.1080/14702436.2011.553109

Milliken, Jennifer. 1999. 'The Study of Discourse in International Relations. A Critique of Research Methods'. *European Journal of International Relations* 5 (2): 225–54. https://doi.org/10.1177/1354066199005002003

Milton-Edwards, Beverley. 2014. 'Islamist versus Islamist. Rising Challenge in Gaza'. *Terrorism and Political Violence* 26 (2): 259–76. https://doi.org/10.1080/0954 6553.2012.690791

Mohamedou, Mohammad-Mahmoud Ould. 2018. *A Theory of ISIS. Political Violence and the Transformation of the Global Order*. London: Pluto Press.

Moravcsik, Andrew. 1997. 'Taking Preferences Seriously. A Liberal Theory of International Politics'. *International Organization* 51 (4): 513–53. https://doi.org/10.1162/002081897550447

Mouffe, Chantal. 1996. 'Democracy, Power, and the "Political"'. In *Democracy and Difference. Contesting the Boundaries of the Political*, edited by Seyla Benhabib, 245–56. Princeton, NJ: Princeton University Press.

Mouffe, Chantal. 2000. *The Democratic Paradox*. London/New York: Verso.

Mouffe, Chantal. 2009. 'Democracy in a Multipolar World'. *Millennium. Journal of International Studies* 37 (3): 549–61. https://doi.org/10.1177/0305829809 103232

Mouffe, Chantal. 2013. *Agonistics. Thinking the World Politically*. London/New York: Verso.

Mueller, John. 2006. 'Is There Still a Terrorist Threat? The Myth of the Omnipresent Enemy'. *Foreign Affairs* 85 (5): 2–8.

Mufti, Aamir R. 2013. 'Why I Am Not a Postsecularist'. *boundary 2* 40 (1): 7–19. https://doi.org/10.1215/01903659-2072846

Mukherjee, Rohan. 2022. *Ascending Order. Rising Powers and the Politics of Status in International Institutions*. Cambridge: Cambridge University Press.

Mullin, Corinna. 2011. 'The US Discourse on Political Islam. Is Obama's a Truly Post-"War on Terror" Administration?' *Critical Studies on Terrorism* 4 (2): 263–81. https://doi.org/10.1080/17539153.2011.586208

Mura, Andrea. 2015. *The Symbolic Scenarios of Islamism. A Study in Islamic Political Thought*. Farnham/Burlington, VT: Ashgate.

Nabers, Dirk. 2016. 'Local Practices of European Immigration. The "Right of Death and Power over Life" in German Asylum Discourses'. *Global Society* 30 (3): 484–506. https://doi.org/10.1080/13600826.2016.1173019

Nagle, John. 2016. 'Between Entrenchment, Reform and Transformation. Ethnicity and Lebanon's Consociational Democracy'. *Democratization* 23 (7): 1144–61. https://doi.org/10.1080/13510347.2015.1058361

Netterstrøm, Kasper Ly. 2015. 'After the Arab Spring. The Islamists' Compromise in Tunisia'. *Journal of Democracy* 26 (4): 110–24. https://doi.org/10.1353/jod.2015.0055

Nilsson, Desirée, and Isak Svensson. 2020. 'Resisting Resolution. Islamist Claims and Negotiations in Intrastate Armed Conflicts'. *International Negotiation* 25 (3): 389–412. https://doi.org/10.1163/15718069-25131250

Nilsson, Desirée, and Isak Svensson. 2021. 'The Intractability of Islamist Insurgencies. Islamist Rebels and the Recurrence of Civil War'. *International Studies Quarterly* 65 (3): 620–32. https://doi.org/10.1093/isq/sqab064.

Noe, Nicholas, ed. 2007. *Voice of Hezbollah. The Statements of Sayed Hassan Nasrallah*. London: Verso.

Noe, Nicholas. 2017. 'In the Levant, the Balance of Terror Is Falling Apart'. *Mideastwire Blog*. 7 April. http://mideastwire.us12.list-manage1.com/track/click?u=dfabb20a87095d6a87fba7306&id=96e3c18d86&e=a70ffa230b (accessed 20 October 2023).

Norris, Pippa, and Ronald Inglehart. 2011. *Sacred and Secular. Religion and Politics Worldwide*. Cambridge: Cambridge University Press.

Norton, Augustus Richard. 2014. *Hezbollah. A Short History*. 3rd ed. Princeton, NJ: Princeton University Press.

Ochoa Espejo, Paulina. 2014. 'People, Territory, and Legitimacy in Democratic States'. *American Journal of Political Science* 58 (2): 466–78. https://doi.org/10.1111/ajps.12064

Ogden, Chris. 2022. *The Authoritarian Century. China's Rise and the Demise of the Liberal International Order*. Bristol: Bristol University Press.

Ounissi, Sayida. 2016. 'Ennahda from Within. Islamists or "Muslim Democrats"?' Washington, DC: Brookings Institution. https://www.brookings.edu/wp-content/uploads/2016/07/Ounissi-RPI-Response-FINAL_v2.pdf (accessed 20 October 2023).

Owens, Patricia. 2012. 'Human Security and the Rise of the Social'. *Review of International Studies* 38 (3): 547–67. https://doi.org/10.1017/s0260210511000490

Pahwa, Sumita. 2017. 'Pathways of Islamist Adaptation. The Egyptian Muslim Brothers' Lessons for Inclusion Moderation Theory'. *Democratization* 24 (6): 1066–84. https://doi.org/10.1080/13510347.2016.1273903

Pasha, Mustapha Kamal. 2005. 'Islam, "Soft" Orientalism and Hegemony. A Gramscian Rereading'. *Critical Review of International Social and Political Philosophy* 8 (4): 543–58. https://doi.org/10.1080/13698230500205235

Peter, Fabienne. 2009. *Democratic Legitimacy*. New York: Routledge.

Peter, Fabienne. 2021. 'Political Legitimacy'. In *Stanford Encyclopedia of Philosophy (Summer 2021 Edition)*, edited by Edward N. Zalta. https://plato.stanford.edu/archives/sum2021/entries/legitimacy/ (accessed 20 October 2023).

Petito, Fabio. 2009. 'Dialogue of Civilizations as an Alternative Model for World Order'. In *Civilizational Dialogue and World Order. The Other Politics of Cultures, Religions, and Civilizations in International Relations*, edited by Michális S. Michael and Fabio Petito, 47–68. New York: Palgrave Macmillan.

Pfeifer, Hanna. 2017. 'Islamisten und die Politik des Säkularismus in Ägypten und Tunesien. Autokratische Stabilität und das demokratische Moment der a-säkularen Arabellion'. In *Arabellion. Vom Aufbruch zum Zerfall einer Region?* edited by Thomas Demmelhuber, Axel T. Paul and Maurus Reinkowski, *Leviathan* Sonderband 31, 193–217. Baden-Baden: Nomos.

Pfeifer, Hanna. 2018. 'Beyond Terrorism and Disorder. Assessing Islamist Constructions of World Order'. In *Islam in International Relations. Politics and Paradigms*, edited by Nassef Manabilang Adiong, Raffaele Mauriello and Deina Abdelkader, 100–23. Abingdon/New York: Routledge.

Pfeifer, Hanna. 2019. 'The Normative Power of Secularism. Tunisian Ennahda's Discourse on Religion, Politics, and the State (2011–2016)'. *Politics and Religion* 12 (3): 478–500. https://doi.org/10.1017/s1755048319000075

Pfeifer, Hanna. 2021. 'Recognition Dynamics and Lebanese Hezbollah's Role in Regional Conflicts'. In *Armed Non-state Actors and the Politics of Recognition*, edited by Anna Geis, Maéva Clément and Hanna Pfeifer, 148–70. Manchester: Manchester University Press.

Pfeifer, Hanna. Forthcoming. 'The Politics of Naming. Epistemology and the Study of "Armed Non-state Actors" in the "Middle East"'. In *The Rowman and Littlefield Handbook on Peace and Conflict Studies. Perspectives from the Global South*, edited by Solveig Richter and Siddharth Tripathi. Lanham, MD: Rowman and Littlefield.

Pfeifer, Hanna, Anna Geis and Maéva Clément. 2022. 'The Politics of Recognition, Armed Non-State Actors, and Conflict Transformation'. *PRIF Report* 2022 (4). https://dx.doi.org/10.48809/prifrep2204

Pfeifer, Hanna, and Christoph Günther. 2021. 'Reducing Artefacts and Shrines to Ruins. The Staging of Cultural Heritage Destruction as a Mediatised Conflict Strategy'. In *Thinking through Ruins. Genealogies, Functions, and Interpretations*, edited by Enass Khansa, Konstantin Klein and Barbara Winckler, 159–78. Berlin: Kulturverlag Kadmos Berlin.

Pfeifer, Hanna, and Regine Schwab. 2023a. 'Politicising the Rebel Governance Paradigm. Critical Appraisal and Expansion of a Research Agenda'. *Small Wars and Insurgencies* 34 (1): 1–23. https://doi.org/10.1080/09592318.2022.2144000

Pfeifer, Hanna, and Regine Schwab. 2023b. 'Re-examining the State/Non-state Binary in the Study of (Civil) War'. *Civil Wars* 25 (2–3): 426–49. https://doi.org /10.1080/13698249.2023.2254654.

Pfeifer, Hanna, and Alexander Spencer. 2019. 'Once upon a Time. Western Genres and Narrative Constructions of a Romantic Jihad'. *Journal of Language and Politics* 18 (1): 21–39. https://doi.org/10.1075/jlp.18005.spe

Pfeifer, Hanna, and Irene Weipert-Fenner. 2022. 'Time and the Growth of Trust under Conditions of Extreme Uncertainty. Illustrations from Peace and Conflict Studies'. ConTrust Working Paper 3. Frankfurt am Main: ConTrust. contrust .uni-frankfurt.de/wp-3 (accessed 20 October 2023).

Philbrick Yadav, Stacey. 2013. *Islamists and the State. Legitimacy and Institutions in Yemen and Lebanon*. London: I. B. Tauris.

Philbrick Yadav, Stacey. 2014. 'Progressive Problemshift or Paradigmatic Degeneration?' In *Rethinking Islamist Politics*, edited by Marc Lynch. POMEPS Studies 6, 56–8. Washington, DC: George Washington University.

Phillips, Nelson, and Cynthia Hardy. 2002. *Discourse Analysis. Investigating Processes of Social Construction*. Thousand Oaks, CA: Sage.

Philpott, Daniel. 2001. *Revolutions in Sovereignty. How Ideas Shaped Modern International Relations*. Princeton, NJ: Princeton University Press.

Philpott, Daniel. 2002. 'The Challenge of September 11 to Secularism in International Relations'. *World Politics* 55 (1): 66–95. https:// doi.org/10.1353/wp.2003.0006

Piattoni, Simona. 2010. *The Theory of Multi-level Governance. Conceptual, Empirical, and Normative Challenges*. Oxford: Oxford University Press.

Pickel, Gert. 2011. *Religionssoziologie. Eine Einführung in zentrale Themenbereiche*. Wiesbaden: VS Verlag für Sozialwissenschaften.

Pinfari, Marco. 2019. *Terrorists as Monsters. The Unmanageable Other from the French Revolution to the Islamic State*. New York: Oxford University Press.

Piscatori, James, and Amin Saikal. 2019. *Islam beyond Borders. The Umma in World Politics*. Cambridge: Cambridge University Press.

Pogge, Thomas. 2002. *World Poverty and Human Rights. Cosmopolitan Responsibilities and Reforms*. Cambridge: Polity Press.

Prinz, Janosch, and Conrad Schetter. 2016. 'Conditioned Sovereignty. The Creation and Legitimation of Spaces of Violence in Counterterrorism Operations of the "War on Terror"'. *Alternatives. Global, Local, Political* 41 (3): 119–36. https:// doi.org/10.1177/0304375417700171

Qassem, Naim. 2010. *Hizbullah. The Story from Within.* Updated ed. London: Saqi Books.

Quamar, Md Muddassir. 2015. 'Tunisia. Presidential and Parliamentary Elections, 2014'. *Contemporary Review of the Middle East* 2 (3): 269–88. https://doi.org /10.1177/2347798915603277.

Ranko, Annette, and Najwa Sabra. 2015. 'Sisis Ägypten. Vollendung der Revolution oder zurück auf Null?' *GIGA Focus Nahost* 2015 (1). https://www.giga-hamburg. de/assets/tracked/pure/24404156/gf_nahost_1501.pdf (accessed 20 October 2023).

Ranstorp, Magnus. 2016. 'The Role of Hizbullah in the Syrian Conflict'. In *Lebanon and the Arab Uprisings. In the Eye of the Hurricane,* edited by Martin Wählisch and Maximilian Felsch, 32–49. Abingdon/New York: Routledge.

Rawls, John. 1993. *Political Liberalism.* New York: Columbia University Press.

Rawls, John. 1997. 'The Idea of Public Reason Revisited'. *University of Chicago Law Review* 64 (3): 765–807. https://chicagounbound.uchicago.edu/uclrev/vol64/ iss3/1 (accessed 20 October 2023).

Rawls, John. 1999. *A Theory of Justice.* Revised ed. Cambridge, MA: Harvard University Press.

Rawls, John. 2005. *Political Liberalism.* Expanded ed. New York: Columbia University Press.

Reder, Michael. 2013. *Religion in säkularer Gesellschaft. Über die neue Aufmerksamkeit für Religion in der politischen Philosophie.* Freiburg/Munich: Karl Alber.

Reus-Smit, Christian. 1997. 'The Constitutional Structure of International Society and the Nature of Fundamental Institutions'. *International Organization* 51 (4): 555–89. https://doi.org/10.1162/002081897550456

Reus-Smit, Christian. 2005. 'Liberal Hierarchy and the Licence to Use Force'. *Review of International Studies* 31 (S1): 71–92. https://doi.org/10.1017/S0260210505 006790

Reuters. 2016a. 'Lebanese Banks Say Blom Bank Attack Targets Them All'. 13 June. http://www.reuters.com/article/lebanon-financial-banks-idUSL8N1951CW (accessed 7 November 2023).

Reuters. 2016b. 'Lebanon Central Bank Says Must Comply with U.S. Hezbollah Law'. 17 May. http://www.reuters.com/article/us-lebanon-banking-hezbollah -idUSKCN0Y8219 (accessed 7 November 2023).

Reuters. 2019. 'How Lebanon's Hariri Defied Hezbollah'. *Middle East Monitor.* 30 October. https://www.middleeastmonitor.com/20191030-how-lebanons- hariri-defied-hezbollah/ (accessed 7 November 2023).

Reuters. 2022. 'Tunisian President Purges Judges after Instituting One-Man Rule'. 2 June. https://www.reuters.com/world/africa/tunisias-president-sacks-57-judges-accuses-them-corruption-2022-06-01/ (accessed 7 November 2023).

Richards, Imogen. 2017. '"Good and Evil" Narratives in Islamic State Media and Western Government Statements'. *Critical Studies on Terrorism* 10 (3): 404–28. https://doi.org/10.1080/17539153.2017.1311495

Richmond, Oliver P., Gëzim Visoka and Beate Jahn. 2021. 'Liberal Internationalism'. In *The Oxford Handbook of Peacebuilding, Statebuilding, and Peace Formation*, edited by Oliver P. Richmond and Gëzim Visoka, 30–41. New York: Oxford University Press.

Robinson, Glenn E. 2021. *Global Jihad. A Brief History*. Stanford, CA: Stanford University Press.

Roepstorff, Kristina. 2013. *The Politics of Self-determination. Beyond the Decolonisation Process*. Abingdon/New York: Routledge.

Rogers, Amanda E. 2018. 'Evil™. Islamic State, Conflict-Capitalism, and the Geopolitical Uncanny'. *Critical Studies on Security* 6 (1): 118–35. https://doi.org/10.1080/21624887.2017.1407597

Rousseau, Jean-Jacques. 1994. *Discourse on Political Economy* and *The Social Contract*. Oxford: Oxford University Press.

Roy, Olivier. 1994. *The Failure of Political Islam*. London: I. B. Tauris.

Roy, Olivier. 2004. *Globalized Islam. The Search for a New Ummah*. New York: Columbia University Press.

Roy, Olivier. 2012a. 'Is "Islamism" a Neo-Orientalist Plot?' In *Whatever Happened to the Islamists? Salafis, Heavy Metal Muslims and the Lure of Consumerist Islam*, edited by Amel Boubekeur and Olivier Roy, 17–26. London: Hurst.

Roy, Olivier. 2012b. 'The Transformation of the Arab World'. *Journal of Democracy* 23 (3): 5–18. https://doi.org/10.1353/jod.2012.0056

Roy, Olivier. 2013a. 'Secularism and Islam. The Theological Predicament'. *International Spectator* 48 (1): 5–19. https://doi.org/10.1080/03932729.2013.759365

Roy, Olivier. 2013b. 'There Will Be No Islamist Revolution'. *Journal of Democracy* 24 (1): 14–19. https://doi.org/10.1353/jod.2013.0009

Rudolph, Lloyd I., and Susanne Hoeber Rudolph. 2010. 'Federalism as State Formation in India. A Theory of Shared and Negotiated Sovereignty'. *International Political Science Review* 31 (5): 553–72. https://doi.org/10.1177/0192512110388634

Rudoren, Jodi, and Said Ghazali. 2014. 'A Trail of Clues Leading to Victims and Heartbreak'. *New York Times*. 1 July. https://www.nytimes.com/2014/07/02

/world/middleeast/details-emerge-in-deaths-of-israeli-teenagers.html (accessed 7 November 2023)

Russett, Bruce. 1994. *Grasping the Democratic Peace. Principles for a Post-Cold War World*. Princeton, NJ: Princeton University Press.

Russett, Bruce, and John R. Oneal. 2001. *Triangulating Peace. Democracy, Interdependence and International Organizations*. New York: W. W. Norton.

Ruys, Tom, and Luca Ferro. 2016. 'Weathering the Storm. Legality and Legal Implications of the Saudi-Led Military Intervention in Yemen'. *International and Comparative Law Quarterly* 65 (1): 61–98. https://doi.org/10.1017/s0020589315000536

Saade, Bashir. 2016. *Hizbullah and the Politics of Remembrance. Writing the Lebanese Nation*. Cambridge: Cambridge University Press.

Sageman, Marc. 2008. *Leaderless Jihad. Terror Networks in the Twenty-First Century*. Philadelphia: University of Pennsylvania Press.

Said, Edward W. (1978) 2003. *Orientalism*. London: Penguin.

Salehi, Mariam. 2022. *Transitional Justice in Process. Plans and Politics in Tunisia*. Manchester: Manchester University Press.

Salehi, Mariam, and Irene Weipert-Fenner. 2017. 'Tunisia's Struggle against Corruption. Time to Fight, Not Forgive'. *openDemocracy*. 16 May. https://www.opendemocracy.net/en/north-africa-west-asia/tunisia-s-struggle-against-corruption-time-to-fight-not-to-forgive/ (accessed 20 October 2023).

Salehyan, Idean. 2009. *Rebels without Borders. Transnational Insurgencies in World Politics*. Ithaca, NY: Cornell University Press.

Salem, Paul. 2019. 'Lebanon'. In *The Middle East*. 15th ed., edited by Ellen Lust, 509–27. Thousand Oaks, CA: CQ Press.

Sandel, Michael J. 1984. 'The Procedural Republic and the Unencumbered Self' *Political Theory* 12 (1): 81–96. https://doi.org/10.1177/0090591784012001005

Sanger, David E. 2012. 'Rebel Arms Flow Is Said to Benefit Jihadists in Syria'. *New York Times*. 14 October. http://www.nytimes.com/2012/10/15/world/middleeast/jihadists-receiving-most-arms-sent-to-syrian-rebels.html (accessed 11 October 2023).

Saouli, Adham. 2018. *Hezbollah. Socialisation and Its Tragic Ironies*. Edinburgh: Edinburgh University Press.

Sargent, Lyman Tower. 2010. *Utopianism. A Very Short Introduction*. Oxford: Oxford University Press.

Schaer, Cathrin. 2022. 'Lebanon–Israel Maritime and Gas Deal: Who Benefits Most?' *Deutsche Welle*. 14 October. https://www.dw.com/en/lebanon-israel-maritime -and-gas-deal-who-benefits-most/a-63442266 (accessed 7 November 2023).

Scharf, Michael P. 2016. 'How the War Against ISIS Changed International Law'. *Case Western Reserve Journal of International Law* 48 (1), article 3. https://scholarly commons.law.case.edu/faculty_publications/1638/ (accessed 20 October 2023).

Scharpf, Fritz W. 1999. *Regieren in Europa. Effektiv und demokratisch?* Frankfurt am Main: Campus.

Schmitt, Carl. (1985) 2005. *Political Theology. Four Chapters on the Concept of Sovereignty*. Chicago: University of Chicago Press.

Schmitt, Eric. 2012. 'C.I.A. Said to Aid in Steering Arms to Syrian Opposition'. *New York Times*. 21 June. http://www.nytimes.com/2012/06/21/world/middle east/cia-said-to-aid-in-steering-arms-to-syrian-rebels.html (accessed 7 November 2023).

Schreier, Margrit. 2012. *Qualitative Content Analysis in Practice*. Los Angeles: Sage.

Schumann, Christoph. 2013. 'Die politische Artikulation der Gesellschaft. Politische Ordnung und Revolte in der Arabischen Welt'. In *Was hält Gesellschaften zusammen? Der gefährdete Umgang mit Pluralität*, edited by Michael Reder, Hanna Pfeifer, and Mara-Daria Cojocaru, 67–89. Stuttgart: Kohlhammer.

Schwab, Regine. 2018. 'Insurgent Courts in Civil Wars. The Three Pathways of (Trans)formation in Today's Syria (2012–2017)'. *Small Wars and Insurgencies* 29 (4): 801–26. https://doi.org/10.1080/09592318.2018.1497290

Schwab, Regine. 2023. 'Same Same but Different? Ideological Differentiation and Intra-jihadist Competition in the Syrian Civil War'. *Journal of Global Security Studies* 8 (1): ogac45. https://doi.org/10.1093/jogss/ogac045.

Schwedler, Jillian. 2011. 'Can Islamists Become Moderates? Rethinking the Inclusion-Moderation Hypothesis'. *World Politics* 63 (2): 347–76. https://doi.org/10. 1017/S0043887111000050

Sebei, Hatem, and Carmen Fulco. 2022. 'Rethinking the Legacy of Tunisian Pact-Making in the Post-July 2021 Order'. *Journal of North African Studies*. https:// doi.org/10.1080/13629387.2022.2150172

Sen, Amartya. 2006. *Identity and Violence. The Illusion of Destiny*. New York: W. W. Norton.

Senghaas, Dieter. 1998. 'A Clash of Civilizations. An Idée Fixe?' *Journal of Peace Research* 35 (1): 127–32. https://doi.org/10.1177/0022343398035001010

Senghaas, Dieter. 2002. 'Some Untimely Reflections on the Dialogue between Christians and Muslims, or Pleading for a Reorientation of the Intercultural Dialogue'. In *Religion between Violence and Reconciliation*, edited by Thomas Scheffler, 545–60. Beirut/Würzburg: Ergon.

Sengupta, Kim. 2013. 'Revealed: What the West has Given Syria's Rebels'. *The Independent*. 12 August. http://www.independent.co.uk/news/world/middle-east/revealed-what-the-west-has-given-syrias-rebels-8756447.html (accessed 7 November 2023).

Shah, Timothy Samuel. 2012. 'Religion and World Affairs. Blurring the Boundaries'. In *Rethinking Religion and World Affairs*, edited by Timothy Samuel Shah, Alfred Stepan and Monica Duffy Toft, 1–14. New York: Oxford University Press.

Shanahan, Rodger. 2017. 'Hizbullah as a Regional Brand. Not All Parties Are Equal'. *Australian Journal of International Affairs* 71 (2): 201–15. https://doi.org/10.1080/10357718.2016.1241979

Sheikh, Mona K. 2014. 'Appointing Evil in International Relations'. *International Politics* 51 (4): 492–507. https://doi.org/10.1057/ip.2014.22

Sienknecht, Mitja. 2021. 'The PKK's Zig-zag in Its Global Quest for Recognition'. In *Armed Non-state Actors and the Politics of Recognition*, edited by Anna Geis, Maéva Clément and Hanna Pfeifer, 109–29. Manchester: Manchester University Press.

Slaughter, Anne-Marie. 2005. 'Security, Solidarity, and Sovereignty. The Grand Themes of UN Reform'. *American Journal of International Law* 99 (3): 619–31. https://doi.org/10.2307/1602294

SNHR (Syrian Network for Human Rights). 2016. 'The Six Main Parties That Kill Civilians in Syria and the Death Toll Percentage Distribution among Them'. 14 November. https://snhr.org/blog/2016/11/14/29132/ (accessed 7 November 2023).

Snyder, Jack. 2011. 'Introduction'. In *Religion and International Relations Theory*, edited by Jack Snyder, 1–24. New York: Columbia University Press.

Sørensen, Georg. 2006. 'Liberalism of Restraint and Liberalism of Imposition. Liberal Values and World Order in the New Millennium'. *International Relations* 20 (3): 251–72. https://doi.org/10.1177/0047117806066702.

Sørensen, Georg. 2007. 'After the Security Dilemma. The Challenges of Insecurity in Weak States and the Dilemma of Liberal Values'. *Security Dialogue* 38 (3): 357–78. https://doi.org/10.1177/0967010607081516

Sørensen, Georg. 2011. *A Liberal World Order in Crisis. Choosing between Imposition and Restraint*. Ithaca, NY: Cornell University Press.

Souleimanov, Emil Aslan, and Valery Dzutsati. 2018. 'Russia's Syria War. A Strategic Trap?' *Middle East Policy* 25 (2): 42–50. https://doi.org/10.1111/mepo.12341

Stein, Ewan. 2021. *International Relations in the Middle East. Hegemonic Strategies and Regional Order*. Cambridge: Cambridge University Press.

Stenersen, Anne. 2020. 'Jihadism after the "Caliphate". Towards a New Typology'. *British Journal of Middle Eastern Studies* 47 (5): 774–93. https://doi.org/10.1080/13530194.2018.1552118

Stengel, Frank A. 2020. *The Politics of Military Force. Antimilitarism, Ideational Change, and Post-Cold War German Security Discourse*. Ann Arbor: University of Michigan Press.

Stepan, Alfred. 2012a. 'Religion, Democracy and the "Twin Tolerations"'. In *Rethinking Religion and World Affairs*, edited by Timothy Samuel Shah, Alfred Stepan and Monica Duffy Toft, 55–72. New York: Oxford University Press.

Stepan, Alfred. 2012b. 'Tunisia's Transition and the Twin Tolerations'. *Journal of Democracy* 23 (2): 89–103. https://doi.org/10.1353/jod.2012.0034

Süß, Clara-Auguste, and Irene Weipert-Fenner. 2022. 'One Crisis among Many. Russia's War in Ukraine and Its Implications for the MENA Region'. *Zeitschrift für Friedens- und Konfliktforschung* 11 (2): 255–65. https://doi.org/10.1007/s42597-022-00081-9

Tamimi, Azzam S. 2001. *Rachid Ghannouchi. A Democrat within Islamism*. New York: Oxford University Press.

Taylor, Charles. 2007. *A Secular Age*. Cambridge, MA: Belknap Press.

Taylor, Charles. 2011. 'Why We Need a Radical Redefinition of Secularism'. In *The Power of Religion in the Public Sphere*, edited by Eduardo Mendieta and Jonathan VanAntwerpen, 34–59. New York: Columbia University Press.

Teti, Andrea. 2007. 'Bridging the Gap. IR, Middle East Studies and the Disciplinary Politics of the Area Studies Controversy'. *European Journal of International Relations* 13 (1): 117–45. https://doi.org/10.1177/1354066107074291

Teti, Andrea, and Andrea Mura. 2009. 'Islam and Islamism'. In *The Routledge Handbook of Religion and Politics*, edited by Jeffrey Haynes, 92–110. Abingdon/New York: Routledge.

Thomas, Scott M. 2000. 'Taking Religious and Cultural Pluralism Seriously. The Global Resurgence of Religion and the Transformation of International Society'. *Millennium. Journal of International Studies* 29 (3): 815–41. https://doi.org/10.1177/03058298000290030401

Thomas, Scott M. 2005. *The Global Resurgence of Religion and the Transformation of International Relations. The Struggle for the Soul of the Twenty-First Century.* New York: Palgrave Macmillan.

Tibi, Bassam. 1998. *The Challenge of Fundamentalism. Political Islam and the New World Disorder.* Berkeley: University of California Press.

Tolbert, David. 2014. 'Introduction. A Very Special Tribunal'. In *The Special Tribunal for Lebanon. Law and Practice*, edited by Amal Alamuddin, Nidal Nabil Jurdi and David Tolbert, 1–9. Oxford: Oxford University Press.

Toros, Harmonie. 2008. '"We Don't Negotiate with Terrorists!" Legitimacy and Complexity in Terrorist Conflicts'. *Security Dialogue* 39 (4): 407–26. https://doi.org/10.1177/0967010608094035.

Toros, Harmonie, and Arrliya Sabogal. 2021. '"Al-Shabaab Is Part of Us". Endogeneity and Exogeneity in the Struggle for Recognition in Somalia'. In *Armed Non-state Actors and the Politics of Recognition*, edited by Anna Geis, Maéva Clément and Hanna Pfeifer, 70–87. Manchester: Manchester University Press.

Transfeld, Mareike. 2017. 'Kein Stellvertreterkrieg im Jemen'. *SWP-Aktuell* 2017 (13). https://www.swp-berlin.org/publications/products/aktuell/2017A13_transfeld.pdf

V-Dem Institute. 2022. *Democracy Report 2022. Autocratization Changing Nature?* Gothenburg: V-Dem Institute. https://www.v-dem.net/documents/19/dr_2022_ipyOpLP.pdf

Valbjørn, Morten. 2017. 'Strategies for Reviving the International Relations/Middle East Nexus after the Arab Uprisings'. *PS. Political Science and Politics* 50 (3): 647–51. https://doi.org/10.1017/s1049096517000312

Valbjørn, Morten, and Jeroen Gunning. 2021. 'Bringing in the "Other Islamists". Beyond Sunni-centric Islamism Studies in a Sectarianized Middle East'. *Mediterranean Politics* 26 (4): 476–83. https://doi.org/10.1080/13629395.2020.1718371

Van Vliet, Sam. 2016. 'Syrian Refugees in Lebanon. Coping with Unpreceded Challenges'. In *Lebanon and the Arab Uprisings. In the Eye of the Hurricane*, edited by Maximilian Felsch and Martin Wählisch, 89–103. Abingdon/New York: Routledge.

Vandeviver, Nicolas. 2019. 'Resisting Orientalism. Gramsci and Foucault in Counterpoint'. In *Revisiting Gramsci's Notebooks*, edited by Francesca Antonini, Aaron Bernstein, Lorenzo Fusaro and Robert Jackson, 248–65. Leiden: Brill.

VDC (Violations Documentation Center in Syria). 2016. 'The Monthly Statistical Report on Victims, December 2016'. https://vdc-sy.net//wp-content/uploads/2017/01/December-report-Eng.pdf (accessed 7 November 2023).

Volpi, Frédéric. 2010. *Political Islam Observed*. London: Hurst.

Volpi, Frédéric, and Ewan Stein. 2015. 'Islamism and the State after the Arab Uprisings. Between People Power and State Power'. *Democratization* 22 (2): 276–93. https://doi.org/10.1080/13510347.2015.1010811

Wæver, Ole. 2018. 'A Post-Western Europe. Strange Identities in a Less Liberal World Order'. *Ethics and International Affairs* 32 (1): 75–88. https://doi.org/10.1017/s0892679418000114

Wählisch, Martin, and Maximilian Felsch. 2016. 'Lebanon and the Arab Uprisings. In the Eye of the Hurricane'. In *Lebanon and the Arab Uprisings. In the Eye of the Hurricane*, edited by Martin Wählisch and Maximilian Felsch, 1–18. Abingdon/New York: Routledge.

Walker, R. B. J. 1993. *Inside/Outside. International Relations as Political Theory*. Cambridge: Cambridge University Press.

Walker, Stephen G. 1983. 'The Motivational Foundations of Political Belief Systems. A Re-analysis of the Operational Code Construct'. *International Studies Quarterly* 27 (2): 179–202. https://doi.org/10.2307/2600545

Walter, Barbara F. 2017. 'The Extremist's Advantage in Civil Wars'. *International Security* 42 (2): 7–39. https://doi.org/10.1162/ISEC_a_00292

Waltz, Kenneth N. 1979. *Theory of International Politics*. Reading, MA: Addison-Wesley.

Walzer, Michael. 1977. *Just and Unjust Wars. A Moral Argument with Historical Illustrations*. New York: Basic.

Walzer, Michael. 1980. 'The Moral Standing of States. A Response to Four Critics'. *Philosophy and Public Affairs* 9 (3): 209–29. https://www.jstor.org/stable/2265115

Walzer, Michael. 1983. *Spheres of Justice. A Defense of Pluralism and Equality*. New York: Basic.

Walzer, Michael. 1998. 'Drawing the Line. Religion and Politics'. *Soziale Welt* 49 (3): 295–307. https://www.jstor.org/stable/40878238

Weber, Max. 1922. *Wirtschaft und Gesellschaft*. Tübingen: J. C. B. Mohr.

Weber, Max. (1920) 1972. 'Die protestantische Ethik und der Geist des Kapitalismus'. In *Gesammelte Aufsätze zur Religionssoziologie, Teil 1*, 17–206. Tübingen: J. C. B. Mohr.

Weipert-Fenner, Irene. 2021. 'Go Local, Go Global. Studying Popular Protests in the MENA Post-2011'. *Mediterranean Politics* 26 (5): 563–85. https://doi.org/10.1080/13629395.2021.1889286

Weipert-Fenner, Irene. 2022. 'Still und leise. Die Abschaffung der tunesischen Demokratie'. *PRIF Blog*. 6 May. https://blog.prif.org/2022/05/06/still-und-leise-die-abschaffung-der-tunesischen-demokratie/ (accessed 20 October 2023).

Weipert-Fenner, Irene, and Jonas Wolff. 2015. 'Socioeconomic Contention and Post-revolutionary Political Change in Egypt and Tunisia. A Research Agenda'. PRIF Working Papers 24. Frankfurt am Main: Peace Research Institute Frankfurt. https://www.hsfk.de/fileadmin/HSFK/hsfk_publikationen/PRIF_WP_24.pdf (accessed 20 October 2023).

Weiss, Jessica Chen, and Jeremy L. Wallace. 2021. 'Domestic Politics, China's Rise, and the Future of the Liberal International Order'. *International Organization* 75 (2): 635–64. https://doi.org/10.1017/s002081832000048x

Welsh, Jennifer, Carolin Thielking and S. Neil MacFarlane. 2002. 'The Responsibility to Protect. Assessing the Report of the International Commission on Intervention and State Sovereignty'. *International Journal* 57 (4): 489–512. https://doi.org/10.2307/40203689

Werenfels, Isabelle. 2022. 'No Time to Lose as Tunisia's President Consolidates Authoritarian Turn. Europe Waits, Watches, Misses Opportunities'. *SWP Comment* 2022 (41). https://doi.org/10.18449/2022C41

Wieland, Carsten. 2016. 'Syrian–Lebanese Relations. The Impossible Dissociation between Lebanon and Syria'. In *Lebanon and the Arab Uprisings. In the Eye of the Hurricane*, edited by Martin Wählisch and Maximilian Felsch, 167–80. Abingdon/New York: Routledge.

Wiener, Antje. 2018. *Contestation and Constitution of Norms in Global International Relations*. Cambridge: Cambridge University Press.

Wiktorowicz, Quintan. 2006. 'Anatomy of the Salafi Movement'. *Studies in Conflict and Terrorism* 29 (3): 207–39. https://doi.org/10.1080/10576100500497004

Wilson, Erin K. 2012. *After Secularism. Rethinking Religion in Global Politics*. Basingstoke: Palgrave Macmillan.

Wilson, Erin K. 2014. 'Theorizing Religion as Politics in Postsecular International Relations'. *Politics, Religion and Ideology* 15 (3): 347–65. https://doi.org/10.1080/21567689.2014.948590

Wintour, Patrick. 2016. 'Peace Talks between US and Russia over Syria Stall at G20 Summit'. *The Guardian*. 4 September. https://www.theguardian.com/world/2016/sep/04/syria-peace-talks-us-and-russia-stall-g20 (accessed 7 November 2023).

Wohlrab-Sahr, Monika, and Marian Burchardt. 2012. 'Multiple Secularities. Toward a Cultural Sociology of Secular Modernities'. *Comparative Sociology* 11 (6): 875–909. https://doi.org/10.1163/15691330-12341249

Wojczewski, Thorsten. 2018. 'Global Power Shifts and World Order. The Contestation of "Western" Discursive Hegemony'. *Cambridge Review of International Affairs*: 33–52. https://doi.org/10.1080/09557571.2018.1476464

Wolf, Anne. 2017. *Political Islam in Tunisia. The History of Ennahda*. New York: Oxford University Press.

World Bank. 2014. 'The Unfinished Revolution. Bringing Opportunity, Good Jobs and Greater Wealth to All Tunisians'. Development Policy Review, report no. 86179-TN. 24 May. https://openknowledge.worldbank.org/entities/publication/326c48af-2863-5cf9-9c57-5b0ca1073072 (accessed 6 November 2023).

World Bank. 2021. 'Lebanon Sinking into One of the Most Severe Global Crises Episodes, amidst Deliberate Inaction'. 1 June. https://www.worldbank.org/en/news/press-release/2021/05/01/lebanon-sinking-into-one-of-the-most-severe-global-crises-episodes (accessed 7 November 2023).

World Bank. 2022. 'Lebanon's Crisis. Great Denial in the Deliberate Depression'. 25 January. https://www.worldbank.org/en/news/press-release/2022/01/24/lebanon-s-crisis-great-denial-in-the-deliberate-depression (accessed 7 November 2023).

Worrall, James, Simon Mabon, and Gordon Clubb. 2015. *Hezbollah. From Islamic Resistance to Government*. Santa Barbara, CA: Praeger.

Yack, Bernard. 2001. 'Sovereignty and Nationalism'. *Political Theory* 29 (4): 517–36. https://doi.org/10.1177/0090591701029004003

Yee, Vivian. 2023. 'Tunisia Arrests a Leading Opposition Figure'. *New York Times*. 18 April. https://www.nytimes.com/2023/04/18/world/middleeast/tunisia-ghannouchi-arrest.html (accessed 7 November 2023)

Yerkes, Sarah. 2022. 'Introduction. Global Lessons for Tunisia's Stalled Transition'. In *Global Lessons for Tunisia's Stalled Transition*, by Sarah Yerkes, Jennifer Mccoy, Paul Stronski, Thomas De Waal, Saskia Brechenmacher, Marc Pierini, Yezid Sayigh and Hamza Meddeb. Carnegie Endowment for International Peace. 21 July. https://carnegieendowment.org/2022/07/21/global-lessons-for-tunisia-s-stalled-transition-pub-87541#introduction (accessed 20 October 2023).

Yıldırım, Ramazan. 2017. 'Transformation of the Ennahda Movement from Islamic Jama'ah to Political Party'. *Insight Turkey* 19 (2): 189–214. https://doi.org/10.25253/99.2017192.10

Yilmaz, Hüseyin. 2012. 'The Eastern Question and the Ottoman Empire. The Genesis of the Near and Middle East in the Nineteenth Century'. In *Is There a Middle East? The Evolution of a Geopolitical Concept*, edited by Michael E. Bonine, Abbas Amanat and Michael Ezekiel Gasper, 11–35. Stanford, CA: Stanford University Press.

Zarakol, Ayşe. 2019. '"Rise of the Rest". As Hype and Reality'. *International Relations* 33 (2): 213–28. https://doi.org/10.1177/0047117819840793

Zarakol, Ayşe. 2022. *Before the West. The Rise and Fall of Eastern World Orders*. Cambridge: Cambridge University Press.

Zelin, Aaron Y. 2016. 'Jihadism in Lebanon after the Syrian Uprising'. In *Lebanon and the Arab Uprisings. In the Eye of the Hurricane*, edited by Martin Wählisch and Maximilian Felsch, 50–69. Abingdon/New York: Routledge.

Zürn, Michael. 2016. 'Survey Article. Four Models of a Global Order with Cosmopolitan Intent. An Empirical Assessment'. *Journal of Political Philosophy* 24 (1): 88–119. https://doi.org/10.1111/jopp.12070

Zürn, Michael. 2018. *A Theory of Global Governance. Authority, Legitimacy, and Contestation*. Oxford: Oxford University Press.

Zürn, Michael, and Nicole Deitelhoff. 2015. 'Internationalization and the State. Sovereignty as the External Side of Modern Statehood'. In *The Oxford Handbook of Transformations of the State*, edited by Stephan Leibfried, Evelyne Huber, Stefan Lange, Jonah D. Levy, Frank Nullmeier and John D. Stephens, 193–220. Oxford: Oxford University Press.

Zürn, Michael, and Johannes Gerschewski. 2021. 'Sketching the Liberal Script. A Target of Contestations'. *SCRIPTS Working Paper* 10. Berlin: Cluster of Excellence 'Contestations of the Liberal Script' (SCRIPTS). https://www.scripts-berlin.eu/publications/working-paper-series/Working-Paper-No_-10-2021/SCRIPTS_Working_Paper_10_WEB.pdf (accessed 20 October 2023).

Primary Sources

Ennahda. 2011a. Ennahda Party Chairman's Speech. 28 October.

Ennahda. 2011b. 'For Freedom, Justice and Development in Tunisia'. Electoral Programme 2011.

Ennahda. 2011c. Interview with Rached al-Ghannouchi in *Foreign Policy*. 5 December.

Ennahda. 2011d. Interview with Rached al-Ghannouchi in *Libération*, by Christophe Ayd. 8 July.

Ennahda. 2011e. Interview with Rached al-Ghannouchi in *Religioscope*, by Mahan Abdein. 30 January.

Ennahda. 2011f. Interview with Rached al-Ghannouchi in *Weekly Zaman*, by Esma Basbaydar. 24 September.

Ennahda. 2011g. Interview with Rached al-Ghannouchi on Al Jazeera, by Nazanine Moshiri. 7 February.

Ennahda. 2011h. Interview with Souad Abdelrahim in *La Presse*, by Cécile Feuillatre and Hassan El Fekih. 1 November.

Ennahda. 2011i. Opinion Piece by Rached al-Ghannouchi in the *Guardian*. 'A Day to Inspire All Tunisians – Whether Islamic or Secular'. 17 October.

Ennahda. 2011j. Opinion Piece by Souad Abdelrahim in the *Guardian*. 'Tunisia's New Beginning'. 22 November.

Ennahda. 2011k. Party Statement 2. 6 December.

Ennahda. 2011l. Party Statement 3. 18 December.

Ennahda. 2011m. Press Statement on the Opening of the Tunisian National Constituent Assembly. 23 November.

Ennahda. 2011n. Statement by the Head of the Ennahda Party. 23 October.

Ennahda. 2011o. Statement by the Secretary General 2. 15 November.

Ennahda. 2011p. Statement of the Executive Committee of Ennahdha Party's Regional Branch in Sfax. 15 October.

Ennahda. 2011q. Summary of Ennahda's Press Conference. 19 October.

Ennahda. 2011r. Transcript of a Conversation with Rached al-Ghannouchi at the Council of Foreign Relations in Washington, DC. 30 November.

Ennahda. 2012a. Concluding Statement of the 9th Ennahda Party Conference. 16 July.

Ennahda. 2012b. Government Statement 1. 15 November.

Ennahda. 2012c. Interview with Hamadi Jebali in *Le Soir*, by Baudouin Loos. 2 October.

Ennahda. 2012d. Interview with Rached al-Ghannouchi at the Woodrow Wilson International Center, by Robin Wright. 2 November.

Ennahda. 2012e. Interview with Rached al-Ghannouchi in *Le Monde*, by Isabelle Mandraud. 19 October.

Ennahda. 2012f. Interview with Rached al-Ghannouchi on Al Jazeera, by Yasmine Ryan. 13 September.

Ennahda. 2012g. Interview with Rached al-Ghannouchi on the BBC, by Owen Bennett-Jones. 6 February.

Ennahda. 2012h. Letter of Complaint to *Foreign Policy* on Its Global Thinkers Profile of Ahlem Belhaj. 7 December.

Ennahda. 2012i. Opinion Piece by Mehrezia Labidi in the *Guardian*. 'Tunisia's Women are at the Heart of Its Revolution'. 23 March.

Ennahda. 2012j. Party Statement 1. 9 January.

Ennahda. 2012k. Party Statement 2. 15 January.

Ennahda. 2012l. Party Statement 3. 3 February.

Ennahda. 2012m. Party Statement 4. 8 February.

Ennahda. 2012n. Party Statement 5. 22 February.

Ennahda. 2012o. Party Statement 12. 14 June.

Ennahda. 2012p. Party Statement 16. 15 September.

Ennahda. 2012q. Party Statement 17. 20 September.

Ennahda. 2012r. Party Statement 19. 18 October.

Ennahda. 2012s. Party Statement 20. 23 October.

Ennahda. 2012t. Party Statement 22. 29 November.

Ennahda. 2012u. Party Statement 23. 13 December.

Ennahda. 2012v. Party Statement at Ennahda Press Conference. 24 February.

Ennahda. 2012w. Press Release. 15 October.

Ennahda. 2012x. Press Statement 1. 11 October.

Ennahda. 2012y. Press Statement 3. 5 December.

Ennahda. 2012z. Press Statement of the Coordination Committee of the Coalition Government Parties. 5 October.

Ennahda. 2012aa. Response Letter to *Time* Magazine on Its Article 'The President and the Islamist'. 8 October.

Ennahda. 2012ab. Statement on the Coordinating Committee of the Coalition Government Parties. 25 September.

Ennahda. 2012ac. Summary of a Lecture Delivered by Rached al-Ghannouchi on Secularism and the Relationship between Religion and the State. 5 March.

Ennahda. 2012ad. Summary of a Speech by Rached al-Ghannouchi. 4 October.

Ennahda. 2012ae. Summary of Rached al-Ghannouchi's Statement at a Press Conference. 4 December.

Ennahda. 2012af. Summary of Rached al-Ghannouchi's Statements at the Davos Debate. 27 January.

Ennahda. 2012ag. Transcript of a Lecture Delivered by Rached al-Ghannouchi at the Center for the Study of Islam and Democracy. 2 March.

Ennahda. 2012ah. Transcript of a Q&A Session with Rached al-Ghannouchi at Chatham House in London. 26 November.

Ennahda. 2012ai. Transcript of a Speech by Mehrezia Labidi at Chatham House in London. 21 March.

Ennahda. 2012aj. Transcript of a Speech by Rached al-Ghannouchi at Chatham House in London. 26 November.

Ennahda. 2012ak. Tunisia Government Coalition Parties' Statement. 18 October.

Ennahda. 2013a. Concluding Statement of a Press Conference. 15 August.

Ennahda. 2013b. Extracts from an Interview with Rached al-Ghannouchi. 14 August.

Ennahda. 2013c. Extracts from an Opinion Piece by Rached al-Ghannouchi in *al-Wihda*. 13 August.

Ennahda. 2013d. Interview with Ali Larayedh in *Le Monde*. 26 March.

Ennahda. 2013e. Interview with Rached al-Ghannouchi in *Adhamir*, by Mohammed al-Hamrouni. 27 October.

Ennahda. 2013f. Interview with Rached al-Ghannouchi in *al-Dameer* Newspaper, by Mohamed Al-Hamrouni. 9 June.

Ennahda. 2013g. Interview with Rached al-Ghannouchi in *Asharq al-Awsat*, by Nadia al-Turki. 1 August.

Ennahda. 2013h. Interview with Rached al-Ghannouchi in *Le Monde*, by Isabelle Mandraud. 6 July.

Ennahda. 2013i. Interview with Rached al-Ghannouchi in the *Washington Post*, by Lally Weymouth. 12 December.

Ennahda. 2013j. Joint Statement by Different Tunisian Parties. 3 September.

Ennahda. 2013k. Joint Statement by Political Parties and National Figures. 30 July.

Ennahda. 2013l. Opinion Piece by Rached al-Ghannouchi in the *Guardian*. 'We Are Building a Tunisia for All'. 13 January.

Ennahda. 2013m. Party Statement 3. 1 March.

Ennahda. 2013n. Party Statement 5. 20 March.

Ennahda. 2013o. Party Statement 6. 10 April.

Ennahda. 2013p. Party Statement 10. 9 May.

Ennahda. 2013q. Party Statement 11. 15 May.

Ennahda. 2013r. Party Statement 14. 6 June.

Ennahda. 2013s. Party Statement 17. 2 July.

Ennahda. 2013t. Party Statement 18. 8 July.

Ennahda. 2013u. Party Statement 23. 25 July.

Ennahda. 2013v. Party Statement 30. 21 September.

Ennahda. 2013w. Party Statement 33. 19 October.

Ennahda. 2013x. Party Statement 34. 21 October.

Ennahda. 2013y. Party Statement 36. 24 October.

Ennahda. 2013z. Party Statement 37. 30 October.

Ennahda. 2013aa. Party Statement 38. 5 November.

Ennahda. 2013ab. Party Statement 43. 17 December.

Ennahda. 2013ac. Press Statement 1. 6 February.

Ennahda. 2013ad. Speech by Rached al-Ghannouchi. 15 August.

Ennahda. 2013ae. Statement by Ennahda Party Consultative Council. 6 October.

Ennahda. 2013af. Summary of Ali Larayedh's Speech. 29 July.

Ennahda. 2013ag. Summary of Ali Larayedh's Statements 1. 28 May.

Ennahda. 2013ah. Summary of Ali Larayedh's Statements 2. 23 October.

Ennahda. 2013ai. Summary of Rached al-Ghannouchi's Statements at a Press Conference 1. 15 May.

Ennahda. 2013aj. Summary of Rached al-Ghannouchi's Statements at a Press Conference 2. 15 August.

Ennahda. 2013ak. Summary of Statements by Ali Larayedh and Rached al-Ghannouchi. 25 July.

Ennahda. 2013al. Transcript of a Video Message by Rached al-Ghannouchi. 14 January.

Ennahda. 2014a. Electoral Manifesto. 4 October.

Ennahda. 2014b. Interview with Rached al-Ghannouchi in *al-Chourouk* Newspaper, by Saïda Amri, Khaled Haddad and Massoudi Abdeljalil. 26 September.

Ennahda. 2014c. Interview with Rached al-Ghannouchi in *Asharq al-Awsat*, by Hatim Betioui. 6 June.

Ennahda. 2014d. Interview with Rached al-Ghannouchi in *Le Monde*, by Isabelle Mandraud. 15 February.

Ennahda. 2014e. 'Mhabet Tounes'. Manifesto. 12 October.

Ennahda. 2014f. Opinion Piece by Rached al-Ghannouchi in the *Huffington Post*. 'Islam, Democracy and the Future of the Muslim World'. 2 January.

Ennahda. 2014g. Opinion Piece by Rached al-Ghannouchi in the *New York Times*. 20 November.

Ennahda. 2014h. Opinion Piece by Rached al-Ghannouchi in the *Washington Post*. 24 October.

Ennahda. 2014i. Opinion Piece by Rached al-Ghannouchi in the *Washington Post*. 'Tunisia Shows There Is No Contradiction between Democracy and Islam'. 27 October.

Ennahda. 2014j. Opinion Piece by Rafik Abdessalem on Al Jazeera. 'Tunisia: A Pioneer of Arab Democracy'. 18 January.

Ennahda. 2014k. Party Statement 2. 14 January.

Ennahda. 2014l. Party Statement 3. 16 February.

Ennahda. 2014m. Party Statement 5. 20 March.

Ennahda. 2014n. Party Statement 6. 25 March.

Ennahda. 2014o. Party Statement 7. 30 March.

Ennahda. 2014p. Party Statement 12. 2 May.

Ennahda. 2014q. Party Statement 14. 6 June.

Ennahda. 2014r. Party Statement 15. 7 June.

Ennahda. 2014s. Party Statement 18. 22 July.

Ennahda. 2014t. Party Statement 19. 22 July.

Ennahda. 2014u. Party Statement 24. 8 October.

Ennahda. 2014v. Party Statement 26. 23 October.

Ennahda. 2014w. Party Statement 29. 30 October.

Ennahda. 2014x. Press Statement 1. 16 June.

Ennahda. 2014y. Press Statement 2. 20 November.

Ennahda. 2014z. 'A Rising Economy. A Secure Country'. Ennahdha Party Electoral Programme 2015–2020.

Ennahda. 2014aa. Statements by Rached al-Ghannouchi at Voice of America's Press Conference in Washington, DC. 27 February.

Ennahda. 2014ab. Summary of Ali Larayedh's Statements 1. 11 January.

Ennahda. 2014ac. Summary of Rached al-Ghannouchi's Statements 1. 7 June.

Ennahda. 2014ad. Summary of Rached al-Ghannouchi's Statements 4. 9 October.

Ennahda. 2014ae. Transcript of a Lecture by Rached al-Ghannouchi at the US Institute of Peace in Washington, DC. 29 September.

Ennahda. 2014af. Transcript of a Talk by Rached al-Ghannouchi at Columbia University, New York. 1 October.

Ennahda. 2014ag. Transcript of Rached al-Ghannouchi's Speech at the Carnegie Endowment in Washington, DC. 26 February.

Ennahda. 2014ah. Transcript of Rached al-Ghannouchi's Speech at the US Institute of Peace in Washington, DC. 24 February.

Ennahda. 2015a. Ennahdha Party Consultative Council Statement 3. 22 March.

Ennahda. 2015b. Interview with Rached al-Ghannouchi in the *New York Times*, by Robin Wright. 27 January.

Ennahda. 2015c. Interview with Rached al-Ghannouchi on Al Jazeera, by Ahmed El Amraoui. 14 November.

Ennahda. 2015d. Interview with Rafik Abdessalem on openDemocracy. 11 December.

Ennahda. 2015e. Opinion Piece by Amel Azzouz in the *Financial Times*. 'Help Tunisia to Complete the Transition to Democracy'. 30 March.

Ennahda. 2015f. Opinion Piece by Rached al-Ghannouchi in *Le Monde*. 'Musulmans modérés unis contre le terrorisme en Tunisie'. 26 March.

Ennahda. 2015g. Opinion Piece by Rached al-Ghannouchi in the *Boston Globe*. 'Progress in Tunisia, but Much Still to Be Done'. 1 May.

Ennahda. 2015h. Opinion Piece by Rached al-Ghannouchi in the *Middle East Monitor*. 'Why Did Ennahda Accept an Unequal Partnership'. 6 March.

Ennahda. 2015i. Opinion Piece by Rafik Abdessalem in *Global Policy Journal*. 'Addressing Extremism. Lessons from Tunisia'. 15 April.

Ennahda. 2015j. Opinion Piece by Soumaya al-Ghannouchi in the *Huffington Post*. 11 May.

Ennahda. 2015k. Opinion Piece by Soumaya al-Ghannouchi in the *Huffington Post*. 'Erdogan, Sisi and Western Hypocrisy'. 11 May.

Ennahda. 2015l. Party Statement 2. 14 January.

Ennahda. 2015m. Party Statement 5. 18 February.

Ennahda. 2015n. Party Statement 7. 20 March.

Ennahda. 2015o. Party Statement 14. 12 April.

Ennahda. 2015p. Party Statement 17. 22 April.

Ennahda. 2015q. Party Statement 20. 17 May.

Ennahda. 2015r. Party Statement 24. 5 July.

Ennahda. 2015s. Party Statement 25. 10 July.

Ennahda. 2015t. Party Statement 28. 8 September.

Ennahda. 2015u. Party Statement 29. 13 September.

Ennahda. 2015v. Party Statement 33. 3 December.

Ennahda. 2015w. Summary of Rached al-Ghannouchi's Statements 1. 21 January.

Ennahda. 2015x. Summary of Rached al-Ghannouchi's Statements 3. 23 March.

Ennahda. 2015y. Summary of Rached al-Ghannouchi's Statements 6. 26 April.

Ennahda. 2015z. Summary of Rached al-Ghannouchi's Statements 7. 7 June.

Ennahda. 2015aa. Summary of Rached al-Ghannouchi's Statements 8. 28 June.

Ennahda. 2015ab. Summary of Rached al-Ghannouchi's Statements at the Global Forum on Modern Direct Democracy. 14 May.

Ennahda. 2016a. Concluding Statement of the 10th Ennahda Party Conference. 27 May.

Ennahda. 2016b. Ennahdha Party Consultative Council Statement 2. 16 October.

Ennahda. 2016c. Interview with Rached al-Ghannouchi in *al-Chourouk*. 18 January.

Ennahda. 2016d. Interview with Rached al-Ghannouchi in *Le Monde*, by Frédéric Bobin. 20 May.

Ennahda. 2016e. Interview with Rached al-Ghannouchi in the *Financial Times*. 18 January.

Ennahda. 2016f. Interview with Rached al-Ghannouchi in the *New Arab*. 17 March.

Ennahda. 2016g. Opinion Piece by Mehrezia Labidi in *Politico*. 'Why Women Should Lead in Tunisia'. 9 March.

Ennahda. 2016h. Opinion Piece by Rached al-Ghannouchi in the *Atlantic*. 'Tunisia's Answer to ISIS Is Democracy'. 1 February.

Ennahda. 2016i. Opinion Piece by Rached al-Ghannouchi in the *Huffington Post*. 'Islam, Democracy and the Future of the Muslim World'. 1 October.

Ennahda. 2016j. Opinion Piece by Rached al-Ghannouchi in *Time* Magazine. 'Tunisia Holds the Key to Defeating ISIS'. 25 January.

Ennahda. 2016k. Opinion Piece in *Die Welt*. 'Islam und Demokratie vertragen sich durchaus'. 9 June.

Ennahda. 2016l. Party Statement 1. 10 January.

Ennahda. 2016m. Party Statement 4. 20 February.

Ennahda. 2016n. Party Statement 7. 6 April.

Ennahda. 2016o. Party Statement 14. 21 August.

Ennahda. 2016p. Transcript of Rached al-Ghannouchi's Opening Speech at the 10th Party Conference. 20 May.

Hezbollah. 2011a. Hizbullah SG Full Speech. 1 June.

Hezbollah. 2011b. Hizbullah SG Sayyed Hassan Nasrallah Speech on Arbaeen of Imam Hussein in Baalbeck. 25 January.

Hezbollah. 2011c. Hizbullah SG Sayyed Hassan Nasrallah Speech on Parliamentary Consultations. 23 January.

Hezbollah. 2011d. Hizbullah SG Speech in Full. 6 June.

Hezbollah. 2011e. Sayyed Nasrallah on the Ceremony for Consolidation with the Arab Peoples. 19 March.

Hezbollah. 2011f. Speech Delivered by Hizbullah Secretary General Sayyed Hassan Nasrallah during the 'Dignity and Victory' Festival Held by Hizbullah at Raya Stadium. 27 July.

Hezbollah. 2011g. Speech Delivered by Hizbullah Secretary General Sayyed Hassan Nasrallah during the Central Ceremony Held by Hizbullah to Commemorate the 40th Day (Arbaeen) for the Martyrdom of Imam Hussein (pbuh) Held in the City of Baalbeck. 14 January.

Hezbollah. 2011h. Speech Delivered by Hizbullah Secretary General Sayyed Hassan Nasrallah During the Ceremony Held to Commemorate the Blessed Birthday of the Holy Prophet Mohammad (Peace Be upon Him and His Household) and the Islamic Unity Week Held in Sayyed Ashuhada Compound – Rweiss. 7 February.

Hezbollah. 2011i. Speech Delivered by Hizbullah Secretary General Sayyed Hassan Nasrallah during the Iftar of the Women's Branch in the Islamic Resistance Support Association. 17 August.

Hezbollah. 2011j. Speech Delivered by Hizbullah Secretary General Sayyed Hassan Nasrallah on the Occasion of al-Quds International Day (26-08-2011) in 'Iran Garden' in the Southern Village of Maroon Al Ras at the Lebanese–Palestinian Borderline. 26 August.

Hezbollah. 2011k. Speech Delivered by Hizbullah Secretary General Sayyed Hassan Nasrallah on the Occasion of the Martyr's Day Held by Hezbollah at Sayyed Ashuhada (pbuh) Compound in Rweiss. 11 November.

Hezbollah. 2011l. Speech Delivered by Hizbullah Secretary General Sayyed Hassan Nasrallah on the Resistance and Liberation Day. 25 May.

Hezbollah. 2012a. Political Section of the Speech Delivered by Hizbullah Secretary General Sayyed Hassan Nasrallah during the Ceremony Commemorating the Leader Martyrs' Day Held in Nabi Sheath. 24 February.

Hezbollah. 2012b. Sayyed Nasrallah Speech during Conclusion of Waad Project to Rebuild Beirut's Southern Suburb. 11 May.

Hezbollah. 2012c. Speech Delivered by Hizbullah Secretary General Sayyed Hassan Nasrallah During the Ceremony Marking the Resistance and Liberation Day Held in Bint Jbeil. 15 May.

Hezbollah. 2012d. Speech Delivered by Hizbullah Secretary General Sayyed Hassan Nasrallah during the Ceremony of Loyalty to the Leader Martyrs. 16 February.

Hezbollah. 2012e. Speech Delivered by Hizbullah Secretary General Sayyed Hassan Nasrallah on the Ceremony Marking the Anniversary of the Demise of Imam Khomeini Which Was Weld in UNESCO. 1 June.

Hezbollah. 2012f. Speech Delivered by Hizbullah Secretary General Sayyed Hassan Nasrallah on the Occasion of the Forum Entitled 'Declaration of al-Quds as the Capital of Palestine, the Arabs and Muslims'. 4 March.

Hezbollah. 2013a. Sayyed Nasrallah Delivers Speech on Resistance and Liberation Day. 15 May.

Hezbollah. 2013b. Sayyed Nasrallah: 'Resistance Ready to Receive Unique Armor'. 10 May.

Hezbollah. 2013c. Sayyed Nasrallah: 'Resistance Will Not Stand Still on Any Aggression against Lebanon'. 16 February.

Hezbollah. 2013d. Sayyed Nasrallah: 'We are Keen on Ignoring Atttempts of Sowing Strife, Rumors on Hizbullah False'. 27 February.

Hezbollah. 2013e. Sayyed Nasrallah's Speech during the Memorial Ceremony for Martyr Leader Hassan Lakkis. 20 December.

Hezbollah. 2013f. Speech [by] Hizbullah Secretary General His Eminence Sayyed Hassan Nasrallah Delivered While Celebrating Prophet's Blessed Birth at Sayyed Shuhada Complex in Rweiss. 25 January.

Hezbollah. 2013g. Speech by Hizbullah Secretary General, His Eminence Sayyed Hassan Nasrallah, Commemorating the 'Day for the Wounded'. 14 June.

Hezbollah. 2014a. Full Speech Delivered by Hizbullah Secretary General, His Eminence Sayyed Hassan Nasrallah, at the Launch of the Jabal Amel Culture and Literature Forum in the Southern Town of Ainatha. 29 March.

Hezbollah. 2014b. Full Speech Delivered by Hizbullah Secretary General, His Eminence Sayyed Hassan Nasrallah, Commemorating the Day of Resistance and Liberation Held in the Southern Village of Bint Jbeil. 25 May.

Hezbollah. 2014c. Full Speech Delivered by Hizbullah Secretary General, His Eminence Sayyed Hassan Nasrallah, via Al Manar Channel Marking the Anniversary of the Martyr Leaders. 16 February.

Hezbollah. 2014d. Full Speech Delivered by Hizbullah Secretary General, His Eminence, Sayyed Hassan Nasrallah, during al-Quds Day Ceremony Held by Hizbullah in Sayyed al-Shuhada Complex in Rweiss. 25 July.

Hezbollah. 2014e. Full Speech Delivered by Hizbullah Secretary General, His Eminence, Sayyed Hassan Nasrallah, during the 8th Anniversary for Victory Broadcasted. 15 August.

Hezbollah. 2014f. Speech Delivered by Hizbollah Secretary General, His Eminence Sayyed Hassan Nasrallah, on the Tenth Day of Muharram in Raya Field. 4 November.

Hezbollah. 2014g. Speech Delivered by Hizbullah Secretary General Sayyed Hassan Nasrallah on the Tenth Night of Muharam Commemorating Ashura during the Central Council Held in Sayyed Ashuhada (pbuh) Complex in Haret Hreik. 3 November.

Hezbollah. 2014h. Speech Delivered by Hizbullah Secretary-General, His Eminence Sayyed Hassan Nasrallah, during a Memorial Ceremony for Late Sheikh Mustafa Kassir. 6 June.

Hezbollah. 2015a. Full Speech Delivered by Hizbullah Secretary General His Eminence Sayyed Hassan Nasrallah during the Memorial Ceremony in Honor of the Great Quneitra Martyrs Held on January 30, 2015. 30 January.

Hezbollah. 2015b. Full Speech Delivered by Hizbullah Secretary General His Eminence Sayyed Hassan Nasrallah on al-Quds International Day. 10 July.

Hezbollah. 2015c. Full Speech Delivered by Hizbullah Secretary General Sayyed Hassan Nasrallah during the Memorial Anniversary of the Resistance Leader Martyrs Held in Sayyed Ashuhada Compound. 16 February.

Hezbollah. 2015d. Full Speech Delivered by Hizbullah Secretary General Sayyed Hassan Nasrallah on the Day of Resistance and Liberation Held in Nabatiyeh. 24 May.

Hezbollah. 2015e. Full Speech Delivered by Hizbullah Secretary General, His Eminence Sayyed Hassan Nasrallah, during the Ceremony Held on the Holy Prophet's (Peace Be upon Him and His Household) Birthday and al-Imdad Association Day. 9 January.

Hezbollah. 2015f. Full Speech Delivered by Hizbullah Secretary General, His Eminence Sayyed Nasrallah, in the Ceremony Held to Mark a Week on the Martyrdom of Hassan al Hajj in Lweizeh. 18 October.

Hezbollah. 2015g. Full Televised Speech Delivered by Hizbullah Secretary General Sayyed Hassan Nasrallah 1. 5 May.

Hezbollah. 2015h. Full Televised Speech Delivered by Hizbullah Secretary General Sayyed Hassan Nasrallah 2. 16 May.

Hezbollah. 2015i. Full Televised Speech Delivered by Hizbullah Secretary General, His Eminence Sayyed Hassan Nasrallah. 27 March.

Hezbollah. 2015j. Full Televised Speech Delivered by Hizbullah Secretary General, His Eminence Sayyed Nasrallah, on the Martyrdom of the Chief of the Freed Detainees Samir al-Quntar. 21 December.

Hezbollah. 2015k. Political Section of the Speech Delivered by Hizbullah Secretary General Sayyed Hassan Nasrallah during the 30th Anniversary of Al Mahdi Scouts. 5 June.

Hezbollah. 2015l. Sayyed Nasrallah's Full Speech on [. . .] Yemen. 17 April.

Hezbollah. 2016a. Full Speech Delivered by Hizbullah Secretary General, His Eminence Sayyed Hassan Nasrallah, during Ashura Rally on the Tenth of Muharram 1438. 12 October.

Hezbollah. 2016b. Full Speech Delivered by Hizbullah Secretary General, His Eminence Sayyed Hassan Nasrallah, During Day of the Islamic Resistance Wounded Fighters Marked. 12 May.

Hezbollah. 2016c. Full Speech Delivered by Hizbullah Secretary General, His Eminence Sayyed Hassan Nasrallah, during the Ceremony Held to Honor the Islamic Resistance Support Organization. 6 May.

Hezbollah. 2016d. Full Speech Delivered by Hizbullah Secretary General, His Eminence Sayyed Hassan Nasrallah, during the University Students Meeting. 23 December.

Hezbollah. 2016e. Full Speech Delivered by Hizbullah Secretary General, His Eminence Sayyed Nasrallah, during the Festival Held to Honor Late Resistance Leader Ismail Ahmad al-Zahri in Nabatieh al-Fawqa. 29 July.

Hezbollah. 2016f. Full Speech Delivered by Hizbullah Secretary General, His Eminence Sayyed Nasrallah, during the Honoring Memorial Commemorating the Anniversary of Late Leader Mustafa Shahadeh. 4 November.

Hezbollah. 2016g. Full Speech Delivered by Hizbullah Secretary General, His Eminence Sayyed Nasrallah, during the Memorial Commemorating Forty Days after the Martyrdom of the Senior Jihadi Leader Sayyed Mustafa Badreddine Held in the Shahed Educational Complex. 24 June.

Hezbollah. 2016h. Full Speech Delivered by Hizbullah Secretary General, His Eminence Sayyed Nasrallah, during the Memorial Held to Honor Martyr Leader Sayyed Mustafa Badreddine. 20 May.

Hezbollah. 2016i. Full Speech Delivered by Hizbullah Secretary General, His Eminence Sayyed Nasrallah, on the Commemoration Ceremony Held in Honor of Sheikh Mohammad Khatoun. 3 January.

Hezbollah. 2016j. Full Speech Delivered by Hizbullah Secretary General, His Eminence Sayyed Nasrallah, on the Divine Victory Anniversary Ceremony Held in Bint Jbeil. 13 August.

Hezbollah. 2016k. Full Speech Delivered by Hizbullah Secretary General, His Eminence Sayyed Nasrallah, on the First Week Commemoration Ceremony Held in Honor of Martyr Leader Ali Ahmad Fayyad (Alaa of Bosnia) in Ansar Village. 6 March.

Hezbollah. 2016l. Full Televised Speech Delivered by Hizbullah Secretary General Sayyed Hassan Nasrallah on al-Quds Day. 2 July.

Hezbollah. 2016m. Full Televised Speech Delivered by Hizbullah Secretary General, His Eminence Sayyed Hassan Nasrallah, on the Lebanese Presidential Elections. 29 January.

Hezbollah. 2016n. Speech Delivered by Hizbullah Secretary General Sayyed Hassan Nasrallah on the Tenth Night of Muharram during the Central Council Held in Sayyed Ashuhada [pbuh] Complex. 11 November.

Hezbollah. 2016o. Speech Delivered by Hizbullah Secretary General, His Eminence Sayyed Hassan Nasrallah, during the Ceremony Held to Commemorate the Death of the Late Allamah Sheikh Abd Nassr al-Jabri. 27 December.

INDEX

EU representative:
Easy Access System Europe
Mustamäe tee 50, 10621 Tallinn, Estonia
Gpsr.requests@easproject.com

www.ingramcontent.com/pod-product-compliance
Lightning Source LLC
Chambersburg PA
CBHW070841300326
41935CB00039B/1341